Theopompus the Historian

In *Theopompus the Historian,* Gordon Shrimpton examines the evidence concerning the life and lost works of Theopompus of Chios, the fourth-century B.C. historian and orator, providing the first comprehensive study of the man and his work. The work includes a translation of the fragments (surviving citations of Theopompus' work) and testimonies (references made to Theopompus' work by other writers) which makes available all that remains of Theopompus' writings.

Theopompus was primarily known in antiquity for his historical works, which included an Epitome of Herodotus, *Hellenica,* a twelve-book history of Greece, and the fifty-eight book *Philippica,* which focused on the career of Philip II of Macedon. All these works were lost by late antiquity, except fifty-three volumes of the *Philippica* which survived into Byzantine times only to disappear by perhaps the tenth century.

Before these works were lost, geographers, lexicographers, biographers, collectors of anecdotes, and later historians all quoted Theopompus in their writings. Critics of historical style also reacted strongly to the asperity of both his language and his work. Shrimpton studies the fragments and testimonies to reveal what can be learned about the scope and content of Theopompus' two major works. He deals systematically with problems of interpretation and makes clear the methodological background of his reconstructions and evaluation. Theopompus' moral and political views are discussed, as are his treatment of two of the most important figures of the middle fourth century B.C., Philip and Demosthenes. Shrimpton also provides a comprehensive index of proper names found in the fragments and reassesses the authorship of the *Hellenica Oxyrhynchia,* suggesting that it is most plausibly identified with Cratippus.

GORDON S. SHRIMPTON is an associate professor in the Department of Classics, University of Victoria.

Theopompus the Historian

GORDON S. SHRIMPTON

McGill-Queen's University Press
Montreal & Kingston • London • Buffalo

©McGill-Queen's University Press 1991
ISBN 0-7735-0837-6

Legal deposit second quarter 1991
Bibliothèque nationale du Québec

Printed in Canada on acid-free paper

This book has been published with the help of a grant
from the Canadian Federation for the Humanities,
using funds provided by the Social Sciences and
Humanities Research Council of Canada.

Quotations from D.A. Russell and M. Winterbottom,
eds., *Ancient Literary Criticism* reprinted by permission of
Oxford University Press.

Quotation from F.W. Hall, *A Companion to Classical Texts*
reprinted by permission of Oxford University Press.

Quotations from the Loeb Classical Library Series
reprinted by permission of Harvard University Press.

Translated portion of Thucydides, *The Peloponnesian
War* reprinted by permission of Everyman's Library.

Canadian Cataloguing in Publication Data

Shrimpton, Gordon, 1941–
    Theopompus the historian
    Includes bibliographical references.
    ISBN 0-7735-0837-6
    1. Theopompus, of Chios, b. 378 B.C.?
    2. Historiography—Greece. 3. Hellenica
    Oxyrhynchia. 4. Historians—Greece—
    Biography. I. Title.
    DF212.T45S57 1991   938'.07   C90-090517-4

To the spirits who guided me:
Malcolm (1910–1989), Lionel (1908–1988),
and my beloved parents

Contents

Tables and Maps

Preface and Acknowledgments

I began to prepare for this book in 1975 when I first thought that I should translate Theopompus' fragments and publish them with a brief commentary. To collect materials for that undertaking, I was awarded a research grant from the Canada Council, as it then was. However, I soon decided that Theopompus needed something more ambitious and reluctantly set the task aside. The project was never completely abandoned, and by 1986 I knew the time had come to start work on a comprehensive book. The University of Victoria generously gave me a year of study leave, a further research grant enabling me to visit the libraries at Stanford and Berkeley. At that time I was able to visit the late L.I.C. Pearson and A.E. Raubitschek at Stanford, where I received some excellent suggestions and much encouragement. I also discussed the idea with the late Malcolm McGregor, who was very encouraging and read a draft of the introduction and chapter 1 and made many useful notes. At about this time (Spring 1988) I also talked to Jane Fredeman, then senior editor at UBC Press, who gave me much help and encouragement. Along the way I have received suggestions and advice from a number of scholars. Malcolm McGregor again, George Paul (McMaster), Iain Bruce (Memorial), and especially Phillip Harding (UBC), who read the whole work and offered a great deal of constructive criticism, have all been generous with their time and interest. Richard Talbert (University of North Carolina) lent me one of his books (by mail!) and listened to some of my ideas. He read a preliminary version of Appendix A and made a number of excellent suggestions. My colleague Keith Bradley kindly read a proposed portion of my work and persuaded me to discard it. My dear friend David Campbell (Victoria) was extremely generous with criticism and advice, saving me from not a few blunders in the Greek translation. He also read a late version to the end of chapter 5.

Thanks to the University of Victoria's Lansdowne Fund, Paul Cartledge (Clare College, Cambridge) visited Victoria and endured several hours of Theopompus one March afternoon. His probing questions were most stimulating, and I remember his visit fondly. Catherine Rubincam (Erindale College) has also shown generous interest and support, supplying me with some useful bibliography as well. An anonymous referee for the Canadian Federation for the Humanities gave me much encouragement. It has been my hope to make Theopompus accessible to students. Accordingly, a few of my students have had to wade through chapters in various stages of preparation. I thank Richard Ross (chapter 5), J. Ainslie Wilson (chapter 4), and Deanna Koch (Introduction and chapter 1).

I am extremely grateful to all of the above people and agencies, but it would be wrong to neglect others closer to home. The Department of Classics at the University of Victoria continues to provide a most congenial environment for research. Last year the department secured money to purchase an Ibycus system, something that I have found extremely valuable. The patience of our secretary, Mrs. A. Nasser, in typing this script for a "computer-illiterate" has never ceased to impress me.

Thanks are also due to Chris Mundigler for the professional way he prepared the maps and Table 2.

To the McGill-Queen's University Press and Peter Blaney in particular I owe an enormous debt of thanks for interest and support. This book has benefited immeasurably from Jane Fredeman's outstanding editorial skills.

Last of all, I thank my family for doing without me without complaint while I struggled to put this together.

Introduction

Theopompus' works are lost. How, then, can they be studied, and why should modern students try to do so if the ancients did not consider them important enough to ensure their preservation? These two questions are based on two unsound assumptions: that a lost work cannot be studied and that only unimportant manuscripts were lost. In the first place, significant lost works leave an impression on subsequent literature that can be studied, and, secondly, importance was far from being the only criterion of literary survival in antiquity.

Those two assumptions deserve separate attention. It is easier to understand how a "lost" work can be saved from total oblivion by imagining an extreme, hypothetical case. If, by some tragic accident, all the printed copies of Shakespeare's works in all versions and translations were lost, the scholarship on Shakespeare would still survive, and from these countless books it would be possible to collect many thousands of *verbatim* quotations, plot-summaries, and descriptions of his plays and other poetical works. The quotations might be called "fragments," the descriptions, summaries, and other references to Shakespeare and his work, "testimonies." This is essentially what happened in antiquity to the works of Theopompus (and to many histories, treatises, and poems by other authors). The ancients who read Theopompus sometimes quoted him and sometimes wrote down criticisms of his works or recorded their reactions to them. Felix Jacoby collected these quotations and comments and furnished a succinct commentary.[1] Unfortunately, Theopompus was not as important to the ancients as Shakespeare is now, but Jacoby was still able to collect in excess of four hundred fragments and fifty-one testimonies (or *testimonia*). Naturally the fragments (FF) and *testimonia* (TT) vary in size and significance. Some "fragments" are as small as a single word, usually cited by a lexicographer interested in an unusual word or a special usage or by an ancient geographer collecting place-names from literary sources. Even these small items can be informative. An unusual word or special usage reveals something about the author's style. In the case of a place-name, if the geographer has reported the work and the number of the book in which he found the reference, it provides a potentially valuable clue to the contents of the book and, hence, to the structure of the work. Places tend to be in the limelight of history at significant times and then disappear. Another hypothetical example will illustrate this point. If someone trying to reconstruct a lost history of the nineteenth century had information that the place-name Waterloo was found in chapter two of a lost work, the suspicion that the author was dealing with the famous Battle of Waterloo would be unavoidable. Any attempt to reconstruct the plan of the treatise would begin with that notion as a working hypothesis.

More about what can be deduced from fragments will become apparent in the main chapters of this book. What of the other assumption: that the disappearance of a work means that it was considered too insignificant for preservation? It is important to know how and why literature was lost. In fact, even the briefest summary of the facts concerning the preservation of ancient texts turns the question on its head. It would be better to ask, "How can we explain the miraculous survival of so much ancient literature, much of it not greatly different (or corrupted) from the original autographs?"

According to the authorities on the subject,[2] ancient literature was extensively preserved in well-stocked libraries in various parts of the Roman empire until the first half of the second century A.D. What happened after that time is succinctly explained by F.W. Hall:

Men could no longer appreciate or even understand the ideals of the past, which were embodied in works which breathed the spirit of ancient freedom. For a time, indeed, the classics survive as a fashion among educated men. But the public which could find pleasure in them, and in the archaistic imitations of them that were produced by a Lucian and an Alciphron slowly passes away. Even while such a public still exists it is clear that its range of reading is severely contracted. Some authors gradually disappear (e.g. the Tragedians, with the exception of the three; Comedy except Aristophanes; and the Lyric poets except Pindar). Those that remain do not survive entire but in selections or in anthologies, which rapidly lead to the extinction of all parts of an author's work that they do not include.[3]

At about the same time the scroll began to lose its popularity and was slowly replaced by the codex, essentially a handwritten book with leaves made from folded sheets of papyrus or, more often, fine leather prepared from the skins of young goats or sheep (*vellum*). In general any work not transcribed from scroll to codex in the desperately troubled centuries after the Severan emperors did not survive into Byzantine times. Of Theopompus' works, Photius, the great Byzantine scholar (fl. 858–86), knew only the *Philippica*, and his copy of it lacked five books. Thus a nearly complete *Philippica* survived to within a few centuries of the age of printing. The precise circumstances of its final disappearance are not known.

Theopompus' output was voluminous; he wrote some seventy-two books of histories and numerous other treatises. Chapter 1 gives an estimate of the average length of his books; suffice to say for the moment that if all his historical works had survived, they would probably occupy some six to ten times the space of a Herodotus or Thucydides on library shelves. Therefore, the acquisition of a complete Theopompus must have been expensive for an ancient library. Quite possibly smaller "provincial" libraries would be sorely pressed to find the money to purchase so voluminous a collection or the space to store so many rolls of papyrus beneath the name of a single author.

There is some information about the loss of Theopompus' main work, the *Philippica*. Photius claims to have read fifty-three surviving books of "histories." It soon becomes clear that he means the *Philippica*. He cites an otherwise unknown Menophanes who claimed that book 12 was lost, but Photius says that he had read that book. To prove it he gives a precious summary of its contents. He identifies four lost books: 6, 7, 29, and 30. Already something is wrong with the figures, for another source shows that there were fifty-eight books. Perhaps Photius thought that originally there had been only fifty-seven, or perhaps he has neglected to mention one of the lost books, or possibly Wachsmuth's restoration of the words "and the eleventh [book]" to Photius' text is correct.[4]

It is tempting, if not unavoidable, to associate Photius' information with a notice in Diodorus of Sicily, the first-century-B.C. compiler of a "universal history." Speaking of the year 360 B.C., Diodorus says (16.3.8 = T17): "Theopompus of Chios made this year the beginning of his *Philippica*, and wrote 58 books of which five are lost." This statement makes it seem as if the five books were lost very early but that afterwards the rest of the *Philippica* survived intact well into Byzantine times. Presumably the fifty-three books known in Diodorus' time are the same as the ones read by Photius.

This assumption may well be correct, but it is nevertheless true that authors who lived after Diodorus were able to provide citations from books that Photius did not have: namely 6, 11 (if correctly restored), and 30. How then could Diodorus be missing these books while other scholars were still citing them? Perhaps Diodorus and Photius were at different ends of one manuscript tradition or "stemma." By this theory other, more complete manuscripts were in existence in antiquity, but no one took the trouble to fill the gaps in the Diodorus-Photius tradition from the more complete versions until it was too late. To judge from the locations of the authors who cite the more complete versions it seems that they were to be found in Alexandria and perhaps Athens. Books 6, 11, and 30 are cited by Harpocration, an Alexandrian whose dates are unknown, but he must have been later than Diodorus. Porphyry, the second-century philosopher, refers to book 11 in a work probably written in Athens. There are also citations of book 6 in a work by the Byzantine grammarian, Stephanus (late fifth–early sixth centuries). However, it is possible that Stephanus was not using Theopompus directly but some lost intermediary source instead.

One other observation deserves to be made in connection with the Diodorus-Photius "stemma." The lost books were allegedly 6 and 7, 29 and 30, and, perhaps, 11 and 12, except that 12 was restored to the "stemma" from some unknown source. One way of cutting costs and saving space in "provincial" libraries was to resort to the otherwise inconvenient opisthographs, papyrus scrolls with writing on both sides. There is reason to believe that an average book by Theopompus would go comfortably onto one side of a scroll of average length. If the subsequent book were written on the back, a single scroll would take two consecutive books with it if lost.

In general, the frequency with which Theopompus was cited in antiquity suggests that his works were kept in extensive if not complete collections at major centres of learning such as Athens (where masters of rhetoric still advocated the use of Theopompus as a stylistic model in the third century A.D.)[5] and Alexandria throughout most of antiquity. He was known to Latin authors; so it is likely that he was well represented in libraries in the Italian peninsula too. Probably the Diodorus-Photius "stemma" originated in a "provincial" collection of opisthographs; how many other opisthographs and partial collections existed cannot be known.

The distribution of the manuscripts provides some indication of the esteem in which the ancients held Theopompus. It seems that he would have been represented in any library with pretentions. Another way of estimating his importance would be to consider the subject-matter of his major works and the interest later generations took in the topics he covered. He wrote historical works: an *Epitome of*

Herodotus (two books), a *Hellenica* (twelve books on Greek history continuing Thucydides' unfinished *Peloponnesian War*, covering the years 411–394), and the *Philippica* (packed with digressions on the life and times of Philip II of Macedon). He also wrote many smaller tracts and speeches. With the exception of letters to Alexander the Great and Philip, an encomium of Philip, and a diatribe against the teaching of Plato, his minor works are not quoted and are scarcely noticed in surviving ancient literature. In this case their loss is attributable to their lack of importance both stylistically and in contents. It is arguable that the letters were noticed only because of their addressees, and the treatise and encomium because their subjects were the teaching of the famous Athenian philosopher and the greatness of Alexander's father. The orations must have been little more than stylistic curiosities. Further, as examples of style they were set at a disadvantage at a date not more than a century or two after Theopompus' death. The problem arose from a theory (or tradition) that became current, even orthodox, at a quite early date. Someone decided or recorded that Theopompus had been a pupil of Isocrates, the great Athenian orator, and the idea won general acceptance.[6] Apparently it was not a difficult view to accept for, according to all reports, Theopompus' and Isocrates' styles were very similar. However, since the orations of the master were generally well preserved, the speeches of his pupils would naturally disappear in his giant shadow with the passing of time. This fate, namely, falling into neglect because of the perceived superiority of the reputed master, befell the orations of many who were reportedly Isocrates' students. They are known by name alone.

With the histories, the story is different. The *Epitome of Herodotus* received scant attention, but there were ancient readers who took an interest in the events and heroes of the great age of Greek history toward the end of the Peloponnesian War and thereafter. Therefore, the *Hellenica* was more widely known and read. Plutarch must have used it, perhaps extensively, in his lives of Alcibiades, Agesilaus, and Lysander. However, the *Philippica* was easily the most important work. Philip V of Macedonia (238–179 B.C.), adopted descendant of Philip II and successor to his throne after several generations, found himself in opposition to the growing dominion of Rome. Perhaps to inspire his generals with stories of early Macedonian invincibility, he had scribes go through the *Philippica* and excerpt all the passages that dealt directly with Philip II (T31). So digressive had Theopompus been that out of the fifty-eight books, a scant sixteen books' worth of material was compiled.

Philip II had been the principal architect of Macedonian greatness.

He had created and trained the army used by Alexander to conquer the Persian empire. With their strong military traditions, the Romans naturally admired Alexander. Some must have looked further to find the reasons for his success in the life and career of his father, Philip. Nevertheless, the *Philippica* never became a classic. Its cumbersome length and chronic digressiveness made it something of a literary monster.

There are other ways whereby ancient texts have survived in precious quantities. A few charred scrolls of disappointing value have been found at Herculaneum, and the unwrapping of some late Egyptian mummies bound in papyrus scrolls has brought to light some important texts. Three substantial historical passages were found at Oxyrhynchus, all written by the same author, and at first it was believed they were fragments of the lost *Hellenica* of Theopompus. While uncertainties remain, the best judgment now seems to be that Theopompus was not the author. It was someone unknown (called, therefore, the Oxyrhynchus historian or, more simply, P for papyrus historian) or possibly the shadowy historian Cratippus.[7]

There still may be room for hope. If there were readers of obscure historians of Greece in Roman Egypt, why not more famous ones too? Is there still the mummy of some ancient Egyptian buried wrapped in a few books of the *Philippica* waiting to be found? If such a discovery is ever made, it might be too much to expect to find the author and title clearly identified. This information was usually on tags that easily became separated from the scroll. In the event of such a discovery, information from the existing fragments and *testimonia* would likely have to be used to effect an identification of the author and work – all the more reason for care in the study of what might be called "the echo" of Theopompus in surviving ancient literature.

Theopompus the Historian

CHAPTER ONE

Theopompus: Life, Works, and Style

Ancient and Byzantine sources provide information about Theopompus' life, but some of it is contradictory, some is questionable, and all of it is distressingly vague. There is a range of choices for the date of his birth. Photius says that he fled into exile from his native island of Chios with his father, who had been charged with "Spartanizing," but that when he was forty-five years old, he was restored to his home by the intervention of Alexander the Great in "a letter to the Chians." Alexander's letter to the Chians can be dated to 334.[1] Simple arithmetic therefore makes 379 the year of Theopompus' birth. This date (or 378/7) has won wide acceptance, but variants are recorded. A tenth-century Byzantine lexicon, the *Suda*, gives between 408 and 403 (that is, the 93rd Olympiad) and 404/3 (the year of anarchy in Athens, that is, the year of the Thirty Tyrants) both in the same line of text.[2] Cornelius Nepos, a Roman biographer of the first century B.C., simply offers the vague information that Theopompus was born "some time" after Alcibiades' lifetime. Alcibiades was assassinated in 404.[3]

Nepos' information is too vague to be of much use, and it remains to see what can be said for the *Suda*'s 408–403 or for Photius' more precise 379. When the early biographers could not give an exact date for someone's birth, they sometimes estimated it from the supposed time of the individual's acme, assumed to be at age forty. If an important, datable event could be found in the person's lifetime, it would be used arbitrarily to "pin-point" the acme, and the birthdate would be placed forty years before.[4] Could this formula have been used to "establish" either or both of the alternative dates (or range of dates) given for Theopompus' birth?

Forty years after 408–403 gives 368–363, and it is hard to imagine anything pertinent to Theopompus between those dates. A date for the exile of Theopompus' father might be helpful. On the assumption that being pro-Spartan meant being anti-Athenian and oligarchic, Wormell argued some time ago that shortly before 340/39 was a likely date for known anti-Athenian Chians to be driven into exile by their fellow citizens. In that year Chios joined an anti-Macedonian and somewhat pro-Athenian alliance with Byzantium.[5] If Theopompus was born in 379, he was about forty by late 340/39. It is possible, therefore, that the date 379 was produced by the application of a dubious formula.

It is not known where Photius got his information. He reproduced comparatively extensive, if factually vague, biographical material about Theopompus. In it, to be sure, he sometimes drew inferences directly from clues provided by Theopompus himself, apparently in the introduction to the *Philippica*: "He himself [Theopompus]," says Photius, "says that he was in his prime [acme] at the same time as Isocrates, the Athenian, Theodectes of Phaselis, and Naucrates of Erythrae." Theodectes, Naucrates, and Isocrates were among Theopompus' opponents in the oratorical contest at the funeral of Mausolus in 352 B.C. (T6a, b). Mausolus' wife, Artemisia, held commemorative games for her husband in which, among other contests, orators competed to see who could deliver the best encomium of the dead king. Apparently, what Photius is summarizing is a passage in which Theopompus mentioned the competition and boasted of his victory. Isocrates' lifespan was 436–338, Theodectes' was c. 375–334, and Naucrates' dates are unknown. Like Theopompus, Naucrates and Theodectes are reported to have been students of Isocrates. Clearly this information does little to establish the lifespan of Theopompus. The more precise information that he was forty-five when restored to Chios is introduced by λέγεται (it is said) and placed in the accusative and infinitive construction, one Greek method of marking off a quotation. Perhaps Photius turned to an unknown biographical source for Theopompus' birthdate. It is by no means impossible that this source somehow dated the exile to c. 339, assumed it to be the date for the acme, and, reckoning inclusively, arbitrarily put Theopompus in his fortieth year and added five years to get to 334, the date of Alexander's letter, to make Theopompus forty-five at the time of his restoration. Another pivotal date suitable for an ancient "acme-reckoning" would be 338, the decisive battle of Chaeronea, Philip's most significant historical achievement. This must have been the culminating event of Theopompus' *magnum opus*, the *Philippica*. Chaeronea took place forty-one years after 379, perhaps close enough for a vague formula. Whatever the truth is, if Photius had other information from Theopompus' works, he neglected to provide it. He was probably completely in the dark himself, and there is no reason to suppose that his source was any less so.

Nevertheless, if 379 is not certainly the date for Theopompus' birth, it may not be too wide of the mark. Theopompus was a prolific author, and the writing of his historical works seems largely to date from after 360, and, indeed, there is no act or event in his life that can be securely dated to before that time. Things that might be earlier can be explained otherwise. A survey of his literary work and of the sparse biographical information will illustrate this point. His first historical enterprise was probably the *Epitome of Herodotus* in two books.[6] An epitome of the father of history sounds like an exercise for a youthful, would-be historian. A letter attributed to the Platonist Speusippus[7] (which may be spurious) clearly implies that Theopompus was at the court of Philip in c. 343 and enjoying his patronage after the publication of the *Hellenica*. Presumably, Theopompus was beginning his researches toward the *Philippica*. Philip had come to power in 360. At first his position was so tenuous that few outside of Macedonia would have regarded him as worthy of special attention. He did not catch the eye of Demosthenes until 352.[8] From this date onward his reputation must have grown rapidly as his successes continued and his empire expanded. By 347/6 Isocrates was addressing him in the *Philippus*.[9] Some time between about 352 and 346 would, therefore, seem right for Theopompus to entertain thoughts of a comprehensive history of Philip's career. Speusippus' letter makes reference to circumstances prevailing in winter 343/2 and, if genuine, must have been written at that time.[10] This letter would fit with another piece of evidence. Theopompus wrote a letter to Philip denouncing Hermeas of Atarneus in c. 343 (F250), and it predates 341 when Hermeas was captured and killed by the Persians. I suspect that the young Theopompus was posing as a pro-Macedonian agent in an attempt to secure Philip's patronage. So the *Hellenica* was finished before c. 343 and begun some time in the 350s, for a passage in Eusebius on ancient plagiarisms brings the charge that Theopompus stole entire passages from the *Hellenica* of Xenophon the Athenian (c. 428–c. 354) and incorporated them in his own.[11] Xenophon's work covers the period from 411 to the battle of Mantinea in 362. It appears to have been divided into three parts, but there is no evidence that it was published piecemeal. Therefore it is unlikely that any of it was in circulation for Theopompus to use until the very late 360s or early 350s. If this is the case, Theopompus' historical activity would fit into the mid- to late-360s for the *Epitome of Herodotus*, the 350s for the *Hellenica*, and the 340s and some considerable time thereafter for the *magnum opus*, the *Philippica*. None of this is certain, but it looks reasonable.

For ten or more years after the death of Philip in 336, Theopompus must have been very busy. The enormous *Philippica* had to be put in its final form, but the historian still seems to have had time for writing a letter or letters of information and advice to the campaigning Alexander. His behaviour during these years is paradoxical to the modern eye, a fitting culmination to his turbulent life. While posing again as an agent and supporter of the Macedonian regime by sending friendly communications to the son, he was writing an incredibly bitter account of the allegedly pernicious habits and career of the father. In anticipation of the conclusions to be reached in chapter 5 about Theopompus' treatment of Philip, it is worth pausing to wonder what might be at the roots of his hostility. Two of Philip's actions could easily have alienated Theopompus. One was the appointment of Aristotle as tutor to the young Alexander (343), and the other was Philip's immoderate celebration of his victory at Chaeronea (F236). Philip dismissed the ambassadors from the defeated Athenians and began a scene of drunken debauchery, which Theopompus recorded in the *Philippica* with obvious disgust. When Aristotle's appointment is considered in conjunction with the information in Speusippus' letter, a little more is revealed about Theopompus' early relationship to Philip.

The appointment coincides exactly with the date of Speusippus' letter and, therefore, with the date of Theopompus' visit to Philip alleged therein; hence it takes little imagination to suppose that Theopompus could have been Aristotle's rival for the position.[12] By 343 Aristotle had not established his independence from Plato's school of philosophy. Therefore, Theopompus' maligning of Plato, of which Speusippus complains, would have to be seen as an attempt to discredit Aristotle. Further, Wormell has dated the letter about Hermeas of Atarneus, Aristotle's uncle by marriage, to Philip to about this same time on independent grounds.[13] Finally, there seems no reason to doubt that Theopompus produced his *Encomium of Philip* at this time also. It was most likely written to secure a favourable reception at the Macedonian court, but securing a lucrative and prestigious tutorship would be a natural secondary objective. After his flattery of Philip and the attack on Aristotle through his family and education, the adoption of Aristotle as Alexander's tutor will have done nothing to cheer Theopompus's already melancholic soul.

Every reference to Philip in the fragments of the *Philippica* is scathingly bitter. It has recently been pointed out[14] that they are all written in the past tense, which probably means that Theopompus set his *magnum opus* in its final form in the years after Philip's death. The uniform negativity suggests that the work was entirely written, or comprehensively revised, in those years. However, there is no solid indication of a date for the *Philippica*'s final publication. Schwartz once argued for 334, a scant two years after Philip's death. But his date seems too early for the writing or reworking of fifty-eight books, and the idea has been well disposed of by Truesdell Brown.[15] The best guess appears to be approximately 323, the year of Alexander's death. At about this time, Theopompus' popularity reached perhaps its lowest ebb. The publication of the malicious *Philippica* might well explain his renewed exile and the general hatred directed toward him.

The minor works, mostly known only by title, seem generally to address people and events from the 350s down to the 330s and, perhaps, to the 320s.[16] A possible exception might be a "To Evagoras," if it is authentic (T48). The famous Evagoras was active in Cyprus until 374/3, when Theopompus says he was assassinated. However, he had a grandson called Evagoras who could just as well be the subject or addressee of this work. He was put to death about 346 after controlling Cyprus and Sidon for a time.[17] There is a small handful of names of works for which dates cannot be suggested, but the *Mausolus* (T48), or *Ecomium of Mausolus*, was delivered at the funeral of the Carian king in 352 (D.S. 16.36.2). Presumably Theopompus would have needed a considerable reputation to have become a finalist in this rhetorical competition. A short epitome of Herodotus and some other exercises, which may or may not have been published by c. 352, are not enough. It is tempting to propose that readings from the early books of the *Hellenica* or even the publication of the finished work could have brought Theopompus to the attention of the mourning widow, and there is a tradition that Theopompus won first prize.[18]

Amongst the minor works there is also a *Panathenaicus* (T48). If it is genuine, its title, bearing the same name as one of Isocrates' famous speeches, was possibly an imitation of or a response to Isocrates' oration. In his own *Panathenaicus* at any rate Isocrates does not seem aware of an already existing work by that name, and his speech seems to have been published in 339.[19] Theopompus' work, therefore, was probably published sometime later. Other minor works addressed to or written about Philip or Alexander, who ascended the throne in 336, are noted. Two sources mention some "Chian Letters," which the *Suda* says were written to Alexander "against the Chians" during the period of exile.[20] Letters to Alexander blaming other Chians might be one means by which the historian hoped to win his restoration. They are datable, therefore, to between 336 (Alexander's accession) and 334 (the restoration). So, if the "to Evagoras" was addressed to Evagoras the younger, the lesser works seem to fit into the same period as the major historical exercises: 350s to 330s B.C.

There remain a few biographical *anecdota* to consider. First, Photius found information about the later life of Theopompus in the same biographical source that pin-pointed Theopompus' age at forty-five in the year of the restoration. The story makes the historian something of an outcast, which is none too surprising considering that most of the Greek world's new rulers were, or were descended from, former friends and partisans of Philip.

After the death of Alexander, driven out everywhere, he [Theopompus] came to Egypt, and Ptolemy, king of Egypt, did not accept him but wanted to do away with him as a meddler — had not some of his friends interceded and saved him.

If this anecdote is trustworthy, Theopompus outlived Alexander, but not necessarily by many years, for this seems to be the latest datable item from Theopompus' life. Further, if the publication of the *Philippica* was indeed the cause of the general hostility to Theopompus, then c. 323 or perhaps a little later would be a reasonable approximate date for its appearance.

Secondly, it is tempting to see more in the reported Spartanizing of Theopompus' father. From the last years of the Peloponnesian War and the overthrow of the Athenian empire there is reason to believe that Athens had generally favoured democracies in her allied states, and Sparta, oligarchies. After 404, when the Spartans had established their maritime empire, their subject states had been governed by "harmosts," usually ten in number and appointed by Lysander. Most of the harmosts were deposed by Sparta c. 403 and replaced by puppet oligarchies. Many of these governments will surely have been overthrown after Conon's defeat of the Spartan navy at Cnidus in 394, but thereafter a pro-Spartan agitator in an Aegean community is likely to have been thought of as an advocate of a totalitarian oligarchy. If those were the politics of Theopompus' father, were they his too? It has been customary to assume so, but chapter 4 will show that the *Philippica* reveals no clear preference for any form of government. However, the historian's family may be reasonably supposed to have had strong oligarchic leanings, and perhaps it was wealthy too, for Theopompus insisted that he never had to give lessons like Isocrates and others. However, he must have financed his extensive travels in some way if Dionysius is right about their extent.[21]

Nonetheless, Theopompus was apparently a democrat, for Alexander's decree generally restored exiled democrats in opposition to the established oligarchies of the time.[22]

Despite apparent unanimity among the ancients that Theopompus was a student of Isocrates,[23] the tradition has been denied in several modern studies and warmly supported and used to flesh out the skeletal knowledge of Theopompus' life by others.[24] The debate has made the question seem rather more important than it probably is. It is by no means impossible that Theopompus knew and studied under Isocrates. Theopompus visited Isocrates' home city, Athens, to judge from his first-hand knowledge of Athenian public inscriptions.[25] As a rich man with literary ambitions, he will scarcely have avoided contact with any of Athens' *literati* during his visit. There is also a tradition that Isocrates opened a rhetorical school on Chios.[26] Unfortunately, since its dates are not recorded, it is not known whether it was operating during Theopompus' youth. Furthermore, Theopompus seems to have been familiar with Isocrates' work. He is accused of reproducing a passage *verbatim* from the master's *Areopagiticus* in the eleventh book of the *Philippica*,[27] and a *Panathenaicus*, if authentic, was probably written in response to Isocrates. However, possibly the most important piece of evidence is, once again, Speusippus' letter. Its importance stems from its earliness. If genuine, it is a contemporary testimony to Theopompus and other intellectuals, and even if it is a forgery, it is based on an extensive knowledge of the people and circumstances of the time. The letter begins with a full-scale attack on Isocrates with specific reference to his *Philippus*. The general quality of this work, the sincerity of its praise for Philip, and even Isocrates' scholarship are all impugned. There is a brief slur on Isocrates' "Pontic student" (Isocrates of Apollonia), and then the denunciation of Theopompus begins. It has been argued that the juxtaposition of Theopompus with a student of Isocrates of Athens must imply that the writer thought he too was a pupil of Isocrates. In this view, the letter is essentially an attack on Isocrates and his school. Some question the strength of this argument on the grounds that the letter does not explicitly identify Theopompus as a student of Isocrates.[28] However, the structure of the entire letter certainly favours the idea. The epistle begins and ends with Isocrates and his alleged insincerity toward Philip. It recommends the bearer, a student of Speusippus named Antipater of Magnesia, and the quality of his historical work over historical notions in Isocrates and, implicitly, over Theopompus' *Hellenica*. The context is the rivalry of two schools, and if the letter does not presume some sort of association between Isocrates and Theopompus, Theopompus' inclusion in it would be something of an anomaly. Finally, Speusippus and Aristotle remained friends after Aristotle left the academy in 347.[29] Therefore, it is not unreasonable to see in the letter a counterblow to Theopompus' *Diatribe against the Teaching of Plato*. If the historian could impugn Aristotle's educator (and, by extension, his education), Speusippus could reply in kind, supporting his school and erstwhile colleague with an attack on Theopompus' alleged master. In other words, the most natural interpretation is that the letter assumes a pupil-master relationship between Theopompus and Isocrates.

Masters may influence the thinking of their students, but they seem never to control it. Isocrates was a stylistic model for Theopompus according to many authors from later antiquity. However, if he did instruct Theopompus, he taught him something about style alone. The master advocated a form of Panhellenism that dreamed of a united Greece and Macedonia campaigning against Persia.[30] No commitment to that ideal can be traced in Theopompus. On the contrary, the dream he imputed to Philip in the lost *Eulogy* was not the conquest of Persia but only of Europe. This theme is highly significant, for it had been Isocrates' aim in advocating the Persian invasion to *deflect* Philip from the conquest of Europe, particularly Greece, and call for voluntary Hellenic alliance against the barbarian.[31] Again, Isocrates wrote a eulogistic treatise on the life of the elder Evagoras. Theopompus, on the other hand, is known to have emphasized Evagoras' sexual scurrility and the sordid circumstances surrounding his assassination, on all of which Isocrates is silent. Similarly, Nicocles, Evagoras' son, is flattered by Isocrates, but Theopompus makes him a dedicated debauchee.[32] No doubt Theopompus wrote much more of which Isocrates would have disapproved. On the other hand, the moralizing tendency of many fragments from the *Philippica*, pointing out as they often do the dire consequences of profligacy, is not out of keeping with the sentiment of Isocrates' *Antidosis*, the work in which he outlines his educational philosophy.[33]

Plato and his school, with their claims to be able to define such abstract notions as "the good" and "justice," attracted Theopompus' attention also. Arrian recorded the following barbed comment:

[Theopompus] charges Plato with wanting to define everything. Why else does he say? "Did no one of us before you say anything good and just? Or do we utter our voices meaninglessly and emptily by not paying meticulous attention to what each of these things is?"[34]

The context of this remark is not known. It might come from the *Philippica* when Theopompus gave his account of Hermeas of

Atarneus. A digression on Plato's school might have included a speech of criticism. Otherwise, it is perhaps more reasonable to associate it with a diatribe against Plato delivered at Philip's court. However, one adherent of the Socratic school was treated kindly: Antisthenes the Cynic (F295). He is described as a concerned and skilful educator (D.L. 6.14). As a consequence of this remark, it has been argued more than once that Theopompus was somehow a follower of the Cynic branch of the Socratic school.[35] The famous Diogenes was the prime mover in this offshoot from the Academy. It is certainly true that Theopompus' moral judgments seem universally damning and that they are delivered with a snarl worthy of Diogenes. Chapter 4 treats these fragments in detail, but no true practitioner of Diogenes' thought would have written so much history. For all his sarcastic morality Theopompus seems too interested in instructing the world like an Isocrates to have rejected it as totally as a Diogenes.

The survey of the evidence relating to the life and career of Theopompus invites the following conclusions. Born about 379 he was of an age and had the opportunity to have studied under Isocrates. If he did, he learned something about style from him. However, Isocrates' influence otherwise seems limited except that Theopompus would have probably agreed with those passages where the master advocates educational programs for improving the morals of the improvable. On the other hand, in some ways Theopompus would have felt at home with the moral attitudes of the early Cynics. His hatred of the Platonists may stem from a bitter and failed attempt to snatch the tutorship of Alexander from Aristotle. Finally, in the political arena, it will be argued that Theopompus was something of a self-styled supporter of Demosthenes in opposition to Philip. Of course, this partisanship does not mean that he abrogated the right to criticize Demosthenes, especially for failure.

A more significant and more complicated question is the matter of Theopompus' relationship to other historians of his time. Present knowledge of most of them is rarely much more substantial than for Theopompus himself, but it is useful to rehearse the few relevant facts about their lives and possible relationship to Theopompus. Xenophon of Athens (c. 424–c. 354) was a friend of Socrates. He left Athens in 401 to accompany his friend Proxenus, a mercenary in Cyrus' expedition, to capture the Persian throne from Artaxerxes, Cyrus' brother. When he returned with the Greek survivors of the expedition, he became son-in-law to Agesilaus, the Spartan king. The Athenians exiled him, probably in 394,[36] but he was able to return to Athens in 366/5 and died there, probably toward the middle of the next decade. He wrote a number of works, but the ones that would be regarded as historical include the *Anabasis* (c. 386), covering Cyrus' expedition and the return of the Greek survivors; the *Agesilaus*, a historical-biographical treatise about his father-in-law; and the *Hellenica*, covering Greek affairs from 411 (the termination of Thucydides' *Peloponnesian War*) to 362 (the second battle of Mantinea). Theopompus knew the *Hellenica* and mined it for his own work of the same name (F21).

The dates usually accepted for Ephorus of Cyme, c. 405–330 B.C., make him an older contemporary of Theopompus.[37] Like Theopompus he was a reputed student of Isocrates, which, if true, need mean nothing more than that his style and, perhaps, his moral outlook were Isocratean. His *magnum opus* was a "universal history" from the earliest time down to 341 in twenty-nine books. The work was broken off by his death. He wrote by subject and had not yet given an account of the Sacred War. It was supplied in a thirtieth book by his son Demophilus. Though termed a "universal history" ('Ιστορίαι), his work focused almost exclusively on Greeks. There seems to have been a presumption by Greeks of this time that they were the only people who had history; barbarians did not. This idea seems to have lasted in the minds of some Greeks at least until the first century when Dionysius of Halicarnassus begins his history of Rome with an elaborate demonstration that the Romans, far from being barbarians, were really Greeks![38]

Nothing is known about Daemachus of Plataea except that he lived in the fourth century and wrote a *Hellenica*.[39] Along with Anaximenes and Callisthenes he is identified by Porphyry as a source from whom Ephorus plagiarized (Jacoby no. 65, T1). Anaximenes of Lampsacus[40] is another shadowy figure. He lived c. 380–320 and wrote a *Hellenica*, a *Philippica*, and *On Alexander*. The *Suda* (no. 72, T1) makes him a teacher of Alexander. His *Hellenica* went from the birth of the gods to Epaminondas' death at Mantinea in 362 in just twelve books (D.S. 15.89.3 = Jacoby no.72, T14). His *Philippica* was almost as compendious. What Theopompus had covered in fifty-eight books, he skimmed through in a mere eight. Pausanias makes him a bitter enemy of Theopompus in a revealing story (T10 = Paus. 6.18.2):

Having a quarrel with Theopompus the son of Damasistratus, he wrote a treatise abusing Athenians, Lacedaemonians and Thebans alike. He imitated the style of Theopompus with perfect accuracy, inscribed his name upon the book and sent it round to the cities. Though Anaximenes was the author of the treatise, hatred of Theopompus grew throughout the length of Greece.

The work of which Pausanias speaks was apparently entitled

Tricaranus, which means "Three-headed (monster?)" (no. 72, TT20–1). A work entitled *Philippica* written by an enemy of Theopompus sounds like an attempt to set the record straight. Since the *Tricaranus* did not parody Theopompus' famous assaults on Philip, perhaps this "teacher of Alexander" wrote his own *Philippica* to answer or "correct" his rival's vicious attacks on Philip to please that monarch's greater son and ingratiate himself. Perhaps the *Suda* is mistaken, however, when it goes so far as to make Anaximenes Alexander's tutor. After Aristotle, Callisthenes of Olynthus, Aristotle's nephew, became the king's philosophical mentor.

If Theopompus' relationship to Anaximenes had been one of bitter rivalry, that with Callisthenes (Jacoby no. 124)[41] looks more respectful. In a way that, at first, looks astonishingly polite for an age of literary piracy, these two historians seem to have maintained a polite distance from each other's topics. Diodorus (14.117.8, 16.14.4 = T27) says that Callisthenes' *Hellenica*, in ten books, covered the thirty-year period from the King's Peace (387) to the beginning of the Sacred War (357). His other major work was *The Deeds of Alexander*. Apparently, therefore, the two historians complement each other nearly perfectly: Theopompus' *Hellenica* covered c. 412–394, Callisthenes' 387–357; Theopompus' *Philippica*, 360–336, Callisthenes' *Deeds of Alexander*, 336-unfinished. However, deference is not the only possible explanation of this distribution of labour. Polybius observed Theopompus' neglect of Greek affairs from 394 to 360 with considerable outrage. Perhaps Callisthenes' decision to devote ten books to the period was motivated by a similar sense of disapproval.

This latter alternative looks a little more attractive in the context of the Oyrhynchus historian or P. Though substantial fragments exist, this work's commencement and termination dates are not known, nor the number of books. Presumably P's work would have been called a *Hellenica*, and there is good evidence[42] that it continued the unfinished *Peloponnesian War* of Thucydides. If so, it began with the year 412 or 411. Its termination is less certain, but 386 has been suggested,[43] and that would seem to be the earliest appropriate date for a history like the *Hellenica Oxyrhynchia* to aim for. P shows decisive interest in mainland history. His meticulous description of the constitution of the Boeotian League (11.2–4) is the only one that survives, and it would be surprising if when he wrote it he did not intend to take his narrative down to the dissolution of that constitution by the Spartans in 387/6. P is always careful to cover major events in the Aegean (Pedaritus' death on Chios, the mutiny of some of Conon's men in the Persian fleet, reports of troop movements in Asia), but his attention to mainland history is extraordinary in detail, and his history was doubtless written from the point of view of a Greek mainlander, perhaps an Athenian.[44] Similar, it seems, was the *Hellenica* of Callisthenes. It began with the King's Peace, P's probable target, and went down to the outbreak of the Sacred War, two crucial events in the history of Central Greece. The greatest events he would have to record would be Thebes' destruction of Spartan land-power followed by her own decline. That Callisthenes followed this thread of mainland history seems certain, which would make his *Hellenica* a continuation of P, and not of Theopompus, who seems far less interested in the mainland, as I shall try to demonstrate in the next chapter.

There was also a Cratippus, an Athenian who lived at the same time as Thucydides and continued his work down to at least the late 390s if not the King's Peace (Jacoby no.64, TT1, 2).[45] Harding[46] has shown that Cratippus could have been another of Ephorus' sources, used for Athenian history after 411, but since P was Ephorus' source for that period, the conclusion that P and Cratippus are the same person is attractive. P was writing early enough to be Ephorus' source. Indeed, he was apparently ignorant of the Sacred War, which seems to put his date of publication before 357. Therefore, there is every possibility that Theopompus knew this *Hellenica*, but the extent of his use of P is impossible to estimate. In the next chapter and in Appendix A I show that Theopompus' *Hellenica* was in some sense a response to P aimed at correcting his historical perspective. If that view is adopted, P was a source for Theopompus to some degree and Callisthenes grouped himself with a historiographical tradition that rivalled Theopompus.

Before leaving the subject of Theopompus' relationship to his fellow historians, it is useful to indicate how they relate to my conclusions that Theopompus made himself a maverick by adopting the point of view of an outsider, someone aloof from the power struggles of the mainland: "A pox on all their houses." In the *Hellenica* he rejected the mainland orientation of the P (Cratippus)-Callisthenes-Ephorus tradition and wrote as a Chian or Ionian. To correct P he may have reflected his wording and arrangement at times, but he brought scathing judgments of states and individuals into both the narrative and special summations, such as obituaries, the sort of thing from which P seems to have abstained. In addition, I argue that he further "corrected" P by including a strain of Sicilian history in the *Hellenica*; there is no sign that P paid any attention to Sicily. On that subject Theopompus' possible sources can only be guessed at, but the works of Philistus of Syracuse and Hermeas of Methymna were probably available.[47] The effect of Theopompus' approach seems well represented by Anaximenes' *Tricaranus*. Anaximenes only parodied his rival's style; he did need to invent his negative attitudes. The Spartans are praised for their personal self-control only on the rare occasions when they displayed it; otherwise, they and their state are condemned, even ridiculed. Athens too was excoriated as a house of greedy imperialists out to steal as much as possible in tribute and bribes from her subjects; only in defeat and at the time of the Second Confederacy, which at least made a show of respecting allied autonomy, can softer words be found. Thebes, for her part, is given the most contemptuous treatment of all. She never got significantly embroiled with Greek states in Sicily or the Aegean. From Theopompus' perspective her brief period of supremacy could be largely and systematically ignored, confined as it was to the mainland and to a few short decades of conflict with a rapidly declining Sparta.

So much for Theopompus' life and age. What sort of writer was he? The longer fragments, most of which are from the *Philippica*, reveal a yarn-spinner and passionate moralist. It cannot be assumed that they are a representative sample,[48] but along with the ancient descriptions and criticisms of and reflections on his style collected by Jacoby, they give ground for observations.

In the *Philippica* Theopompus included some digressions that won fame, or notoriety, enough to receive their own title in antiquity. A digression on Athenian political leaders from Themistocles (c. 528–c. 462) to Eubulus (c. 405–c. 330) was found in book 10. It came to be known as "On the Demagogues."[49] This much-studied digression is treated in chapter 3. For his style another famous digression is more informative: the *Mirabilia*, or "Marvels," found in book 8 and, apparently, early in book 9.[50]

In the books of the *Philippica* leading up to this digression Theopompus had covered Philip's rise to power, his early struggles with the Illyrians, and his first intrusions into Thessaly.[51] In the meantime, a war had broken out between Phocis and Thebes over control of the famous oracle at Delphi, the so-called Sacred War (357–347). By 353, the Phocians, under their commander Onomarchus, were enjoying considerable success, pressing north into Thessaly where they encountered Philip pushing down from the north. Their success had been bought at a shocking price, however. They had taken control of the vast treasures at Delphi and used the oracle's riches to make coins with which to hire mercenaries. Using these forces, Onomarchus had succeeded in driving Philip from Thessaly by the end of 353.

But what is the connection with the "Marvels"? How did a digression on wonderful things fit this context? To answer that question it is necessary first to consider the content of the "Marvels" as revealed by the fragments. It is convenient to work through them in the order in which they are arranged by Jacoby, though the order in which Theopompus himself narrated them is not known. There was a section on Persian religion in which Theopompus gave the names of the two great eastern divinities, Ahriman (Angra Mainyu), god of evil, and Oromasdes (Ahura Mazda), a god of good. Further, he apparently claimed that the Persian Magi believed in resurrection to immortality "and that substances will endure through their own [the Magi's] imprecations."[52] This comes from Diogenes Laertius, a chatty, third-century(?) A.D. collector of anecdotes about the lives and teachings of ancient philosophers. Plutarch, the famous biographer and moralist of the first to second century A.D., records a fuller account of a Persian myth of creation and cosmic eschatology, mostly, if not totally, derived from Theopompus (F65 = Plut. *Mor.* 370A–C):[53]

Oromazes, born from the purest light, and Areimanius, born from the darkness, are constantly at war with each other; and Oromazes created six gods, the first of Good Thought, the second of Truth, the third of Order, and, of the rest, one of Wisdom, one of Wealth, and one the Artificer of Pleasure in what is Honourable. But Areimanius created rivals, as it were, equal to these in number. Then Oromazes enlarged himself to thrice his former size, and removed himself as far distant from the Sun as the Sun is distant from the Earth, and adorned the heavens with stars. One star he set there before all others as a guardian and watchman, the Dog-star. Twenty-four other gods he created and placed in an egg. But those created by Areimanius, who were equal in number to the others, pierced through the egg and made their way inside; hence evils are now combined with good. But a destined time shall come when it is decreed that Areimanius, engaged in bringing on pestilence and famine, shall by these be utterly annihilated and shall disappear; and then shall the earth become a level plain, and there shall be one manner of life, and one form of government for the blessed people who shall all speak one tongue. Theopompus says that, according to the sages, one god is to overpower, and the other to be overpowered, each in turn for the space of three thousand years, and afterward for another three thousand years they shall fight and war, and the one shall undo the works of the other, and finally Hades shall pass away; then shall the people be happy, and neither shall they need to have food nor shall they cast any shadow. And the god, who has contrived to bring about all these things, shall then have quiet and shall repose for a time, no long time indeed, but for the god as much as would be a moderate time for a man to sleep. (F.C. Babbitt, tr. L.C.L.)

The lexicon of the Byzantine scholar Photius provides an illuminating entry. Under the heading Zopyrus' talents (as in money) he includes the story of Zopyrus' self-mutilation before the Persian capture of Babylon. Here Theopompus seems to have repeated a story in Herodotus wherein Zopyrus made himself a spy credible to the Babylonians by severely mutilating himself and telling the Babylonians the wounds were inflicted by Darius, the Persian king. The ruse worked; the Babylonians trusted Zopyrus, who was then able to betray the city to the Persians. Theopompus referred to Zopyrus' scars metaphorically as his "talents" because they secured a rich reward from Darius. The ancients seem to have found this characteristic of Theopompus' use of language rather outlandish.[54]

It is evident from a number of sources that Theopompus also included the remarkable story of Epimenides the Cretan. He is the Greek Rip van Winkle. Sent by his family to fetch in the sheep, he was overtaken by nightfall and fell asleep — in a cave according to Apollonius' paraphrase of Theopompus' account. He slept there for fifty-seven years and later died at the age of 157. Other stories told by Theopompus about Epimenides are summarized by Diogenes Laertius (1.115 = F69):

Theopompus says that while Epimenides was preparing a temple for the Nymphs, there broke a voice from heaven which said: "Epimenides, not for the Nymphs, but for Zeus." He predicted to the Cretans the Spartan defeat by the Arcadians ... And indeed they were defeated at Orchomenus. He also says that he became an old man in as many days as he had slept years.

Pherecydes of Syros (mid-sixth century B.C.) was a mythographer and theogonist thought by some ancients to have been the teacher of Pythagoras. Theopompus told two stories illustrating his prowess as a seer. In the first he quenched his thirst with a drink from a well and predicted an earthquake "after a couple of days"; and in the second he predicted the disappearance of a ship, which immediately happened even as he and his companions were watching it approach the harbour. Porphyry (A.D. 232/3–c. 305), the anti-Christian follower of Plotinus, found these same mantic accomplishments attributed to Pythagoras by the fourth-century author Andron of Ephesus. Porphyry blames Theopompus for plagiarizing the stories from Andron and changing the locations and attributing them to the wrong person in a lame attempt to hide his theft. However, if anyone did alter the tradition, Porphyry probably blamed the wrong person. Andron seems to have been the inventor, creating another Pherecydes whole-cloth; and, anyway, the transfer of anecdotes from the lesser known Pherecydes to the more famous Pythagoras seems a more natural process of ancient biography-building.[55] Again, Diogenes Laertius, using Theopompus as his source, provides two otherwise unknown anecdotes. In one Pherecydes predicts the fall of Messene, and in the other he advises the Spartans, on direct authority from Heracles, not to honour gold or silver (F71 = D.L. 1.116–17). It is not clear whether Theopompus agreed with the sources who made Pythagoras a pupil of Pherecydes. The attribution to Pherecydes of prophetic achievements that others gave to Pythagoras could be an indication that Theopompus was cool to Pythagoras, a suspicion seemingly confirmed by the one reference, probably from the "Marvels," to Pythagoras' teaching. In an apparently sarcastic tone, Theopompus seems to have claimed that the Pythagorean doctrine promoted tyranny.[56]

The most famous and extensively quoted anecdote in this digression was the story of the land of Meropis told to Midas by Silenus. Midas got Silenus drunk by mixing a spring at which he used to drink with wine. Once drunk, Silenus was subdued by Midas and compelled to answer questions "about nature and things of old." Silenus told Midas about a boundless other world beyond the stream of Ocean. The inhabitants of this other world are twice as large as the denizens of the known world and live twice as long. Two states great in size are found there, Wartown and Saintsbury. The Saintsburgers lead a beatific, long, and effortless life, while the Wartowners, though they enjoy much power and wealth, have short lives, dying either of diseases or struck down in battle. Gold is so abundant that it is "of less value to them than iron is to us."

People called Meropes live among them in large cities, and in a remote corner of their land is a place called No Return.

It is like a chasm covered by neither darkness nor light, and the air hangs over it a mixed muddy red. Two rivers flow around this place one called the river of pleasure, the other, of sorrow. Trees the size of tall plane trees grow beside these two rivers. The trees by the river of sorrow bear fruit of the following nature: if anyone tastes of it, he sheds so many tears as to dissolve away his entire life in lamentation and so dies. On the other hand, the trees that grow by the river of pleasure bear the opposite fruit. Whoever tastes of them ceases from all his former cares. Even if he loved anyone, of this too he gains forgetfulness; and he becomes young little by little. He regains the earlier, bygone phases of his life. He sheds old age and returns to his prime, next he rejoins the age of youthfulness, then becomes a boy, then a babe and after that he ceases to be.[57]

Two more items are known to have been included in the "Marvels." One reference sadly plucked from its context briefly mentions sacrificial meats at the Olympic Games remaining untouched by birds circling and screeching above. Finally, a note copied in two Byzantine works and assigned to book 9 of the *Philippica* says tantalizingly that Theopompus retailed many incredible (παράδοξα) stories about a Bakis who was recommended by Apollo himself to purify certain Spartan women who had gone mad.[58]

Prophets, priests, and portents are obvious recurring themes in the "Marvels." At first glance Zopyrus looks like a misfit among the group of divines present in the "Marvels." The full story of Zopyrus was told by Herodotus (3.152–9) whose work Theopompus knew. In Herodotus, the episode of Zopyrus' self-mutilation was introduced by a portent. While the Persians were besieging Babylon, the occupants of the city had been taunting the besiegers: "Till mules foal you will not take our city." Of course, one of Zopyrus' mules immediately foaled, and it was this miracle that prompted Zopyrus' drastic action to bring about the capture of the city and, no doubt, that made him a candidate for inclusion in this digression in the *Philippica*.

The Persian Magi are by no means misfits. Their priestly role and the fabulous revelatory nature of the Zoroastrian mythology are perfectly suited to the context. It is tempting to believe that Theopompus would have included an account of Zoroaster himself in which portents and prophesies abounded, but unfortunately there is not a scrap of evidence that he did so. While it is true that his account of the myths of creation and judgment sound authentically Zoroastrian, the fragments do not reveal what Theopompus knew about Zoroaster himself: whether he made him the great prophet he was reported to be or whether he blended conflicting aspects of Iranian religion and cult into one uncritical report. It would be surprising if he was ignorant of Zoroaster, but the fact that he seems to make the Magi the priests of Zoroastrianism, when they are generally thought to have been amongst its bitterest enemies, may suggest that he failed to distinguish pure Zoroastrianism from other ancient Iranian cult practices.[59]

To judge from these fragments, the themes of the "Marvels" included famous prophets and the miracle stories associated with them, persons in history visited by some miraculous portent, and substantial accounts of the "truths" revealed by the prophets themselves or through the mantic occurrences in their lives. These themes have an obvious, if somewhat loose, connection with the Delphic oracle, the most important mantic source for most mainland Greeks. In some cases individuals in the stories had more specific connection with Delphi. Herodotus saw Midas' throne in the Corinthian treasury (1.14.2), and Bacis was recommended to the Spartans by Apollo, the oracle's inspiring divinity. Other Greeks in the "Marvels" are likely to have visited Delphi or dedicated something there, but there is no reason to suppose that any Magi or Zoroaster did anything of the kind. Therefore, the overriding connection between Delphi and the anecdotes in the "Marvels" seems merely to have been the subject of mantic occurrences and the miracles and, perhaps, teachings of famous mystics and prophets.

From this summary, the "Marvels" look like a somewhat rambling digression collecting varied anecdotes around a broadly defined theme. The ancients themselves describe Theopompus as an author whose digressions frequently got the better of him. Photius' story that Philip V could find material about Philip II to fill a mere sixteen books exaggerates a notorious truth (T31). The second-century orator Aelius Theon cited Theopompus as an example of an author whose digressions are so long that his reader becomes "unable to recall the thread of the story." Even the admiring Dionysius of Halicarnassus found some of the digressions unnecessary, inopportune, even childish.[60] Nevertheless, ancient commentators seem to have thought Theopompus talented as a teller of tales. Aelius cites myths in Herodotus, Philistus (Sicilian historian, c. 430–356 B.C.), Theopompus, and Xenophon as examples to be imitated, and Aelian calls Theopompus a formidable yarn-spinner ($\delta\epsilon\iota\nu\grave{o}\varsigma$ $\mu\upsilon\theta o\lambda\acute{o}\gamma o\varsigma$). Cicero found countless stories (*innumerabiles fabulae*) in Theopompus, and they were not all confined to books 8 and 9.[61] Photius gives a summary of the topics included in book 12 that suggests that there was a digression on the geography of Pisidia and Aspendus, on how certain localities were named after men and women from the bronze age, on the bronze age origins of Greek doctors from Cos and Cnidus, and on how Pamphylia was colonized by Greeks, all placed at the end of an account of the career of Evagoras I; the digression was introduced by the dealings of Evagoras' ally, the Egyptian king Acoris, with southern Anatolia. Scattered fragments from many books suggest that Theopompus rarely missed an opportunity to pause and digress. There are tantalizing sketches of Paeonian kings using large horns from cattle for drinking cups in book 2, hints at a ramble into ancient Egyptian history in book 3, and in book 21 Strabo found a treatment of the legendary origins of the names of the Ionian and Adriatic seas and some claims about their geography that he found ridiculous. Technically speaking, the eight-book excursus on eastern history (*Philippica* 12–19) and the five books on western events and geography (*Philippica* 39–43) should also be counted as digressions, for their relevance to Philip's career is very remote. However, it will be shown in chapter 3 that these digressions are integral to the meaning of the work. They both continue the *Hellenica* and end in 344/3, from which year the *Philippica* pursues the career of Philip with a singlemindedness no less remarkable than the chronic digressiveness of the previous books. The point is clear: from 344/3 on there is no more Hellenic history; all is Philippic. Everything Hellenic pales into insignificance beside Philip. Unfortunately for Greeks, however, Philip's success was no blessing for them.

So Theopompus was noted by the ancients as something of a compulsive rambler, but the asperity of his moral judgments provoked considerably more comment. Dionysius of Halicarnassus praised the loftiness of his moralizing excursuses on themes of "justice, propriety, and other virtues in many fine passages." His description of Theopompus' moralizing style is worth quoting at length (T20a = D.H. *Pomp.* 6[2.244].7):

[Theopompus has] the ability not just to see and report what was obvious to all in each transaction but to scrutinize both the hidden reasons for deeds and the inner feelings of their doers also, things not easily seen by the many, and to bring to light the mysteries of apparent virtue and undetected vice. I should think that the mythical scrutiny of bodiless souls in Hades before the infernal judges is about as keen as that throughout the writings of Theopompus. Therefore, he has seemed to be even a slanderer, because he takes up certain needless charges against important persons, over and above the essential ones.

Dionysius finds Theopompus' moral probing occasionally excessive, likening him to a doctor who overcauterizes wounds. His style is compared to that of Isocrates: "pure, unaffected and clear, also lofty, magnificent and full of solemnity." However, "when he denounces cities and generals for bad plans and wicked practices," he becomes more bitter than the master. This side of him is apparent in many passages, but especially in the *Chian Letters*. There, apparently, his style becomes more affected and artificial.

There are also many passages surviving from the *Philippica* in which Theopompus "denounces cities and generals." Here too his style occasionally lapses into offensive pretentiousness. Perhaps the best example is from book 49. In this passage, which Polybius found utterly execrable, he launched into a scathing diatribe against Philip and his men. Demetrius, Hellenistic(?) author of a work *On Style*, cites lines from this diatribe as an example of how stylistic affectation can destroy the forcefulness of the message: "Men-killers were they by nature, men-kissers by habit; ... they were called [the king's] Friends, but were really his 'boy-friends.'"[62] It seems unlikely that Theopompus was trying to introduce humour with these hideous puns. On the whole, the fragments and *testimonia* make him seem quite humourless. There are two near exceptions to that rule where Theopompus indulges in some sarcastic irony. In the first he began his *Philippica* by introducing Philip in terms that made it sound as though he were beginning a eulogy. According to Polybius, Theopompus began by announcing the great importance of Philip as a subject for history, for "Europe had never born such a man at all as Philip, son of Amyntas." Polybius continues (F27 = Polyb. 8.11[13].1):

> Straightaway after this, both in the introduction and throughout the entire history, he shows him to be a most uncontrolled womanizer to the point of destroying his own household as far as he could through his impetuosity and ostentation in that regard; moreover a most unjust and conniving man in his manipulations of friendships and alliances; a man who enslaved or seized unexpectedly a very great number of cities either by treachery or by force; and a natural maniac in uncontrolled drink so as frequently to be seen among his friends manifestly drunk in broad daylight ... For, having set out to write about a king very well born and disposed towards excellence, he has not omitted a single shameful or terrible story.

Attempts will be made to unravel the introduction in chapters 3 and 5, but it looks as if Polybius read it as an encomium followed by a denunciation with mostly negative characterizations throughout the work thereafter. He seems to have found the apparent contradiction puzzling, if not outrageous.

It is possible that Polybius has been misled by Theopompus' introduction. "Europe had never born such a man at all as Philip" might sound encomiastic, but in truth it is ambivalent. Perhaps Polybius failed to detect the sarcasm of an equivocating proem. There is one other passage at least where Theopompus clearly reveals a penchant for sarcastic irony. An unknown author [Longinus] in a work called *On the Sublime* finds the following passage badly written (F263):

> Similarly, Theopompus first gives a magnificent setting to the descent of the Persian king on Egypt and then ruins it all with a few words:
> "What city or nation in Asia did not send its embassy to the King? What thing of beauty or value, product of the earth or work of art, was not brought him as a gift? There were many precious coverlets and cloaks, purple, embroidered, and white; there were many gold tents fitted out with all neces-

sities; there were many robes and beds of great price. There were silver vessels and worked gold, drinking cups and bowls, some studded with jewels, some elaborately and preciously wrought. Countless myriads of arms were there, Greek and barbarian. There were multitudes of pack animals and victims fattened for slaughter, many bushels of condiments, many bags and sacks and pots of onions and every other necessity. There was so much salt meat of every kind that travellers approaching from a distance mistook the huge heaps for cliffs or hills thrusting up from the plain."

He passes from the sublime to the mean; the development of the scene should have been the other way round. By mixing up the bags and the condiments and the sacks in the splendid account of the whole expedition, he conjures up the vision of a kitchen. (D.C. Innes, tr.)

[Longinus] has failed to recognize that the description is intended to ridicule the pomp of the king of Persia and not merely to describe his invasion of Egypt. Thus, the impression of Theopompus' humourlessness is not helped by the insensitivity of the ancient commentators.[63]

Cicero referred to the bitterness of Theopompus on two occasions. However, in one of them it is possible that he was thinking of the *Chian Letters* rather than any historical work.[64] On the other hand, Lucian, a second-century rhetorician and author of satirical essays, leaves little doubt in his essay on *How to Write History* that Theopompus could be scathing in his historical works as well (T25a):

your characters are not in court. You do not want to find yourself liable to the same criticism as Theopompus who condemns most of his personages with real malice and makes a regular business of it, acting as prosecutor rather than historian.[65]

To understand the criticisms of the ancient commentators more fully it is useful to consider what they thought of history and what it was that they expected of a historian. For them prose was written to be read aloud, which made it a form of oratory. In his *Rhetoric*, Aristotle divided oratory into three main classes: epideictic, or "display oratory," forensic, or rhetoric for the law courts, and political, that is, the technique of political persuasion. Since history is not for the law courts and its ostensible purpose is not (or should not be) to persuade politically (otherwise it becomes propaganda), it falls into the general category of epideictic oratory. This categorization usually has to be inferred because the ancient manuals on style rarely say much about history. Aristotle's treatment of epideictic oratory does little to accommodate the specific needs of the historian. His advice seems aimed at the author of set speeches of the sort that would have been given, for example, in competition at the funeral of Mausolus. Nevertheless, it might be reasonably supposed that the section in which Aristotle gives advice on how to compose narrative in epideictic oratory would be relevant to the study of historical narrative. His remarks on that subject are worth quoting in part: "One's narration should sometimes be broken up ... the achievements that show his courage are different from those that show his wisdom or justice."[66] It might follow that a historical narrative that set out the great achievements of an illustrious man would be difficult to distinguish from narrative components of an encomiastic set speech about him. Perhaps this approved method helps explain Polybius' outrage at Theopompus' treatment of Philip, for the historian had seemingly promised an account of Philip's achievements. If Polybius accepted Aristotle's views on oratory, then a narrative of great accomplishments would have to be read as encomiastic, and the passages of derision and abuse in which Theopompus periodically indulged would read like violent contradictions to the main thesis and the apparent tone of much of the narrative. This is not to say that history and encomium were indistinguishable – despite the fact that, to judge from advice given by Lucian, some historians probably did pull out all the stops of encomiastic oratory from time to time. Lucian's own comments about Theopompus, however, suggest that his failings lay in the opposite area. Here the criticism is easier to articulate. The historian errs by resorting to the techniques of forensic oratory, putting his characters on trial, when he should be restricting himself to a straightforward epideictic narrative whose criteria are the measures of truth and usefulness to the reader.

There was another feature of Theopompus' style that may well have added to Polybius' annoyance. A.J. Woodman has recently shown that Roman historians generally accepted the need to suit the style to the type of subject.[67] If the theme was celebratory or encomiastic, the full, smooth style should be used. On the other hand, for a negative theme recording a decline or a period of decadence, the abrupt and choppy style was suitable. Polybius (c. 200–118 B.C.) was a Greek by birth but a Roman by adoption, so to speak. A friend of Scipio, his main historical enterprise was a massive (forty-book) history of Rome's rise to greatness. Unlike Dionysius of Halicarnassus, he could impute history to the Romans and recognize in them a high degree of political sophistication without first having to argue that they were really Greeks by ethnic descent. Dionysius, who approached the Romans as a Greek steeped in Greek traditions, saw no difficulty with Theopompus' mixing of the full style with a nega-

tive subject (the spreading evil of Philip), but Polybius' criticisms probably reflect the Roman ideas that were to be so clearly enunciated by
Cicero in the next century: an account of a person's achievements in
the full style meant that the history was intended to be encomiastic.
The problem with encomium was credibility. Therefore, some
criticisms should be introduced just to show that the author has not
lost all sense of proportion, but Theopompus had been merciless and
relentless in his attacks on Philip. This interpretation best explains the
following remark by Polybius (8.11[13].2):

So that either this author [Theopompus] must be a liar and a flatterer in the
prefatory remarks at the outset of his history, or he is entirely foolish and
childish in his assertions about particulars, *imagining that by senseless and
far-fetched abuse he will insure his own credit and gain acceptance for his laudatory
estimate* (ἐγκωμιαστικὰς ἀποφάσεις) of Philip. (W.R. Patton, tr., L.C.L., my
emphasis)

The point is that Polybius found excessive abuse of Philip in the
Philippica. Why then did he not conclude that the work was a diatribe?
Probably the work met all the technical requirements of an encomium
when judged by the standards adopted by Polybius.

As for political oratory, Plutarch recognized that it has a place in
historical writings. Speeches may be written for statesmen and
generals when they are trying to persuade the citizens or encourage
their armies. The temptation to take flight at such moments must
have been great indeed. Plutarch comments: "But as for the orations
and periods of Ephorus, Theopompus and Anaximenes which they
declaim after arming and arraying their forces, it is possible to say,
'No one near the steel prates thus.' "[68]

In a similar vein, Polybius found the descriptions of battles in
historians from Theopompus' time to be more artificial than real. Of
Ephorus' land battles in particular he says: "If we take [Ephorus'
descriptions of the battles of Leuctra and Mantinea] point by point
and examine the formations and reformations during the actual
battles, he does seem ridiculous, entirely inexperienced, and ignorant
of such things." Polybius remarks on the impressive description of the
engagement at Mantinea provided by Ephorus, but its factual
shortcomings "become clear if you examine the terrain and accurately measure out the movements described by him. The same
thing," he goes on to say, "is found in Theopompus."[69] This practice
of the historians of producing fanciful narratives of actions that could
not have happened as told perhaps finds its justification in the
seminal teaching of the sophist Gorgias of Leontini (483–376). Not

much of Gorgias' work survives, but one quotation from his *Helen* is illuminating:

If everyone had a memory of all that is past, a conception of what is happening at present and a foreknowledge of the future ... [text uncertain] But as it is, there is no easy way of either recollecting the past or investigating the present or divining the future, so that on most subjects most men have only opinion to offer the mind as counsellor; and opinion is slippery and insecure.[70]

Despite the uncertainty over the apodosis of the first sentence, the meaning of the utterance is clear. In Guthrie's words: "knowledge is in general impossible and fallible opinion the only guide." In the *Gorgias* Plato attributes to the famous sophist the view that if a person were only trained in rhetoric, he could speak persuasively whether he knew anything of the subject or not. Plato is not necessarily committed to being fair to the sophists, but in this case it is reasonably certain that Gorgias probably did teach something like that since it seems entirely compatible with the view expressed in the *Helen*.[71] Gorgias was one of the first of the authors of rhetorical manuals, and his influence on the theory and practice of style in the late fifth and early fourth centuries b.c. was considerable. He is said to have been Isocrates' master. The apparent practice of historians of putting too elaborate speeches into the mouths of leaders and providing grandiose but groundless descriptions of battles looks like an application of Gorgias' theory: to rely on plausible opinion and extemporize persuasively since the facts are beyond recovery.[72]

History had been written by Greeks before the rhetorical manuals began to appear. Herodotus had blazed his own trail, making a virtue of the investigation (Ionic: *historiē*) and collection of both opinion and knowledge about the past presented in a narrative style that owed more to the old age of epic poetry than the new era of sophistic rhetoric. The purpose of this narrative blending of knowledge and opinion in a way less haphazard than it might seem at first was to commemorate or celebrate great and marvellous accomplishments from the past and, as far as possible, to provide them with credible explanations. Thucydides is close to Herodotus in these aims. He still wishes to commemorate and explain, but he has deliberately jettisoned epic ornamentation from his narrative and added utility to his purpose: "those who wish to observe the past and what will once again happen in the future ... will consider my work sufficiently useful."[73]

The early rhetoricians helped to introduce a new style of Greek prose called "periodic," usually to be equated with the "full" or "smooth" style. Demetrius explains what that means and how it differs from the older style.

A period is a combination of clauses and phrases which has brought the underlying thought to a conclusion with a neatly turned ending, as in the example: "it was especially because I thought it in the interest of the state for the law to be repealed and secondly because of Chabrias' son that I have agreed to be, to the best of my ability, my client's advocate" ... Suppose we turned round the period cited above from Demosthemes, and said: "I shall be my clìent's advocate, Athenians; for the son of Chabrias is dear to me, and much dearer still is the state, whose interest it is right for me to defend." The period is now lost.

Demetrius goes on to explain further the difference between the newer, periodic style and the older one, sometimes called paratactic.

One kind of style is called the neatly ended style, such as the wholly periodic style found in the artifices of Isocrates' school, Gorgias, and Alcidamas, where period succeeds period no less regularly than the hexameters of Homer. The other style is called the disjointed style and consists of loosely related clauses with little interlocking, as in Hecataeus, most of Herodotus, and all the early writers generally. Take this example: "Hecataeus of Miletus relates as follows. I write of these things as I believe them to be true. For the stories of the Greeks are, it seems to me, both many and absurd."[74]

Demetrius' examples bring out well the differences between the older and newer styles. A typical period introduces an idea, works through a series of subordinated clauses that relate to it, and finally returns to it and finishes it off. In the older style, in its simplest form, the clauses, as Demetrius puts it, "seem to be piled one on top of the other and thrown together without any integration and interdependence and they do not give the mutual support found in periods." Isocrates was, of course, one of the first great masters of the periodic style, and to judge from the number of times the ancients group Theopompus with Isocrates stylistically, there is little doubt that he was an accomplished practitioner of it too. Modern scholars have attempted to demonstrate some very close relationships between the two authors in points of stylistic minutiae. Unfortunately, the fragments of Theopompus are too few and may be too inaccurately copied to inspire confidence in these results.[75]

This last point deserves reinforcement. Photius says that Theopompus boasted of having written "more than 150,000 lines in which it was possible to learn the transactions of Greeks and barbarians reported down to the present."[76] Roughly speaking, if the historical works filled 150,000 or more lines of papyrus text, the average historical book of Theopompus would be equal to more than one-third, but less than one-half the size of Thucydides' book 1. Four

The Aegean

or five books would have gone into the average volume of Oxford text, and the entire historical output of Theopompus would have needed at least eight and perhaps as many as twelve Oxford volumes to print. As it is, there exist a few hundred quotations from these works of varying length and quoted with an accuracy (or inaccuracy) that is generally beyond verification. Collected together these surviving lines would scarcely fill fifteen Oxford pages. If their verbal reliability is doubtful, it is even more certain that they are not representative. Of the fifty quotations that are three lines or more in length, a full thirty-six are from one author, Athenaeus, who is interested primarily in the bizarre and sensational. This leaves little of substance with which to try to compensate for the special focus of Athenaeus. There is much useful work to be done with the surviving material, but these facts and figures are reminders of the severe limitations of the evidence.

CHAPTER TWO

How to Study
Theopompus' Fragments:
The Hellenica

This chapter begins the consideration of Theopompus' fragments. Therefore, it seems appropriate to invest a little time and space outlining what I hope to achieve and how to coax the maximum amount of reliable information from the few random quotations from and references to a lost work. Further, it is a good time to lay down some of the axiomatic ideas, the working hypotheses, that will be used regularly in the argument of the next four chapters.

When I tell people that I am studying the fragments of a lost author, they usually respond with an "Oh, I see, you are examining the surviving bits and trying to guess what was in between them – fill in the blanks, so to speak." In fact, "filling in the blanks" is rarely the objective. Usually the contents of the "blanks" must be known in a general way in order to begin. That is to say, it is necessary to know the story that ought to have been told. In the case of the *Hellenica* there are some nineteen fragments (seven are single-word entries in Stephanus' list of geographical expressions) from twelve books. The longest of these fragments is F22: about eleven lines of Greek text in Jacoby's collection. By themselves, these pathetic remnants are not likely to reveal very much. Fortunately, however, Diodorus provides the vital information (13.42.5, 14.84.7) that Theopompus' *Hellenica* began where Thucydides left off (411), included twelve books, and ended with the battle of Cnidus in 394. Therefore, it began where Thucydides' history of the Peloponnesian War abruptly breaks off, covered the period of the rise and supremacy of Sparta, and ended with the decisive destruction of the Spartan fleet by the Persian navy commanded by the exiled Athenian Conon.

This crucial information makes it possible to set the fragments into a context. Thanks to the *Hellenica* of Xenophon, "Lives" of Plutarch (notably the *Alcibiades*, *Lysander*, and *Agesilaus*), and the narrative of

Diodorus, who made extensive use of the *Hellenica* of Ephorus, Theopompus' contemporary, much is known about how the Greeks narrated the events of those years, and the fragments can be examined for clues to the peculiar features of Theopompus' version. In sum, the primary objective is to get the maximum from each fragment by working from what is generally known of the context to the fragment.[1]

No one will deny that there are difficulties with this method. In any given case its results will rarely be more than tentative. However, no one in antiquity complained that Theopompus substantially altered the traditional versions of events. His reputation as a maverick stems from his negative moral judgments. Both Athenaeus and Dionysius of Halicarnassus used the word "truth-loving" to describe him as a reporter. Polybius, his severest critic, finds fault with his battle narratives, his omission of the period of Greek history that included the battle of Leuctra, and his bitter characterization of Philip, but otherwise he does not even hint at factual distortions or wild variations in content. Therefore, it seems reasonable to expect that Theopompus followed tradition in its broad outline at least. Second, the method is useful only as part of a larger plan of attack. Each tentative result must be added to the next and the next to see if a generally coherent picture emerges. One result may be of little help, but several that point toward a consistent view of the work may be worth something. This is called accumulation.

In this context it is appropriate to turn to a major feature of the fragments of the *Hellenica* and, particularly, the *Philippica*. Many passages are cited because of their sensational stylistic or evaluative content. The judgments generally have a strong moral twist. Now it is frequently true that applauding a politician implies the approval of his politics. Again, the denigration of an entire city, for example, on moral grounds might well be taken to imply disapprobation of its image, its role in history conventionally perceived. The temptation, therefore, is to try to read a program of political sympathies into the body of moralizing fragments, to read politics between the lines of moral praise and criticism. If this approach could be justified, it would be a major forward step toward the goal of finding maximum meaning in the fragments. The approach will be refined in chapter 4, but for the time being the following procedural rule is offered in anticipation of later conclusions. There is a strong circumstantial (cumulative) case for a correlation of moral and political views in Theopompus. However, five notes of caution must be sounded.

First, the context must be determined as far as possible in order to be sure which political posture is likely to be under fire. A case in point would be the Byzantians. There are two places where they would probably have figured prominently in the *Philippica*: the account of their role in the dismantling of the Second Athenian Confederacy (the Social War against Athens, 357–355) and their resistance to Philip's siege of their city in 340/39. The next chapter shows that the revolt was probably recorded in books seven and eight, and the siege in books forty-seven and forty-eight. Their democracy is criticized in F62 from book 8. Therefore, if any political posture is being criticized as the position of "undisciplined eaters and drinkers" (as the fragment describes them), it will have to be the one they adopted in the mid to late 350s (the period under scrutiny in book 8), namely, to help dismantle Athens' Second Confederacy or at least to profit from its demise by annexing Calchedon. Since no other long fragment deals with Byzantium, it is not known how Theopompus judged their war effort against Philip.

The example of the Byzantians is also useful to introduce the second caution: the evaluative statement is not always integrated with a narrative; rather, it may be isolated from it as the comment about the Byzantians in F62 probably was from the narration of Philip's siege of the city, but it was perhaps integrated with the account of the Social War. The ideas of integration and isolation can be illustrated with reference to historians whose works still exist. An interesting case of what I am calling isolation was recently discussed by T.J. Luce in connection with the Roman historian Tacitus' (c. 55 A.D.–after 115) treatment of the emperor Tiberius in his *Annals of Imperial Rome*. Tiberius' death is reported at the end of book 6, and a brief obituary is provided (6.51.3). As Luce points out, it is difficult to see a relationship between the obituary summation of Tiberius' reign and the preceding full narration of it. The obituary brings out six distinct phases of Tiberius' life marked by clear behavioural changes. By contrast, the narrative took no notice of these phases and merely emphasized the uniform evil of Tiberius' character. Luce's conclusion is that the narrative and obituary were written from two perspectives: the narrative emphasized Tiberius' character, the obituary his behaviour. Theopompus may or may not have adopted a similar style, but the possibility is there nonetheless. Obituaries are not necessarily integrated with the preceding narrative. On the other hand, their effect should not be to destroy the general tenor of the narrative. On that score at least both Tacitus' narrative and obituary agree: Tiberius was evil. To be sure, the obituary allowed him an early phase of excellence "both in achievement and reputation, as long as he was a private citizen or held commands under Augustus." However, he soon deteriorated; he was:

given to concealment and an artful simulator of virtue (*occultum ac subdolum fingendis virtutibus*), as long as Germanicus and Drusus survived; a similar mixture of good and evil during his mother's lifetime; then a period of loathsome cruelty, but concealed lusts, as long as he had Sejanus to love or fear; then, finally, he threw himself into crimes and vices alike, casting aside all sense of shame and fear, following no inclination but his own.

This sample (R. Martin, tr.)[2] points up an expected feature of the obituary: rhetorical balance. In the narrative the historian presumably concentrates on recording the actions of his characters in the light of his assumptions about their true nature. In the obituary he steps back and seeks to make a balanced rhetorical statement. For an evil character an early attempt can be made to say something good. The feebleness of the result or total failure of the effort serves only to intensify the condemnation. The impression is conveyed that even after a serious, detached attempt at impartiality little or nothing of merit can be found in the subject.

Three obituaries from Theopompus are included in the fragments. One, from the *Hellenica*, has been used by Professor Meyer as a key to understanding the central purpose, or tendency, of the work. The other two, from the *Philippica*, are also of considerable importance.It is worthwhile, therefore, to spend a little more time understanding how ancient historians used the obituary. Tacitus showed the fully developed form; does its original appear in historical writing before Theopompus? Thucydides (2.65) intrudes editorially to extol the wisdom of Pericles' war policy over the folly of his successors after noticing the statesman's death. The subsequent narrative illustrates the point but never returns to it explicitly. Clearer is Thucydides' terse remark about Nicias, the Athenian general captured and executed by the Syracusans after the collapse of the Sicilian expedition (Thuc. 7.86.5): "a man who, of all the Hellenes in my time, least deserved such a fate, seeing that the whole course of his life had been regulated with strict attention to virtue" (Richard Crawley, tr.). This brief note illustrates well the principle of isolation as I identify it. Readers of Thucydides' narrative will not doubt that he generally approved of Nicias' politics, particularly his opposition to the proposed Sicilian expedition, but, on the other hand, the narrative and obituary are not integrated so that the obituary flows logically from the narrative. The previous narrative is not a concerted demonstration of Nicias' virtue (*aretē*). Just as in Tacitus' treatment of Tiberius, Thucydides has stepped out of his narrative and looked at Nicias from a broader perspective.

It remains to show what the term integration is intended to mean. It will be argued at the end of chapter 3 that Theopompus' narrative was tendentious because he worked editorial judgments into his narration. By so doing he made his sympathies clear by characterizing the deeds described as being those of men of such-and-such a moral disposition. The notion needs illustration, and, once again, Tacitus provides a suitable passage (*Ann.* 4.52.1):

But in Rome, the imperial house was already shaken; and now, to open the train of events leading to the destruction of Agrippina, her second cousin, Claudia Pulchra, was put on trial, with Domitius Afer as accuser. Fresh from a praetorship, with but a modest standing in the world, *and hurrying towards a reputation by way of any crime,* he indicted her for unchastity, for adultery with Furnius, for practices by poison and spell against the life of the sovereign. Agrippina, *fierce-tempered always and now inflamed by the danger of her kinswoman, flew* to Tiberius, and, as chance would have it, found him sacrificing to his father. (J. Jackson, tr., L.C.L., my emphasis)

The italicized words are examples of integrated editorializing. They could be removed, "flew" could be changed to "went" (perhaps a better translation of *pergit* anyway), and the account would be largely neutralized. Integration certainly adds life to the narration. It also serves to involve and manipulate the unwary reader.

A political program can be traced in a body of Theopompan moral judgments, therefore, provided context, integration, and three other cautions are taken into account. The third on the list might be called the principle of mediation. The correlation of morals to politics is not necessarily as simple or direct as it has been described so far. Chapter 4 shows that there is probably a mediating notion that could at times have the effect of deflecting the moral evaluation to something other than the political program under scrutiny. Key concepts in Theopompus' moral program include lack of self-control or self-discipline on one hand and diligence and industry operating through experience on the other. Generally, people who submitted to Philip without a struggle are called uncontrolled or undisciplined, and others who put up ineffective resistance are similarly described, but there is some evidence that criticisms were softened somewhat in the treatment of more determined opponents to Philip. However, the tempting conclusion that Theopompus systematically praised Philip's opponents and vilified his agents for their politics may be pushing the scant evidence a little too far. Nonetheless, the historian did register approval of diligence, industry, and experience wherever he found it; and since those characteristics were required to offer concerted, effective resistance to the notorious blandishments and bribes of the

Macedonian king, the ultimate effect is the apparent approbation on moral grounds of a political program of resistance to Philip.

Since it makes no effective difference in this case, why consider the mediating principle at all? The answer is twofold. First, there is evidence that it is there, and, therefore, it must be considered. Second, it helps make sense of the *Hellenica*, the subject of the second part of this chapter. The moral judgments that relate to the *Hellenica* do not reflect on the politics of the subjects in the same way. Experience makes the difference. In F342 Theopompus is made to claim that experience in battle makes the best soldiers and that the best politician must have experience at public speaking. Now the *Hellenica* covers the period of maximum Spartan influence in the Aegean, and Spartans were notoriously inexperienced statesmen. Their educational system (*agōgē*) trained soldiers. Therefore, it is possible that diligence and industry credited to Spartans reflects on their military prowess, not necessarily their politics.

The fourth cautionary note falls under the rubric of comparison, and the fifth, completion. The two complement each other and can usefully be taken together. It is not enough merely to note that Theopompus criticizes someone; the severity of the criticism has to be estimated by extensive comparison of individual judgments with all the others. Chapter 4 examines the language of the editorial fragments to establish a scale of their intensity. However, it will only be useful if the fragments are generally representative of Theopompus' entire judgment. If it should be that the fragments are only excerpts and mitigating remarks have been occasionally, or even systematically, omitted by the excerpters, then the comparisons are vitiated to an unknown extent. How representative are the fragments?

In this case the testimonies come to the rescue. Since most of the judgments are condemnations, the most serious worry will be the significant loss of complimentary sentiments. However, the testimony of readers who knew the *Philippica* and *Hellenica* provides assurance that there were hardly any such remarks to lose. The only likely loss is further negative material. Here, too, excessive concern seems unnecessary. Reporters like Athenaeus who relish the sensational were scarcely likely to omit the juiciest lines. Therefore, with these *caveats* and the further need for a cumulative case before conclusions are drawn in mind, the straightforward use of most of the fragments in the ways outlined above is likely to be a safe enough procedure. In two cases, however, completion will prove to be a legitimate concern. These are the obituaries of Lysander and Agesilaus. Their surviving parts are demonstrable or suspected extracts from fuller statements whose overall tendency is of greater importance than the apparent meaning of the excerpt. Fragments like these must be approached with great caution indeed.

One other principle must be advanced before considering the *Hellenica* in detail. The working hypothesis that Theopompus wrote history as a Chian, a spokesman for his native island, the Aegean islands nearby, and the Ionians on the Asiatic coasts is less susceptible of proof, but all that is expected of a working hypothesis is that it contradicts no known evidence and explains a good deal of otherwise puzzling material.

Of course, most people have a special interest in their home towns, and the fragments show that Theopompus was no exception. The references to Chios come from the *Philippica*. In F104 an example of Chian aid to Athens is commemorated. As a result, the Athenians include the Chians in their prayers to the gods. F122 separates the Chians from other Greek enslavers because they only bought and sold barbarians, whereas other Greeks, like the Spartans and Thessalians, enslaved fellow Greeks. Again, F164 is a speech put into the mouth of Philocrates clearly in advocacy of the peace treaty with Philip that Athens was soon to sign and that bore his name. Athens was too isolated to resist Philip, Philocrates was made to argue, since the Chians, Rhodians, and other allies had abandoned her. In F276 the Chians become the first ever makers of wine, learning the art from Oenopion, son of Dionysus (the wine-god). And in F291, the tattered papyrus remains of what I identify as an obituary on Hermeas of Atarneus, Hermeas was excoriated for mistreating the Ionians, Chians, and Mytilenaeans, and some editors restore Chians a second time as once again having been exploited by Hermeas. But when does a natural interest in one's native state or region become a fixation and manifest itself in a persistent literary perspective? Theopompus took a keen interest in whether Lysander had embezzled money from the Spartan imperial treasury (FF20, 332, 333). Why should he not? The question was intrinsically interesting, more so, of course, to a tribute-paying islander whose money some of it had been. Again, what should be made of the report in F94 that Cleon accepted an otherwise unknown bribe from unspecified "islanders" to secure them favours in the Athenian law-courts? Or, should the text of F153 be amended as it is by most scholars to make it read as something other than what it says: namely, that the peace treaty signed between Athens and Persia in the fifth century (the Peace of Callias, or Epilycus) was "against the Hellenes"? An islander might have no difficulty seeing peace between Persia and fifth-century Athens as opening the door to further exploitation of "the Hellenes" in the Athenian empire. The three historical works of Theopompus were the *Epitome of Herodotus*, the

Hellenica, and the *Philippica*. The topics of interest to him, therefore, were the Persian War, the period of Spartan rule over the Aegean, and the rise of Philip. However, it is also true that the first two works covered periods in which Chios came to the forefront of Hellenic affairs. For Herodotus the Persian War was touched off by the Ionian revolt in which the Chians were among the leaders and heroes (Herodotus 5.97, 6.15). More significantly, the period of the *Hellenica* corresponds exactly with the time of Spartan maritime ascendancy in the Aegean. Thucydides himself says that the Spartan opportunity to enter this arena, formerly dominated so completely by Athens, was created by a Chian-led revolt of some major allies (Thuc. 8.5). From that moment until the Spartan fleet was destroyed at Cnidus Chios was at or near the centre of Greek history. After Cnidus, the main arena for the struggle for power shifted to the mainland where, gradually, Thebes was to arise as the spoiler. Later, Chios again became something of a power-broker in the Aegean. She was a principal ally of Athens in the founding of the Second Confederacy (378) and again led in the break-up of that Confederacy in 357. These events were probably covered in books 7 and 8 of the *Philippica*, and yet another fully seven to eight books, the longest digression in the work, possibly the longest in all ancient historiography, were devoted to the eastern coastal region of the Mediterranean and Aegean, of which Chios was at least at or near the centre on a rough north-south axis. While none of this proves anything, it is all perfectly consistent with the hypothesis that Theopompus wrote from the perspective of his native Chios.

Perhaps there was a general feeling amongst the islanders and Asiatic Greeks that they had been too much overlooked in the reporting of Greek history. Ephorus hailed from Cyme just north of Chios on the Asiatic coast. He was notorious for forcing his native town onto the attention of his readers even at inappropriate times (Jacoby, no. 70 F236 = Strabo 13.3.6). Otherwise, he wrote to appeal to mainlanders. He was kind to both Athens and Philip as far as the remains of his *Hellenica* show. Apparently, he was concerned to cultivate a broad readership. Theopompus, on the other hand, seems to have vilified all his major players. In his introduction he boasted of his freedom from dependence on teaching for an income. Therefore, he did not need to attract students; perhaps he felt independently wealthy enough to alienate the majority of his world's rich and powerful. Despite his apparent interest in sponsorship by Mausolus and Philip, he seems to have been ultimately content to antagonize nearly everyone and ended his life "driven out from everywhere." All these factors are consistent with the thesis that he made himself the spokesman for an otherwise ignored and relatively powerless constituency, an angry man, a self-relegated outsider, relentlessly attacking the main power-brokers of history and exposing their insensitivity and corruption.[3]

When all methods fail, as they frequently do, I resort to ascertaining what is known of a given subject in the *Philippica* and arguing back to the *Hellenica*. What was in this work of which there are such scant remains? At least the sources have been generous in identifying the books from which excerpts were taken. Only books 3, 5, and 12 have no fragments at all assigned to them; the others have anywhere from one to four. As a result, the work is substantially lost. No master structure emerges with any clarity as it does for the larger *Philippica*, and the fragments suggest little more than an inevitable treatment of Sparta and the Spartans.

These considerations notwithstanding, the probable general contents of the work can be ascertained, which makes it possible to set the preserved fragments in some context. The twelve books of the *Hellenica* embraced the period from 411 (or 412 as I shall suggest below) to the battle of Cnidus in August 394. For comparison there is the *Hellenica* of Xenophon. It also began with the year 411 (continuing Thucydides) but went well beyond Cnidus to the second battle of Mantinea (362) in seven books. Clearly, Theopompus' history was much fuller than Xenophon's, for there is no reason to suppose that Theopompus' books were inordinately small. Furthermore, Xenophon's *Hellenica* was apparently known to Theopompus, and the late Greek philosopher Porphyry actually accused Theopompus of plagiarizing and somehow debasing a long section of Xenophon's work. Theopompus' work was written after the publication of Xenophon's, therefore, and used it as a source.

Did it begin like Xenophon's, abruptly (if somewhat loosely) picking up Thucydides' narrative, or did it recapitulate portions of Thucydides in order to establish a discrete beginning for itself as an independent work? Some of the early fragments suggest a retailing of events of 412–411 in the first two books. F5 reveals that Theopompus described the fighting off Abydus in late 411 as the "second battle of Cynossema." Clearly, therefore, unlike Xenophon, he must have at least mentioned the one that had already been described by Thucydides (8.104). More significantly, F8, from book 2, is a remark about Pedaritus, the first Spartan harmost of Chios. Thucydides had already reported how he was killed fighting the Athenians on Chios sometime in the winter of 412/11 (Thuc. 8.55.2–3).[4]

What these fragments say about the organization of the opening books of the *Hellenica* is puzzling. Perhaps Theopompus devoted the first book to the tying up of "loose ends" from Thucydides, following the course of events in the Hellespont and Propontis. FF6 and 7, geographical entries from book 1, mention locations in the Thracian Chersonese and the Bosporus. They suggest a comprehensive treatment of naval operations in that area (X. *HG* 1.1.22). If that is correct, perhaps the detailed account of developments in the southern and central Aegean were saved for book 2; and again the story would have been taken back to material already covered by Thucydides. Indeed, the events of 412 as narrated by Thucydides could not fail to be of considerable interest to a Chian historian. In that year Chios and Erythrae instigated a revolt in Ionia from the ruling Athenian power (Th. 8.5.4–9.3), and Theopompus would scarcely have been able to ignore the famous judgment on the Chians Thucydides inserted into his record of 412 (8.24.4–5):

Indeed, after the Lacedaemonians, the Chians are the only people that I have known who knew how to be wise in prosperity, and who ordered their city the more securely the greater it grew. Nor was this revolt, in which they might seem to have erred on the side of rashness, ventured upon until they had numerous and gallant allies to share the danger with them, and until they perceived the Athenians after the Sicilian disaster themselves no longer denying the thoroughly desperate state of their affairs. And if they were thrown out by one of the surprises which upset human calculations, they found out their mistake in company with many others who believed, like them, in the speedy collapse of the Athenian power. (Richard Crawley tr.)

This quotation introduces two notions: the greatness of Chios and the islanders' ability to remain levelheaded whilst in the possession of power and influence. These ideas could easily have become themes to bind together a narrative of Aegean events between the beginning of the revolt in 412 and the battle of Cnidus in 394, and they are themes that seem perfectly tailored to the mind of Theopompus.

Despite the efforts of Eduard Meyer, Theopompus' method of organizing his narrative is simply not known. The ancients had two main choices: they could proceed year-by-year (κατ᾽ ἐνιαυτόν) or collect their material into subjects or episodes (κατὰ γένος) and narrate the events discretely. One method keeps close track of chronology but chops up major campaigns or movements that cover more than one year. The other approach solves that probable but risks chronological confusion. Practices varied from author to author. Herodotus wrote by subject; Thucydides' narrative was divided into campaigning seasons. Xenophon began following the Thucydidean model closely but later became less meticulous about it. Ephorus proceeded by subject, while P (the author of the anonymous *Hellenica Oxyrhynchia*) followed Thucydides' example quite strictly. There is no way of determining what choice Theopompus made. The fragments permit both possibilities. Those from book 1 seem best related to the events of 411/10 (with, perhaps, some preparatory material from 412), but book 2 flashes back to Chios in 412, perhaps in a digression. In other words, the procedure could be year-by-year with digressions, subject-by-subject (first operations in the north, next the struggle in the south-central Aegean), or even a combination of the two styles.

Theopompus' choice of a termination for the *Hellenica* has been a matter of some controversy. A little background information will help put the question into perspective. From 399 an army under Spartan command had been operating in Persian territory, laying waste regions of the western Asiatic satrapies. Unable to drive this army away by force of arms, the Persians resorted to bribing the states of mainland Greece to revolt from Spartan hegemony. Their hope was to draw off the Spartan army and engineer its recall to deal with rebellions closer to home, and they were successful. By the beginning of the campaigning season of 394 the Spartans at home had decided that their situation was grave. They mobilized the home troops and recalled Agesilaus, the Spartan king who was commanding the Asiatic army. The army at home invaded Corinth and won a somewhat indecisive victory. Meanwhile, Agesilaus marched home through Thessaly, not without some difficulty. He had not left things in a state of peace in Asia. The year before his departure (395) the Spartan state had taken the unprecedented step of adding the navy to his command. This move unified under one man the control of both the land and maritime forces. Never had a Spartan, or any Greek for that matter, wielded such power. He promptly delegated the naval command to his brother-in-law Peisander, who is described by Xenophon as possessing more ambition than ability (X. *HG* 3.4.29). Perhaps this decision was a mistake on Agesilaus' part, but he probably calculated that he had nothing to fear from the Persian fleet. The *Hellenica Oxyrhynchia* (19–20) reports that its organization was in a shambles in 395. The men had not been paid for many months (fifteen according to Isocrates, *Panegyricus* 142), and some were in revolt. Unfortunately, the papyrus breaks off before the story of how Conon regained complete control is finished, but it is clear that he did. On 14 August 394 Agesilaus was approaching the borders of Boeotia when he observed a partial eclipse of the sun. At about the same time news came to him that Conon had destroyed the Spartan fleet at Cnidus with his once mutinous navy and that Peisander was dead. Agesilaus concealed the information from his men and invaded Boeotia to fight an allied force at Coronea. The result was a nominal but indecisive victory for Sparta. The sources report no other major events in this connection from that year.

The obvious question is why end with Cnidus and not finish the year off to include Coronea? How did Theopompus organize the narration of this year? While it is impossible to prove which alternative he selected, the possible choices can be evaluated to estimate which is most likely. There are three possible solutions. The first could be called the ragged termination thesis: the return of Agesilaus was described down to the march through Thessaly and dropped for a description of Cnidus. After describing the sea-battle, Theopompus abandoned the manifestly incomplete *Hellenica* to begin work on the *Philippica*. The second possibility might be called the subordination thesis: Agesilaus' return was described down to, perhaps beyond, 394 prior to, and in effective subordination to the main narrative, namely the events leading up to and including the battle that eliminated Sparta as a maritime power (the later battle of Naxos in 376 nothwithstanding). This view would seem to necessitate the assumption that Theopompus narrated the conclusion of the *Hellenica* more by subject (κατὰ γένος) than synchronistically by year (κατ' ἐνιαυτόν). The third is the elimination hypothesis: the departure of Agesilaus from Asia was merely reported but not narrated. The clear implication of this last thesis is that at the end of his work at least if not throughout it Theopompus had little or no interest in the struggle for control of the mainland but only of the Aegean.

Fortunately, there is some more information with which to work. Polybius (8.11.3 = T19) complained that the termination of the *Hellenica* (in 394) and subsequent commencement of the *Philippica* (in c. 360) effectively omitted an important period called by him the times (or circumstances) of Leuctra (*Leuktrikoi kairoi*). Now Leuctra was the battle fought in 371 in which Thebes finally secured a decisive land victory over Sparta. After it the Thebans successfully dismantled Sparta's old Peloponnesian League by supporting the foundation of the strategic Megalopolis and peopling it with implacable Spartan enemies. This is what Polybius says about Theopompus:

Indeed, no one would applaud the aforementioned historian for his overall divisions (ὁλοσχερεῖς διαλήψεις) for he set about writing up Hellenic affairs from the point where Thucydides left off and, when he got near to the times of Leuctra (συνεγγίσας τοῖς Λευκτρικοῖς καιροῖς) and to the most notable of Hellenic deeds, Greece and her struggles he threw away abruptly, changed his subject, and began to write up the deeds of Philip.

Unfortunately this passage has been variously interpreted. It was the view of Jacoby, recently reiterated by Bruce, that Theopompus was writing up the events of Greece and was planning to continue past 394, indeed, that he had notes for the ensuing narrative but changed subjects abruptly when Philip caught his attention. On the other hand, Meyer, and Lane Fox took the view that Cnidus was the planned termination all along.[5]

At first, this seems inconclusive, but in fact Polybius has broadened the question. He talks about the historian's "overall divisions," that is to say, the way he divides up his entire historical enterprise. The implication is that the omission of the *Leuktrikoi kairoi* is not a fault of the *Hellenica* alone, but also of the *Philippica*. Jacoby suggests that the period would have been covered by digressions in the *Philippica*. Indeed, if Theopompus had gone to the trouble of preparing notes, it would be a surprise had he elected not to make use of them in a work as notorious for its digressions as the *Philippica*. In view of the time period, at least twenty-three years (394–371) and at most thirty-four (394–360) of eventful Greek history, an adequate digression on the subject would scarcely fit into a tiny corner of the *Philippica*, and there is no evidence for a substantial digression on this period. All there is is the possibility that a part of book 45 covered some Theban history (F212), but the reference appears to be to an obscure, early episode. The principle of the subordination of mainland history to that of the eastern Mediterranean is well illustrated by F103, a Byzantine scholar's summary of the contents of *Philippica* 12. It tells the story of Evagoras' leadership of his native Cyprus' revolt from Persian domination (391–380). A few years after the outbreak of this revolt the Great King obtained a free hand against Cyprus by imposing a peace agreement on the mainland Greeks with the help of Sparta, the so-called King's Peace (or Peace of Antalcidas) of 387/6. This treaty is one of the major events in what Polybius calls the *Leuktrikoi kairoi*. Significantly, its circumstances were reported by Theopompus not in a connected narrative of mainland history but in a subordinate, illustrative role in an account of eastern events. Similarly, Evagoras' assassin is identified as Thrasydaeus of Elis. Elis is in the Peloponnese, the province in which the Olympic Games were celebrated, and Thrasydaeus was described in Xenophon's *Hellenica* (3.2.23–31) as a drunken democrat, leader of an Elean revolt from Sparta. Again mainland history is brought in only when it serves the eastern narrative and then, apparently, piecemeal and only insofar as it is necessary. Finally, one other mention of this period from the *Philippica* survives. In FF322–3 there are references to the Theban general Epaminondas' invasion of the Peloponnese in 370/69 shortly after the battle of Leuctra. The best guess is that these fragments come from a somewhat unkind obituary on Agesilaus, of which the thesis was that Agesilaus began his career as the most illustrious Greek history knew but that he sank in a few decades to the point where he had to bribe his worst enemies to spare his homeland and that in a few more years he died a lonely death after selling his services as a mercenary to the king of Egypt. Theopompus' knowledge of the King's Peace, Thrasydaeus of Elis, and Epaminondas' invasion of the Peloponnese does not prove that he had prepared "copious notes" on the *Leuktrikoi kairoi*. It shows only that he had read Xenophon, something that was never in doubt, and that he was as knowledgeable and opinionated about the main events of the period as any well-informed Greek of the day.

It is worthwhile to call to mind what is actually known about what Polybius calls the "overall divisions" of Theopompus' historical work. The *Philippica* was devoted to the career of Philip and the threads of eastern (Greek) and western (Sicilian) history from the late 390s to 344/3 when Philip's final conquest of Greece becomes the sole topic. There is also room for a digression on Black Sea history, but nothing is known about it. Now the obvious reason for commencing the eastern and western digressions in the late 390s is that they are continuations of the *Hellenica*, which had broken off in 394. Eastern history was inevitably central to the *Hellenica*, but beginning Sicilian history in 394 in the *Philippica* can only mean that that work was picking up a thread of Sicilian history that had been carried through the *Hellenica*. Thucydides had brought Sicily into the mainstream of Greek narrative when he devoted most of books 6 and 7 of his work to the abortive Athenian attack on Syracuse (415–413), and it would be perfectly natural to maintain the interest since Syracuse turned to active support of the Spartan effort after the defeat of the Athenian invaders.

As a result, Sicilian history was a loose end dangling from the *Hellenica*, for 394 is near the middle of the reign of Dionysius I (reigned c. 406–367) and no natural stopping point at all. In recognition of the inappropriateness of the date as a termination, Theopompus went back to it and "tied off the loose end" with a suitable digression in the *Philippica*. However, he did not feel the same way about mainland history from 394 to 360. He left it out of the *Hellenica* and did not feel the need to pick it up in the *Philippica*. The elimination thesis therefore seems the most probable; that Theopompus probably did not describe Agesilaus' homeward march; that this left him free to end with Cnidus, his intended stopping point; and that this is precisely the matter about which Polybius is complaining. He was upset because Theopompus had abruptly "thrown away

Greece and her struggles" in the *Leuktrikoi kairoi*. Despite their importance ("the most notable of Hellenic deeds"), Theopompus had described everything else relevant to Greek history from that period while omitting the period itself. The omission was systematic and deliberate. Perhaps he was content to leave the story to Callisthenes' *Hellenica*; perhaps he was just not interested.

This apparent lack of interest in the mainland was possibly not just confined to the *Leuktrikoi kairoi*. Plutarch's *Lysander* offers a clue. The central historical sources for this "life" seem to have been the *Hellenica*s of Xenophon (probably) and more certainly those of Ephorus and Theopompus, who are mentioned by name (17.2, 20.6, 25.3, 30.2–3). One story is of considerable interest. According to it, Lysander hatched an elaborate but abortive plot to use a corrupted oracle (first Delphi, then Dodona, then Ammon in Libya) to support his planned attempt to alter the Spartan constitution. It is an episode full of bribery, discovered secret documents, and political scandal of the sort that Theopompus should have found irresistible. Plutarch, however, gives an unusually extensive account of his sources for this story when the episode is first introduced and Lysander runs afoul of the ephors, the investigative magistrates who had got possession of a letter condemning Lysander, and makes it clear that his main source was not Theopompus but Ephorus. He declares "some sources" (ἔνιοι μέν, *Lys.* 20.5) claim that Lysander really saw the god Ammon and so determined to visit the oracle and propitiate the god. However, "the majority" (τοῖς δὲ πλείστοις δόκει, 20.6) considered the god "a mere pretext" (πρόσχημα) for Lysander's desire to elude the ephors and have a compelling, religious excuse to go travelling and "escape the yoke" (20.6) at home. "The reason Ephorus records," continues Plutarch, "I shall relate shortly." It comes in full in section 25, where he notes for a second time that the source is Ephorus. Again, the sequel is given in 30.3. Here the context is the death of Lysander and what the Spartans discovered when the contents of his estate became known. According to Theopompus (30.2) it was his personal poverty, but according to Ephorus it was his speech on the constitution, which he had caused to be written to support his revolutionary designs. Agesilaus suppressed the document. When Plutarch introduces the story, he implies that he found it only in Ephorus. Perhaps Theopompus was counted either amongst the "some" (ἔνιοι μέν), or, more probably, his version, being the most important early alternative to Ephorus (Xenophon is silent), was the source for "the majority" (πλείστοις δέ). Of course, Plutarch says nothing to rule out the possibility that Theopompus mentioned the conspiracy. On the other hand, nothing Plutarch says makes it necessary to believe that the story was found in any source but Ephorus, and it would be surprising to see the scandalmongering Theopompus being outdone at his own game by the notoriously mild Ephorus. However, of the non-Ephorean sources Plutarch's information makes it clear only that some (obviously laudatory ones) sent Lysander away from Sparta on a religious quest while others scoffed at the "quest" theory and made him leave because life in Sparta was too oppressive. This sounds like Theopompus, for the idea that Spartans who had seen something of the world found life at home insufferable and so turned to travel is found in the *Philippica* (F232). The implication must be that Ephorus alone fully reported the story of the attempted overthrow of the Spartan constitution. One obvious reason Theopompus ignored it or gave it less time and space despite its obvious attractions would be that he was not interested in the subject.

On the other hand, if Theopompus did ignore or downplay Lysander's conspiracy, he was careful to report his refusal to embezzle money from the allied treasury (F333). By way of contrast, from another story in the *Lysander* told by both Ephorus and Theopompus (17.3), money embezzled by Gylippus is described cryptically by a household slave as "owls sleeping under the roof-tiles" (*Lys.* 16.2). This money does not sound like Persian plunder or "loans" from Cyrus. The "owl" was the Athenian four-drachma piece. This was money taken from the now defunct Athenian empire, something in which the Chians and all the coast-dwellers and islanders of the Aegean had a special interest. The story fits with the hypothesis that Theopompus was concerned to bring a Chian or eastern Aegean perspective to the history of his time: not generally concerned about Spartan constitutional crises, but keeping a watchful eye on the money collected from Sparta's subjects.

The theory that the *Hellenica* was written from an Aegean perspective contradicts the only other existing explanation of this work. The opposing thesis was advanced in a book entitled *Theopomps Hellenica* published in 1909. In that work Eduard Meyer advanced the view that the *Hellenica* was a deliberate celebration of the pinnacle of Spartan power from which the Greek world had sadly declined ever since. Meyer held that Theopompus "placed beside the lamentable conditions of his own time the picture of the brief epoch in which wise conditions prevailed and his ideal [government] was very nearly realized."[6] Meyer's reasoning is not convincing today, but it is worth a brief recapitulation, for a discussion of his hypothesis brings forward a few more of the important questions relevant to Theopompus' historiography.

Meyer's theory was founded on a general observation, another theory, and a dubious textual emendation. The observation was that Spartans are usually treated gently in the fragments of the *Hellenica*. Meyer also accepted the theory, popular for a time, that the *Hellenica Oxyrhynchia* could be identified with Theopompus' history. It is rich in otherwise lost details of mainland as well as Aegean history, and it is written synchronistically by year (κατ' ἐνιαυτόν). To all this Meyer added what is now Jacoby's F23 which he assigned to book 3 since he accepted Schwartz's emendation of the text which supplied "book 3 of the *Hellenica*" to the preamble. The contents of F23 seemed to him to have reference to Lysander's siege of Samos in 404/3, and suddenly an astonishing picture of the structure of the *Hellenica* seemed to emerge. If Theopompus wrote year-by-year and had reached 404/3 by book 3, then even if the siege of Samos was placed at the end of book 3, he would have covered the first eight years of the period under scrutiny in a bare three books, and the remaining nine books would have been devoted to the decade of supreme Spartan power. Clearly, Meyer felt, that was the main focus of the work. Unfortunately, the Oxyrhynchus historian continues to elude positive identification, but (see Appendix A) there are grave difficulties with the belief that he could have been Theopompus. Further, the restoration of F23 looks very doubtful, and it is not accepted by Jacoby, who also points out that the fragment's contents are too vague for it to be assigned to the siege of Samos. It could be a reference to almost any period of Ionian history. The only part of Meyer's argument that remains is the treatment of individual Spartans.

The two principal representatives of Sparta in the Aegean were, of course, Lysander and Agesilaus. Both are awarded high praise in fragments from the *Hellenica*. While the praise is only for their personal restraint in refusing to indulge or enrich themselves, or in the case of Agesilaus, to enjoy eating as many delicacies as enormous power and vast quantities of money make possible, it nonetheless could be argued that praise of administrators implies approval of their respective administrations. On close scrutiny, however, this line of argument loses some of its attraction. The remarks about Lysander are preserved by Athenaeus, who assigns them to book 10. Coming so late in the work, the context must be Lysander's death, years after his administration had been dismantled. In other words, the reference is from an obituary in some considerable isolation from the narrative in question. Moreover, as valuable as the excerpt is, it does not necessarily represent Theopompus' full and final verdict. An attractive strand in an obituary, the whole of which does not survive, does not imply approval of the whole garment. Indeed,

Plutarch paraphrases the same passage in his account of Lysander's death (F333) and adds the revealing comment: "So records Theopompus whom a person would rather trust when he praises than when he blames, for he blames more readily them he praises." Apparently, the kind remark about Lysander was rare, even isolated. Since it apparently comes from an obituary, the vital principle of "completion" comes into play. Plutarch does not make it sound as if the context was generally one of high praise for Lysander and his administration.

It is hardly likely to have been so if the traditions about Theopompus' (and his brother's) rich and comfortable life are reliable. From Plutarch's report of Lysander's settlements in the Aegean, his was not a system designed to appeal to the established elites of Greek society. "For Lysander did not appoint rulers out of consideration of good birth or wealth," says Plutarch (*Lys*.13.4), in a vitriolic denunciation of Lysander's organization of the Aegean that culminates in a biting quotation from "Theopompus, the comic poet," likening the Spartans to tavern-girls because they "gave the Greeks a very pleasant taste of freedom, then dashed the wine with vinegar" (B. Perrin, tr., L.C.L.).

Xenophon, whose focus on Lysander is restricted to his military and diplomatic efforts against Athens, is silent on this subject, and Ephorus seems to have tried to be kind, excusing Lysander as a mere agent of Spartan policy. Whence came the substance of Plutarch's negative characterization of Lysander's regime? Its bitterness sounds unlike Ephorus, more like Theopompus or no identified source.[7] Plutarch's entire summary of Lysander's regime substantively supplements Xenophon and is full of a viciousness worthy of Theopompus; by elimination the latter alone emerges as the likely source for the material. But even if the criticism of Lysander's administration is not derived from Theopompus, Plutarch's inability to report a positive tradition is significant. He seems to want to set Lysander's achievements in the best light; therefore, if he found fulsome praise of Lysander's "near ideal" exercise of Spartan power in Theopompus, why did he not reflect that tradition in the *Lysander*?[8] Finally, F5, a summary of the contents of the opening books of both Xenophon's and Theopompus' *Hellenica*, implies that Theopompus did not deviate from the standard ancient view of the reign of The Thirty at Athens, Lysander's arrangement for that city after he had deposed the democracy. The word used to describe their regime is "tyranny." That Theopompus had many kind words for Lysander's administration looks doubtful indeed.

Lysander's decarchies were overthrown c. 403, about the same time as the deposition of The Thirty and the restoration of democracy in

Athens. For the next six or seven years the cities were apparently governed by oligarchies, which, Xenophon says, were in chaos (*HG* 3.4.7) when Agesilaus came to Ephesus in 396. What Theopompus said about the interval between Lysander and Agesilaus cannot be known; and even if it could be ascertained that he spoke well of Agesilaus' administration, there was little time left to develop the theme. A scant three seasons after Agesilaus' arrival (August 394) would be the termination of the *Hellenica*. From the fragments it can be guessed that Agesilaus first appeared in any major way in book 10, and then he probably dominated the last two books, 11 and 12. It might be argued that admiring Agesilaus would be consonant with an approval of the Spartan regime since the deposition of Lysander's decarchies. But caution is needed. The evidence that Theopompus admired Agesilaus is equivocal, for there are two fragments regarding Agesilaus, both from book 11, and taken together they suggest that Theopompus was ambivalent toward the Spartan king. The laudatory passage is preserved by Athenaeus, and it illustrates precisely what he claims for it: the ability of Spartans to control their bellies (Athen. 14.657 B–C = F22 from book 11):

Fatted geese and calves are mentioned by Theopompus in the thirteenth book of his *History of Philip* and the eleventh book of his *History of Greece*; in these passages he illustrates the abstemiousness of the Lacedaemonians in relation to the belly-appetites, writing as follows: "The Thasians, too, sent to Agesilaus when he went to their aid all kinds of small cattle and steers well fattened, and besides these cakes and every possible variety of sweetmeats. Agesilaus accepted the sheep and the large cattle, but as for the cakes and the sweetmeats, at first he did not know what they were, since they were kept covered. But when he saw them, he commanded that they be taken away, saying that it was not lawful for Spartans to use such viands. And when the Thasians insisted he replied, pointing out the Helots to them, 'Take and give them to those fellows yonder,' explaining that it was much better for them to be corrupted by eating the stuff than that he and the Spartans with him should be." (C.B. Gulick, tr., L.C.L.)

It must be admitted that to infer that Theopompus admired both Agesilaus' government and another similar one that preceded it is to demand a great deal from a fragment that merely says that Agesilaus knew how to control his appetite for food.

However, if Theopompus' Agesilaus could control his belly, was he in control of his other appetites and his government as well? Was he an effective administrator? The other surviving "fragment" raises serious doubts. It is not so much a quotation from the historian as an accusation that he plundered a whole scene from Xenophon (4.1.29–41) where Agesilaus met the satrap Pharnabazus (T27, F21). After a dignified exchange and a further demonstration of Spartan asceticism by Agesilaus (who, after all, was being scrutinized at every move by sixty piercing Spartiate eyes [X. *HG* 3.4.2, 8; 4.1.34]), the two part as nominal enemies but personal friends. Porphyry's complaint is that Theopompus took Xenophon's account, which was "dignified and becoming to both men," and described the business in a "fruitless and sluggish ... and unproductive style."[9] Elsewhere, Theopompus was reputed to have been anything but dull, but that is how Porphyry saw it. Nonetheless, by implication the story was not "dignified nor becoming to both men." He probably besmirched the dignity of both Agesilaus and Pharnabazus in his more characteristic way. In sum, the chances that Theopompus might have admired Lysander's leadership are not strong despite his approval of Lysander's personal self-control. He might have been kinder to Agesilaus, but his ambivalence toward the man suggests nothing more. At best, there may be reason to suppose that the Spartan leadership of Greece received a few indifferent nods of approval in the closing books of the *Hellenica*; but even that is far from certain.

Meyer's theory is, therefore, difficult to accept. However, despite a lack of evidence to support it, not everything about it has to be rejected. The possibility still remains that the later years received fuller treatment than the earlier ones. Textual problems in F23 notwithstanding, F12 (from book 6) seems datable to 402/1 and F13 (from book 7, if the number is not corrupt), on the wretched life and historical background of Sparta's subjugated Helot population, seem most naturally to be associated with an uprising led by Cinadon in 399/8.[10] It is quite possible, therefore, that books 1 to 6 covered the first eleven or twelve years and that the last five years occupied the remaining six books. However, there was also probably a strand of Sicilian history, as will be argued in the next chapter, which would have affected the arrangement of the work's contents.

If Theopompus did not idealize the Spartan regime between 404 and 394, it remains to show how he did treat it. Doing so, of course, is rather more difficult than disproving Meyer's thesis. The evidence only goes so far. Following my introductory remarks, the correct procedure is to suggest that it was the diligence and industry of the Spartan high command in doing what it was most experienced in that won applause from Theopompus, and these Spartans were trained as soldiers, not administrators.[11] The victorious Lysander had brought the Peloponnesian War to an expeditious conclusion by negotiating money from Cyrus of Persia and by maintaining strict discipline in his navy. Agesilaus had amassed large sums of money by plundering extensive tracts of Persian territory. Neither enriched himself personally despite their vast power and countless opportunities. Part of the verdict on Lysander exists (F20 from book 10):

He was industrious and able to cultivate the friendship of both private men and kings, a man of moderation too strong to be ruled by any of the pleasures. Indeed, he became master of almost all Hellas but in no city will it be shown that he engaged in sexual pleasures or got involved in drunkenness and unseasonable tippling.

Somewhere in this appraisal (almost certainly an obituary) his refusal to embezzle any of the money that came to him "both from the cities and the King" was praised (F333), but there the flow of kind words probably stopped, and the remainder turned more characteristically negative as Plutarch's remark suggests, confirming the earlier narrative of an incompetent administration. Much the same treatment was probably afforded to Agesilaus. As for Sparta herself, there is only F13, in which Theopompus characterized the state of the Spartan Helots as "thoroughly harsh." It would be hasty to conclude from this fragment alone that Theopompus deplored their treatment, but other evidence to be considered below does lead to that conclusion.

It is significant that a similar approach to Sparta and leading Spartans can be found in fragments of the *Philippica*. Agesilaus comes off well only when the subject is his personal self-control. As a governor he is rarely made to look good. F240 from book 56 makes him appear to be a most ungallant king. According to the story certain Spartans killed Xenopithea, the most beautiful woman in Sparta, and her sister with her. Apparently her "crime" was that she was the mother of one of Agesilaus' personal enemies. Of course, the story does not directly implicate Agesilaus, but it scarcely reflects well on his kingship. Again, F103 characterizes the actions of Sparta under Agesilaus' leadership at the time of the conclusion of the King's Peace. That agreement had included a clause giving autonomy to the Greek states. Agesilaus undertook to impose his understanding of autonomy on each leading state insofar as he could. Primarily, he made it mean that Thebes had to dismantle her Boeotian League while Sparta kept the Peloponnesian League intact. Theopompus apparently called the Spartan behaviour "presumptuous."

Sparta in general does not do well either. When her leaders get away from home, they do not all avoid temptations despite their disciplined training (F192, Pharax; 232, Archidamus). Moreover, the state itself was based upon the brutal enslavement of fellow Greeks as F122 from book 17 makes clear. There, Theopompus commends the Chians for enslaving only barbarians and faults Thessalians and Spartans for subjugating Greeks. The Thessalian "serfs," called *penestai*, were originally Perrhaebians and Magnesians, while the Spartans had reduced Achaeans to wretched servitude (cf. F13 where they are called Messenians and former occupants of Helos, a region in southern Laconia). Now Perrhaebians, Magnesians, and Achaeans are all listed as founding member tribes of the central Greek Amphictiony in F63. Members of the Amphictiony took an oath to defend, not enslave one another. Theopompus therefore probably disapproved of the Spartan treatment of the Helots.

Agesilaus' fortunes were most completely bound up in those of his native state. His strengths and weaknesses were hers, the product of her system of education. He shared with Sparta his hour of highest glory, and his personal decline was coincident with that of his state. Theopompus' account of his last months and what is known or can be reconstructed of his obituary proved highly quotable in antiquity. Sections of his description of the aged king's visit to Egypt to hire himself out as military adviser to the Egyptian rebels were quoted by Athenaeus and paraphrased by Plutarch and Nepos. F107 is from Plutarch's *Agesilaus* (36.6). The source is identified as Theophrastus, but it echoes FF106 and 108 of Theopompus' *Philippica* so faithfully that the whole section may be taken as ultimately from Theopompus. Indeed, Wichers emended Theophrastus to Theopompus since it looks to be such an obvious mistake (Plut. *Ages.* 36.4–6):

As soon as he landed in Egypt, the chief captains and governors of the king came down to meet him and pay him honour. There was great eagerness and expectation on the part of the other Egyptians also, owing to the name and fame of Agesilaus, and all ran together to behold him. But when they saw no brilliant array whatever, but an old man lying in some grass by the sea, his body small and contemptible, covered with a cloak that was coarse and mean, they were moved to laughter and jesting, saying that here was an illustration of the fable, "a mountain is in travail, and then a mouse is born." They were still more surprised, too, at this eccentricity. When all manner of hospitable gifts were brought to him, he accepted the flour, the calves, and the geese, but rejected the sweetmeats, the pastries, and the perfumes, and when he was urged and besought to take them, ordered them to be carried and given to his Helots. He was pleased, however, as [Theophrastus] tells us, with the papyrus used in chaplets, because the chaplets were so neat and simple, and when he left Egypt, asked and received some from the king. (B. Perrin, tr., L.C.L.)

The sentiment echoes F22 cited above very closely. This is certainly

the Agesilaus of Theopompus. The three specific citations of Theopompus in Plutarch's life are to be assigned with great probability to
the obituary that must have appeared in the *Philippica* not long after
this eloquent description of Agesilaus' arrival in Egypt, and they have
an eloquence of their own. It is hard to imagine a context for them
other than an obituary. In their most likely order, chronological, they
reveal in skeletal outline a merciless evaluation of the pathetic
deterioration of this once-great man.

F321 = *Ages.* 10.5: And he was confessedly the greatest and most illustrious
man of his time, as Theopompus also has somewhere said. (B. Perrin, tr.,
L.C.L.)

Plutarch is describing the moment when Agesilaus became supreme
commander of both army and navy, the most powerful Greek in all of
history. The highly rhetorical reference from Theopompus must be
to the same moment, the beginning of Agesilaus' decline.

F322 = *Ages.* 31.2. Epaminondas entered Laconia (a country that had
remained inviolate for centuries): For Agesilaus would not suffer the
Lacedaemonians to fight against such a "billowy torrent of war," to use the
words of Theopompus. (B. Perrin, tr., L.C.L.)

Once again, this is a highly rhetorical passage from the so-called
Leuktrikoi kairoi, in this case the aftermath of the battle of Leuctra.
Since this period was not given a full narration by Theopompus, its
most likely home is Agesilaus' obituary where some of the main
events would have been cited. The same must be said of the next
and last quote (F323 = *Ages.* 32.8):

As for the reason why the Thebans withdrew from Laconia, most writers say
that it was because winter storms came on and the Arcadians began to melt
away and disband; others, because they had remained there three entire
months and thoroughly ravaged most of the country; but Theopompus says
that when the Theban chief magistrates had already determined to take their
army back, Phrixus, a Spartan, came to them, bringing ten talents from
Agesilaus to pay for their withdrawal, so that they were only doing what they
had long ago decided to do, and had their expenses paid by their enemies
besides. (B. Perrin, tr., L.C.L.)

So the erstwhile "greatest and most illustrious man of his time" was
reduced in three short decades to bribing his most hated enemies
to do (the irony is classic Theopompus) what they were going to do
anyway.

It would be useful to contrast the treatment of Sparta with that of Athens. Unfortunately, no fragment of any substance from the *Hellenica* mentions Athens or any Athenians. Therefore, with two possible exceptions all the items of evidence will be taken from the *Philippica*. These exceptions, the Delphic oracle's advice to save Athens and the treatment of Alcibiades, will be considered below. First, the hostile treatment of Athens should be noted. F281 is a good example; it cannot be associated with any specific context, but it is tempting, if somewhat dangerous, to take it as generally representative of the treatment of the city (F281 = Athen. 6.254B):

The Pythian oracle calls [the city of Athens] the hearth of Hellas, but the malevolent Theopompus calls it the town-hall of Hellas; *and in another passage* he says that Athens was full of shyster-actors, sailors, and highway robbers; also false-witnesses, swindlers and fabricators of summonses. (My emphasis)

It is possible that the text of the first half of this passage is in error, for in 5.187D Athenaeus says: "The Pythian god proclaimed it [Athens] 'the hearth and town-hall of the Hellenes' " (C.B. Gulick, tr., L.C.L.). Where Athenaeus found the report of this Delphic response is uncertain. At first it appears that 5.187D provides the correct form of the oracle – namely, that the Pythian called Athens the hearth and town-hall of Hellas – and that Athenaeus found it in an unknown source. In this view, 6.254B would be a confused account of the oracle, attributing part of it mistakenly to Theopompus. The alternative would be that 6.254B actually identifies the source of the oracle as Theopompus. 6.254B would, then, be derived from two distinct passages in Theopompus. If this second alternative is the correct one, then the oracle must derive from the *Hellenica*. This conclusion comes as the result of a somewhat roundabout line of reasoning. First, if 6.254B is drawn from two passages in Theopompus, the first one would be the "hearth and town-hall" maxim attributed to Delphi and the second would be the remainder of F281. The context for the quotation from the Pythian is provided by Aelian (*VH* 4.6), who frequently derives material from Theopompus. He says that when Lysander had taken Athens (404), the Spartans were cautioned by Delphi not to "upset the common hearth of Hellas." Now Theopompus was an expert on Delphi, and of all the known historians of this period he is the most likely to bring in references to Delphi in this manner. Therefore, his account of Athens' fall in the *Hellenica* (book 4 or 5?) is a likely enough source for Aelian *VH* 4.6 and Athenaeus 5.187D; and since part of Athenaeus 5.187D is attributed to Theopompus in Athenaeus 6.254B, it is possible that the

entire "hearth and town-hall" passage is an attribution to Delphi
originally recorded in the *Hellenica*. There is no way to even guess at
the exact origin of the rest of Athenaeus 6.254B. However, if the above
argument is plausible, two conflicting streams of thought may appear
concerning Athens: the one predictably malevolent, the other sympathetic. The often detested Athens may have received generous
treatment in defeat. Theopompus' respect for Delphi was profound.
He is not likely to have quoted it frivolously. In other words, it is
possible that he recorded the idea on Delphi's authority that, despite
its corruption, there was something worth sparing in Athens at the
end of the Peloponnesian War.[12]

Athens was a big and varied historical subject. A brief sketch of her
fortunes will help to set the few relevant fragments into some sort of
context. The Persians invaded Greece in 480 B.C. As their forces
withdrew, the Athenians moved aggressively into the Aegean to
replace them. In 477 the Delian Confederacy (or Delian League) was
established, and all Ionians and islanders were invited (if not forced)
to join. Before the outbreak of the Peloponnesian War (431), the
Confederacy had become in reality the Athenian empire. The
Athenians were assessing and collecting tribute (*phoros*) from their
"allies" and policing the empire with a large, well-drilled fleet of ships.
In 415 the Athenians launched the abortive expedition to Sicily that
failed in 413. This had been the period of Alcibiades' greatest
influence in Athens. He fled as the result of a religious scandal in 415
and went to find asylum in Sparta. By 411, however, after a brief stay
with Tissaphernes, satrap of Sardis, he was a commander of the
Athenian fleet, and his personal energy seems to have contributed
much to the prolongation of the Athenian war effort against a Sparta
now supported with Persian money and despite the widespread revolt
in the empire. However, by 404 the Spartans were triumphant, and
thirty puppet tyrants were put in control of Athens. By 403/2 they
were gone and Athens was a democracy again, allied, of course, to
Sparta.

After the Persian fleet defeated Sparta at Cnidus (394), the
Athenians began to rebuild the fortifications dismantled at the end of
the war. They can scarcely have entertained serious dreams of a
revived empire through this period.[13] Most of their efforts in the
Aegean seem best understood as attempts to secure the vital grain
supply down a sea-corridor from the Black Sea and Hellespont. In
387/6 the King's Peace seemed to have settled Greek affairs. It
included some sort of autonomy clause that implicitly forbade the
construction of new empires but apparently did not restrict free
alliances (X. *HG* 5.1.31). In 378, nearly a full century after the

founding of the first Confederacy, the Second Athenian Confederacy apparently grew out of an earlier bilateral alliance between Athens and Chios (384/3).[14] Thebes was added as a third major ally by 378/7. Fortunately, the charter of this Confederacy has been preserved on an inscription set up in Athens in the founding year. It will be useful to note some of its contents:[15]

If anyone *wishes*, of the Hellenes, or of the barbarians who are living on the mainland, or of the islanders, *as many as* are not *subject to the King*, to be an ally of the Athenians and of their allies, it shall be permitted *to him* to do so, remaining *free* and autonomous, living under whatever constitution he wants, neither receiving a *garrison* nor having a governor *imposed* upon him nor paying tribute, but he shall become an ally on the same terms as those on which the Chians and the Thebans and the other allies did. (Italics indicate partial restoration of the text: P. Harding, tr., *TDGR*)

In this passage and throughout the inscription the allies seem to be at pains to avoid the mistakes of a previous age of Athenian imperialism. Athenians are expressly forbidden to own allied land, for example. Of course, the allies must also be careful to avoid obvious infringements to the clauses of the King's Peace. Persia rarely had the military strength to suppress Greeks directly, but she had shown a willingness to spend large amounts of money to pay potential troublemakers to create serious difficulties for would-be imperialists who might get too strong in the Aegean. Despite its liberal charter, the Confederacy was to last for a mere two decades. For reasons that are not entirely clear, the Chians and Rhodians instigated a decisive revolt in 357. By the end of it, in 355, Athens was being guided primarily by the cautious Eubulus. So Athens abandoned her war with the allies (the so-called Social War) and turned to securing a few strategic bases in the Aegean and Hellespont, specifically Samos and Sestos.[16] A few years later, in 347/6, Philip would be moving into Phocis to settle the Sacred War, and Athens would be sending out ambassadors to Hellenic communities far and near in the hope of forging a new anti-Macedonian alliance. The ambassadors returned empty-handed.

The fragments of the *Philippica* reveal that Theopompus had something to say about all of this history. Detailed discussion of some of the relevant ones is reserved for the next chapter, but the following observations are appropriate here. First, the fifth-century "demagogues" from Themistocles to Hyperbolus, whose policies led to and advanced the old empire, were all mercilessly attacked in book 10. Second, Athenian imperial rhetoric was also savaged at the time of the embassies. But what did Theopompus think of the Second

Athenian Confederacy? Did he take seriously its avowed aim of forging a voluntary alliance, or did he scorn it as thinly disguised imperialism?

There are some clear signs that Theopompus' attitude to the relatively powerless Athens after 404 was somewhat softer than to the Athens of the earlier period. Indeed, even before 404, the Alcibiades who had struggled against hopeless odds to save Athens' fortunes had won praise from Theopompus, no doubt for his unquestionable diligence on his city's behalf (F288). But what of the city itself? First, in F103 (the summary of book 12), where the Spartans are characterized as presumptuous for trying to exploit the King's Peace, the Athenians "tried to abide by its terms" (F103.7). There is no indication they were attacked for doing so. To the contrary, F104 is quite probably an extension of the account of Athenian behaviour in F103, and it looks to be rather glowing. It is natural to take F104 as a reference to an alliance between Athens and Chios:

The Athenians pray for the Chians and themselves together when they sacrifice since the Chians would send allies to Athens when the city was in need, according to Theopompus in the 12th book of the *Philippica*. He says, "But the majority(?) refrained from doing so, and the result was that they began to make common prayers for them as well as themselves; and in making libations at their public sacrifices they began to offer joint prayers to the gods that they give blessings to the Chians as well as to themselves."

Obviously, the quotation is torn violently from its context, but the actors seem to be the Athenians and the subject is gratitude to the Chians in connection with some sort of an alliance. F103 shows that book 12 covered eastern Aegean history, especially the revolt and later career of Evagoras of Cyprus (391–374). The only known alliance between Athens and Chios from this time is the one already noted from 384/3, which apparently served as a preliminary to the generation of the Second Athenian Confederacy.

The founding of this Confederacy was another event from Polybius' *Leuktrikoi kairoi*. Like all the others that Theopompus bothered to report from that period, it found its way into the *Philippica* as an adjunct to a major digression, in this case to "On the Demagogues" in book 10. This digression (see pp. 68–71) came after the narration of the first few years of Philip's reign, the outbreak of the Sacred War, and (probably) the destruction of Athens' Second Confederacy by the allies in the Social War. The probable effect was to accuse Athens of failing to hold on to her confederacy because of her compulsive imperialism, which was documented by the long, scathing digression. The demagogues are relentlessly attacked until the last two: Callistratus and Eubulus. Their treatment is ambivalent. Now Callistratus was influential in Athens at the time of the Confederacy's foundation, and Theopompus noted his direct involvement in it, as F98 makes clear. In order to remove the stigma of the fifth century and make a show of abiding by the King's Peace, the Athenians had agreed with the Chians and other allies to bring a fresh approach to the administration of the new Confederacy, as is reflected by the charter. One of the many things they consented to was that there would be no more tribute (*phoros*), the old word for enforced payments to the central *fiscus* housed in Athens since 454 and under the direct control of the Athenians. The new system implied more voluntary assessments in keeping with the autonomy of the allies. For the new system, a new word was coined, says Theopompus (F98), by Callistratus. The word was *syntaxeis* meaning something like "assessed contributions." The new word was in one sense no different in meaning from the old one, but it was free of negative connotations from the past. Did Theopompus scoff at this as a mere tinkering with words to conceal the ruth as G.T Griffith believed?[17] I think not. The few scraps of evidence that remain suggest otherwise. First, F104 commemorates the Chian inclusion in Athenian public prayers, and Theopompus did not scoff at Greek religious convention. More to the point, Callistratus himself is characterized in F97 (Athen. 4.166E): "Callistratus ... the demagogue ... was uncontrolled in [private] pleasure but diligent in political business." For Theopompus, diligence is a key word. A "diligent" politician was a good politician, and the politics he noted included a decision to modulate the Confederacy in tune with the allies' desire for autonomy. The modulation was done in deed as well as word, at first. How long it took before Theopompus saw, or thought he saw, the old imperialism re-emerging cannot be known.

Again, at the time of the break-up some profited from the dissolution of the Confederacy. They include the Byzantians, who are called lazy and corrupt (F62), and Mausolus, who is called greedy (F299). In this characteristic way Theopompus probably blamed both the Athenians and their allies for the debacle: Eubulus became Athenian demagogue at about this time. He is credited with a reorganization of Athenian finances that tended to inhibit the direction of money toward military adventures.[18] To me, the adoption of this approach to public finances can only imply a certain willingness to let the recalcitrant allies go. Theopompus saw two aspects of Eubulus' career; in the first he curbed spending and built up Athenian cash reserves. For these accomplishments he is awarded the highest praise of any public figure in the fragments. Theopompus looked for diligence and industry in the few people he chose to applaud, and Eubulus is the only person whose political efforts are characterized by both these words. However, Theopompus identified a contrasting phase of Eubulus' career in which he distributed those reserves to the people. Theopompus deplored that decision. F99 (= Harp. *Euboulos*): "[Eubulus] was a most prominent demagogue, diligent and industrious. He provided the Athenians with great wealth but distributed it. The result was that the city became most cowardly and indifferent under his governance as Theopompus records in book ten of the *Philippica*."[19]

Apparently, Theopompus considered the one side of Eubulus' career altogether praiseworthy. His fiscal control gave Athens the opportunity to prepare for some future enemy (such as Philip), but the money was squandered and the city enervated as a result. I will return to this point in chapter 5. Here, it is important to note that the Athenian demagogues who advance the cause of the empire in the fifth century are all attacked without mercy, but in the fourth century Callistratus, who helped fashion a new Confederacy that attempted to respect allied autonomy, is praised, apparently in direct connection with his efforts in that regard. Eubulus is praised as lavishly as Theopompus knows how but only in connection with the manner in which his financial arrangements had the effect of steering the Athenians away from imperialism. His image became sadly tarnished as a result of his corrupting decision to distribute to the people the funds he had preserved for the city's treasury. Thus, the Second Athenian Confederacy met with some approbation; its dissolution was deplored. Otherwise, when Athenians advocate aggressive imperialism toward the Aegean they are excoriated, but the few who practised moderation or renounced aggression toward the allies are applauded for their policies. This seems to make Theopompus and advocate of the autonomy of the Aegean islanders and Ionians and a supporter of voluntary alliances between them and Athens.

CHAPTER THREE

The Philippica

The *Philippica* was Theopompus' *magnum opus*, fifty-eight books of generally smoothly written historical narrative broken up by digressions of interminable length, all liberally sprinkled with classic Theopompan vitriol. In the caustic moments, he apparently abandoned the smooth style for a seething turgidity punctuated by wretchedly contrived puns (T20). From the citations, or fragments, there is enough information to produce an outline of the work's structure, a fairly detailed "Table of Contents," if you will, but before examining them, it is useful to consider what they are and how they survived. The scholarly world after Theopompus' time was primarily preoccupied with rhetoric. Orators thrive on anecdotes; and the ancient rhetorical enterprise seems to have been served by collections of them culled from the major authors. Someone ransacked the *Philippica* for a list of thumb-nail sketches of intemperate boozers and their riotous lives. The list he compiled was substantial, but not exhaustive.[1] Perhaps great rhetoricians, grammarians, geographers, and lexicographers set their "graduate students" the task of scanning ancient works like the *Philippica* for pithy quotes and spicy anecdotes to relieve the numbing horror of speeches lasting up to five hours (orators),[2] for examples of good and bad grammar or syntax (grammarians), for rare place-names or unusual spellings (geographers), or for new words coined or bizarre uses of old ones (lexicographers). Whoever they were, these molish compilers were sometimes assiduous enough to note down the source of each "tidbit" by author, work, and book number.

The modern collecting and arranging of these citations by book number has been going on since 1829. Scholars today recognize 223 such fragments from the *Philippica* alone, representing some forty-eight of the fifty-eight lost books. More than two hundred fragments, some substantial, will obviously provide solid clues to the contents of the books, but a few words of caution are timely.

The book numbers provided by these compilers are not always reliable. Indeed, any thesis that depends upon a single item like a number in an ancient text is taking a calculated risk. The probability that words have been faithfully preserved for two millennia or more is generally good, often excellent, but never certain. Words in context are susceptible of restoration. If a scribe writes, "The hero charged one his horse," the correction to "The hero charged on his horse" is easy, and the meaning of the quotation is not affected if the writer adds, "Homer, book 14," or "book 24." Once a number became corrupt, an easy thing, since a copyist would not always consider it vital information, there was little chance that an ancient or Byzantine scholar would check it for accuracy or try to trace the quotation and restore the correct figure. To do so is not easy with scrolls of papyrus, and it is difficult to imagine why anyone would think of undertaking the laborious task even with a codex, since the information important to the orator or grammarian was the substance of the citation, and not its precise source and location. This fact is best demonstrated simply by noting the nearly two hundred further fragments in Jacoby's collection that lack any indication (some lost, most never provided) of their source other than the author's name. Further, unacknowledged citations can be suspected; in authors like Strabo, for example, there are occasionally close verbal parallels with the known fragments.[3]

Examination of the fragments' texts confirms the uncertainty. There is indeed a significant body of fragments from which the numbers have been lost by scribal carelessness or where the numbers do not command absolute confidence. To make matters worse, there are sometimes reasons to doubt the reliability of ancient attributions to Theopompus. There was another Theopompus, a comic poet, with whom the historian was confused, and a suspected case of confusion of Theopompus with Theophrastus, Aristotle's star pupil and Theopompus' contemporary, was noted in the previous chapter.

However, the purpose of these remarks is to advocate caution, not despair. There is strength in numbers, and the fragments do indeed fall into a pattern. Broadly speaking, they show the outline of a chronological treatment of Philip's career punctuated by digressions of varying magnitude (some enormous), very much what might have been expected from a reading of the *testimonia*.

THE CONTENTS OF THE *PHILIPPICA*

When Dionysius of Halicarnassus began his *Roman Antiquities*, he began with a preface because, as he says, he felt obliged to do so. It was standard procedure for a historian. Nonetheless, he declared that he would not spend a great deal of time in his prologue praising himself

Table 1
The Contents of the *Philippica*

Book	Contents	Dates
	First phase. Philip secures his position.	
1	Introduction. The situation in Greece at the time of Philip's accession and the incursions of the pretenders, FF24–37, 381? 345? 286? 307? 310? 337? 348? 372? 279? 393? 352? 341? 181? (D.S. 16.2–3)	360/59
2	War with the Paeonians and Illyrians, geography of Illyria? FF38–41, 363? 235? (D.S. 16.4)	359/58
3	Capture of Amphipolis, F42, F30? Acquisition of the mines at Mt. Pangaeum, FF43–4. Early Thracian history, tuinvasion of Sesostris of Egypt, FF46–7. (D.S. 16.8; Herodo-2.102–108)	357
3–4	Philip's first intrusion into Thessaly, FF48–9. (Just. 3.18)	357/6?
4	Philip's defeat of Thracian alliance, F51? Capture of Halonnesus, Methone, FF50, 52, 384? (D. *On Organization* 13.23, *Against Aristocrates* 199; D.S. 16.22.3, 31.6, 34.3–5)	356/3
5	Philip's campaign against Pherae, reduction of Pagasae, FF53–8. (D.S. 16.14, 31.6)	354, 353?
6	Onomarchus opposes Philip? FF60–61. Situation in Ionia (Second Athenian Confederacy?), F59, 305? (D.S. 15.28)	353
7–8	Social War – Athens loses Second Athenian Confederacy? F62. (D.S. 16.7.3–4, 21–2)	(357–355)
8	Philip drawn into Sacred War, F63, 298? 336? (D.S. 16.35)	353?, 352?
	Pause for background, digressions.	
8–9	Marvels, FF64–77, 392? 394?	
9	Description of Delphic Amphictiony, descriptive geography of central Greece, FF78–82. War with Cersobleptes of Thrace, FF83, 84. (D.S. 16.38.1; Schol. Aeschin. 2.81)	352?
	Intermediary phase. Philip poised for expansion.	
10	Philip menaces Athenian interests (D.S. 16.42–9?). Digression "On the Demagogues," FF85–100, 261?	
11	End of war with Cersobleptes, F101. Effects of Social War? F102.	
	Turmoil in Western Satrapies.	
11	Introduction to long digression on western satrapies of the Persian Empire? F293?	
12	History of eastern Greeks and western satrapies – reign and assassination of Evagoras I, FF103–4, 346? 351? (D.S. 14.98.1–4, 15.2–5, 8–12, 18–19, 20–1?)	c. 394/374

Table 1 *(Continued)*

Book	Contents	Dates
13	Egyptian revolt from Persia and death of Agesilaus, FF105–9, 321–3? (D.S. 15.29.1–4, 41–43, 90–93). Historical geography of NW coast of Asia Minor, FF110–12.	360
14	Artaxerxes Ochus ascends the throne, moves against Egypt? F113.	360/51?
15	General revolt of western satrapies involvement of Sidon, Cyprus, FF114–16 (D.S. 16.40.3–45.6). More historical geography of W coast of Asia Minor, FF117–18. Digression on political treachery? FF119–20.	351/0
16	History of Caria (SW coast of Asia Minor). Mausolus overthrows democracy on island of Rhodes? F121.	c. 358?
17	Chians aid Mausolus in extending his influence, Social War revisited? FF122–3, 299? 297?	c. 355/51
18–19	Artaxerxes Ochus reduces Egypt, FF124, 263? 368? (D.S. 16.46–51)	346/3?
	First phase of Macedonian expansion. Athenian response fails.	
20	Initiation of Philip's attack on Olynthus, FF125–7, 266? 375? (D.S. 16.52.9)	350/49
21	Geographical digression on regions north of Macedonia, Italy and Sicily, Pontic, Adriatic, and Ionian Seas, and peregrinations of Jason and Medea? FF125–33, 266? 375? 274? 285? 356? 317? Mention of Sicily and her tyrants evokes comparison with milder rule of Athenian Pisistratus? FF134–6.	
22–23	Philip's war with Olynthus, FF137–45.	c. 349
24	Olynthian War, Philip's intervention in Euboea, FF146–9, 287? (D.S. 16.53.9)	
24	Revolt of Euboea, FF147–51. Digression on early Euboean history? F387?	349/8
25	End of Olynthian War, "debunking" of rhetoric of Athenian Empire, FF152–5, 306? 281? Philip moves to settle Sacred War, FF156–8, 301?	347
26	Philon's exposure and execution? FF159, 344? (D.S. 16.56). Philip moves against Cersobleptes in Thracian Chersonese, FF160–1. War against Halus, F162. End of Sacred War, negotiation of Peace of Philocrates begins, FF164–5. (D.S. 16.57–64)	347

346 |
| 27 | Peace of Philocrates concluded, F166. | 346 |

Table 1 *(Continued)*

Book	Contents	Dates
	Second intermediary phase. Philip consolidates.	
28–29	No fragments.	
30	Aftermath of Sacred War. History of Delphic Amphictiony now under Philip's control, FF167–70.	
31	No fragments (unless F30?).	
	Interlude for background.	
32–33	Philip's alliance with Messenia. Digression on early Spartan and Peloponnesian history, FF171–8, 311? 357? 350?	
34	No fragments.	
35	Historical geography of northern Asia Minor and environs? FF179, 388? 389? 370?	
36	F291? (but see book 46).	
37	No fragments.	
38	Historical geography of northern Asia Minor FF181, 363?? Philip in Illyria, F182 (D.S. 16.69.7).	344/2
	Philip consolidates.	
39	Philip in Epirus, F183.	344/2
	More background digression.	
39	Digression on Sicilian history (via Timoleon?), FF184–7, 189–91, 358? 365? 371? 283?	394-344/3
40	Sicilian digression continues, FF188, 192–3, 196. Return to northern Peloponnese, central Greece FF194–5.	
41	No fragments.	
42	End of Sicilian digression? F198.	
42–43	Far western geography: Gibraltar, Iberia, Gaul, Etruria, FF199–205, 335? 354? Philip in central Greece, FF206–7, 382? 319?	343/2
	Final phase of consolidation.	
44	Philip's reorganization of Thessaly into tetrarchies, FF208–9. (D.S. 16.69)	344
	Final phase of Philip's conquests.	
45	Philip's relationship to Thebes, digression on early Theban history, FF210–12, and to Athens, F213. Philip moves against eastern Thrace, prepares to attack Byzantium, F214. (D.S. 16.71.1–2)	343/2

Table 1 *(Continued)*

Book	Contents	Dates
46	Philip's relations with Arcadia? F215. Philip strengthens hold on Thrace by marrying Medea, a Thracian princess, F216. Death of Hermeas of Atarneus, F291.	341
47–48	Outbreak of war between Philip and Athens. Parmenio and Antipater operate in Thrace. Philip's abortive assaults on Perinthus and Byzanthium, his capture of Athenian grain fleet, FF217–22, 360? 292? (D.S. 16.74–77.2)	340/39
49	Philip prepares for final showdown with Greek states, long diatribe against him, FF223–5.	
50	End of Thracian campaign F226. Philip's piracy in the Aegean? F227.	
51	Preliminaries to Chaeronea, Demosthenes forges alliance against Philip, FF229–31, 328?	339/8
52	Sparta's involvement in alliance? End of career of King Archidamus, FF232–4, 318? 312?	
53	Battle of Chaeronea, FF236, 329? 385? (D.S. 16.84–88.2)	338
54	Aftermath of Chaeronea, F237.	
55	Philip enters Peloponnese, FF238–9.	338
	Final consolidation.	
56	Philip's relations with Peloponnesian states, FF240–1	
	Digression.	
	Digression on Arcadia? FF242–4	
	Conclusion. End of Philip's career.	
57–58	League of Corinth established, Philip declares war on Persia, his assassination, FF245–6, 280? (D.S. 16.89–95)	338/7 336

and censuring other authors as Anaximenes and Theopompus had done in theirs (F24 = D.H. *AR* 1.1.1). Photius knew and summarized a lengthy passage in which Theopompus introduced himself and compared himself favourably to other authors (F25, see also F345), and there seems no reason to doubt that Photius was quoting the introduction to the *Philippica*. In this passage Theopompus identified himself as a contemporary of Isocrates, a little known Theodectes, and a Naucrates. Since these orators were his competitors in the funeral oration over Mausolus, he probably mentioned that contest and boasted of his success. He claimed that the four competitors were the leading rhetoricians of the age, but he and Naucrates outshone the other two because Isocrates and Theodectes had been obliged to teach rhetoric for pay. Free of the burden of teaching, he and Naucrates could devote their time to the pursuit of wisdom and knowledge. However, he thinks he should be given pride of place because of his voluminous literary output, both historical and purely rhetorical. He had written on subjects whose importance was still acknowledged and had scarcely left an important Greek city unvisited. In each place he had given declamations and left behind an enduring memory of his rhetorical prowess. According to two other sources (Athenaeus and Dionysius of Halicarnassus, FF26, 181), he emphasized the enormous cost of his travels and the authenticity they lent his history. Photius concludes:

So he speaks about himself and declares the pre-eminent authors of former time to be greatly inferior, not even up to second-rate standard of his own day. He claims that this is clear both from the best wrought works of the two groups [ancients and moderns] as well as their neglected ones; for according to him, literary knowledge made great progress in his generation.

Photius wonders who could have been meant by the "pre-eminent authors of former times." He speculates for a moment but can think of no previous historian whom he would agree to have been so greatly inferior to Theopompus, certainly not Herodotus and Thucydides if they were meant.[4]

Neither Herodotus nor Thucydides had introduced himself with such fanfare. After trumpeting his own importance, however, Theopompus probably became more businesslike and introduced his work and its main topic. At some point, probably in the *Philippica*, he admitted to the practice of retailing yarns (μύθοι), and the introduction would be a likely place to do that (F381). If so, the conclusion that he deliberately rejected a Thucydidean principle would be difficult to avoid. In his famous introduction Thucydides had warned his readers not to expect the element of yarn-spinning (τὸ μυθῶδες) in his work. So Theopompus was declaring a closer affinity with Herodotus, who was famous for his marvellous digressions. Perhaps without mentioning either Herodotus or Thucydides by name, therefore, he was able to imply that he would do better than Thucydides, on the one hand, by reintroducing the element of entertainment to history and than Herodotus, on the other, by using his extensive travels for "research" and writing them up in a better, "more modern" style.[5]

Eventually he would have to come to the direct introduction of his subject. According to Polybius (8.11.1 = F27) he had turned to Philip as a subject because he perceived him as unique: "Europe had never born such a man." As chapter 5 will show, he probably followed this with the generally accepted genealogy that traced Philip back to Heracles (or, at least, a version of it), thereby declaring him to be a Greek by descent (FF29, 279, 393) and of the finest lineage, a king, as Polybius puts it, "born with the finest natural disposition toward manly excellence." Next Polybius summarizes Theopompus' characterization of Philip as a womanizer and drunkard who manipulated his friends and enslaved cities by treachery and force. Most of the points Polybius makes are reflected in the preserved fragments. Athenaeus repeats several passages where Philip's wild drinking was recorded, and he and Polybius both record descriptions of Philip's manipulation of his friends. On Philip's womanizing the fragments are silent, but there is no reason to doubt Polybius' report. Satyrus the Peripatetic listed eight wives for Philip, though his version apparently explained most of Philip's early marriages as political opportunism. They cemented key alliances with Illyrians, Thracians, Molossians, and Thessalians (Athen. 13.557B–E). However, Polybius' description of the *Philippica* makes it sound as if Theopompus dealt with Philip's uxuriousness less as a tool of imperialism than as a destructive, pathological compulsion, a view taken by Satyrus and most others only in connection with the last marriage to Cleopatra. In that case Philip is generally alleged to have been smitten with love. The union would have been a threat to the youthful Alexander, who would otherwise have had undisputed claim to succeed Philip, had it produced male offspring, and it seems that Olympias, Alexander's mother, saw it that way. In 336 the assassination of Philip by Pausanias, which was probably engineered "by a person or persons unknown," secured the throne for Alexander and made it possible for Olympias to triumph over her female rival.[6] Tradition has Alexander devoted to his mother (Plut. *Alex.* 25.6, 27.8), and probably Theopompus, who posed elsewhere as Alexander's agent and adviser, saw to it that his account of Philip's marriages suited her views. Indeed, in some context now lost he provided, perhaps formulated, the standard genealogy of Olympias that traced her to Priam, king of Troy, on one side and Achilles, hero of the *Iliad*, on the other; that could scarcely have displeased her (F355).

The introduction appears to have been lengthy, but eventually Theopompus will have addressed himself to his narrative. A detailed discussion of the possible contents of the *Philippica* could fill a separate book. Table 1 is a summary of the contents based on the fruits of the labours of Wichers, Schranz, and Jacoby. In a few cases I have expanded a little on the work of these scholars, and in one place I have boldly presumed to settle the dispute over the location of the important fragment 291 on Hermeas of Atarneus.

The first seven and a half books of the *Philippica* predictably covered Philip's brilliant initial successes in securing his throne and then his expansion into territories captured largely at the expense or to the embarrassment of Athens: Amphipolis, Mt. Pangaeum (book 3, FF42-4), Methone on the coast, and the island of Halonnesus (book 4, FF50-2), even his operations at Pagasae so close to the northern tip of Euboea (353? book 5, FF53-8). However, from book 6 two, or perhaps three, geographical fragments seem to testify to a sudden change of scene to the Aegean and the disintegration of the Second Athenian Confederacy. Jacoby's ordering of these fragments is simply one of convenience and need not be followed slavishly. Indeed, I argue that the correct order is 60/61, 59. F61 is from Stephanus of Byzantium. It simply mentions a Euaemon, "a city of the Orchomeians." There were two places called Orchomenus, one in the Peloponnese (in Arcadia, just north of Mantinea) and the other in Boeotia (near the border with Phocis), but only the Arcadian city owned a town called Euaemon. About 360, or a little before, Euaemon and Orchomenus had joined together in sympolity. F60 is expressly a reference to Arcadia ("Eua, a city of Arcadia"), but do these two fragments really add up to a digression on "the situation in the Peloponnese" as Jacoby suggested? Pausanias also knows of a Eua, but he makes it a village of Corinthia (2.38.6). It was the location of a shrine to Polemocrates, son of Machaon, "heroic" physician in the *Iliad*, but it was otherwise of little significance and hardly central to any important Peloponnesian issues of the 350s. Euaemon is also the name of a hero, the father of the Homeric Eurypylus, who hailed from southern Thessaly. Eua, for its part (F60), is also to be associated with southern Thessaly, but more remotely. The shrine to Polemocrates mentioned by Pausanias was a place of healing, and the hero's therapeutic powers were apparently inherited from his father Machaon, a Thessalian from Tricca. Machaon was son of the healer-god Asclepius whose cult emanated from Thessaly. Both F61, therefore, on Euaemon, and F60, on Eua, can reasonably be taken as part of a digression of the sort sometimes indulged in by Theopompus (cf. F103) at the end of a sustained narrative before he began a new one. Its theme was perhaps the legendary history of southern Thessaly, giving some of its cult associations and connections with Arcadia.[7]

Table 2
Theopompus' Main Narratives Compared to His Principal Rivals or Sources.

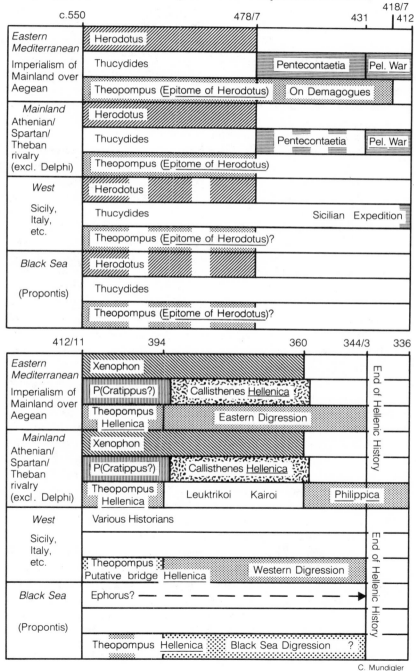

C. Mundigler

F59 provides the most dramatic change of scene and subject. A place called Pygela is the topic of a fragment preserved by the Alexandrian lexicographer Harpocration. He says that the place was in Ionia and took its name (according to Theopompus in book 6)[8] from a disease of the buttocks (Gr. *pygoi*) contracted by some of Agamemnon's men. The diseased men were left there to found the place and give it its name. A slightly fuller version of the same story is given by Strabo (14.1.20), who identifies the place as a Samian possession on the mainland, part of the Ephesian littoral near Priene. This Pygela is certainly to be identified with the Phygela of F305, which is an inscription from Priene. According to this inscription, a panel of experts had been appointed to determine who owned Phygela. The judges had consulted various histories, including Theopompus', and concluded that most ancient accounts agreed in making the place Samian. The variation in spelling is easily explained. The local Ionian dialect had a tendency to drop "h" sounds, a process called psilosis. The same confusion was found in a similar place name, to give but one of many possible examples: The *Suda* has an entry, "Pygella – place we call Phygella, a place whence the ferry-crossing to Crete is made." This place must have been much further south than Theopompus' Phygela for it to be convenient for the Cretan ferry. The form Pygella is the Ionic variant of the more usual Phygella.

A consideration of F59 suggests that it is from a detailed account of Ionia and the Aegean islands including its pre-history and its territorial distribution; otherwise, it would be hard to see how Theopompus could be cited as an authority for the Samian ownership of Phygela. Since an account of this nature has no conceivable place interrupting a narrative of events and cult associations in and around southern Thessaly, it seems probable that F59 belongs to the later part of book 6, part of a new topic which Jacoby reasonably identified as the situation in Ionia. There are no fragments from book 7, but the denunciation of the Byzantians and Chalcedonians for succumbing to the enervating beguilements of democracy (F62) must surely come somewhere near the opening of book 8. The Byzantians had democracy first, and the Chalcedonians learned it from them. That F62 belongs early in book 8 seems hard to deny. The end of this book was dominated by the excursion known as the "Marvels," which "spilled over" into book 9 (FF77–8). They were almost certainly introduced by a return to central Greece and the circumstances of the Sacred War and a description of the membership of the Delphic Amphictiony (F63). This organization leaves only the beginning of the book for a mention of the Byzantians and Chalcedonians. Demosthenes mentions an apparent annexation of "Chalcedon, which belonged to the

King, and Selymbria, once our ally" by Byzantium in his speech *For the Rhodians* (26, from the year 353 or 351?) when the Chalcedonians probably had democracy introduced to them by a Byzantian-sponsored coup. The grab for territory is most naturally associated with the annulment of Athenian authority in the region, in other words, the Social War. There was an account of Ionia in some detail at the end of book 6. There is nothing of book 7, but the Byzantians were annexing territory early in book 8, probably taking advantage of the complete collapse of Athenian power in the Aegean. Therefore, the most likely topic for the end of book 6 and the beginning of book 7 would be the Second Athenian Confederacy and its dissolution by the successful revolt of the allies in 357–355. Further, it is difficult not to recognize an attempt to see historical cause in this leap from Philip's intrusions into the coasts of the Thermaic Gulf, the Chalcidic peninsula, and southern Thessaly to the disintegration of Athenian power in the Aegean. Philip could take these coastal places because there was no sea-power to resist him. This is the "power vacuum" thesis. According to Plutarch, a similar case was argued by the orator and historian Callisthenes, Aristotle's nephew and Alexander's court historian until he fell from grace. At a banquet the Macedonians asked him to give a speech praising them, which he did with great success and much to their pleasure. They then suggested that praising the great was easy. The real challenge to his rhetoric would be to denounce these same Macedonians. In response, Callisthenes allegedly advanced the thesis that dissension (στάσις) among the Greeks was the cause (αἰτία) of the growth of Philip's power. He ended with a quotation from Euripides: "In time of sedition, even the vilest wins honour" (Plut. *Alex.* 53.5). His ability as a rhetorician was clearly established, but his utter lack of tact probably contributed in no small part to his ultimate undoing.[9] Years later the second-century Greek traveller Pausanias, who never had a good word for Philip, explained his conquests as opportunism, taking advantage of the weakness and turmoil in Greece after the Peloponnesian War. The line of narrative presented by Theopompus looks perfectly compatible with the sort of argument advanced by Callisthenes and Pausanias.

Theopompus' native Chios had been a ringleader in provoking the Social War, along with Cos, Rhodes, and later, Byzantium (D.S. 16.7.3), but it is not clear that he approved of their actions. The Byzantians at least were described as undisciplined "barflies," and if F59 treated a local territorial dispute between Samos and Priene or Ephesus, it is possible that he emphasized corrupt shortsightedness or petty greed leading to territorial squabbles amongst the allies as a cause of the Social War. One of the prime movers promoting the revolt had been Mausolus of Caria.[10] Theopompus characterized him as a man who would do anything for money (F299).

Theopompus was not excusing Athens, of course. For there is reason to regard the scathing attack on the political leadership of Athens placed toward the end of book 10 as an explanation of and lament for Athens' inability to mount an effective resistance to Philip in his more vulnerable early years. The digression has been extensively studied by Connor, and I intend to add little to his results. It focused on Athenian political leaders from Themistocles to Hyperbolus (c. 483–c. 416) and again from Callistratus to Eubulus (c. 380–c. 350). It is not certain that the fragments give an exact indication of its scope, but Connor gives reasons for believing that they may. First, the fragments suggest that the known subjects were treated in some detail, and if there had been substantially more politicians in it, there could well have been a problem of space, since the entire digression occupied only a part of a single book. Second, the argument from silence may have some weight here. The digression was justifiably famous and, by all reports, sensational. After the "Marvels," it is the most quoted section of all of Theopompus. The Athenian political leaders were, of course, intrinsically interesting to later compilers of anecdota and biographies. Under these circumstances, it would be odd if there were a substantial treatment of a famous Athenian politician in this treatise that has left no identifiable trace whatsoever in later sources.

However that may be, the known subjects of the digression illustrate certain themes. Connor points out the persistent notions of corrupt leaders buying popular support with their own fortunes – Cimon (FF89, 90) – or with public money – Eubulus (F100) and probably Pericles – or acquiring funds rapaciously – Themistocles (F86), Cimon (F90), and Cleon (F94). The victims of their greed are not always specified in the fragments, but Theopompus probably identified them generally as Aegean islanders and Ionians. He would have known Herodotus' story that Themistocles pocketed a bribe from the Euboeans (8.5), and he directly accused Cleon of taking five talents from unspecified "islanders" (F94) who wanted him to persuade the Athenians to lighten their tribute. A further point not emphasized by Connor is that all the politicians known to have been included in the digression played key roles in shaping Athenian imperial policy vis-à-vis the Aegean and Ionia at a time when desperation was not the order of the day and there were real political options. Figures like Alcibiades, Thrasybulus, and Iphicrates were involved in Aegean politics in desperate times.[11] Their actions in this arena were aimed primarily at keeping open a.corridor for the vital shipments of grain from the Black Sea to Athens. As far as is known, they were not included in the digression. Another demagogue not known to have been included, Cleophon, advocated a senseless persistence in the Peloponnesian War, a policy disastrous for Athens but of little significance to the Aegean at the time. Therefore, the apparent structure of the digression is not implausible given that it was written by a historian who hailed from an Aegean island, and not Athens.

The previous chapter suggested that the remarks made about Callistratus and Eubulus are compatible with a sympathetic treatment of the Second Athenian Confederacy. If that view is correct, book 10 ended with a sympathetic treatment of the short-lived Second Confederacy, or, at least, of its ideals followed by the scathing attack on Eubulus for squandering the public monies, so laudably amassed, on frivolities like state festivals and undermining public morale (FF97–100). Since this digression follows an account of early Macedonian expansion and was probably located near the Social War and its aftermath, it was possibly Theopompus' way of explaining Athens' inability to maintain the support of her allies and use her Confederacy to offer resistance to Philip at this most crucial time.

FF101 (on Cersoleptes' father) and 102 are assigned to book 11, and it would be nice to be certain of their correct order. Whatever it was, F102 is easily the more important. It indicates that part of book 11, quite likely the beginning, continued a commentary on conditions in Athens in the aftermath of the allied victory in the Social War. The "fragment" is a peculiar one. It is not a quotation from Theopompus but an allegation that he plagiarized a section of a speech of Isocrates, the *Areopagiticus*. Now it has long been recognized that this speech must have been written by Isocrates at the time of or shortly before the Social War.[12] Part of its purpose was to comment on Athens' sorry plight at the time and draw some instructive lessons from alleged past mistakes. Porphyry, who supplies the information, simply says that the plagiarism began with Isocrates' words (*Areopagiticus* 4): "nothing of either good or evil visits mankind unmixed" and so on. He gives nothing that reveals where the citation ended. The remainder of the sentence reads: "but ... riches and power are attended and followed by folly and folly by license; whereas poverty and lowliness are attended by sobriety and great moderation; so that it is hard to decide which of these lots one should prefer to bequeath to one's own children" (G. Norlin, tr., L.C.L.). This sentence alone would make a very apt conclusion to the digression "On the Demagogues," but Isocrates' point does not end it here; it goes on to draw parallels with Spartan history:

For we shall find that from a lot which seems to be inferior men's fortunes generally advance to a better condition, whereas from one which appears to be superior they are wont to change to a worse. Of this truth I might cite examples without number from the lives of individual men, since these are subject to the most frequent vicissitudes; but instances which are more important and better known to my hearers may be drawn from the experiences of our city and of the Lacedaemonians. As for the Athenians, after our city had been laid waste by the barbarians, we became, because we were anxious about the future and gave attention to our affairs, the foremost of the Hellenes: whereas, when we imagined that our power was invincible, we barely escaped being enslaved. Likewise the Lacedaemonians, after having set out in ancient times from obscure and humble cities, made themselves, because they lived temperately and under military discipline, masters of the Peloponnesus; whereas later, when they grew overweening and seized the empire both of the sea and of the land, they fell into the same dangers as ourselves. (G. Norlin, tr., L.C.L.)

How much of this Theopompus used is uncertain, but the sentiment suits him well.

It appears that books 12 to 19 were devoted to Greek relations with the turbulent and often disloyal western satrapies of the Persian empire from Dascylium in the north to Egypt in the south spanning the five decades from c. 394 to the mid-340s when Artaxerxes Ochus finally recovered Egypt (343). Before leaving the opening books of the *Philippica*, however, I should point out also that if my suggestions about the arrangement of the material are correct so far, it is quite possible that the first nineteen books of the *Philippica* exhibit a structure known as ring-composition, or bracketing. The first five and a fraction books are mainly a narrative of Philip's early expansion, punctuated by relatively brief geographic digressions. They are "balanced" by the seven books from 12 to 19, a narrative of western Persian history again adorned by relatively short geographical digressions. Book 7, along with parts of 6 and 8, was a narration of the Social War. Book 8 discussed the Delphic Amphictiony, no doubt in the context of the Sacred War. Next came the "Marvels," followed by more on the Amphictiony. The end of book 10 and part of 11 return to Athens in the aftermath of the Social War, and finally the new narrative of western Persian history is taken up. In short, then, the structure was probably as follows: long narrative, Social War, Delphic Amphictiony, "Marvels," Delphic Amphictiony, Social War, long narrative.

Book 12 of the *Philippica* provides another clear instance of ring-composition. Its contents were summarized comprehensively by

Photius to prove that he had read it and that it was not lost as Menophanes had claimed. F103 indicates that the main topic of book 12 was the career of Evagoras I and particularly his revolt from Persian domination (c. 390– c. 380). The main narrative is framed by Acoris, king of Egypt, who is shown making alliances at the beginning of the narrative and again at the end. The book opened with an account of an alliance Acoris concluded between Egypt and Carthage (c. 390); then he "acted in support of Evagoras of Cyprus in resisting the Persian king." There is a flashback to Evagoras' unexpected accession (c. 411 or earlier) and a further flashback to bronze age pre-history to show how Cyprus was legitimately a part of the Greek world, having been once taken by Agamemnon on his way to (or from?) Troy. Next comes the narration of the revolt. The Persian king commits forces against Evagoras, who is defeated in a sea-battle at about the same time as the signing of the Peace of Antalcidas (387/6). (This is known as the battle of Citium, dated by most scholars to 381.) There follows some intrigue involving the Persian high command, and Evagoras manages to hold out until after Nectenibis has succeeded Acoris on the Egyptian throne (380). Finally, Evagoras negotiates a generous surrender, but a few years later (374/3) he is assassinated by a eunuch amidst some salacious harem intrigue. Now Acoris is reintroduced, and Theopompus relates how he had made alliances with Pisidia and Aspendus on the south coast of Asia Minor. This is unquestionably a flashback. The most likely time for Acoris to have been negotiating alliances with regions of southern Asia Minor would have been near the beginning of his reign at the same time as his negotiations with Cyprus. The return to Acoris and his alliances brings the section back, full-circle, to the start in the true manner of ring-composition. The information concludes the narrative section, while mention of the regions with which Acoris made alliance ushers in the next topic: the geography and legendary "pre-history" of southern Asia Minor, itself echoing the flashback to the Bronze Age at the opening of the narrative. With that the book comes to an end.

Only the merest glimpses into the contents of the following books survives. The death of Agesilaus (360, FF105–8) was narrated in book 13. Other topics it covered included the betrayal of the island of Syros to Samos by a certain Theagenes (F111) and something about mining zinc near Troy (F112). This book probably also included a sketch of the twenty years from Nectenibis' ascension (380, F103) to the time of Agesilaus' visit to Egypt. If so, FF105-8 should be assigned to the end of the book.

Agesilaus' visit to Egypt is securely dated to the year 360. Two years later in 358 Artaxerxes II (surnamed Memnon) died, and Artaxerxes

III (surnamed Ochus) ascended the Persian throne. Memnon had been ineffective in his attempts to reduce Egypt, and his control over other western satrapies had been far from impressive. With Memnon's death most of these satrapies seized the opportunity to join Egypt in revolt. F113 from book 14 is about the crippling costs inflicted on Persian grandees when they were obliged to entertain their monarch. Perhaps the context is the young Ochus moving about his kingdom trying to restore order. Circumstantial detail is lacking, and generally there is no reason to believe that Theopompus claimed any special knowledge of Persian history or geography beyond what could be gleaned from the coastal communities immediately accessible to Greeks.

Book 15 has seven fragments. The subject ought to have been the revolt of the western satrapies, and F114 lends confirmation to that suspicion, mentioning Straton, the debauched ruler of Sidon, and his competitor in profligacy, Nicocles of Cyprus. The jaundiced treatment of these two puppets can only be taken at face value. Both rulers permitted themselves to be corrupted by wealth and power, and both came to bad ends. FF115–16 are simply Cypriot place-names. FF117–18 return to Ionia, at or near Colophon, describing how the Colophonians became fabulously wealthy by selling purple dye. However, their wealth corrupted them; they fell into political turmoil and thence into the clutches of a tyrant (cf. Strabo 14.1.29). F120, and, probably, F119 proceed to the mainland for stories of pro-Macedonian treachery. It seems that moralizing, the affairs of the Aegean, and the insidious advance of Macedonian fortunes were never far from Theopompus' mind.

F121 from book 16 mentions the corrupt oligarchy led by Hegesilochus of Rhodes. That island had been a democracy and an ally of Athens as late as 357, when she became a ringleader for the allies in the Social War. Hornblower suggests that the coup that brought Hegesilochus to power took place during the Social War and was aided by Mausolus of Caria, who was interested in expanding his own sphere of influence, in this case at the expense of Athens. Scholars who think that Theopompus generally favoured oligarchies over democracies might well ponder this fragment. According to F121 Hegesilochus openly gambled with his cronies to see which free-born women would be debauched and which men would have the job of bringing in each unfortunate woman willy-nilly to the victor. There is nothing to tell whether Theopompus pointed out that the women to be humiliated were wives of the disgraced former democrats. However that may be and whether or not the anger of the fragment reveals a sympathy for the disfranchised democrats, it would be difficult to believe that the historian saw Hegesilochus' oligarchy as an improvement over anything the Rhodians might have had before. Further to Mausolus' interference with erstwhile Athenian allies, F123 from book 17 is probably from a full description of the Carian king's attempts to exploit Athenian misfortune to expand his small empire. It may be a lot to build on a single place-name, Assessus, but this city, near Miletus, is known to have been one of Mausolus' key strategical objectives.[13] The other fragment from book 17, F122, mentions Chios' well-known slave trade. Chians, Rhodians, and Mausolus falling together in a narrative of Aegean events in the mid-350s can only mean that the context is the Social War once more. Is it likely that Theopompus narrated the war twice? Perhaps it was a mistake to put the account of the war into book 7. On the other hand, it was an important event with relevance both to the earlier subject of Philip's phenomenal success and to the fortunes of the coastal satrapies, the current topic. Much of their freedom was attributable to the absence of a sustained Greek maritime power such as the Athenian alliance. It would surely be possible to tell the story from two points of view: first, from the vantage point of Athens and her inability to hold the Hellespont and keep Philip out of Amphipolis, and second, from the perspective of the rebels and the satraps like Mausolus, the principal agents of the war in the southeastern Aegean.

Jacoby's suggestion that books 18 and 19 covered Artaxerxes Ochus' final reduction of Egypt (346–343) seems reasonable. Only one fragment is positively assigned to these books, F124 from book 18. The subject is Nicostratus of Argos, who is described as an outrageous flatterer of the Persian king. Fortunately, Diodorus (16.44.2) identifies Nicostratus as the commander of three thousand Argive soldiers sent at the request of the Persian king to help him reconquer Egypt. Diodorus assigns Nicostratus' mission to the year 351/0, but it is generally held that he has misdated it.[14] This fragment on Nicostratus helps establish the context, but it also adds to an understanding of Theopompus' treatment of barbarians. It is not just the flattery that is censured; what seems to make things worse is that Nicostratus went to excess, seeking "honour from the barbarian." Nicostratus was a "leader of the Argive state" who had inherited "status, money, and much substance from his forebears." He was, in short, a ruler amongst Greeks, a people whom Chians regarded as natural masters anyway, fawning excessively on "the barbarians," and barbarians were more suited for a life of servitude.

If there was a message in books 12 to 19 it is not easy to divine. Jacoby's description of the digression as "Persian history" is perhaps misleading.[15] The vast majority of the fragments are identified with places in the Aegean and coastal communities from the Troad through Ionia, Caria, Rhodes, and Cyprus, southern Asia Minor, and Sidon down to Egypt. The focus therefore was apparently on areas of Greek-Persian interaction. Three fragments are purely Persian, but they lack any precise location. One, F109, is a lexical entry giving the "Persian word" for ambassadors: "angaroi." This is probably no more than a Persian mispronunciation of the Greek word for messenger: *angeloi*. The Persians probably thought they were being clever speaking Greek. The Greeks failed to recognize the mispronounced word as their own and took it for Persian. F113 is on the lavish and costly living of the Great King. Its location appears to be somewhere in the heart of the Persian empire. Finally, F263, which must belong to book 18 or 19, is slightly less vague. It records in mocking terms the staggering requirements of the Persian king, his court and army, in their assault on Egypt. Food was stockpiled (perhaps on Cyprus) to such heights that approaching people took the piles for hills or ridges.

A Panhellenist such as Isocrates would have seized on the themes of the lavish resources of the Persian empire and its lack of political cohesion to advocate a Hellenic invasion of the King's territory. If Theopompus was sympathetic to the Second Athenian Confederacy, if he took careful note of the Persian king's inability to control his western satrapies, and if he believed in the suitability of barbarians to slavery, then he did have the makings of a Panhellenist like Isocrates. His disgust at the behaviour of Nicostratus of Argos and of Nicocles of Cyprus and Straton of Sidon is not incompatible with a view that Greeks, being natural commanders, should keep themselves aloof from the flattery of servile barbarians and apart from their sumptuous living. Further, from the fragments it is difficult to avoid the impression that he believed that a troubled Persian empire was ripe fruit for Greeks to pluck and that if only they could avoid servility to the barbarians and unite in some form of voluntary federation rather like the Second Athenian Confederacy, then Persian wealth would be theirs and there would be nothing to fear from Macedonia or anywhere else.

It would not be surprising if Theopompus thought that way. However, how many other Greeks would have felt the same? It would be easy for them to acquiesce in the general notion that Greeks really should not be fighting Greeks and would do better to unite and go plundering the vulnerable Persian empire. The problem was how to do it. The apologist for Panhellenism must argue for a leader, a unifier, since Greeks had not shown the will or ability to unite voluntarily. The candidates for hegemon in recent years had been Athens, Sparta, Jason of Pherae, and Philip. Despite the hopes raised by the Second Confederacy, Athens had failed, and the historian's impression of Spartan leadership was no better, perhaps worse, despite the apparent promise of the rigid *agogē*. Jason of Pherae's moment of glory was short-lived and belongs to the 370s, about the time of the battle of Leuctra. Polybius complains specifically that this period in Greek history was ignored by Theopompus; and that leaves Philip. In chapters 4 and 5 I will examine evidence that suggests Theopompus found Philip and his foreign policy utterly execrable. If that is so, then Theopompus was no Panhellenist in any special, Isocratean sense of the term.

It is more likely that Theopompus would have been content if the digression left behind the general impression of Greek shortsighted-ness and ineptitude. In the period covered the King had been able to exercise little or no control over his western provinces. Even his forced reduction of tiny Cyprus had taken a decade, and it had only been accomplished by negotiation in which Evagoras succeeded in winning very generous terms for an erstwhile rebel. In the course of the revolt the Carian satrap Hecatomnos, charged with building a fleet and attacking Cyprus, went through the motions of obedience, Diodorus says (14.98.3–4), but he was reportedly sending Evagoras money to support his revolt (D.S. 15.2.3). Since this event was already known to Ephorus, Diodorus' source, it would be surprising if Theopompus missed it. F105 from book 13 also deserves attention in this context because it shows that Nicostratus and Agesilaus were not the only Greek military commanders who figured in this narrative. The subject is Chabrias, the Athenian general (Athen. 12.532A–B):

But he was unable to live in the city [Athens], partly on account of his licentiousness and the lavish expense of his manner of living, partly also on account of the Athenians; for they are harsh toward everybody; hence their distinguished men chose to pass their lives outside the city, Iphicrates in Thrace, Conon in Cyprus, Timotheus in Lesbos, Chares at Sigeum, and Chabrias himself in Egypt. (C.B. Gulick, tr., L.C.L.)

Chabrias had gone from Athens to Cyprus to help Evagoras in his revolt (narrated in book 12, see F103); thence he had gone to Egypt to aid the rebels there until the King protested to Athens that he was in violation of the Peace of Antalcidas and forced the Athenians to recall him. Diodorus dates the recall of Chabrias to 377 (16.29.4). He goes on to say that Iphicrates was sent out upon Chabrias' return, this time to support the Persian cause. Around 360 Agesilaus was to go adven-turing from Sparta in support of the Egyptian rebels, and again in the 340s Nicostratus of Argos went to fight on the side of the King. This looks like sunshine for a lot of rhetorical hay-making about Greeks unable to unite and exploit the tottery Persian empire but – scandal of scandals – fighting now on one side, now on the other, even fighting each other at times to keep the empire alive. FF105, 113, 114, 124, and 263 are perhaps the merest glimpses into what Theopompus the orator was able to do with this material; and when the digression finally came to an end, Ochus, the "sumptuary," had won back Egypt and was in better control of his western regions than any Persian king since the fifth century.

The next eight books, 20 to 27 inclusive, were primarily devoted to the narration of Philip's attack on Olynthus, the further isolation of Athens as a result of the settlement of the Sacred War, and the negotiation and conclusion of the first peace treaty between Athens and Philip: the Peace of Philocrates. A brief sketch of Olynthian history will help put these fragments in context. Olynthus is on the Chalcidic peninsula near Macedonia. Chalcidice's three "fingers" jut prominently into the northern Aegean. After the collapse of the Athenian empire in 404, Olynthus united the peninsula into the Chalcidic League, which was strong enough to threaten Macedon in 382. In that year Sparta, as self-appointed "policeman" of the King's Peace, and Macedon united to dismantle the League in a campaign that ended in 379. After this time Sparta was too preoccupied with Thebes and Megalopolis to interfere, and the League grew again like a phoenix. In 360, the year of Philip's accession, it was a considerable power, and Philip had the good sense to win its alliance. The League rivalled Athens for control of places like Potidaea and Amphipolis, and Philip quickly saw that Olynthus and Athens could be played off against each other. However, by 350 Philip's relations with the League were strained. Olynthus was becoming a haven for Philip's exiled political enemies, and so, Theopompus says, Philip recited to the Olynthians the "story of war and hybris" (F127 from book 20). The story's content was recorded by the second-century fabulist Babrius. The version he gives runs like this (#70):[16]

The gods married and, when they had all been paired up, War was the last to be allotted a mate. So he married Hybris [Arrogance] and has held fast to her alone. Indeed, they say that he fell exceedingly in love with her; he follows close upon her everywhere she goes. Hybris alone may not come upon a nation anywhere, or a city of men, smiling on the people, since War will be right on her heels.

The likely date for the telling of this story would be 350 or 349, the year the Macedonian invasion began. Olynthus and Athens became allies, but Athenian aid came too little and too late. In 348 Olynthus was razed by the victorious Macedonians. From that date there could be little doubt about the true nature of Philip's power, his potential ruthlessness, and Athenian effectiveness. The fragments suggest a rather conventional approach to the narrative on the whole, with the exception of two interesting digressions to which I will return below. The story of Philip's invasion of Olynthian territory was apparently given in considerable detail, since it filled or occupied parts of books 20 (FF125–7) and 22 to 24 (FF137–46) and was perhaps brought to a conclusion in book 25 (F152). FF147–51 mention places in Euboea, and they doubtless reflect an account of the revolt of the island from Athens (winter 349/8). It is natural to suspect that the revolt was stirred up by Philip in an attempt to distract Athens from sending help to the besieged Olynthians.[17] How Theopompus told the story, however, is not known.

Of the two most eye-catching parts of books 20 to 27, one is a geographical treatise on regions to the north of Macedonia, Paeonia, and Illyria, and the second is a diatribe against Athens placed somewhere in book 25 not far from the account of the conclusion of the Peace of Philocrates. Two fragments of this diatribe (FF154, 155) reveal that Theopompus impugned an inscribed version of the treaty with Darius, the King of Persia (probably a renewal of the so-called "Peace of Callias" of the fifth century), on the grounds that it was inscribed in forth-century letter-forms. The lettering he described as Ionian or "Samian" and he gave the date and the circumstances of its introduction to Athens as a replacement for the older Attic letter-forms. It was a certain Archinus, the story goes, who got the Athenians to change "in the archonship of Euclides" (403/2).

A third fragment from this digression (F153) attacks exaggerated Athenian claims about the battle of Marathon and a certain "oath of Plataea."[18] Marathon (490) and Plataea (479) were key land battles in what is generally called the Persian War, the subject of Herodotus' history, and the Athenians had used their contributions to the Greek effort at that time to justify their later acquisition of an empire. In book 1 (73.2–5) Thucydides put a speech into the mouths of unnamed Athenian ambassadors to Sparta, men who happened to be in Sparta in 432 just at the time when the Spartans and certain of their allies, such as Corinth, were debating whether Athens was in breach of the treaty that existed between the two states. The result was the Peloponnesian War (431–404). The Athenians acknowledge that their empire had become extremely unpopular, but they insist, nevertheless, that it was their due reward for their contributions to the Hellenic victories at Marathon and Salamis (the sea-battle of 480). In the fourth century, when Athenian naval supremacy was not at all the assured thing it had been through most of the fifth, perhaps their shift in rhetorical emphasis away from the naval victory and to the final, decisive land battles of Marathon and Plataea is understandable.

Plutarch provides a little more information about the way the Athenians justified their empire and the style of leadership to which they felt entitled. In his *Pericles* (12) he makes the Athenian statesman deny the need to give the allies an accounting of the monies collected from them as tribute because the Athenians were (or had been) "prosecuting the war on their behalf and keeping off the barbarian." It would be interesting to know where Plutarch got this information, but he was widely read in sources from the fifth and fourth centuries, and it is by no means unreasonable to imagine that it went back at least to the fourth and was known to Theopompus. Plutarch's context is the famous Periclean building program of the 440s–430s, which used allied monies. Theopompus also seems to have had some interest in the way the allied tribute money was used. Perhaps the high-handed way the Athenians used it helped provoke his attack on their policies in the fifth century.

Theopompus was a Chian, and Chians and other islanders and Ionians had paid tribute to Persia in the sixth century and early fifth, to Athens through much of the fifth, to Sparta into the fourth, and to Athens again until the Social War. In this light his sensitivity to the behaviour of tribute collectors would be understandable. Perhaps this explains the obvious concern for the Hellenic victims that permeates F153. Notice how many times Hellene or Hellenic occur in the "fragment," which is partly an elliptical paraphrase and partly (the last sentence) a quote:

The Hellenic oath which the Athenians say the Hellenes swore against the barbarians before the battle of Plataea is falsified, and the treaty of the Athenians with King Darius against the Hellenes. Moreover, the battle of Marathon did not happen as everyone hymns it up and " ... all the other things that the city of the Athenians crows about and uses to dupe the Hellenes."

As an islander, Theopompus quite possibly thought of the Hellenes as Ionians and islanders first and mainlanders second. Insofar as the treaty with Darius secured the temporary continuation of the Athenian empire, it is easy to see how the historian could have described it as a virtual act of war "against the Hellenes."[19]

The oath of Plataea itself is known from a stele found at Acharnae in Attica and datable to about the last third of the fourth century.[20] A similar text is given in Diodorus (11.29.2), and it was also quoted by the fourth-century Athenian orator Lycurgus in a speech delivered in 330 (*Against Leocrates* 81). In some of the versions, the text of the oath looks innocent enough, and one wonders what the historian found objectionable. In Diodorus it is simply a promise made by the soldiers that they will do their duty in battle and bury fallen comrades afterwards, that the present allies will not destroy each others' cities in any future war, and that they will leave sanctuaries destroyed by the barbarian unrepaired as a memorial to his sacrilege. The Acharnae stele mentions an intention to lay a tithe on Thebes, no doubt as a war indemnity for siding with Persia. The text given in Lycurgus goes further, mentioning an intent to tithe all cities that had sided with the King. This is potentially poisonous, for the Ionians and islanders had been perforce members of the Persian empire until after Plataea. Perhaps some orators were citing this last version of the oath, assuming that "tithing" meant collecting tribute and then using the text to "prove" that the collection of tribute was a sacred right of the Athenians as heirs to the Hellenic hegemony that began somehow in the days before Plataea. In the absence of supporting evidence, however, this can only remain an attractive possibility. It would certainly help explain Theopompus' interest in the oath.

The authenticity of the Peace of Callias has attracted endless debate. Very little, indeed, is known about it with any certainty. In a recent study Badian has argued that the Peace was first negotiated with Xerxes by Callias and ratified c. 463 only to be broken on the instigation of Pericles, who sent an expedition against Cyprus and Egypt c. 450. At the conclusion of this campaign Callias renegotiated the shattered Peace with Artaxerxes, and it was again in place by 448. Finally, after Darius II came to the throne in the 420s, it was necessary for the Athenians to reconfirm the treaty with the new King. This was done through the agency of an otherwise little known Epilycus.[21] The terms of the Peace were described somewhat vaguely by fourth-century rhetoricians. Nothing of the inscribed text survives. From the orators it seems that the Athenians extracted a commitment from the Persians not to attack the empire and, particularly, not to bring a fleet into Aegean waters. For their part, the Athenians undertook not to plunder the King's territory. Badian argues that there was also a clause by which the allies were to have a certain autonomy, but even if this is true, nothing is known of its wording or how it was to be enforced. Whether or not there was an autonomy clause, the Athenians can be trusted to have interpreted it and the whole treaty to suit their own ends: the King had acknowledged the Athenian empire and conceded them the right to administer it as they saw fit. The Spartans had participated in the oath of Plataea as history well knew.

History also told of their voluntary withdrawal from the grand Hellenic alliance against Persia only a few years after Plataea, leaving the Athenians alone to the hegemony. Therefore, the Peace of Callias, or, more particularly, of Epilycus, extracted explicitly from Persia what the oath of Plataea and subsequent events got implicitly from Sparta: recognition of Athens' right to hegemony.

Whatever the precise details, Connor's conclusion that the digression is an attack on fifth-century Athenian foreign policy looks about right. If my suggestions are correct, "particularly with regard to the fifth-century empire" should be added. It will be useful to return now to the context of the digression, which was probably introduced by the narration of the last few years of the Sacred War. The digression probably also looked forward to the ensuing events, preparing the reader for the failure of Athens' effort to form an alliance of Hellenes to keep Philip out of southern Greece.

F157 mentions a mountain called Hedyleum. This, according to Demosthenes (*On the Embassy* 148), was a place from which the Phocians were plundering Theban territory in 347. Tilphossaeum was another, and its mention in F301 suggests that the fragment also belongs with this book. The suffering of the Thebans was severe (D.S. 16.56, 58.1, and Demosthenes, *On the Embassy*, 148); they were driven to seek the support of an ally. They turned to Philip, and so a small number of Macedonian soldiers entered the Sacred War on Thebes' side. Theopompus is not likely to have ignored this momentous arrival of Macedonian forces in southern Greece. The Macedonian presence stiffened Theban resistance, and it was perhaps in response that the Phocians dug deeper into the oracle's treasures to finance their own countermeasures. Sometime earlier, perhaps when Thebes first made overtures to Philip, the Athenians had sent out ambassadors on the motion of Eubulus with the aim of fashioning an anti-Macedonian alliance with various unspecified Aegean states. The ambassadors returned empty-handed. Despite some initial successes in Thrace, probably in an attempt to draw Philip away from southern Greece, the Athenian effort against Macedon now seemed doomed. A new glimmer of hope came toward the end of 347 when the now hard-pressed Phocians offered to turn over key strategic towns near the Thermopylae pass to be manned by Athens and Sparta. Athens and Sparta both committed forces to this objective. Alarm over the Macedonian presence in southern Greece was natural. Ellis and Markle have argued that yet another host of emissaries now fanned out from Athens to the Hellenic cities to call for a congress to decide whether there should be war or peace.[22] These embassies, too, if historical, proved fruitless, as did the attempt to occupy Thermopylae.

Phalaecus, the Phocian general, refused to turn over the fortresses to
the allies. Apparently, he was reaching terms with Philip whereby he
and his fellow mercenaries would ultimately be given safe passage out
of the region in exchange for their immediate cooperation with
Macedonia (D.S. 16.57-64).

In fact the position was lost, but the Athenians still saw one flicker
of hope. Some sixty kilometres northeast of Thermopylae, near the
coast of the Gulf of Pagasae was a town called Halus. It was not on the
best of terms with Pharsalus, Philip's ally, and with Athenian support
from the sea it could well hope to hold out in a siege. Unless the place
were bottled up to landward by siege, it could be a useful base from
which to harass the left flank of any Macedonian march into southern
Greece. Therefore, Philip had to commit forces and his two best
generals to trouble-spots created or supported by Athens: Antipater
to Thrace, where he "waited" (F160 from book 26), and Parmenio to
besiege Halus. It is quite probably to this attack on Halus that the
famous "editorial" fragment (F162 from book 26) belongs as Jacoby
suggests. There Theopompus excoriates the Thessalians for permitting themselves to be "conquered more with parties than by bribes."

It is difficult to see just how Theopompus organized his narrative
of all these events and just where he was at the end of book 25. F159
(from book 26) is a small item of lexicography attributing the
expression "wooden, sacred objects" to the twenty-sixth book of
Theopompus. Now F344 on the visit of Magnes (or the Magnesian) to
Delphi (discussed in the next chapter) mentions sacred objects quite
probably of wood that were carefully tended by the poor but
diligently pious Clearchus of Methydrium, and Jacoby suggests that
perhaps F344 is from book 26 and provides the context for the lexical
entry of F159. This is very ingenious.

If correct, it tends to support what seems likely anyway: that the
context is Delphi, although F159 might have been assumed to be
about the venerable objects in the shrine destroyed or despoiled by
the mercenaries. However, the oreichalcum (Oreian bronze) of F158
described by the Scholiast as "a form of bronze named after its
discoverer Oreius" according to some authorities while others "say it
got its name from [Oreius the] sculptor, so ... Theopompus, book 25"
does suggest statuary, probably votive offerings at Delphi. A likely
reason for their appearance in the narrative would be the exposure
and execution of Philon narrated by Diodorus after the fall of
Olynthus (16.55) and after the successful Phocian occupation of
outposts in Boeotia (16.56.1-2) but before the arrival of Macedonian
support for Thebes (16.58). Apparently, some Phocians were shocked
at the rapacity of their own mercenaries. They deposed the general

Phalaecus (but only temporarily as things turned out) and called his senior administrator, Philon, to give an accounting of his handling of the funds. The extent of the pillaging is alleged to have reached appalling dimensions, and because Philon could offer no acceptable explanation, he was tortured and executed. Theopompus could scarcely have ignored this story. If my interpretation of FF158 and 159 is correct, the story must have occupied the end of book 25 and the early part of 26.

However that may be, a substantial part of book 26 must have been devoted to the negotiation of the Peace of Philocrates between Athens and Philip. F165 gives the names of the ambassadors Philip sent to Athens in this connection, and F164 from Didymus' commentary on Demosthenes quotes from a speech Theopompus put into Philocrates' mouth in defence of the proposed treaty. These two fragments are from book 26. F166, however, also from Didymus, is located by him in book 27. It is a quotation from a speech opposing the Peace that is attributed to Aristophon.[23] It is reasonable, therefore, to conclude that the debate over whether to agree to the treaty finished book 26 and extended into 27.

The two quotations provided by Didymus deserve attention, for they give a precious glimpse at Theopompus' summing up of Athens' desperate situation. The speeches owe nothing stylistically to the compressed abruptness of Thucydides. If their subject is somewhat gloomy, their style is easy and graceful. Philocrates (F164):

Consider, moreover, how there is no chance at all for us to seek victory and that our city is in no fortunate state; rather, many and great are the dangers surrounding us. We know that the Boeotians and Megarians are ill-disposed toward us, of the Peloponnesians, some lean toward Thebes and others toward Sparta, as for the Chians and Rhodians and their allies, they are hostile to our city; indeed, they talk friendship with Philip.

And Aristophon's reply (F166):

Consider how we would be behaving of all things most cowardly if we should agree to this peace and abandon Amphipolis – we who occupy the greatest of all the Hellenic cities! We have a great number of allies, we own three hundred war galleys, and take income of nearly four hundred talents. This being so, who would not censure us if we, cowering before the Macedonian power, should agree to anything unjust?

These speeches show the effect of the diatribe against Athenian foreign policy in book 25. It must have prepared the reader for the inevitable failure of the embassies to the various Hellenic states. "The Hellenes" wanted no more Athenian rhetoric, no more Athenian hegemony. The claims of Philocrates were authenticated by the preceding narrative, that of Aristophon shown to be empty bluster, dreaming, as it does, of long lost Amphipolis (lost nearly eighty years before) and pretending to see a host of allies at Athens' back, allies who were in reality no more than ghosts from a vain past.

For the next eleven or twelve books information is just too scant for even the most speculative of reconstructions. There are no more fragments from book 27, none at all from books 28 and 29. If the main protagonists in the debate over signing the Peace were made to be Philocrates and Aristophon, one can only wonder about the role assigned to Demosthenes. Most of the fragments that mention him seem to be tied to the preliminaries and aftermath of Chaeronea. With such scant information it would be foolish to draw firm conclusions.

The digression "On the Demagogues" in book 10 demonstrated Athens' need for Demosthenes' policies (see pp. 171–3, below), and book 11 probably had a section dwelling on Athens' depressed state in the aftermath of the Social War (F102). Demosthenes was starting to become politically active at about this time, and by all accounts he was very active during the peace negotiations of 346 and afterwards. Regrettably, there is no indication of what notice, if any, Theopompus took of him.

Books 28 to 33 are altogether badly represented in the fragments, but if there is any theme discernible at all, it is a general survey of Greece and Philip's new relations with its various parts in the months and years immediately following 346. Book 30 returns to Delphi and the Amphictiony. Indeed, F168 identifying Pylae as the earliest seat of the Amphictiony and F169 on the "hieromnemones," the name of the delegates to the Amphictionic synod, suggest that Theopompus postponed a full history of the Amphictiony until the moment when Philip reorganized it. This arrangement would probably have emphasized how far the new measures were in breach of the Amphictiony's venerable traditions.

From book 31 there are no fragments, but the eight from books 32 and 33 suggest an extensive description and history of the Peloponnese, especially the Spartan conquest of Messenia (c. 8th-c. 7th centuries B.C.) and the reduction of the Messenians to helotage. This digression was likely prompted by the cementing of Philip's alliance with Messenia, freed from Spartan domination in 370/69 when Epaminondas invaded the Peloponnese in support of the Messenians and the Arcadians who were founding Megalopolis.[24] From that time the Messenians had remained independent of Sparta thanks to the impregnability of Megalopolis, Spartan weakness, and a Messenian alliance with Thebes. In 346, however, Thebes was totally eclipsed by Macedon as "the power" in central Greece. Accordingly, the Messenians transferred their allegiance to Philip.

Therefore, central Greece is the subject in books 30 and perhaps 31, the Peloponnese in books 32 and 33, and the sketchy clues from the next five books reveal a change of scene to northern Asia Minor and Illyria. Consequently, if Athens and her relations to Philip in the period after 346 were treated, the most likely place would appear to be books 27 to 29, plenty of space for a thorough treatment of Athenian politics in this crucial age. If only there were some clues. It might be objected that I am being too cautious. Of course, Theopompus would not have ignored so important a topic nor so significant a contributor as Demosthenes. However, while the ancients often agreed remarkably well on what happened, there is not always the same high level of consensus on who made it happen. For example, when Xenophon narrated the decade of Theban supremacy (c. 372–362), he managed to mention Epaminondas, the architect of Theban power, and, by all other accounts, the man of the decade, only a few times and only in connection with his last invasion of the Peloponnese in 362.[25]

Books 34 to 38 are very badly represented. Only three short fragments are assigned with any certainty, and one (F180) is an entry from Stephanus of Byzantium that is worthless because it is the name of a city whose general location has fallen from the text. Of the other two F179 from book 35 is about King Thys of Paphlagonia on the Black Sea coast of Asia Minor, who "provided his table with a hundred of everything, starting from cattle, when he dined," a habit he continued right up to his captivity and death at the hands of the Persian King. He was captured by Pharnabazus, the local Persian satrap until his transfer to the Egyptian front in the 380s (D.S. 15.41 puts it in 374/3). Therefore, the fragment may suggest a digression on Euxine geography and history going back to the early 370s and probably earlier.

Theopompus (F181 = Athen. 3.85A–B):

in his account of Clearchus, tyrant of Heraclea in Pontus, contained in the 38th book of his *Histories*, tells how he forcibly put to death many persons, giving most of them aconite to drink "when then," he says, "all had come to know this loving-cup of his, they never went out of doors without eating rue"; for those who eat this beforehand are not in the least injured by drinking aconite, which, he says, received its name from a place called Aconae, near Heraclea. (B. Gulick, tr., L.C.L.)

A minimum of two complete books separate F179 (set in Paphlagonia) from F181 (set in Heraclea Pontica, in Bithynia). Now Bithynia is a region immediately adjacent to Paphlagonia, and it strains credibility to think Theopompus required two full books to move about five hundred kilometres along the south Pontic coast. There are too many choices: a book number in one of the fragments could be wrong; Theopompus could be digressing within his digression; the two fragments could even be isolated digressions for an otherwise lost narrative that had nothing at all to do with the Pontic Sea.

The fragments are inconclusive, but there are some structural features of the *Philippica* that provide a further clue that a full digression on the history and geography of the Euxine was needed to complete the *Philippica*. The books in question are a suitable, perhaps the only possible place for such a digression to find a home as the next section of this chapter shows.

After Philip reorganized the Delphic Amphictiony in 346 (FF167–70, book 30), he embarked on a further Illyrian campaign and entered and reorganized Epirus (345–342). Mention of a place in Illyria (F182, book 38) and another in Epirus (F183 with Strabo 7.7.9, 9.5.2, book 39) probably means that that now became Theopompus' subject. However, Philip apparently remained at centre stage for perhaps a book and a half before the scene and subject moved into the western parts of the Mediterranean for a five-book digression on Syracuse, Sicily, Italy, and a quick survey of more remote western regions as far as Gibraltar, Spain, and southern France (books 38 to 43 inclusive).

Despite the survival of more than twenty fragments, no clear, cohesive theme or point of view is discernible. The Syracusan fragments are either scathing attacks on the tyrants Dionysius the Elder and the Younger, their families, and their associates, like Dion, the famous friend of Plato, or single place-names from Stephanus. This part of the digression attracted the anecdote hunters mentioned at the start of this chapter. Someone compiling a catalogue of famous boozers was able to do so with no difficulty from the scrolls of Theopompus. Most of the entries came from this very digression: names of Syracusan tyrants and their immediate relatives; but providing anecdotes can scarcely have been Theopompus' prime objective.

Diodorus does give a general description of the digression (16.71.3), but it only deepens the confusion:

Theopompus of Chios in his *Philippica* composed three books embracing Sicilian history. He began from the tyranny of Dionysius the elder, covered 50

years and ended with the expulsion of Dionysius the younger (344/3). There
are three books, from the forty-first to the forty-third.

Some of this is puzzling. The digression discerned in the fragments
ends with the 43rd book, to be sure, but by this time the subject is no
longer Sicilian history but Italy and the far west. While 344/3, the
expulsion of Dionysius the Younger, is a reasonable halting place for
the Syracusan part of the digression, fifty years before this, 394/3, is
no natural starting place. Dionysius the Elder came to power about
406, and it would seem odd for the narrative to begin in the middle of
his reign. Finally, Athenaeus, who seems generally reliable, assigns all
his Syracusan quotations to books 39 and 40. Diodorus may not have
been too familiar with this part of Theopompus. He was a Sicilian
himself and likely to be interested in sources for Sicilian history, but
recent scholarship has shown that he probably did not use Theopompus as a source for his own Sicilian sections.[26] Therefore, there is no
need to suppose that his description of the digression stems from a
direct and immediate examination of it.

He might have recalled that the Sicilian section proper filled three
books and that the digression ended with book 43. In this case, the
only useful information from Diodorus would be that the western
digression devoted the equivalent of three books to Sicilian history
and that the two remaining books then covered the remainder of the
western Mediterranean. This may be substantially true. It appears
that Philip's arrangements in Epirus spilled over from book 38 into
the beginning of 39 (F183 with Strabo 7.7.9, 9.5.2). Otherwise, the
five fragments from F185 to F190 are all Sicilian or Syracusan, and
F191 (with Strabo 6.3.5) specifies a location in southern Italy that is
nearby and not likely to be irrelevant. Much the same is true of book
40. Two fragments from this book deserve special notice in this
regard. F195 is an apparent anomaly. From Stephanus, it simply
names Eleutheris, a city of Boeotia founded by the Athenian heroes
Cothus and Aïclus. Jacoby suspects the book number in Stephanus'
text, but only because a discussion of a colony on or near the
Athenian-Boeotian border looks out of place in what is otherwise
taken to be a digression on fourth-century Sicilian history. F194
reveals how such anomalies can arise and how misleading a one-time
entry from Stephanus can be. The first line, usually all that Stephanus
preserves, merely mentions a city of Achaea. It gives the form of the
proper adjective and cites Theopompus, 40. The debate would centre
on whether to emend the number or whether there were some cause
for the historian to divert his attention to Achaea were it not for the
further citation from Theopompus' actual text that Stephanus gives,

contrary to his usual custom: "The leaders of the city were, of the Syracusans Athenis and Heraclides, and, of the mercenaries, Archelaus the Dymaean." Stephanus cites the line to verify the classical form of the proper adjective Δυμαῖος; however, the citation shows that the conclusions that might have been drawn with only the first line as a guide would have been wrong. The subject was clearly Syracuse, not Achaea. The remaining five fragments are Sicilian. F192 on the visit of Pharax, the corrupt Spartan, and F193, on the lavish gifts sent to Delphi by the fifth-century Sicilian tyrants Gelon and Hieron, make the digression look like a full, circumstantial account with flashbacks. Delphi never seems far from Theopompus' mind. Curiously, there are no fragments at all from book 41, but F198 (from book 42), another Sicilian place-name, suggests that Sicily was still the topic, unless the one-line entry is as misleading as F194 might have been. However, following the clue from Diodorus, it seems reasonable enough that the Sicilian part of the digression was accurately described as occupying the equivalent of three books; most of 39, all of 40 and 41, and the opening of 42, leaving most of 42 and 43 for Italy and the far west.

One of the longest fragments that exists (F204) comes from book 43. It is a lengthy description of the Etruscans and their style of living (see p. 104, below). In a roundabout way two other fragments can be added to this context. Clement of Alexandria found in the forty-third book of the *Philippica* a record that dated the Trojan War to five hundred years before Homer's time (F205). What possible connection could there be between Homer and the subject of this part of the *Philippica*? There may be a hint in the remark of a Scholiast (F354) according to which Theopompus made Odysseus, the hero of Homer's *Odyssey*, die in great honour amongst the Etruscans. FF206 and 207, both from Harpocration, return to southern Epirus whence the digression was launched. Jacoby's ordering of the fragments looks reasonable here. It would be natural to return to Epirus at the end of book 43. That was the apparent jumping-off point for the digression.

With F208 from book 44 Philip and his reorganization of Thessaly into tetrarchies (344) reappear as the subjects. The narrative now moves relentlessly forward to Chaeronea. Suddenly there are no more digressions of any size. In fact, not one can be identified with any certainty. Table 1 shows a possible digression on Arcadia in book 56; but this is only an inference from four place names. It is just as likely that they are sites along or near Philip's route into and out of the Peloponnese after Chaeronea. It seems reasonable to suppose that the establishment of the League of Corinth (338/7) whereby Philip cemented his hold on southern Greece, the marriage to Cleopatra,

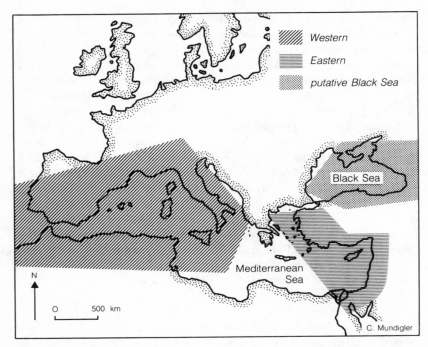

2   The long digressions and their geographical relationship to Macedonian expansion under Philip

and the assassination of Philip by Pausanias were all to be found in books 57 and 58, but only two of the briefest fragments survive from 57 and nothing from 58. The main issues of concern in these last fifteen books, the treatment of Philip and Demosthenes, are treated in the subsequent chapters, and I turn now to a consideration of the *Philippica*'s structure.

THE STRUCTURE OF THE *PHILIPPICA*

It could be argued with an element of truth that a history faithful to its age should exhibit no more structure than the randomness of the age's events. To a certain extent the *Philippica* follows the outline of Philip's career. The linear narrative of Philip's development from a struggling young ruler to an expansionist monarch to an altogether intimidating military strongman cut down by an assassin in his prime and at the height of his power holds the enormous work together. However, Philip's career did not entirely shape the work; it seems to have been used rather like a coat rack from which to hang some very extensive excursions into various parts of the Hellenic world never conquered by, indeed unknown to Philip except by hearsay. These digressions all together fill approximately twenty-nine books or one-half of the entire work, and the way they interrupt the linear narrative gives the work its peculiar structure.

The early books seem to exhibit a style known as ring-composition, but the later fragments are too scant to trace its continuation with confidence. It is by no means unlikely that other books were structured the same way as book 12. For example, the far western digression was introduced after some treatment of Philip's intervention in Epirus in 345, and Theopompus returned to Epirus at its end. Further, the geographical and myth-historical excursus on southern Asia Minor was postponed until after the end of Evagoras' revolt, indeed, until after his assassination some six or seven years after Acoris' death. It was placed where it would emphasize a natural break in the narrative, despite the fact that the alliances made by Acoris were most likely fashioned at the beginning of his reign, chronologically near the beginning of the narrative. However, Theopompus may not have postponed all digressions till natural breaks came along. Book 12 also has a digression on early history at the beginning of the story of Evagoras' revolt, if digression is the correct word. Photius' summary of the book's contents clarifies the point:

The twelfth book includes: concerning Acoris, king of the Egyptians, how he concluded a treaty with Cyrene and acted on behalf of Evagoras of Cyprus against the Persians, how, unexpectedly, Evagoras had come into the kingdom of Cyprus subduing Abdymon, the ruler of the island; how the Greeks with Agamemnon had taken Cyprus having expelled Cinyras and his followers, the remainder of whom were Amathusians.

There is a relevance to the "digression" on Agamemnon's capture of Cyprus. It makes the island part of the Hellenic world from ancient times and explains, if it does not justify, Evagoras the Greek's claim to legitimate rulership over that of Abdymon, whose name sounds distinctly barbarian.

On the other hand, the digression at the end of the story goes further afield, is more substantial, and, partly because it is more distant, is less relevant to Cyprus and Evagoras. The connection to the narrative is tenuous, rather mechanical. Acoris is remembered from the first part of the story, and his alliance with Pisidia is described. The object is no longer to elucidate the story of Evagoras' revolt but to find a bridge to the mainland, a hook from which to hang a digression.

The larger digressions have features peculiar to themselves alone. The largest and best known, the excursion on the Persian littoral (books 12 to 19), is a good example. It follows the narrative that completes the description of how Philip secured the facing coastline of Macedonia. The "bridge" across the Aegean is the collapsed Second Athenian Confederacy. The digression covered about fifty years from the late 390s to 344/3 when Ochus recovered his western kingdom. The next best-known digression had to wait until Philip had secured the coastline on the other side of the Balkan peninsula after the bloody Dalmatian and Illyrian campaign of (probably) 345 and the reorganization of Epirus. According to Diodorus, it too covered fifty years ending in 344/3. The "bridge" in this case might have been the departure of Timoleon from Corinth to Syracuse in 344 (F334). Timoleon went to Syracuse as something of an adventurer and did much to aid the Greeks in their wars with the Carthaginians. He was instrumental in the expulsion of the younger Dionysius, the event that, Diodorus implies, ended the digression (Plut. *Tim.* 13).

Among the problems with Diodorus' description of the western digression was the fact that c. 394 is not a natural place from which to begin a narrative of Dionysius the Elder's reign. However, Theopompus' *Hellenica* had ended with Cnidus in 394, which certainly makes the late 390s a reasonable place for him to begin his account of the Persian littoral. With the apparent exception of Evagoras' seizure of the Cypriot throne, the history of this region before that time must have been covered in the *Hellenica*. Much the same is probably true of Sicilian history. Xenophon records that Syracusans had fought actively on the Peloponnesian side since about 413.[27] His *Hellenica* was much sparser than that of Theopompus. He had taken only a little over three books to get from 411 to 394. Theopompus took twelve books to cover the same ground. Generous helpings of Sicilian history would be one natural filler.

In short, the two digressions began c. 394 because they were both continuations of the *Hellenica*. They had their own separate reasons for ending in 344/3: Ochus reconquered Egypt; Dionysus the Younger was expelled. But is it possible that 344/3 could have further significance? In Sicily there was much more to tell with the arrival of Timoleon on the scene, an event whose significance Theopompus can scarcely have ignored, and to which I will return at the end of this section.

The large digressions seem to bear a relationship to Philip's expansion. The eastern digression begins when Philip has control of the facing littoral; the same is true of the west. In both cases the topic includes territory occupied or controlled by non-Greek peoples, but the narrative seems to have spent very little time exploring non-Greek territory, and there is no evidence at all that Theopompus ever credited barbarians with a history. The "Persian digression" is really about the Greek-occupied Persian coastline. Similarly, three-fifths of the "western digression" focused exclusively on Greek Sicily, and some of the rest of it probably centred on Greek settlements in the south of Italy and France. His interest was primarily in the Greek world, and there is one part of it as yet untreated, the Propontis and Black Sea. Following the pattern of the eastern and western digressions, the opportunity for an excursus on those regions would be provided by Philip's gaining control of the adjacent littoral through the invasion and conquest of eastern Thrace and southern Scythia. Now it is not known how Theopompus described Philip's annexation of Thrace as far as the Hellespont and the Propontis. As early as 352/1 he seems to have been operating against Cersobleptes (FF83, 84, 101?) in alliance with Byzantium and Perinthus, which puts him in direct contact with the shores of the Propontis. His last military presence in the area (in person) was the abortive attempt on Perinthus and then Byzantium (FF217–22, books 47–8) in the year 340/39. This failed assault was followed by the successful invasion of Scythia (339), perhaps narrated in book 50 (F227?). However, there is no place for a digression of any substance in the surrounding books. On the other hand, Philip had been in the region some seven years previously as well, about the time of the negotiation of the Peace of Philocrates, which was probably narrated in book 26 (FF160–1). Therefore, soon after book 26 would be another reasonable place to expect a Black Sea digression, if Theopompus was behaving true to form; and it is here (books 28 to 32) that the possible presence of a substantial digression on the peoples and geography of the Black Sea seems likely. However, nothing is known about its nature and scope. There had certainly been some substantial treatment of the Black Sea region in the *Hellenica*, and if there was a digression in the *Philippica*, it was in all likelihood another "up-date" of the *Hellenica*. Accordingly, it would have opened with events of the 390s, but its termination date (or dates, if it went region by region or city by city) is unknown.

The following general conclusions about the probable structure of the *Philippica* are indicated by the discussion so far: the large digressions were most likely continuations of the *Hellenica*, which ended with Cnidus in 394; the two known digressions ended with the year 344/3; they were attached to Philip's career by the rather mechanical expedient of first narrating Philip's successful establishment of a sustainable presence on the coastline facing the area to be explored; they were geographical and historical in content, generally treating Greek communities, but occasionally peering into the barbarian hinterland; the historical segments focused primarily, if not exclusively, on Greeks; some sort of mechanical "bridge" (such as the Second Athenian Confederacy, Timoleon's crossing from Corinth to Sicily) was used to obtain an "entry" into the digression. However, it is impossible to guess what the "bridge" could have been to get into the putative Black Sea digression.

One further point emerges from a consideration of the *Philippica*'s structure. If the work is ostensibly about Philip and his career, then the first forty-three books down to 344/3 contain more digressive material than main narrative; by stark contrast, the last fifteen books follow the line of Philip's career with but one or possibly two short digressions. After that date, there seems to have been no more Hellenic history for Theopompus. The implication seems to be that from that date Hellenic affairs no longer existed as a discrete concept; they had become Philip's affairs. Theopompus loved word-play, and in 360, when Philip came to power, there still were Hellenic affairs, "Hellenica," but by the end of it, Philip had made them his affairs, "Philippica." The title of the book is a conscious word-play.

GEOGRAPHY IN THE *PHILIPPICA*

The long digressions demonstrate that it was a matter of some importance to Theopompus to survey the world with which the Greeks had become familiar, namely, the coastline of the entire Mediterranean, particularly the more northerly parts, and, perhaps, the Black Sea. Generally, therefore, his geographical work took the form of what the Greeks called a *Periodos Gēs*, a circuit tour of the world.

Another aspect of geography entails the mapping of land forms. The substantial remains from the twenty-first book show that the historian embarked on just such an enterprise. He apparently tried to sketch a verbal map of the outflow of the Danube and the position of the northern tip of the Adriatic Sea with respect to the western extremity of the Euxine.

The ordering of this fascinating book is hard to make out at first. The numerous fragments clearly show that Theopompus covered the length of the Ionian and Adriatic Seas from Sicily to the Venetians, including some ethnography of the Italian peninsula (F132). Obviously, he included some ground that was to be revisited in the large five-book western digression that appeared some eighteen books later. Unfortunately, the relationship of this digression to the later one is not clear. Moreover, there is very little in the fragments even to show their correct order within the book. However, from the context, a reasonable guess at the book's internal arrangement can be made. The immediately preceding book (20) introduced the momentous events of 350/49, Philip's declaration of war on the united league of the Chalcidic peninsula with its capital at Olynthus. Theopompus gave the Olynthian war a good deal of attention, as it deserved. He did not finish his narrative of it until book 25. The destruction of Olynthus enabled Philip to consolidate his hold on Macedonia by removing a powerful rival and making its land and riches available as rewards for his loyal followers. The geographic location of this major operation would be worthy of attention, therefore, and it would scarcely be surprising to see a digression on the Chalcidic peninsula and its environs early in the narrative of the war.

However, no one today would be inclined to count the Adriatic, the mouth of the Danube, and the west coast of the Black Sea among the environs of the Chalcidic peninsula, but that is the peculiar point of this book, for it appears that Theopompus did. The key passage is F129 from the geographer Strabo (7.5.9). Strabo scoffs at a number of geographical misconceptions in Theopompus, most notably the claim that the "seas [Adriatic and Euxine] are connected by a channel." That they were Theopompus had apparently inferred from alleged discoveries of Thasian and Chian pottery "near the Naro river." He also claimed that one mouth of the Ister (or Danube) river empties into the Adriatic, and that "both seas" (presumably again the Adriatic and Euxine) were visible simultaneously from the same mountain.

Strabo seems to be summarizing a substantial argument about the geography of the region found in Theopompus. The Chian and Thasian pottery near the Naro, a river located in the southern quarter of the Dalmatian coast (unless Theopompus wrote Narex), was apparently used as proof of a heavy sea-trade between the Adriatic and the Aegean. Theopompus must have denied the plausibility of a southern route from Chios and Thasos around the extremity of the Peloponnese and northwards past the Corinthian Gulf and Corcyra or even across the Corinthian isthmus via the famous ancient *diolkos*. Perhaps he cited the notorious treachery of the capes of Malea and Messenia, two of the Mediterranean's worst graveyards, as deterrents to such a trade. Moreover, other sources reveal that popular reports made "the two seas" visible from a mountain called Haemus. Now Haemus is actually the name of an imposing ridge that formed the boundary between the Roman provinces of Thrace in the south and Lower Moesia to the north. From places on it, it is just possible that one might have glimpsed both the Aegean and Pontic seas, but certainly not the Adriatic, as Strabo is careful to point out. It appears that Theopompus believed that the Adriatic and Pontic were much closer together than they really are on the basis of misconstrued information about what could be seen from Mt. Haemus (or Delphium, as he perhaps called it). He further inferred from alleged pottery finds that there had to be some trade link with the northern Aegean through the Euxine to the Adriatic. Bunbury suggested[28] that Theopompus knew of the region called Istria in the northern Adriatic and assumed that it was so named because the Ister (that is, the Danube) issued into both the Adriatic and the Euxine, thus providing the desired channel. If that were true, one could possibly have sailed up one branch of the Ister mouth from the Black Sea and down another into the Adriatic. For this to be possible, Theopompus must have believed that the two seas were separated by a narrow neck of land somewhere to the north of Olynthus on the Chalicidic peninsula.

The pictured proximity of the two seas was known to the anonymous author of a geography written in verse to which a date c. 110 B.C. has been assigned. It describes the Adriatic as "sharing an isthmus" with the Pontic Sea. It goes on to describe the Adriatic as enjoying a different climate from the Euxine despite their proximity. It gives other details about the peoples and islands around the northern Adriatic and mentions that there were people called Eneti (Venetians) who were settlers from Paphlagonia, a region of the southern Black Sea coast. The authority cited for all this information is given as an otherwise unknown Theopemptus. It is customary to emend the name to Theopompus, an emendation accepted by Jacoby, who makes the citation F130.

Of course, this notion of the proximity of the seas is palpable nonsense. At 45° N, the approximate latitude of the mouth of the Danube, the distance between the seas is more than eleven hundred kilometres. How could Theopompus have made such a mistake? It is not likely that he got the idea from some previous authority writing in a less sophisticated age. Herodotus' description of the Danube had no hint of this strange idea (4.48). Nor is there another author before Theopompus to whom it can be attributed. Indeed, the empirical evidence used in Theopompus' presentation of the concept shows that it was not based on received tradition but had to be argued for as an innovation. Why did he feel it necessary to do this? The pottery evidence is scarcely sufficient. After all, there was a southerly route from the Aegean to the Adriatic, the route, indeed, by which it must really have got there.

The two remaining passages in ancient literature that mention the two mouths of the Danube connect the geographical concept with the legendary story of Jason's flight with Medea from the Colchians after he had captured the golden fleece. Theopompus no doubt took the legend of Jason as seriously as he did the reported wanderings of Agamemnon to various parts of the Aegean (FF103, 59). According to a work whose title translates to something like *On Marvellous Things Heard* (105), found among the works of Aristotle but certainly not written by him, the Ister "divides, and one part flows into the Pontus, and the other into the Adriatic" (W.S. Hett, tr., L.C.L.). This work goes on to show how extensively the case was argued to support this wild contortion of geography: "for they say that Jason made his entry to the Pontus by the Caynean rocks [the Bosporus], but his exit by the Ister; and they produce a considerable number of other proofs, and in particular they show altars in the district dedicated by Jason, and in one of the islands of the Adriatic a temple of Artemis built by Medea." (W.S. Hett, tr., L.C.L.).

It is natural to suspect that the author of this remarkable work ransacked the *Philippica*. No less than nine of its anecdotes (including the above quotation) closely parallel fragments of the *Philippica*.[29] There is another passage that bears obvious relevance to the present case:

There is said to be a mountain between Mentorice and Istriane called Delphium, having a high peak. When the Mentores who live near the Adriatic climb this peak they can apparently see ships sailing in the Pontus. There is a spot in the gap in the middle in which, when a common market is held, Lesbian, Chian and Thasian goods are brought up from the merchants who come up from the Pontus, and Corcyrean amphorae from those who come from the Adriatic. (W.S. Hett, tr., L.C.L.)

This looks like a fuller version of part of the argument summarized by Strabo and attributed to Theopompus. It is difficult to know what the "spot in the gap in the middle" is, but it might be an awkward way of referring to the isthmus of land that separated the two seas according to "Theopemptus" (F130). This picture of the region's geographical configuration and the associated bificuration of the Danube to provide a navigable channel connecting the two seas by which Jason fled from the Colchians informs the version of Jason's escape set down by Apollonius of Rhodes in the third century (*Argonautica* 282-337; in 289 "Ionian" must be wrong). If invented by Theopompus, therefore, it seems that the idea rapidly won the status of orthodoxy.

The reconstruction of book 21 must be approximately along the following lines, therefore: it began with Philip's declaration of war on

Olynthus; the event was so important that a full account of the geographic position of Olynthus was felt obligatory; the immediate coastal environs were well known to the Greeks, but as they probed further north, they would be more and more dependent on hearsay; the story that came to Theopompus was about a mountain from which the two seas were visible; considerations of pottery and the legend of Jason compelled him to conclude that these seas were the Euxine and Adriatic; altars and a shrine in places on the Adriatic and Ionian seas allegedly put up by Jason and Medea attested to their flight by that route; but the only way Jason could have gained the Adriatic from the Euxine would have been by some sort of navigable channel; hence the splitting of the Danube. Apollonius calls the channel on the Adriatic side not the Naro but the Narex (312). This line of narrative would probably have involved the tracing of Jason's southward flight from the region of Istria to Corinth.

This reconstruction has its attractions, but much of it, particularly the precise order of the argument, remains highly speculative. It is simply advanced as the tidiest explanation of the fragments and other related information. Perhaps it would be worthwhile to return to a more detailed examination of Strabo's critique in search of more clues (7.5.9):

According to Theopompus the old name [Ionian Sea] was derived from the name of a man [Ionius, see F128] who used to rule the region – his family was from Issa – and Adrias derived from the name of a river. The distance from the Liburnides islands to the Ceraunian mountains is a little more than 2000 stades [c. 250 miles]. Theopompus makes the length of the entire [Adriatic] gulf to be six days' sail: the entire length of Illyria thirty days on foot. I reckon that this is too long. He makes other incredible claims. He infers that the two seas are connected by a channel from the discovery of Chian and Thasian pottery at the Naro; he claims that both seas are visible from a certain mountain. He claims that one of the Liburnides islands is large enough to have a circumference of 500 stades and that the Ister empties by one of its mouths into the Adriatic.

Is this a random list of Theopompan geographical errors, or is it a priceless reflection of Theopompus' argument in the exact order of its presentation? For a random list it exhibits structure: after discussing the nomenclature, it begins near the northern tip of the Adriatic Gulf (the Liburnides) and then measures the distance from there southward to the Ceraunian mountains, the narrows between the heel of the Italian boot, and the modern Albanian coast. It then returns to the very northern tip of the Adriatic to a putative channel connecting the two seas, and the high mountain. Then it returns to the Liburnides for a more detailed geographical investigation of the whole region, then north again for the conclusion that there was a second mouth of the Danube. It could be ring-composition: geography, channel, geography. The claim at the centre that there was a channel connecting the seas is then repeated as the conclusion of the excursus, Q.E.D.

The connection with Jason must remain tenuous. It is true that the measurement of the length of Illyria is made from north to south, and that would be compatible with the direction of Jason's putative flight, but, alas, that is as far as these fragments go. On the other hand, FF285 and 356 certainly show that the story of Jason and Medea was told in some detail somewhere by Theopompus, and it would be hard to think of a better context for it than here. Perhaps one final consideration should be added. Normally, Theopompus does not repeat himself or return to a geographical or narrative subject once treated. Therefore, the overlap between this digression and the upcoming western one is something of an anomaly that calls for an explanation. The search down the Adriatic for traces of Jason's visit to reinforce the argument about the alleged configuration of the terrain north of Olynthus would provide one.

As he passed along the Italian coast, Theopompus found occasion to mention the Umbrians (F132). Their manner of life was compared to that of the Lydians of Asia Minor, says Athenaeus (12.526F–7A). However, it is not necessary to follow Jacoby's suggestion that F317 belongs to this book. It is from Pliny's *Natural History* (3.57). Pliny recorded a remark in Theopompus to the effect that Rome had been captured by the Celts as the earliest direct reference in literature to the city of Rome. However, if my view of book 21 is correct, the treatment of the Italian peninsula was cursory and generally subordinated to the search for clues to the passing of Jason and Medea. I should think it better to assign F317 to the western digression, to book 42 or 43 where the Celts are known to have received some attention.

Three other fragments from book 21 (FF134–6) suggest that a discussion of tyrants and tyranny was included somewhere. If the proposed outline is correct, it could have been placed near the end, for the first part was apparently a geographical continuation of book 20. Once that was complete, Theopompus had to find his way back to Philip and his war on Olynthus. Perhaps Jason's ambitions for power in Corinth, which prompted his marriage to the daughter of the Corinthian king and consequent divorce of Medea, got him onto the subject of vain political ambition; or, possibly, a southward sweep down the Italian peninsula brought him too close to Sicily, the home

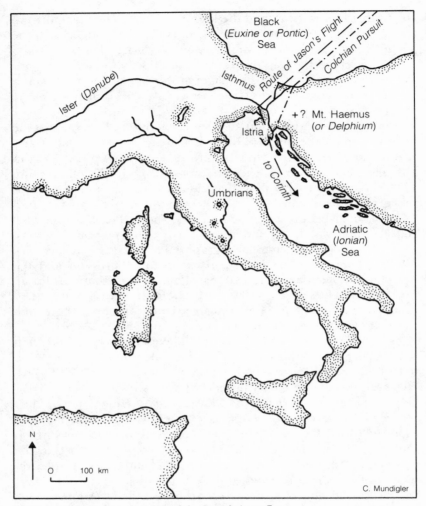

3   Theopompus' reconstruction of the Danube's outflow

of one of his "pet hates," the Syracusan tyrants and their undisciplined drinking (F134). At least he had the good grace to remember that not all tyrants had been profligate sots. Pisistratus of Athens had been such a model of decorum that he had needed no bodyguards (F135) and even had the foresight to give the Athenians a useful place to spend their leisure time, a gymnasium called the Lyceum (F136), perhaps to be thought of as a salutary alternative to taverns and brothels. There is a natural "bridge" to this digression. The Ionius who gave his name to the sea hailed from Issa, a place colonized by

Dionysius the Elder of Syracuse (F128c). With book 22 the subject was once more Philip and his assault on Olynthus.

GREEKS AND NON-GREEKS: ETHNOGRAPHY IN THE *PHILIPPICA*

Most Greek historians wrote something about non-Greeks, or barbarians as they called them.[30] The fact that non-Greeks were lumped together under one term suggests a certain lack of discrimination on the part of the Hellenes. Aristotle regarded barbarians as natural slaves and Greeks as natural rulers,[31] and his contemporary, Theopompus, had a similar view.

The difference between Greeks and barbarians inevitably exercised the mind of Herodotus. His treatment of one people, the Scythians, has been the subject of a recent study by the French scholar François Hartog. Hartog speaks of a rhetoric of "otherness": the way Herodotus describes Scythia and its people reveals something about that land and those people, but it says much more about how Herodotus defined "otherness" or "non-Greekness." His description of Scythians provides a mirror or negative image of Herodotus and his idea of "Greekness."

For the most part Herodotus wrote history about Greeks and ethnography about barbarians. The Greeks had war and the politics of their city-states. This gave them history. Barbarians like Scythians and Egyptians fought wars but had no politics and, therefore, no history despite their considerable antiquity as nations. By contrast, the Persians did have history. Their nobles at least were political. This Herodotus is at pains to assert over the objections of his fellow Greeks. The most famous occasion is the sophisticated political debate he puts into the mouths of three Persian grandees (3.80-81) in the late 520s when, he says, they discussed whether Persia should have a monarchy or be governed by an oligarchy or even a democracy.

A century after Herodotus, Aristotle would speak in the *Politics* of hunting barbarians as being much like trapping and ensnaring animals (1256b, 23–26), but there is no reason to attribute so extreme a view to Herodotus. In his account of the battle of Thermopylae (480), he spoke of the barbarian warriors under Persian command as inferior in courage to the Greeks (7.210.2): "many human males" (ἄνθρωποι) they had, "but few men" (ἄνδρες). On the other hand, the Greeks' behaviour is explained to King Xerxes by the exiled Spartan Demaratus. They are not there in service to some master but in willing obedience only to the laws of their state, which laws they will obey to the death. In an ensuing mêlée the barbarians have to be flogged forward into battle like slaves, while the Greeks stand their ground against hopeless odds. The discussions Herodotus gives to Xerxes and Demaratus set up the military conflicts as tests of the two political systems: Persian monarchy and Greek political freedom (7.101–4). The Persians won the pass, but Herodotus leaves no doubt about which system engendered the more courage in its males.

Theopompus would doubtless have liked to be able to write about the sort of heroic Greeks who people the history of Herodotus. Alas, his was a different day. His Greeks lived under a general "peace" (the Peace of Antalcidas) that was dictated from the Persian throne. They offered themselves as hirelings to the Great King to prop up his empire, or they sold their services to various of his minions like Mausolus and squabbled among themselves to the detriment of their own alliances, or they fought for rebellious Pharaohs, but they did nothing for Hellas, for themselves collectively.

Theopompus seems to have thought along these lines, but can his picture of "the barbarian" be brought into sharper focus? Did he treat barbarians differently from Greeks?

The Persian king was a barbarian. The two fragments that mention him emphasize the enormity of his resources or of his empire. F113 pretends to know the obligatory cost of entertaining him for one dinner: twenty or thirty talents, enough money for about two weeks' wages for the entire Peloponnesian navy in the last years of the Peloponnesian War.[32] Similarly F263 concludes with a near comic description of the King's enormous stockpiles of food and supplies, dumped in heaps of improbable size, in preparation for the assault on Egypt. In both fragments Theopompus invites his fellow Greeks to look at the Great King and feel dwarfed. Only the few Greeks who were with Alexander or one of his successors could have known such opulence. Otherwise, which of them could contemplate entertaining a friend at dinner at a cost of twenty to thirty talents, and who could imagine owning such stockpiles of meat?

A full translation of F263 appeared in chapter 1. There it was suggested that Theopompus' narrative is freighted with irony. The progression from the magnificent treasures to the mundane piles of meat is a deliberate reversal of normal, climactic, rhetorical order. The passage opens with a series of rhetorical questions that serve both to alert the sensitive reader to the tone of mockery and to show that Theopompus was well aware of the usual order:

What city or nation throughout Asia did not send embassies to the King? What good or product of things that grow in the earth or are devised by human skill was not brought him as a gift?

The tents and coverlets he received would be useful in a field campaign, as indeed would be the "countless myriads of arms ... Greek and barbarian." However, he also received "silver vessels and worked gold, drinking cups and bowls, some studded with jewels, some elaborately and preciously wrought." These are the adornments of court not the battlefield. However, the King's treasures were his weapons too, for he needed to pay his mercenaries. How much irony did Theopompus find in that? He seems never to have shrunk from imputing base motives to the giving and receiving of "gifts," or "bribes" as he usually thought of them. On the other hand, the ironic treatment of the King is noteworthy. There are passages in which Greek leaders' prodigious ostentation is treated, but there is no subtlety to them. They are unambiguous, scathing attacks.

In fact, in the fragments in which Theopompus addresses the subject of luxurious behaviour, there is a change in mood and vocabulary depending on whether the subject of the fragment is Greek or barbarian. The subtle irony of F263 contrasts dramatically with the unambiguous denunciation of the profligacy of the Thessalians (F49) whose "Greekness" was guaranteed by their involvement as founding members of the Delphic Amphictiony (F63, under the name of Achaeans). The fragments on the Persian king focus on the external manifestation of his wealth. The attitude is one of irony, mocking awe. The Thessalians' ostentation, on the other hand, is described in detail from within and the language condemns them (Athen. 12.527A):

Their lives are spent ... in the continual company of dancing-girls and flute-girls, while others pass the livelong day in gaming, drinking, and *the like forms of dissipation*, and *they are more interested in having the tables that are served to them laden with all sorts of dainties than in making their own lives decent*. (C.B. Gulick, tr., L.C.L., my emphasis)

Of course, caution is necessary. More of the Persian context might change the interpretation. What would Theopompus have said about the notorious oriental harems?

A long passage has been preserved in which the eating, drinking, and sex habits of another barbarian people, the Etruscans, are described in detail. In the next chapter I examine the way Theopompus describes Greek excesses. His moralizing diatribes are full of judgmental expressions when the subject is a Greek. Boozing, dicing, excessive eating, and irresponsible or socially destructive sexual practices are variously and persistently described as lack of self-control (ἀϰρασία), lack of self-discipline (ἀϰολασία), profligacy

(ἀσωτία), wanton corruption (ἀσέλγεια), frantic agitation (παρακίνησις), or even mental derangement (μανία). In rare moments of
approval, a person displays diligence (ἐπιμέλεια) or industry (φιλοπονία). These words are not found in the fragment describing the
Etruscans. Despite their obvious dedication to personal gratification,
"pleasure-addiction" (ἡδυπάθεια) is not attributed to them, and
luxury is mentioned only once. Instead, the description is detached,
even clinical. Again and again Theopompus simply emphasizes that
they seem to have no sense of modesty or shame (αἰσχρόν, αἰσχύνομ-
αι), just as one might comment on the way animals copulate in a
farmyard (F204 = Athen. 12.517D–18B):

And Theopompus in the 43rd book of his *Histories* says that it is customary
with the Etruscans to share their women in common; the women bestow great
care on their bodies and often exercise even with men, sometimes also with
one another; for it is no disgrace (αἰσχρόν) for women to show themselves
naked. Further, they dine, not with their own husbands, but with any men
who happen to be present, and they pledge with wine any whom they wish.
They are also terribly bibulous and are very good-looking. The Etruscans
rear all the babies that are born, not knowing who is the father in any single
case. These in turn pursue the same mode of life as those who have given
them nurture, having drinking parties often and consorting with all the
women. It is no disgrace (αἰσχρόν) for Etruscans to be seen doing anything in
the open, or even having anything done to them; for this also is a custom of
their country. And so far are they from regarding it as a disgrace (αἰσχρόν)
that they actually say, when the master of the house is indulging in a love
affair, and someone enquires for him, that he is undergoing so-and-so,
openly calling the act by its indecent name (προσαγορεύσαντες αἰσχρῶς τὸ
πρᾶγμα). When they get together for companionship or family parties they
do as follows: first of all, after they have stopped drinking and are ready to go
to bed, the servants bring in to them, the lamps still being lighted, sometimes
female prostitutes, sometimes very beautiful boys, sometimes also their wives;
and when they have enjoyed these, the servants then introduce to them lusty
young men who in their turn consort with them. They indulge in love affairs
and carry on these unions sometimes in full view of one another, but in most
cases with screens set up around the beds; the screens are made of latticed
wands, over which cloths are thrown. Now they consort very eagerly, to be
sure, with women; much more, however, do they enjoy consorting with boys
and striplings. For in their country these latter are very good looking, because
they live in luxury and keep their bodies smooth. In fact all the barbarians
who live in the west remove the hair of their bodies by means of pitch-plasters
and by shaving with razors. Also among the Etruscans at least, many shops are
set up and artisans arise for this business, corresponding to barbers among us.

When they enter these shops, they offer themselves unreservedly, having no modesty whatever (οὐθὲν αἰσχυνόμενοι) before spectators or the passers-by. This custom is also in use even among many of the Greeks who live in Italy; they learned it from the Samnites and Messapians. (C.B. Gulick, tr., L.C.L.)

This fragment illustrates with remarkable clarity Theopompus' use of what Hartog calls a "rhetoric of otherness." *They* have no modesty; the implication is that *we* do have it (or ought to). *They* have their entire bodies depillitated openly in "barber shops"; *we* do not (except that a few of *us* are learning it via intermediaries from *them*). Curiously, he even seems to resort to the age-old criterion of racial differentiation (not to say bigotry). *Their* sex drive is prodigious. Their lack of modesty places them beyond the perimeter of moral evaluation. Greeks who know shame can lose control of themselves and act shamelessly; barbarians who know not the meaning of the word cannot be described as shameless.

I have already mentioned a fragment (F122) in which the Chians are called the first to enslave non-Greek people. There is no reason to think that Theopompus meant this to the Chians' discredit. On the contrary, he is likely to have been proud of it. He was careful to point out that the Spartans and Thessalians had anticipated the Chians but that they had enslaved Greek peoples, while the Chians "acquired *barbarians* as domestics and sold them for a price" (my emphasis). This is not a defence of the institution of enslaving barbarians, for there is no reason to believe that the institution was under attack. It is simply an assertion of the superiority of the Chian approach to enslavement. The argument seems to presuppose Aristotle's view about barbarians being natural slaves. What does a historian who accepts this view do when he must describe slaves in a barbarian society? His choice would be to accept that some barbarians could become rulers somehow; otherwise, their management of slaves would be inexplicable. Or he could seek to deny the formal institution to barbarian societies, choose not to see any distinction in the society along the lines of slave-master relationships. Herodotus had done both. The underlings of the King of Persia, even grandees like Hydarnes, he seems prepared to regard as, somehow, Xerxes' slaves. Again, early in book 4 he clearly attributes the institution of slavery to the nomadic Scythians (4.2–3). However, in the same book (4.72), he denies any knowledge of "bought slaves" among them. In the earlier passage, he used the normal Greek word δοῦλοι for slaves, as did Theopompus in F122 (he also uses οἰκέται = "domestic slaves" in the last sentence of that fragment). However, in section 72, he drops the standard terminology for the vaguer θεράποντες (attendants) who wait on the king and even the rare and very neutral διάκονοι (also to be translated "attendants"). In his description of the Etruscans, Theopompus avoids the word δοῦλοι to describe their "attendants," selecting instead the rare διάκονοι. So it is possible that he chose not to recognize the institution of bought slavedom in Etruscan society.

More revealing is Theopompus' claim that the Etruscans rear all their children without knowing who the father is. This bizarre, and apparently false,[33] idea is perhaps little more than an inference from the alleged promiscuity of the Etruscans, itself exaggerated if not utterly untrue. The effect is to deny the Greek notion of family (oikos) to these "barbarian" peoples. The Greek oikos, with its power to own slaves (oiketai), arrange marriages, and dispose of family property to (usually male) heirs,[34] was the basic unit of Hellenic society. If I may be Theopompan for a moment and coin a linguistic oddity, Theopompus (and his fellow Greeks, no doubt) chose to see non-Hellenic societies as "anoikic," lacking the oikos. This made possible or perhaps was caused by their "shameless" promiscuity. With no identifiable heirs, there would be no need for concern over deeding "family" property to future generations; and with no oikoi, "domestic establishments," there would be no place for oiketai, "domestic slaves." Again, this is perfectly in keeping with what Hartog calls a rhetoric of "otherness." What is being defined is not Etruscan society but Greek (in some way, perhaps idealized) "through a mirror."

There is a rich abundance of information on barbarians in Theopompus, at least by the standards of poverty for most other topics. Something must be said about his treatment of Thracians. There is one fragment of substance on Cotys, the Thracian king, and a vacuum to be considered. First, the vacuum. The fragments suggest that Theopompus reported Philip's Thracian wars in detail. Thracian place names proliferate in all the appropriate locations. There are some twenty-seven fragments in which Thrace or Thracians are mentioned, most, unfortunately, single-line entries.[35] F307 is a wretchedly fragmentary quotation on papyrus (perhaps from book 1) in which the Thracian Cersobleptes cooperated with two Macedonians, Heraclides and Python, sons of Archelaus, in hiring mercenaries. It appears that they captured a Miltocythes, son of Cotys, the Thracian king, but nothing more is known. This could serve as a fair example of the detail in which Theopompus reported Thracian affairs. If he passed judgment on any of these Thracians for their courage, treachery, or debauchery, no hint of it survives. Considering the number of Greeks who are singled out for scathing rebuke and a few words of reserved approbation, perhaps the silence is significant.

Whatever the truth of that, there is a fragment describing the bizarre behaviour of Cotys. He is one of a small handful of apparent "exceptions" to the rule of differential treatment for barbarians, most of which actually confirm the rule on closer examination. F31 (= Athen. 12.531E–532A) reports that Cotys had established a number of pleasure spots "with groves of beautifully planted trees" that he used as "summer resorts." Next he is called "of all Thracian kings before his time the most given to pleasure-addiction and luxurious living." It looks as if the historian is getting his moral rhetoric "into gear." However, the rest of the fragment actually emphasizes a beatific quality in the chosen places and lifestyle of Cotys. This point will become even clearer in the next section of this chapter which considers Theopompus' sensitivity to the idyllic aspects of nature:

As he travelled about he would establish banquetting spots in places that he saw to be shaded with trees and watered by flowing streams. Whenever he was in the region, he would visit the places, sacrifice to the gods and hold court. So he continued, happy and altogether blessed until he undertook to blaspheme against and offend Athena.

His blasphemy consisted in a decision to marry the goddess Athena. He made the arrangements and proceeded to get very drunk. Two messengers were sent, one after the other, to see if the goddess was in the bridal chamber awaiting the prospective groom. He shot them with his bow when they returned with a negative answer. The third one had the good sense to bring back an affirmative report. On another occasion this same king allegedly cut his wife to pieces in a fit of jealousy. Another reference to this story in Harpocration (see Κότυς) closely parallels this version in Athenaeus. Despite its extreme brevity, there are verbal echoes that suggest a common source. Cotys is described as "carried off into a state of savagery and rage" so that he butchered his own wife "who had borne him children." There are no traces of expressions like derangement or agitation to describe his actions. His life of luxury is called beatific, and his actions of insane brutality are either described objectively (as in Athenaeus) or called "rage and savagery" (Harpocration). Once again this parallels the way one might speak of an animal now feeding blissfully from a trough, now turning inexplicably to sudden acts of vicious rage.

Barbarian drinking habits are also not given the same treatment as those of Greeks. The behaviour of the Illyrians (F39 = Athen. 10.433A–B) is described in neutral language once more, and while a note of approval of some of their acts of restraint may be implied, there is nothing explicit to that effect:

The Illyrians dine and drink seated, and even bring their wives to parties; and it is good form for the women to pledge any of the guests no matter who they may be. They conduct their husbands home from drinking-bouts. The men all have a hard life, and when they drink they gird their bellies with wide belts. This they do, at first, with tolerable looseness; but as the drinking becomes more intense, they pull the belts more and more tightly together. (C.B. Gulick, tr., L.C.L.)

Theopompus possibly recognized the existence of a mixed category of humans: what might be called barbarized Greeks or Hellenized barbarians. Two important persons and an Illyrian tribe can be considered under this rubric: Hermeas of Atarneus, Philip himself, and the [Ardiaeans]. Hermeas was the subject of a long but pathetically mutilated passage in Didymus' commentary on Demosthenes (F291). He was probably described as a "Bithynian by race," and so not a Greek. Unfortunately, the ethnic has to be partially restored, and Jacoby preferred an alternative reading, "deformed in appearance." Other editors, however, claim to be able to see enough of "Bithynian" to regard it as preferable.

The language of F291, such as survives, lacks traces of Theopompus' standard pejorative moral rhetoric. Perhaps this is what misled Kurt von Fritz, who saw the fragment as encomiastic.[36] Hermeas had studied philosophy at Athens in Plato's Academy and, barbarian or not, seems to have been a close friend of Aristotle. Through the 340s he seems to have had a small maritime empire based at Atarneus on the Asiatic coast facing Lesbos. In 341 he was treacherously captured by the Persians and put to death. He had been an ally of Philip, and apparently the Persians hoped to torture him and so learn of Philip's plans. In this, however, they seem to have been unsuccessful.[37]

Didymus' introduction to the fragment leaves little doubt about its negative tone, at least as he saw it: "Some commemorate him [Hermeas] in the best of terms, but others in the very worst. Among the latter is Theopompus." The fragment certainly called him a eunuch, leaving no doubt that Theopompus believed that he had been a slave at one time. He did not come into the territory of Atarneus peacefully but by force. He ruled "with great corruption" actually poisoning some [of the citizens?] and [doing away?] with others by [hanging?]. He came into some disagreement with the Chians and Mytilenaeans and "insulted most of the Ionians." He was described as a money-grubber, "sitting at the table of monetary exchange." The gist of the fragment's last sentence is pretty clear whatever restoration one adopts. He did not altogether get away with his "impious and disgusting" ways but was "dragged off to the King, tortured and crucified, and so ended his life." Like Cotys, Hermeas was capable of impiety, and all editors restore ὠμότατα, "extremely violently," as an adverb to describe his manner of dealing with people. His treatment of the Ionians and islanders, notably the Chians, recalls sentiments expressed in the anti-Athenian digression in book 25, but there is no hint of the rhetoric of self-discipline or self-control that pervades the treatment of known Greeks. The accusation of money-grubbing is reminiscent of the characterization of another barbarian who built himself a small maritime empire, Mausolus, who would do "anything for money." Perhaps Theopompus saw profligacy (ἀσωτία) as a Greek vice, avarice as a barbarian one.

In his treatment of barbarians, Theopompus offers a somewhat fanciful description of real people that is structured by his conception and expectations of his own society. Similar patterns should emerge when he describes unreal people, such as the Meropians in the "Marvels." These descriptions show the polarity of Theopompus' moral view. The Saintsburgers are beatific but lack cities (*poleis*) and families (*oikoi*); their life is simple, agricultural, and blessed by the gods. They are barbarians who somehow know shame and are, thus, able to control their lives. The Wartowners, on the other hand, are imperialists; they subjugate their neighbours. They live in cities and are diseased and unhappy. The Saintsburgers achieve happiness by combining the ideals of barbarism (bucolic simplicity) with those of Hellenism (self-control), while the Wartowners do neither and are utterly wretched. The contrast elaborates a paradigm for the morality of self-control. Similarly, the [Ardiaeans], an Illyrian tribe mentioned in book 2 (F40), present a picture of Hellenized barbarians on the edge of the world. The name is a textual restoration and probably wrong. They were probably Autariatae, a large, more northerly tribe of Illyrians living much closer to that imaginary isthmus between the Adriatic and Euxine, that is, near the boundary where the historian's knowledge ends and fantasy begins. (Illyria is very roughly the same as modern Albania.) They had a society, however, that mimicked venerable Greek ones by its control of large numbers of slaves. By not controlling their appetites, they fall under the control of their enemies. This fragment, set early in the *Philippica* and on the boundary of the world as Theopompus knew it, looks programmatical. Its purpose is to introduce the rhetoric, the moral vocabulary of self-control.

Philip is the last example. If Hermeas was a Hellenized barbarian or, more properly, a Bithynian posing as a Hellene, Philip was the opposite: a Greek with a pedigree that went back to Heracles who lived as a barbarian among barbarians. This point is examined fully in chapter 5.

THEOPOMPUS ON NATURE

The centuries after Theopompus' death witnessed the emergence of an escape literature, accounts of imaginary Utopias and the writing of the famous *Idylls* of Theocritus, pastoral poems set in an idealized landscape.[38] It is difficult to say precisely how far this trend was anticipated in the fourth century, but there are visible signs in Theopompus' fragments of a willingness to dally over the bucolic, if not numinous, peacefulness of forests and streams. This is not necessarily a simple idealization of nature, for one of the relevant passages, the description of No Return in the land of Meropis, turns on an assumed ambivalence of the otherwise idyllic setting. Nature, even at her loveliest, can be sinister. The person who eats the fruit of the wrong tree ends his life in tears and lamentation. In the case of Cotys, his selection and enjoyment of "beautifully ordered groves watered by flowing streams" were central to his beatific life until he became impious and violent.

In Aelian's *Varia Historia* there is an extremely beautiful description of Tempe, the valley of the Peneus river that cuts between the awesome peaks of Mts. Ossa and Olympus. Unfortunately, Aelian does not say where he got the description, but a number of convincing clues point emphatically to Theopompus. The scholar Aelius Theon speaks of a description of Thessalian Tempe in the ninth book of the *Philippica*; he describes Tempe's location and mentions a little of the topography in words that closely echo actual phrases and expressions in Aelian. If that were not enough, an example of a grammatical item preserved by Priscianus, cited again from *Philippica* book 9, provides another fairly extensive and nearly exact verbal echo of a phrase in Aelian. The subject is, in part, Tempe's alleged historic relationship to Delphi, an entirely appropriate topic for *Philippica* 9. On these reasonable grounds it has been inferred that Aelian's description is a close paraphrase or quotation of the text of *Philippica* 9 cited by Aelius Theon and Priscianus. Accordingly, Jacoby prints the description as F80, but in small print to indicate that the attribution falls just a little short of scientific certainty.

The lingering description is a remarkable piece of poetic rhetoric. It is worth reproducing in full, if only for its haunting lyrical beauty (Aelian *VH* 3.1 = Theopompus F80):

Come then let us describe in words the place called Tempe of Thessaly ... it is situated between the two mountains Olympus and Ossa. These are two very high mountains seemingly split apart by some divine will. Between them lies a valley the length of which is about forty stades [8 km] and the width is a plethrum [30 m] or a little wider here and there. The river called Peneus flows through the middle of it. Thither the other streams flow together, blend their waters in it and they make the Peneus large. This spot has places of relaxation rich in texture and variety, no work of human hand but self-grown products of Nature who strove for an effect of beauty when the place came into being. Ivy in abundance and very lush flourishes and luxuriates creeping up and clinging to the soaring trees like select grape-vines. An abundance of holm-oak grows up hard against the cliff itself and shades the rock. The rock itself is completely concealed and only greenery can be seen, a feast for the eyes. In the smooth low-lying places are dappled groves and dense bowers, pleasurable retreats for wayfarers to flee to in summer's heat, affording a welcome coolness. Numerous springs splash through it, and rivulets of cool water flow into it, sweet to drink. These waters are said to be a boon to any who wash in them restoring them to health. Birds cast a spell with their music here and there, especially the melodious singers providing a rich feast for the ears and effortlessly and pleasurably by their sweetness banish the weariness of by-passers, and send them on their way. These are the blandishments and places of repose on either side of the river.

Through the heart of tempe flows the Peneus; its movement is leisurely and gentle with the liquidity of olive oil. Deep is the shade born of the trees by its banks and of the branches that hang from them; so for most of the day it lasts and shields off the sunshine and provides cool for boaters to sail by. All the people who live nearby get together with each other, make sacrifice, hold gatherings, and drink together. Because there are many making sacrifices and frequent burnt offerings, naturally the pleasantest smells are wafted to passing travellers and boaters. Therefore the dignity of the place, age-lasting and uplifting, makes it divine. There, say the sons of the Thessalians, Apollo the Pythian was purified according to the command of Zeus when he shot the Python, the serpent that was guarding Delphi when Earth still possessed the shrine. They say that the son of Zeus and Leto went garlanded with the laurel of Tempe and bearing a shoot of the same laurel in his right hand, and came to Delphi to possess the oracle. There is an altar on the very spot where he donned his garland and plucked the laurel shoot. Every ninth year the Delphians organize a procession of noble youths and a sacred leader from amongst themselves. When they have come and held magnificent sacrifice in Tempe, they weave garlands from the selfsame laurel from which the god made his own long ago and return again. They take the road called the Pythian Way. It passes through Thessaly, Pelasgia, Oete and the land of the Aenianes and that of the Melieis, Dorians and Locrians of the West. They accompany the procession with song and honour no less than they who honour the bearers of the sacred gifts of the Hyperboreans to this same god. And in truth it is from this very same laurel that they make the garlands for the victors in the Pythian Games. That is my account of Thessalian Tempe.

APHORISMS

Theopompus was not only a prolific writer of histories; he was also known in antiquity as an accomplished orator. A few of his rhetorical works, known by title alone, were noted in the first chapter. Of course, the orator in him will not have fallen silent the moment he picked up the historical pen. He will have composed speeches for his characters like most other ancient historians, and his scathing attacks and rare moments of praise directed toward his fellow Greeks throughout the *Hellenica* and *Philippica* are clearly more rhetoric than history.

At the start of this chapter I mentioned the collections of anecdotes and sayings, handy aids for the speech-writers of later antiquity. It is not surprising to find Theopompus' sayings represented among the surviving collections. Of course, scholars receive these aphoristic "morsels," dropped from the groaning tables of ancient rhetorical banqueters with the eagerness of starving dogs though they regret the fact that their position beneath the table makes it impossible to see whence any fragment was torn. Generally, the quotations are wrenched from their context and either grouped together under headings one after another like railroad cars and preserved as anthologies or dropped into a new and foreign context, such as the sort of learned dinner chitchat represented by Athenaeus. So far are these fragments from their original home that they are not necessarily culled from the original works but, in many cases, from previous anthologies now lost.

These introductory remarks are necessary cautions against the hasty misuse of the six aphorisms collected below. They look tempting. The impulse is to regard them as invaluable windows into the mind of Theopompus or signposts toward a sure and accurate assessment of the thought that informs his work. However, most of them cannot be used this way. Only two of the six are assigned to the *Philippica*, and the others could be from that work, from the *Hellenica*, or for some rhetorical showpiece whose purpose and occasion is lost. Even in the *Philippica*, a remark may be composed for a character speaking to a specific situation. In that case, the saying need no more represent the mind of Theopompus than a line or speech from a character in a drama represents the thinking of the playwright. In only one case, the last in the following list, a citation from Polybius, is there enough information to accept the apophthegm as a true representation of the historian's beliefs. Even in this case, lamentably, the source is not certain. Polybius' commentary leaves little doubt that it belongs to a history, and by that he usually means the *Philippica*, but there is always the possibility that it came in this instance from the *Hellenica*.

Once again, I retreat to the principle of cumulation: safety in numbers. The cumulative weight of these aphorisms can be added to the surviving fragments and testimonies to reinforce the undoubted impression of Theopompus as a disillusioned moralist seizing any possible opportunity to rail at the corruption and waste of his times or else sinking back to express his despair over the ubiquity of these human failings in his own words or through the characters in his history.

The first example makes it tempting to part company a little with these general caveats. It is set up as a typical nostalgic comparison of the extravagant customs of "today" with the more reserved standards of a happier "yesterday" (F36 = Athen. 6.275B from book 1):

But today there is nobody even among those in moderate circumstances, who fails to set an extravagant table, or does not own cooks and many other servants, or does not lavish more for daily needs than they used to expend at the festivals and sacrifices. (C.B. Gulick, tr., L.C.L.)

Athenaeus clearly assigns the quotation to book 1 of the *Philippica*, a book in which Theopompus was probably laying a foundation for the themes and ideas that would bind his enormous work together. In other words, coming so early, the sentiment may well be thematic in purpose. If it was part of a speech put into someone's mouth, it is hard to imagine a situation calling for this sort of a sweeping judgment. After he introduced himself and Philip, Theopompus seems to have included in book 1 a general survey of the Greek and barbarian world surrounding Macedonia as it stood at the time of Philip's ascension followed by some account of Philip's struggle against the early pretenders to the Macedonian throne (D.S. 16.2-3). In short, there is no visible situation or crisis on which this remark could be a comment, but it looks like a perfectly suitable remark for a jaded moralist to make about Greek affairs at the time of Philip's accession. If any contextless aphorism is to be associated with the mind of Theopompus on circumstantial and *a priori* grounds, therefore, this is it.

The second aphorism is located in book 5. The book's topic seems to have been Philip's operation in or near Pagasae in southern Thessaly. It would be tempting to see it as just another denunciation of Thessalian lassitude brought on by overeating except that the statement is couched in a language that sounds decidedly Pythagorean, and Theopompus was no admirer of Pythagoras.

First, here is the fragment (F57 = Athen. 4.157D–E from book 5):

Too much eating, as well as meat-eating, destroys the reasoning faculties and makes souls more sluggish, and fills them besides with irascibility, hardness and awkwardness. (C.B. Gulick, tr., L.C.L.)

The keys to this fragment are the caution against eating meat and the concern over the health of the soul, a consideration unparalleled in the other fragments, which generally characterize overindulgence as signs of uncontrolled or undisciplined behaviour. Caring for the soul was philosophical in the fourth century; Plato and his school made much of it, as did the Pythagoreans. Both schools advocated an ascetic way of life, but, according to Aristotle, the Pythagoreans especially had prohibitions against eating various things, including certain meats and special cuts, and they seem to have stressed the avoidance of overeating. Some later traditions attribute to the Pythagoreans a general taboo against eating meat. For these reasons, F57 may be regarded as a Pythagorean sentiment. The occasion for its intrusion into book 5 is beyond recovery. Theopompus would have approved of the self-control advocated, but the details of its supporting arguments about the sluggishness of the soul and other harm it allegedly suffers from overeating probably derive from a philosophy with which he had no sympathy.

The next three aphorisms could easily be excerpts from speeches, display orations of Theopompus' own, or words put into the mouths of historical figures. Indeed, the last one closely parallels a sentiment put into the mouth of Pericles by Thucydides (2.45.1) in the famous Funeral Oration.

F287 = Clem. Al. *Strom.* 6.2.21.4 [439, 14].

For if it were possible for any to escape the present danger and live out the rest of their lives without fear, the desire to survive would not be surprising; but, as things are, so many are the banes that have befallen life as to make death in battle seem far preferable.

F380 = Stob. 3.16.16

If a person should live his life in constant distress though he had acquired the greatest number of good things, he would be of all men, both who are and are to be, the most miserable.

F395 = Theon. *Prog.* 1 (II 63, 18 Sp).

For I know that many people scrutinize the living invidiously, but on the dead, because of the number of intervening years, they are sparing with their envy.

The last and most important of the aphorisms comes from the historian Polybius' long diatribe against what he sees as the incompetence of the historian Timaeus (Polyb. 12.23–8). In the course of this sustained attack, Polybius comes to the question of the best preparation for historical writing. Timaeus had read his previous literary sources, but that was not enough. He should have gained a broader experience by visiting the places of which he speaks and "interrogating living witnesses" (12.27.3). He should have engaged in a personal investigation regardless of the toil and cost. The value of this approach is evident from the statements of other historians, Polybius argues. Ephorus acknowledged the superiority of first-hand knowledge and (F342 = Polyb. 12.27.8–9):

> Theopompus says that the man who has the best knowledge of war is he who has been present at the most battles, that the most capable speaker is he who has taken part in the greatest number of debates, and that the same holds good about medicine and navigation. (W.R. Paton, tr., L.C.L.)

The value of Polybius' remarks is twofold. First, they show that he was not just citing a useful passage, but also attributing a belief to Theopompus and recognizing it by means of the quote. This is important because it shows that Theopompus paid lip-service at the very least to the importance of "first-hand knowledge" or "on-the-job training." However, it says more: "the greater the experience and longevity at a profession, the greater the person's authority." Perhaps it implies even more: "the person with no experience should defer to the expert." Second, Polybius seems to be citing various historians' own statements about their methods, mostly, no doubt, from their introductions. Perhaps this fragment should be assigned to the introduction, therefore, and connected with the claim that the historian travelled far and wide to gather his information. However that may be, the fragment helps explain Theopompus' views on key issues.

PUNS AND JINGLES: THEOPOMPUS AT WORD-PLAY

Puns are by no means uncommon in ancient literature. Both Herodotus and Thucydides employed them, and Gorgias of Leontini, orator, sophist, and master of the master Isocrates, revelled in them as attention-getting tricks of style.[39] It is not certain that ancient puns were meant as jokes. Theopompus especially looks to have been a rather humourless sort. There are moments of sarcastic irony in the fragments, but the jesting pun suggests a lightheartedness that scarcely suits what the ancients say about Theopompus' snarling attitude. However, humour, like beauty, is "in the eye of the beholder"; and if the following items strike the reader as funny, then perhaps there was a lighter side to Theopompus' melancholy.

It would be well to repeat the customary "word of caution." To speak of the intricacies of Theopompus' use of words assumes that the fragments contain them. If a fragment is a paraphrase, then it is by no means clear how far the author's original words may be reflected. Even the quotations are not necessarily taken directly from Theopompus; they may be copies of contextless quotations. In the case of one pun, the punning word has been restored to one of the three texts in which it occurred by emendation. That alone shows the seriousness of the difficulties plaguing the sort of close textual analysis of these fragments. However, considering the small number of fragments, puns and jingles occur in them with notable frequency. This makes them seem a legitimate feature of Theopompus' style, and there is further support of the testimonies. Dionysius speaks of an interweaving of letter sounds in Theopompus, and several critics of style react to an innovating attitude that they saw in his works: he even coined words in a way that they seem to have found offensive. Therefore, the general impression conveyed by the following examples is likely to be reliable even if there are doubts about the authenticity of specific instances.

F113 (= Athen. 4.145A) gives an example of consonance used to emphasize the cost of entertaining the King of Persia at dinner. From the way Athenaeus introduces the fragment, it appears that he is quoting the historian's exact words. They run as follows: "Whenever the King goes to any of his grandees, on the dinner (*deipnon*) for him they spend (*dapanasthai*) twenty talents, sometimes thirty." The jingle is on the d, p, and n sounds of the noun *deipnon* and the verb *dapanaō*. The noun *deipnon* means simply "meal" or "dinner," but the jingle on the verb *dapanaō* (= to spend, spend lavishly) suggests an equation between *deipnon* (dinner) and *dapane* (lavish expense, cost). The jingle is repeated, as if for emphasis, in the next sentence of the fragment. "Some even spend much more (*dapanosi*), for on each of their cities according to size, just as for the tribute, so the dinner (*deipnon*) has been assessed from ancient times." The second use of *deipnon* removes any doubt about Theopompus' intent. Strictly speaking, it is not the dinner that is assessed but its cost (*dapanē*) on each of the cities. The second use of *deipnon* completely confuses the word with *dapanē*. The confusion looks to have been contrived.

This case is an example of a contrivance to emphasize or clinch a point: Persian royal dinners are lavishly expensive. In F75, concerning the Saintsburgers and Wartowners, there is a very similar device, operating this time in anticipation rather than retrospect. The unusual expression is probably introduced first to arrest the flow of the narrative. The puzzle is exploited by the second use of the same word: "[The Saintsburgers] overturn [*katastrephousi*] their own lives ... [But the Wartowners] are always at war overturning [*katastrephontai*] their neighbours." I translate *katastrephousi* "overturn" to bring out the word-play, but considering the context, it must have the metaphorical sense of "turn in," "bring to an end." Theopompus uses it in the active voice, and, so used, it means to overturn or overthrow, an odd thing to do with one's own lifestyle. In an agricultural context, Xenophon (*Oeconomicus* 17.10) uses it to mean to plough or cultivate sown seed into the soil. Perhaps this usage is also relevant because Theopompus had just finished describing how effortlessly the Saintsburgers raise and harvest their crops:

The Saintsburgers live their lives in peace and deep abundance and they take their harvests without ploughs and ox-teams; there is no need for them to work the ground and sow seed. They live healthy and disease-free lives, and *katastrephousi* their own lives with much laughter and happiness. They are indisputably just enough for the gods to think it no condescension to visit them frequently. But the inhabitants of the city, Wartown, are born fully armed.

The progression of ideas seems to be: the Saintsburgers do not toil on the land (presumably they are divinely blest); they do not turn the soil with the plough but overturn (that is, terminate) their lives laughing and happy, living contrary to the norm. On the other hand, the Wartowners are violent and overturn their neighbours with a view to subjugation. However, the power they receive and exercise does not make them happy. The point is enforced by means of a contrived pun that forms a bridge from the agricultural prosperity of the Saintsburgers to the militarism of the Wartowners while at the same time emphasizing how rare, "inverted," the Saintsburgers' lifestyle really is.

This word-play exploits a rare meaning: *katastrephein* "to overturn" is made to carry the metaphorical sense "to terminate" just as *deipnon* "dinner" acquires the meaning of expense, *dapanē*. If meanings can be contrived for words in a special context, so too words can be invented for meanings. F338 gives three examples deplored by the critic, but F262 gives one that was generally admired: "Philip was excellent at stomaching facts" (*anankophagēsai pragmata*, Russell and

Winterbottom, trs.). The coined, or at least extremely rare, word
anankophagesai is assembled from two roots *anankē* = "compulsion,
necessity" and *phagein* "eat." Aristotle (*Politics* 1339) uses the cognate
noun *anankophagia* to describe the strict diet of athletes. In addition,
pragmata means more than facts; it is used to describe political affairs
or events. What then does this fragment mean? Perhaps it is an
expression of admiration for Philip's political dedication; if so, it
would be unique among the fragments. F237 from book 54 describes
Philip as a man of nearly miraculous good luck; does this fragment
recognize that he had a certain political ability? Perhaps it does, but
Theopompus' normal expressions for political dedication were
diligence and industry. Why invent a new term just for Philip unless
the purpose was to show that his political acumen was not of the
regular variety? It is equally possible that the intention was sarcastic.
Does the word imply that Philip's greatest political tool was his
stomach? That notion would be more in keeping with the ideas
expressed in other fragments concerning Philip.

The above puns are taken from texts that seem to be reasonably
authentic. The next one is considerably less certain. It is from a
Scholiast on Aristophanes' *Peace* (l. 363). It gives background
information on a traitor called Cillicon. Theopompus is cited as the
source of the information, a story he apparently told in book 13
(F111). The Scholiast goes on to explain how Cillicon's betrayal of his
native island of Syros to the Samians was avenged by Theagenes:

A certain Theagenes of Syros, a citizen of the island betrayed by Cillicon, was
a butcher in Samos having moved there long before and so was spending his
days. He was enraged at the betrayal of his native land. When Cillicon came to
him to buy meat, he gave it to him to hold down (*kratein*) so that he could trim
it. Cillicon obeyed and held it down (*kratein*, again). On the pretext of
trimming the meat he took up his butcher's knife and lopped off Cillicon's
hand saying, "you won't betray another city with that hand."

It is not clear how closely the Scholiast is reproducing the exact
wording of this source. The word *kratein* is not used to mean "to hold,
hold down" in classical Greek; it usually means "to rule," "control,"
"dominate." It could, therefore, be an expression of the post-classical
Scholiast, or the late classical Theopompus could be anticipating the
later usage in this passage. On the other hand, it is rather attractive to
consider the possibility that the word is used to indicate a deliberate
reversal. Cillicon, by gaining "mastery" over the piece of meat, is
falling under the mastery of Theagenes.

Simpler puns in other fragments seem to be intended to emphasize the author's meaning. Hegesilochus of Rhodes (F121) has no worth (*axioma*) in the eyes of his citizens but deems himself worthy (*axiōn*) of rule. The [Ardiaeans] (F40 from book 2) are devoted quite uncontrollably (*akratesteron*) to drink. Their lack of self-control (*akrasia*) becomes known to their enemies, the Celts, who give them a dinner laced with a drug, which puts them painfully out of control (*akratores*).

There are times when the pun ceases to be the vehicle of meaning and becomes the driver. The description of Philip's court (F225 from book 49) attributes to the Macedonians some flagrant habits of homosexuality. Are they included for any special reason or simply to prepare the reader for the grotesque pun that closes the description of their sexual habits? *Androphonoi* by nature, they were by habit *andropornoi.* Perhaps the best way to bring out this crude pun would be to translate the first word "men-killers," and the second "men-kissers," but it really means "men-whores." A few lines above, Theopompus had ridiculed the court of Philip with an even more telling jibe. Philip had built up an entourage of followers whom he called his companions or friends, *hetairoi.* By the rules of Greek, which observes grammatical gender, this noun is masculine. With the change of a letter or two at the end of the word, it becomes feminine and takes on the meaning "prostitute" or "courtesan." Naturally, Theopompus exploited the punning opportunity offered by this phenomenon: "Wherefore [because of their outrageous sexual mores] a person would rightly understand them to be not friends (*hetairous*), but girl-friends (*hetairas*)." It looks as if this pun had been introduced by Theopompus at least four books earlier. There was a special unit in Philip's army called foot companions (*pezetairoi*), or, pejoratively, "foot boy-friends." Now in F213 (from book 45) Theopompus ridiculed the ineffective Athenian general Chares as a self-indulgent sloth accusing him of taking with him on his expeditions "flute-girls, harp-girls, and foot girl-friends (*pezas hetairas*)." As G.T. Griffith noted, this is an unmistakable sideswipe at Philip and his *pezetairoi.*[40] It would be interesting to know how pervasive this sort of word-play really was.

In the case of the pun on *hetairoi*, it is quite possible that the attraction of the punning possibilities has influenced the author's decision to include or emphasize, even invent, descriptions of sexual mores for the Macedonian court. However that may be, there is another way in which word-play in the form of speculative etymology substantially influences the historian's content. F13 from the *Hellenica* derives the name of the Spartan serf-class, Helots (*Heilot-*) from the Greek word for marsh (*helos*) and finds a home for at least some of them in a place called *Helos* (The Marsh) that was situated near

Gytheum at the mouth of the Eurotas. The "etymology" was probably used as evidence to support Theopompus' contention that the Spartan state was founded on the enslavement of fellow Greeks.

More flagrant, and most amusing of all, is the way the history of a place can change depending on how a person chooses to pronounce its name. Pygela pronounced in the Ionic dialect, is derived from *pygoi*, buttocks (F59). Theopompus apparently thought of the place as Buttville, because Agamemnon allegedly founded the place by leaving some of his crew there after they had contracted a disease of the buttocks. However, pronounced in other Greek dialects, its name is Phygela, Flighttown. So pronounced, the history of the place immediately changes (Plin. *N.H.* 5.114): "founded by fugitives as the name implies."

THEOPOMPUS' NARRATIVE DISCOURSE

The modern view of Theopompus is distorted thanks to the process of selection that preserved the fragments. The majority of the identified quotations were chosen by ancient scholars or scandal-mongers for their sensational contents or points of style. Writers who borrowed from Theopompus' narrative, like Trogus Pompeius in places and, perhaps occasionally, Plutarch, rarely identify their source. In addition, it is possible that there has been stylistic influence on some later historians (Tacitus? Livy?), but the facts are largely beyond recovery in the absence of an extended passage of connected narrative. Many of the fragments, particularly those that come from Athenaeus, are moral judgments on states or individuals. Do they reveal anything about the nature of Theopompus' historical narrative?

The answer is yes – to a limited degree – provided the notions of integration and isolation introduced in chapter 2 are borne in mind. In general, the many moral evaluations can be shown with reasonable certainty to have been integrated with the narrative. Most of them are probably not isolated summations, digressions, or obituaries, but direct intrusions at critical moments of narrative flow. Their purpose can scarcely have been other than to direct the readers' feeling in reaction to the agents and decisions described.

A couple of the more striking examples provide illustrations. The two denunciations of the Thessalians (FF49, 162) come at places in the *Philippica* wherein Thessalian support for Philip was critical. F49 is from book 4, covering events of about 357/6 when Philip was still extremely vulnerable despite some spectacular early victories against Illyrians and Paeonians and various rivals for the throne. A concerted Thessalian resistance by land coupled with an Athenian naval

harassment would have caused him grave problems indeed. Fortunately for him, however, Athens was too distracted by the Social War,
and Thessaly was divided. Some of its leaders were friendly to Philip,
anxious for Macedonian support. It is at this moment that the
Thessalians are attacked as indolent, self-indulgent sots; the Pharsalians are expressly singled out for extreme vilification. Generally,
they seem to have been amongst Philip's most ardent supporters.
When the Thessalians reappear for further excoriation in book 26,
the period c. 347/6 is under scrutiny. By this time Philip was far
stronger than ten years earlier. Nevertheless, history had shown that
the region of Delphi into which he was now moving was potentially a
religious and military powder-keg. He had to be sure of his friends –
that they would not want to drop any lit political matches – in order to
bring off what could well prove to be the greatest diplomatic coup of
his career: seizing control of the Central Greek Amphictiony. Solid
Thessalian support was crucial, and it was forthcoming, but, once
again, the Thessalians are blasted for their indolent submission to
"the buffoon" (F162). The moral denunciations appear to be Theopompus' expressions of disgust over Thessalian cooperation with
Philip. They invite the reader to see the support for Philip as rooted in
indolence, and they must be seen therefore as fully integrated. They
attempt to manipulate the readers' opinions about the decisions
under consideration. In chapter 4 I shall point out a number of similar
examples. The conclusion is that this form of manipulation was a
feature of Theopompus' style.

A more precise idea of the nature of Theopompus' narrative
requires a continuous passage that is either borrowed from or heavily
dependent upon a section of Theopompus. Quite some time ago,
Felix Jacoby suggested (comment to F283) that Justin 21.1-5 is just
such an extended passage, derived from Theopompus' account of the
career of the younger Dionysius of Syracuse.

Justin's work is an epitome of an earlier (and obviously fuller) work
by Trogus Pompeius. It is, therefore, more than once removed from
the source, and it is impossible to estimate the violence done to
Trogus by Justin's epitomization. Nor has it ever been demonstrated
that Trogus followed any source systematically. His work was called
"The Philippic Histories," which seems clearly to indicate his stylistic
model and one of his sources, but echoes of Theopompus prove to be
sporadic whenever they can be tested. If Theopompus was Trogus'
main source for much of the mid-fourth century, he has probably
sewn in material gathered from various other places. Indeed, Justin
described his work as an anthology.[41] Of the five sections mentioned
by Jacoby, only two and five look to have a good chance of being taken

from the *Philippica*. Section one is merely an account of Dionysius' acquisition of power and could be adapted from Timaeus (c. 356–260 B.C.) or any other account of Sicilian history, and section three was assigned to Timaeus by Pearson on plausible but not conclusive grounds.[42] Of course, the inclusion of the material by Timaeus does not preclude the possibility that Theopompus reported it also, but while there are reasonable grounds to suspect influence from another author, the section must be disregarded. Again, section four gives a brief account of some contemporary Carthaginian history. It describes an attempted coup d'état by Hanno, who planned the murder of the entire Carthaginian Senate on the day of his daughter's wedding. The plot was foiled, and a second attempt was also exposed. Hanno was fiendishly tortured and executed as was his whole family. This is clearly an illustration of violent barbarian politics, but it probably does not come from Theopompus. No fragment suggests any substantial treatment of Carthaginian politics, and Theopompus was generally uninterested in barbarian history. On the other hand, Justin 21.2 and 5 do contain echoes of known fragments and exhibit interest in things typical of Theopompus. The two passages are reproduced below in the nineteenth-century translation of John Selby Watson.[43] The narrative will be interrupted here and there to point out the apparent echoes of Theopompus.

Justin 21.2 (the subject is Dionysius the Younger, a short time into his reign in Syracuse):

When his rivals were removed, he fell into indolence, and contracted, from excessive indulgence at table, great corpulence of body, and a disease in his eyes, so that he could not bear the sunshine, or dust, or even the brightness of ordinary daylight.

The emphasis on indolence and excessive indulgence (Lat. *segnitia* and *nimia luxuria*) sound like Theopompus' favourite concerns: *akrasia* and *truphē*. Furthermore, his wild extravagance leading to blindness was apparently emphasized by Theopompus (F283a, b).

Suspecting that, for these weaknesses, he was despised by his subjects, he proceeded to inflict cruelties upon them; not filling the gaols, like his father, with prisoners, but the whole city with dead bodies. Hence he became not more contemptible than hateful to every one.

The connection between the immorality and the decline in political respectability answered by extreme political violence, first, shows the thorough integration of the moral judgments with the political narrative and, second, is a line of reasoning that seems to be closely paralleled by F121 on Hegesilochus of Rhodes, who, lacking all esteem with the people, resorts to violently anti-social sexual games with his cronies. Similarly, FF224–5 explain Philip's political violence as a natural extension of his desperate immorality.

The Syracusans, in consequence, resolving to rebel against him, he long hesitated whether he should lay down the government or oppose them in arms; but he was compelled by the soldiery, who hoped for plunder from sacking the city, to march into the field. Being defeated, and trying his fortune again with no better success, he sent deputies to the people of Syracuse, with promises that "he would resign the government, if they would send persons to him with whom he might settle terms of peace."

Again the integration of moral judgment is to be noted. The corrupt tyrant (like Philip) is incapable of controlling his army. Their greed deprives him of choice and threatens the plundering of his own city.

Some of the principal citizens being accordingly sent for that purpose, he put them in the close confinement, and then, when all were off their guard, having no fear of hostilities, he despatched his army to devastate the city. A contest, in consequence, which was long doubtful, took place in the town itself, but the townsmen overpowering the soldiery by their numbers. Dionysius was obliged to retire, and fearing that he should be besieged in the citadel, fled away secretly, with all his king-like paraphernalia, to Italy.

His lack of self-control results in his disgrace and downfall. However, the arch-villain finds other unsuspecting people to exploit:

Being received, in his exile, by his allies the Locrians, he took possession of the citadel as if he were their rightful sovereign, and exercised his usual outrages upon them. He ordered the wives of the principal men to be seized and violated; he took away maidens on the point of marriage, polluted them, and then restored them to their betrothed husbands; and as for the wealthiest men, he either banished them or put them to death, and confiscated their property.

The theme of the violation of respectable women by the corrupt statesman is easily paralleled in the fragments (FF121, 143). In general, the entire narrative is the sort of thing the testimonies make it natural to expect from Theopompus. No one looks good. Dionysius is corrupt, his army is greedy, and the Locrians seem incredibly passive and gullible. The stubborn and successful resistance of the Syracusan citizenry to the rapacious army is not made heroic.

By section five the same Dionysius is back in power in Syracuse again, and one can only wonder what Trogus' source made of that (3.10 merely says he returned by treachery):

Dionysius, in the meantime, being re-established in Syracuse, and becoming every day more oppressive and cruel to the people, was assailed by a new band of conspirators. Laying down the government, he delivered up the city and army to the Syracusans, and, being allowed to take his private property with him, went to live in exile at Corinth; where, looking on the lowest station as the safest, he humbled himself to the very meanest condition of life.

This deliberate demeaning of himself is arguably more compatible with Theopompus' account of the story than the more widely read version in Timaeus. Polybius (12.4a.2 = F341) says that Timaeus had attacked Theopompus for making Dionysius flee from Syracuse to Corinth in a merchant ship (cf. D.S. 16.70.3) rather than a warship. In giving Dionysius a warship for the crossing, Timaeus was perhaps distancing himself from a version of the story that emphasized the straightened circumstances of the last years of the exiled tyrant's life. If that is true, Trogus' version is more compatible with Theopompus' than Timaeus' account. To return to Trogus, the remainder of section five attributes to Dionysius a life of futility in taverns and among prostitutes and indulging in unseasonable drink in a way reminiscent of known Theopompan discourse (FF20, 62, 143, 210, 213, and more):

He was not content with strolling about the streets, but would even stand drinking in them; he was not satisfied with being seen in taverns and impure houses, but would sit in them for whole days. He would dispute with the most abandoned fellows about the merest trifles, walk about in rags and dirt, and afford laughter to others more readily than he would laugh at them. He would stand in the shambles, devouring with his eyes what he was not able to purchase; he would wrangle with the dealers before the aediles, and do everything in such a manner as to appear an object of contempt rather than of fear. At last he assumed the profession of a schoolmaster and taught children in the open streets, either that he might continually be seen in public by those who feared him, or might be more readily despised by those who did not fear him; for though he had still plenty of the vices peculiar to tyrants, yet his present conduct was an affectation of vices, and not the effect of a nature, and he adopted it rather from cunning than from having lost the self-respect becoming a sovereign, having experienced how odious the names of tyrants are, even when they are deprived of power. He strove, therefore, to diminish the odium incurred from his past by the contemptibleness of his present life, not looking to honourable but to safe practices. Yet amidst all these arts of dissimulation, he was accused of aspiring to the sovereignty, and was left at liberty only because he was despised. (F283[b])

At best, therefore, the two sections of Justin examined above are an epitome of an adaptation of Theopompus' narrative, and at worst they are an illustration of the type of discourse other evidence suggests Theopompus wrote. The process of epitomization has quite possibly concentrated the sensational and rhetorical effects. A fuller version might well have seemed smoother and less tendentious.

Perhaps it would be instructive to consider the tattered remains of F291 in comparison with the sections of Trogus. This fragment is from Didymus' commentary on Demosthenes' *Philippic Orations*, and it gives a brief summary of the life and career of Hermeas of Atarneus, citing Theopompus' book (?)-ty-six, as the source (the papyrus is unreadable in many places). Jacoby assigned it tentatively to book 36 where information about the *Philippica*'s contents is even more sketchy than usual, but the relevant time-frame is c. 346–344. At this time Hermeas was at the height of his power and influence, and he was in communication with Philip, if not allied to him. It would be an appropriate time to introduce him to the narrative. However, it seems better to follow the majority of editors who find 46 a more suitable number to fill the gap in the papyrus, a book which records the events of the year 341, the year of Hermeas' death at the hands of the Great King (D.S. 16.52, who puts the events too early). In all likelihood, therefore, F291 is an obituary and following the terms established at the beginning of Chapter 2, it is a statement isolated from its surrounding narrative. However, the fragment is also a narrative in its own right. It goes from birth (by one reading) to death and characterizes Hermeas' life and reign in a few deft lines. As an obituary it can be expected to exhibit a high degree of rhetorical concentration, but as narrative it perhaps reveals in concentration some of the regular features of more normal Theopompan discourse. I translate its uncertain, lacunose text largely as restored by the Teubner[44] editors from the sadly tattered papyrus. One alternate restoration is shown in parentheses. I make no attempt to differentiate restored from surviving text. The scholar is urged to compare Jacoby's printed text with that of the new Teubner edition or to consult Harding's translation[45] for the exact details (4.63):

Hermeas set out on this path a eunuch and a Bithynian by race (or: disfigured in appearance) [short gap] thirdly [gap], with Eubulus he took Assos and its tower and Atarneus and its environs. Of all people this man accomplished the most violent and wicked things against all, both his citizens and others, doing away with some by poisoning and others by the noose. When the Chians and Mitylenaeans put him in charge of some land over which they were disputing, he played many drunken tricks with unpaid military expeditions and grievously insulted most of the Ionians. A money-grubber and money-changer, he did not hold his peace when the Chians fell into misfortune [large gap] to restore their established constitutions. However, he did not altogether escape nor get off with his impious and disgusting manners, but he was arrested and sent to the King where he was extensively tortured and ended his life in crucifixion.

CHAPTER FOUR

Theopompus' Moral and Political Views

This chapter turns from the content of the *Philippica* to its interpretation. The division between the two is convenient but not as sharp as it might seem. The decision a historian makes to include or exclude material is itself an interpretative act of sorts, and when it is necessary to "reconstruct" nearly 100 per cent of the historian's content, the reconstruction itself is an act (if not a crime) of interpretation. Nonetheless, it rarely seems to suffice to know what an author says. Otherwise, library holdings on Shakespeare would be confined to collections of his works and editorial exercises in which scholars focused exclusively on establishing the precise text of a poem or play. They are not so limited, of course. Any self-respecting collection on Shakespeare will have cases of exegetical studies, and they will only represent a fraction of what is available in journals, theses, and dissertations (not to mention films and live performances, interpretations of a different type). In Theopompus' case, directly or indirectly a significant amount of what he said survives, and, frequently, so does some idea of the context of the preserved remarks. What is the meaning of these words from the past in an ancient language?

A good opportunity to move from text to meaning is provided by the long description of Philip's court (quoted pp. 165–6, below). It well illustrates the problems of interpretation for which a reliable analytical method is needed. Whether it is read in English or in Greek, there is not going to be much disagreement over its superficial meaning – the immediate impression gained from a first perusal of the text. It shows Theopompus' disapproval of the behaviour of Philip and his courtiers; as people he regarded them as the worst humans alive. More meaning is derived, if somewhat tentatively, from the context. The sources place the diatribe at the beginning of book 49 when Theopompus must have just finished his account of Philip's northern conquests. He was turning to the final confrontation with the southern Greeks at this stage of the *Philippica*. What, then, is to be made of the characterization of Philip's henchmen? "Fabulously wealthy, but lusting for more." The comment suggests that Philip's "foreign policy," his decision to mobilize against Athens, was driven, at least in part, by the insatiable greed of desperadoes. Presumably, the historian did not approve of Philip's foreign policy. So, the context implies a political judgment on what looks superficially like a simple moral comment. If the passage is set in the much broader context of the whole work and its main theme, further interpretative problems arise. This attack on Philip is by far the fullest treatment of vitriol in the fragments. Perhaps the centrality of Philip and his court to the work is enough to explain the length of the diatribe. However, it exhibits signs of incoherence not easily explained by observations about Philip's importance. Theopompus repeatedly remarks on the disorderly lives of Philip and his men. Repetition is time consuming. Odd, then, that he should conclude the diatribe with a claim that he is in a hurry to get to other pressing matters. The alleged haste itself looks peculiar given how rambling the *Philippica* really was. Further, the style of the diatribe is occasionally garish. At least one ancient commentator found some of the puns in it offensive (T44, F225C). Perhaps there is a less obvious meaning lurking at some distance behind the words.

The apparent contradictions, the trenchancy, the disorganization, and, most of all, the devotion of such an enormous work to a topic the historian professes to hate all suggest conflict. A Jungian psychologist might argue that Theopompus detests Philip with his conscious mind, but unconsciously admires him.[1] In the next chapter, I shall point out fragments that characterize Philip as a poor general who does not plan things and frequently enters battle drunk. How did his armies succeed so formidably then? "Philip was lucky," Theopompus would probably have replied; and yet, the description of Philip's luck betrays fascination, admiration perhaps (F237 = Athen. 3.77D–E): "in Philip's domain around Bisaltia, Amphipolis and Macedonian Grastonia the fig-trees bear figs, the vines grapes, and the olive trees olives in the middle of spring when they ought to be flowering, and Philip was fortunate in everything."

There is more here than a simple dichotomy between words and meaning. The extent of the conflict between the introduction and the rest of the work depends on the reconstruction of the introduction, and the claim that F237 about Philip's luck explains his successful generalship depends on the observation that the fragment belongs to book 54 when Theopompus was describing the aftermath of Philip's greatest victory (from a Greek perspective), Chaeronea, that is, that F237 is part of Theopompus' explanation of Philip's success. In other words, the interpretation is based on the reconstruction. At this stage the world can become very misty. There is a very real danger of getting lost in the fog and falling down rabbit holes. In the words of Lionel Pearson:

"Writing books about books that don't exist" sounds like a suitable occupation for Wonderland, and it deserves an explanation that would satisfy Alice. "How can you understand the books that exist," they might have told her, "unless you read the non-existent books first?" "Yes, I know, " Alice might reply, "but there are so many lost Greek historians."[2]

Pearson goes on to show that the scholar who wishes to "read the non-existent books first" must have a method. For him, the best method is to work not from the fragments but from the later authors who are generally recognized to have used the author whose work is begin reconstructed. Reading these later sources, the scholar attempts to peer behind them, asking, as Pearson puts it, "What does this presuppose?" Pearson's book is a demonstration of how useful this method can be in the hands of a skilled philologist, but Theopompus does not lend himself as well to this approach as does Timaeus, Pearson's principal subject. There are no continuous narrative sources of any substance that demonstrably follow the *Philippica* exclusively or extensively. Trogus probably used Theopompus but not to the exclusion of other sources, and Trogus' history only exists in the form of Justin's epitome.[3] On the other hand, the fragments of Theopompus survive in substantially greater numbers than do those of many other lost histories; this is particularly true of the *Philippica*. At the beginning of chapter 2 I proposed a general method for gaining maximum meaning from the fragments. It involved defining the context, then asking what the fragment would have to mean in that context. I also noted the importance of evaluating the fragments by comparing them with one another to establish the degree or intensity of meaning.

The urgent need for this method can be illustrated from a brief survey of attempts by scholars to make sense of the *Philippica*. A case in point is the treatment of the Athenians (for example, F213). The Athenians enjoy the corruption of their inept and profligate general Chares. Their young men frequent the brothels; when they are a little older, they are at boozing, dice, and similar incontinence; and the entire populace (*demos*) spends more on festivals than the management of the state. Why did Theopompus attack the Athenians, and where on a putative scale of bitterness should this verbal assault be placed? One thesis (Momigliano's) made Theopompus an Isocratean Panhellenist who wanted Greece to unite and attack Persia under Philip's leadership. The Athenians, of course, resisted Philip, however ineffectively. Therefore, the Athenians were vilified for failing to unite in the great enterprise. According to Kurt von Fritz, however, Theopompus was an aristocrat who hated democracy. Because F213 specifically mentions the corruption of the whole *demos* (τὸν δὲ δῆμον ἅπαντα), it is argued, the attack is really on democracy. The Athenians were defamed because they were governed by a democracy. Can both views be true? According to an argument I advanced some years ago, the Athenians were denounced because they did not exert themselves against Philip sufficiently. This view focused attention on the relative intensity of the attack, the indolence and corruption attributed to the Athenians, the complaints about the dissipation of state resources on festivals, and the uselessness of their most popular general at the time (c. 343/2) when Athenian hostilities with Philip were beginning in earnest. Another view, advanced by Michael Flower, sees a world of utter corruption in the *Philippica*. Philip was a villain who needed no ability. When he needed friends, he simply seduced them into more debauchery from their existing states of corruption, and, generally, his enemies were too indolent to offer him serious resistance. In this view, morality is the overriding concern. The Athenians were attacked because of their morals not their morals because of their politics. This approach is very similar to Connor's. For him Theopompus wrote "history without heroes."[4] From this perspective a final possibility suggests itself: Theopompus despised everyone; therefore, his attack on the Athenians requires no explanation. It is motivated by nothing special – nothing beyond the historian's disgust with every human subject in his work.

This last proposal is an extreme view. It will not withstand close scrutiny, but it is worth stating for two reasons. The first is that it *is* extreme; a careful retreat from it offers hope of a more productive systematization of the information in the fragments. The second is that it has arbitrarily reduced all the signals from the fragments to the same level of what the information theorist would call noise. What is needed is an effective criterion by which to sort out the true information from the "noise."[5] An example should help. Imagine a painter who depicts a great variety of images and forms on many canvasses but uses only one colour, black. Now, obviously, it will be foolish to argue that the painter sees anything sinister in the human left foot "because he always uses black to paint that foot." Of course, all left feet are black in his paintings, just like everything else. Blackness is not information; it is noise. Now suppose that this imaginary painter changes his style a little. He begins to experiment with shades of grey. Most figures remain black, or charcoal grey, but a very few are done in light grey – one here, one there. The eye is immediately drawn to these grey figures. Now it is legitimately possible to look at the various shadings in search of meaning. What did these figures represent to the artist that prompted him to soften his colour? Closer examination makes it easier to differentiate between the charcoal grey and the black.

Theopompus used his own kind of black for most of his characters. His moral and condemning bent is obvious to anyone who glances at the *testimonia* and fragments. Nepos grouped Theopompus with Timaeus, calling him "most malicious" (F288). Plutarch considers praise credible in Theopompus because it is so rare and blame so all-pervasive (F333). Cicero finds it hard to think of anything more bitter than Theopompus (T40); and Lucian saw him as an overzealous prosecuting attorney, always attacking his heroes (T25a). For Dionysius of Halicarnassus he was comparable to a judge who is more searching than Rhadamanthys in the underworld or to a (military) doctor who probes and cauterizes wounds very deeply (T20). Other testimonies could be added. The agreement of these ancient critics has not escaped notice.[6] It offers reassuring illumination of the fragments, otherwise surrounded by total darkness. A great many of them come from only one source: Athenaeus. Without the confirmation of the *testimonia* there would be grave doubts about the sensational impression that they give. Of course, a full understanding of Theopompus' historiography is not possible without a miraculous discovery of his lost works; but because the ancient testimonies conform so closely to the impressions conveyed by many of the fragments, it is reasonable to expect something reliable from a careful analysis of their contents, however one-sided the ensuing picture might ultimately be.

Since Theopompus disliked so many people, those few people or things (if any) that he admired or, at least, on which he heaped less than total abuse provide the greatest meaning. Unfortunately, the full meaning will probably still be beyond recovery. The analogy of the painter works in another way. The black figures themselves can only be seen against a lighter background. If the whole canvas is black, there are no discernible figures. Evil is only recognizable with reference to good. If Theopompus denounces lack of self-control, it follows that he would approve of temperate behaviour if he could ever find it. Otherwise, he "denounces" nothing; he merely writes about things.

In sum, there are two main problems connected with the interpretation of fragments. One is the need to explain a relatively short piece of text in an alien context, and the other is the need to generalize about the author's typical treatment of a topic with only a limited number of examples. Thus, despite the relative length of the description of Philip and his court, it had to be placed in context and related to the argument of the *Philippica*. However, that "argument" must be recovered largely from the fragments, of which this is a major representative. To put it succinctly: the context must be used to interpret the fragment, but if the very context is reconstructed from the fragment, the fragment is being used to interpret itself. The danger is a certain circularity of argument. With reference to the treatment of the Athenians, there is another danger: a certain limitation of vision that comes from a premature focusing on a specific problem. How Theopompus regarded individual X may be a useful question, but surely it is necessary first to address the broader question of how he treated individuals in general? Indeed, rather than begin with certain specific questions, offer answers, and grope aimlessly in search of general principles, it would be better to work in the opposite direction: launch a systematic search for Theopompus' general ideals, or values, and use them to throw light on the various specific problems.

It remains to show that this can really be done. Theopompus' attitude to the sacred can be taken as a test case. An obvious place to begin is a treatise called *On the Treasure Plundered from Delphi*, a work that receives further attention in the next chapter.[7] It was a diatribe perhaps the size of a pamphlet that had few heroes, probably none. The fragments suggest a catalogue of sacrilegious outrages perpetrated by the Phocian mercenaries during the Sacred War. Athenaeus preserves three substantial quotations from it (FF247–9); and FF232 and 312 (of uncertain origin) relate the fate of Archidamus, the Spartan king who did nothing to stop the shrine's desecration, indeed, whose wife profited handsomely from it. The salient themes are simply stated. One precious item after another is identified and details of the donor(s) and circumstances of the dedication are given. Thereby, the value of the object is provided, not in monetary terms, but as an expression of its meaning to the shrine, to Apollo, and to the donor. Then the fate of the treasure is detailed. Some goes to Archidamus' wife, Dinicha, to win her support in influencing her husband in favour of the Phocian mercenaries. Some goes to Chares, the Athenian general, as a reward for defeating Adaeus, the "Rooster," captain of Philip's mercenaries. Chares spends the money on parties for the Athenians. Many unique items are bestowed by the generals on their sexual playthings. The sacrilege nearly went further. Phayllus wanted his flute-girl Bromias to play at the sacred festival itself, but "the people" halted the outrage. Some of the plunderers or at least their accomplices and favourites met with ignominy or worse. Physcidas, the "pretty-boy," was later prostituted to Philip's court, but he left "unrewarded." Pharsalia, the dancing girl, was torn to pieces by certain seers when she went to Metapontum wearing her ill-gotten gains, a golden crown of ivy-leaves, a dedication of the Lampsacenes. Archidamus, struck down in battle, was not permitted burial, perhaps the greatest ignominy of all for a Spartan king. Generally speaking, the two most powerful states of southern Greece, Athens and Sparta, were allied to these Phocian "temple-robbers." So, insofar as they figured in the work, it would have been as accomplices. When the temple-robbing came to an end, Philip let the worst criminals, the mercenary soldiers and their generals, go unpunished and exacted punishment and reparation from the relatively helpless Phocian villagers who were left behind. He broke with the sacred traditions and took for himself the two votes on the Amphictionic Council that had formerly belonged to the Phocians. All the actors in this sordid drama look like villains, and Theopompus probably made them out to be so. However, the apparent complaints about the irreverent behaviour of the Phocians and others will only have meaning if Theopompus himself revered the oracle and the venerable traditions for which it stood. Had he made it clear in the work that he did not care about the oracle because it too was a place of (say) hypocrisy and corruption, telling of its plundering and desecration would have meant little to him. There would seem to be little purpose in writing such a treatise unless the author cared about something, most probably, the shrine itself.

This example suggests one principle of interpretation: a critical preoccupation with something negative implies that Theopompus would have asserted the opposite as a positive value. The criticism of sacrilege in *On the Treasure Plundered from Delphi* implies that the historian venerated the shrine and expected others to do the same. Even more, it suggests that he was a man of reverence for things traditionally held sacred by the Greeks. This contention can be supported by reference to three fragments (or, more precisely, a part of one long fragment and two other substantial ones in their entirety). The first item is a brief remark in the diatribe mentioned above. Philip and his henchmen "readily assumed the odium of perjury and cheating in the most august sanctuary." According to Greek custom, an oath taken in a sacred place was more solemn, and a person offering to take an oath could seek to gain credibility by challenging his opponent to name the location for the swearing.[8] Now Theopompus had already characterized the Macedonian leaders as swindlers in the preceding sentence. Therefore, the additional remark is climactic. They are not only perjurers, but they will take false oaths on a "stack of bibles" or "their mothers' graves." They have no respect for things traditionally venerated by society. Theopompus was shocked at this, or, at least, he expected his readers to be. Either way the point is made. All that it is possible to recover are the attitudes and postures he assumes when writing. The beliefs of his inner heart are beyond recovery.

The second item is more substantial and delightful enough to deserve attention in its own right. It is a long quotation or, more properly, a close paraphrase found in Porphyry's *On Abstinence* (2.16 = F344). It provides a rare opportunity to get some sense of the smoothness and clarity of which Theopompus' narrative style was capable, so different from the turbulence of his more intense moral excursions, and a more refined look at his religious ideas. Whatever the context was, a digression it certainly seems to have been, and it is hard to imagine Theopompus telling the story and disapproving of its message. A certain Magnesian (or Magnes) of Asia, the story goes, was rich in cattle and was accustomed to making great and splendid sacrifices to the gods each year, partly because of the abundance of his possessions and partly because of his piety, and desire to please the gods. He went to Delphi, and after slaughtering a hundred oxen to the god and honouring Apollo lavishly, he approached the oracle to consult it. Supposing that he of all human beings was showing the greatest respect to the gods, he asked the Pythia to signify which person honoured the god best and most zealously and who made the god's favourite sacrifices; he naturally expected first prize. The priestess replied that the person was Clearchus, who lived at Methydrium in Arcadia. Completely thunderstruck, Magnes conceived a desire to meet this man and learn how he conducted his sacrifices. He went speedily to Methydrium, which he found contemptible for its smallness and humbleness. He could not imagine how the entire town, much less one of its private citizens, could honour the gods more satisfactorily or splendidly than himself. Nevertheless, he met Clearchus and asked him to tell how he honoured the gods. Clearchus described how he completed and zealously burned offerings at the appointed time; each month he observed the new moons garlanded and washed Hermes and Hecate and the other sacred objects left him by his forebears. And he said that he honoured them with frankincense, barley cake, and buns. Every year he made the customary public sacrifices, omitting not a single festival. In these same celebrations he revered the gods not by killing oxen or slaughtering sacred animals but by offering whatever was at hand. He took special care to apportion out to the gods the first fruits of all his crops as they ripened, gifts of the earth, some of which he gave intact, some of which he burned. So goes Porphyry's account of Theopompus' story. Porphyry saw in it a divine rejection of animal sacrifice, but for Theopompus the lesson was more likely that the gods want the service of dedicated people however humble their means and are more impressed by it than lavish ostentation. Motive is, of itself, not the issue, for both Clearchus (implicitly) and Magnes (explicitly) were motivated by piety. Clearchus' piety is characterized by its assiduous dedication: no festival is omitted great or small year in and year out. The gods looked for dedication; so too did Theopompus.

The third item, almost as substantial as the last, equally dramatic in a different way, is even less ambiguous because it contains a lengthy direct quotation, and the historian's own words leave little doubt of his opinions. It is F31 concerning the madness of King Cotys of Thrace. Despite his preoccupation with pleasure, he had maintained frequent sacrifice to the gods, and his life was one of pure happiness (εὐδαίμων καὶ μακαριστός), words usually held in reserve by the Greeks to describe the rare state of a genuinely blessed existence. However, he undermined it all by his act of "blasphemy" in announcing that he was going to marry Athena. On another occasion he brutally murdered his wife in a fit of jealousy. Whether he committed the murder before or after the attempted marriage with Athena is not specified, but Harpocration puts it late in his life and in his period of madness. Theopompus' language leaves no doubt that Cotys' beatific existence ended with his act of insane blasphemy. His choice of words suggests that for him happiness was incompatible with sacrilegious behaviour. Even non-Greeks like the Saintsburgers need to respect the gods and are blessed when they do.

Finally, a few matters of procedure remain. Working carefully with the text of the fragments requires translation for the Greekless reader. In this chapter the translations will generally be my own. For the more advanced scholar the Greek will be given in parentheses where it is thought useful. Words that do not go conveniently into English will occasionally be transliterated and the opportunity will thereby be given the Greekless reader to form an independent opinion by examining their usage. Word-studies will help, but Theopompus was not a philosopher, as has been pointed out.[9] Philosophers such as Plato and Socrates spent a good deal of time trying to define words and use them consistently. Whether or not they succeeded, Theopompus probably never tried. Ancient critics of his style suggest that his writing could be turbulent or outlandish at times. The fragments often show an indiscriminate extravagance of language that suggests more of a striving for the pungent expression of vehement indignation than an attempt to develop a systematic moral philosophy. "He is always using his bludgeon upon the characters of his drama," said Gilbert Murray, "there is more denunciation than subtle analysis."[10] The fragments confirm this judgment. Two Macedonian agents, Timolaus of Thebes and Thrasydaeus the Thessalian, are denounced in superlative terms. Thrasydaeus is called "a very great flatterer (κόλακα μέγιστον)"; and, of Timolaus, Theopompus says:

Not a few people have become debauched (ἀσελγεῖς) in their daily lives and drinking, but I know of no one in public life more lacking in self-control (ἀκρατέστερον), more gluttonous, or more of a slave to pleasure (δοῦλος ... μᾶλλον τῶν ἡδονῶν) if not ... Timolaus.

This last quotation is F210 from book 45 of the *Philippica*. When Theopompus wrote it, had he forgotten his earlier judgment of Straton of Sidon from book 15 (F114)? "Straton surpasses all mankind in addiction to pleasure (ἡδυπαθεία) and sumptuous living." Or again, in book 4, it is not an individual, but all the townsmen of Pharsalus who are "of all mankind the most idle and extravagant (F49)." Later, in book 49, he describes Philip (F224) as "of all mankind the worst home manager." No doubt the impression of the historian's uncritical use of verbal excesses would be considerably strengthened if all fifty-eight books of the *Philippica* had survived. This does not necessarily mean that he had no moral system, only that he did not express it by means of a rigid control of his vocabulary.

A failing that Theopompus found in many people is something he calls *akrasia* (ἀκρασία). In the fragment quoted below (F40), I translate it as "lack of control" or "lack of self-control." This expression is of central importance to an understanding of the historian's political and moral views. Indeed, in the preceding chapter it was shown that F40 is probably a programmatic introduction of a key concept and its vocabulary.[11] (F40 = Athen. 10.443B–C):

The [Ardiaeans] have acquired 300,000 *prospeletai*, just like helots. They get drunk every day, hold parties and devote themselves quite uncontrollably (ἀκρατέστερον) to eating and drinking. Wherefore, the Celts, when they made war on them, being aware of their lack of self-control (ἀκρασίαν) instructed all their soldiers to prepare an extremely lavish dinner in a tent.

They put into the food a toxic herb which had the power to devastate the bowels and induce diarrhoea. When this happened, some of them were captured and slain by the Celts, and others threw themselves into the river, having lost control of their bellies (ἀκράτορες τῶν γαστέρων γενόμενοι).

It is always questionable whether an intermediary like Athenaeus has copied his source faithfully. Has he tampered with the text? Are the puns his and not those of Theopompus? There is a difficulty with this text, but not a serious one.[12] More disturbing, perhaps, the transitions from the *prospeletai* to the scene of the Celts preparing the meal and from there to the arrival of the unsuspecting victims are far too abrupt, and it seems likely that Athenaeus has omitted some details. Despite these uncertainties, there are four or five reasons for believing that the language very closely follows the original text. None of them is conclusive, but together they make a cumulative case. On stylistic grounds, the elaborate pun on *akrasia* sounds like the interweaving of letter sounds (συμπλοκή τῶν φωνηέντων γραμμάτων) that Dionysius of Halicarnassus said bedevilled Theopompus' moral diatribes (*Pomp.* 6.10 = T20). The word, not to say the form, *akrasia* (as opposed to the alternative ἀκρατεία) is a favourite of Theopompus. Furthermore, even in places where the word is not found, lack of self-control is a theme of many of the fragments, finding expression in such phrases as "slave of pleasures." F225 provides an opportunity to compare a long quotation of Theopompus by Athenaeus with a citation of the same lengthy passage by Polybius. Both authors give similar wording and are clearly following the same original very closely. In one place, Athenaeus drops two words, and an abrupt transition is created in a way roughly similar to the two awkward transitions noted above. Finally, this fragment exhibits a structural parallel with the diatribe against Philip early in book 49, and in general terms the discussion that follows should leave little doubt that it well represents the style and thinking of Theopompus.

Spartans were trained to a rigid regimen of self-denial. *Akrasia*, therefore, emerges as the opposite of Spartan asceticism in a pathologically one-sided account of the career of King Archidamus of Sparta, again attributed to Theopompus by Athenaeus (F232 = Athen. 12.536C–D). Apparently, Theopompus emphasized Archidamus' luxurious lifestyle and interpreted his decision to become a soldier of fortune in Italy as a spurning of the traditional asceticism of Sparta. He was left dead on a battlefield without the honour of burial. Strangely, Theopompus chose to report that Archidamus' friends, the Tarentines, offered much money for the return of his body, but he did not allow the obvious esteem of the Tarentines to mitigate his condemnation of Archidamus. Here, perhaps, Archidamus' affiliation with Delphi's spoilers, the Phocian mercenaries, has coloured the picture; and F312 includes dark hints of Apollo's wrath against the Spartan king.

If lack of self-control is programmatic to the *Philippica*, it would be worthwhile to trace the origins of this moral concept and its development into the fourth century, for it certainly did not originate with Theopompus. There is a much earlier and very substantial characterization of the condition in the *Hippolytus* of Euripides written in the 420s B.C. In that play the heroine, Phaedra, is smitten with unrequited love for her stepson Hippolytus. She struggles not to give in to the illicit passion, but there are destructive side effects nevertheless. She remains on a sickbed, refusing to eat. Her friends and attendant nurse are all distressed. Hippolytus is devoted to the manly sport of hunting, and Phaedra talks agitatedly about wanting to go hunting. To the nurse, who as yet knows nothing of Phaedra's love, these are the words of madness (μανία, l. 214). Goddesses like Artemis might enjoy the hunt, but respectable Greek women did not. Hippolytus loves horses, and Phaedra wants to tame horses. "Which of the gods," wonders the nurse (l. 238), "is deranging [Phaedra's] wits (παρακόπτει φρένας)." Throughout the scene Phaedra is shown as feeble (she has not eaten for days), distracted (the chorus calls it a wandering of her wits, πλάνον φρενῶν, l. 283), and frequently demanding minute attentions from her frustrated nurse.

To be sure, Euripides does not use the word *akrasia* to describe Phaedra's state, but the words of the soliloquy she gives after the nurse first leaves her alone on the stage are a perfect description of it.[13] The central idea of her speech is the diametric opposite of the view known to have been advanced by Socrates, probably at about the same time as the writing of the *Hippolytus*. To anticipate the argument a little, Plato makes Socrates criticize and reject a certain view of morality in the *Protagoras* (352A–53A) that is very similar to the one advanced by Phaedra. It is primarily through Socrates' argument and secondarily through Phaedra's own language that the word *akrasia* comes to be used of her condition. She addresses the chorus, announcing that she is going to reveal some of her private thoughts. She says that having good sense is quite possible, but the problem is that although "we know and recognize what is right, we do not toil it through (ἐκπονοῦμεν); sometimes we are lazy, and sometimes we prefer some pleasure over honour" (ll. 377–82). After further remarks, she explains how she tried to deal with her illicit love for Hippolytus. She tried to conceal it; then she tried to conquer it by being sensible (σωφρόνειν), but she could not conquer love (Κύπριν κρατῆσαι). The word for "conquer" can also mean "control," and it is from the same root as *akrasia*.

For Socrates Phaedra's faith in knowledge was inadequate. In his view the person who truly knows "the good" cannot help but act in conformity with it and its requirements. True knowledge of "the good" was too overpowering a thing for its influence to be denied. People (or, more properly, people's emotions and desires) were not out of control; they were ignorant (or not being exposed to the influence of true knowledge). Phaedra's claim to know "the good" was an act of self-delusion if she then proceeded to do wrong. As Socrates would have it, either "the good" she claimed to know was not the true one, or her knowledge of it must have been imperfect. In short, he saw *akrasia* in the pure sense of "lack of self-control" as impossible. Only imperfect knowledge makes improper behaviour possible; perfect knowledge of good makes the choice of evil unthinkable.

Theopompus was very likely aware of Socrates' views. He knew Plato's dialogues and attacked them (FF259, 275, 295, 359). He himself was an admirer of Antisthenes, Plato's rival for the leadership of the Socratic school after the master's death and, apparently, more of a moralist than Plato. Another product of the Socratic school was Aristotle himself, Plato's greatest student and close contemporary of Theopompus. He wrote a lengthy analysis of *akrasia* in his *Nichomachean Ethics*.[14] Aristotle's careful systematization and definition of the moral vocabulary helps in identifying the concepts in Theopompus where they are not expressed in such philosophically precise language.

Aristotle divides immorality into three main headings: vice (κακία), lack of self-control (ἀκρασία), and bestiality (θηριότης). Vice is the opposite of manly excellence (ἀρετή), a broad category whose precise meaning is not important here. Lack of self-control is used as an absolute term with reference to the sense of touch (primarily) and taste (secondarily). That is, if it is simply said that a person has *akrasia*, it is assumed that the lack of self-control refers to the bodily senses or to the desire to eat and drink excessively. Otherwise, it is qualified by saying, for example, "he is uncontrolled in anger" or "in his desire for honour" and the like. Bestiality is a rare condition. It resembles a very extreme case of *akrasia*. Bestial people live only on the level of sensation (αἴσθησις). Like the animals they have little or no memory and make no long-range plans. Some barbarians who have never been exposed to the civilizing influence of Hellenism exhibit it. A condition similar to *akrasia* is *akolasia* (ἀκολασία), lack of self-discipline. The difference is that the undisciplined is so by choice, for Aristotle guardedly accepts a notion similar to Socrates', namely, that *akrasia* is at least aided by ignorance; choice is not possible if a person knows nothing else. However, his distinction between *akrasia* and *akolasia* proves to be very subtle, for earlier he had argued that once the person has chosen the life of *akolasia*, he is not likely to leave it (3.5.14–15). In addition, *akolasia* parallels *akrasia* in its relationship to the sense of touch and taste (3.10.8–10). In practical terms, therefore, it will be difficult for an observer to distinguish between the two conditions. Aristotle obviously does not go as far as the Socratic idea that knowledge makes *akrasia* impossible, for he recognizes it as a true condition of immorality. However, he suggests somewhat tentatively that the *actions* of the uncontrolled could be called immoral, but that the *people* are not necessarily so themselves, for they do not exercise choice. He also points out that a person can be said to know and not know at the same time. Intoxication or madness can temporarily suppress knowledge or render it ineffective. His concept of madness resembles that of Euripides. It can be a temporary state of mental derangement brought on by a passion such as love. A sister condition to *akrasia* is softness (μαλακία) or the excessive enjoyment of luxury. Its opposite is toughness or endurance (καρτερία). This too echoes Euripides, whose Phaedra finds laziness and the enjoyment of daily pleasures to be a cause of a person's losing control, and, conversely, for Euripides the way to control is to "toil through" (ἐκπονεῖν).

As a historian Theopompus will pose as an impartial observer of human conduct. Probably he will not be interested in morality in the abstract so much as in specific examples. Many of the incidents that he will report will be from politics, the public life of leading statesmen, and the question will arise: how much does private incontinence influence public behaviour? F143 shows how private (sexual) *akrasia* can interfere with political effectiveness. It concerns the general and politician Charidemus:

He was seen day by day to be cultivating a debauched lifestyle even so as to be always drinking and drunk. He would dare to debauch respectable women. Indeed, he sank to such a level of *akrasia* that he set about asking for a captured boy, who was very attractive and graceful in appearance, from the Council of the Olynthians.

The arrangement of the fragment seems to be climactic, and one may wonder how desiring a captured boy is more outrageous than corrupting respectable women (γυναῖκας ἐλευθέρας). The progression is not from one misdemeanour to a more serious to a yet more serious one, but rather from private incontinence (drinking) to mischief with negative social implications (debauching respectable women) to the ultimate degradation: taking one's depravity out into the open world of politics. Charidemus' appearance before the Olynthian Council with a request is a political event. His sexual appetite is disrupting his public career. The progression from private incontinence to a loss of political equilibrium parallels in a small way the total loss of self-determination suffered by the [Ardiaeans] thanks to their Sybaritic excesses.

However, *akrasia* did not necessarily work like Christ's leaven, which "Leaveneth the whole lump [of dough]." For Theopompus a person's life could be uncontrolled behind closed doors but the opposite in public. The famous Athenian general and statesman Alcibiades was praised by Theopompus (F288 = Nep. *Alcib*. 11), no doubt largely for his energetic generalship. But the historian will have scarcely been ignorant of his personal life, famous for its wild self-indulgence. Callistratus (died 361 BC.), one of the architects of the Second Athenian Confederacy, is a clearer example (F97 = Athen. 4.166E). He was "in pleasure uncontrolled (ἀκρατής), but diligent (ἐπιμελής) in political business." I shall return to diligence in considering what Theopompus approved. In the meantime it is worth observing that the historian's use of terminology is un-Aristotelian. Callistratus seems to fit Aristotle's category of *akolasia*, lack of self-discipline, better than *akrasia*. The undisciplined are so by choice; therefore, they should be able to "switch on or off" more readily than the one who is truly out of control. This is what was to be expected: Theopompus moves from one Aristotelian category to another without adjusting his vocabulary. He is not a philosopher and certainly not an Aristotelian.

Indeed, there is no hint that Theopompus knew of Aristotle's distinction between *akolasia* and *akrasia*. The two terms were synonymous for him. Of seven noteworthy places where Theopompus used the expression *akolasia* (or its cognate ἀκόλαστοι), six provide a context that illustrates the type of undisciplined activity meant. It is most commonly associated with excessive drinking and only slightly less frequently with dicing and desporting with flute-girls (FF62, 134, 139, 162, 185, 236). Like *akrasia* it becomes the means and opportunity whereby the undisciplined become dominated by their enemies. In an important passage, one to which Plutarch took grave offence (Plut. *Mor*. 856B), Theopompus explains the ease with which Philip annexed Thessaly (F162); he did not conquer it by military prowess, but instead, knowing that the Thessalians were already undisciplined, he prepared them parties and so conquered them by corruption.

In the analogy of the painter, these are the darker figures – or some of them. To determine whether this has been the black or merely the dark grey, some contrast will be useful. In other words, to find levels or shades of denunciation in the fragments, it is important to ascertain what things, if any, met with Theopompus' approval. There is a limited choice of fragments with which to begin, but perhaps the most useful is his statement about how people get to be good at what they do. F342 (= Polyb. 12.27.8–9) suggests that experience is the best teacher: "Who has experienced the most risks is best in war, and the most powerful orator is he who has endured the most political fights. The same principle is true for doctors and navigators." The choice of these four professions suggests that perhaps another principle besides experience is also in operation. The incompetent soldier will probably not live to experience the "most risks," and poor navigators will soon find the reefs or the sea-bed for their permanent homes. Similar, metaphorical shipwrecks are usually in store for political and medical quacks. Experience teaches, and longevity and endurance are a test of quality.

The *Hellenica* contained a story abut King Agesilaus spurning certain luxurious foods, which Athenaeus introduces as an illustration of Spartan control over the belly, as if the context was not Agesilaus' personal greatness but the famous Spartan asceticism. More informative are remarks recorded about Lysander in Athenaeus (F20 = Athen. 12.543B–C) and Plutarch (F333 = Plut. *Lys.* 30.2). The passage in Athenaeus reveals the formulaic expressions that describe the Theopompan moral man. He is a dedicated worker (φιλόπονος), not a flatterer of kings but a man who can cultivate both private citizens and kings (θεραπεύειν δυνάμενος καὶ ἰδιώτας καὶ βασιλεῖς). He is moderate (σώφρων) and above all pleasures (τῶν ἡδονῶν ἁπασῶν κρείττων). Despite his supreme power in Greece, there is no city where he will be found to have been an addict of sexual pleasures (ὁρμήσας πρὸς τὰς ἀφροδισίους ἡδονάς), nor was he given to intoxication and unseasonable drinking (μέθαις καὶ πότοις ἀκαίροις χρησάμενος). In chapter 2 I noted that the passage from Plutarch looks like a continuation of this same encomium. Plutarch says that Lysander's poverty, which became apparent upon his death, made his quality (ἀρετή) the more manifest. The reckoning of his estate proved that he had not enriched himself from the quantities of allied money that had been under his control. This is high praise for a ruler. However, it reflects primarily on his personal morality; the only thing it says about him as a governor is that he did not embezzle state funds. Plutarch's remark at the end of the quotation, "So records Theopompus, whom a person would believe more readily when he praises than when he finds fault. He is happier at fault-finding than praising," suggests the rarity of passages like this. So, while *akrasia* usually undermines good government, self-control does not of itself promote it.

At first it seems a little odd to argue that Lysander's administration was not applauded in view of the obvious praise of Lysander himself. However, the remarks are apparently from the end of the *Hellenica* when the topic was not Lysander's governance of the Aegean, but the circumstances of his death. As I argued in chapter 2 Theopompus probably donned his orator's hat to make a general statement about the man and his qualities and failings as exemplified through his career. If Theopompus was true to the maxim cited by Polybius (F342), it was open to him to claim that Lysander had succeeded in the skills for which he had been trained in the narrow and rigorous Spartan system of education. It taught personal self-control, good soldiery, and unquestioning obedience to authority, but not the arts of diplomacy and statecraft. Neither Lysander nor Agesilaus had had experience in government as the Aegean Greeks knew it. Therefore, Theopompus probably saw these men as capable of success only as soldiers and disciplinarians, not as diplomats or administrators.

If Theopompus is dissatisfied with people who are out of control, then it follows that he wants to see some sort of control in people. It would be useful to know how he thought they should gain control of themselves. Aristotle expected them to control the appetites for luxurious living, anything that indulges or titillates the senses of touch and taste, especially when taken to an excess. For Euripides the antidote to *akrasia* seemed to be toil; similarly, for Aristotle the controlled person exhibits toughness, no doubt won through toil. Theopompus' view was essentially the same. Clearchus of Mythydrium distinguished himself in the eyes of the gods by his painstaking diligence in sacrifice. In the digression "On the Demogogues" Callistratus was singled out for his diligence (ἐπιμέλεια) in politics and Eubulus was called diligent and industrious (φιλόπονος = "toil loving") in amassing great wealth for the Athenian treasury. Otherwise, Theopompus' concern was to see people managing their personal affairs properly, unlike Philip (FF224–5).

The example of the Saintsburgers suggests another way whereby the effect of self-control can be achieved. Not surprisingly it is through great piety and, moreover, through deliberate abstinence from warfare. The idea that the description of their country, Meropis, is an original composition of Theopompus for an allegorical purpose was advanced in 1951 by Italo Lana and later, in altered form, by myself. There are seven definite citations of or references to the story in antiquity, and they all attribute it to Theopompus (FF74, a, b, 75 a, b, c, d, e). This means that it was generally regarded as Theopompan: that he either invented it or first brought it from the oral tradition into the mainstream of Greek literature. However,

Chapter 1 showed that the story was allegedly told to Midas by a captured Silenus somewhere in (northern) Macedonia. Before Theopompus the capture of Silenus was already known to Herodotus (8.138) and Xenophon, who, however, did not put it in Macedonia (X. *An.* 1.2.13). It was also known to Aristotle, who said that the Silenus told Midas something to the effect that it was better "never to have been born." Did Aristotle know of the place called No Return described by Theopompus in this same passage? There, he wrote that if people choose to eat from trees by the river of sorrow, they die in misery. If they eat from those by the river of joy, the life process stops and goes immediately into reverse. The moral of a story like that could well be "better never to have been born," but the motto does not fit the Wartown-Saintsburg part of the fragment nearly so well. Indeed, the Saintsburgers have "long and happy lives." This part of the fragment also exhibits the contrived, punning style of Theopompus that pervades his moralizing editorials. The other part does not. It is tempting to suggest, therefore, that No Return was the traditional part of an old story encountered by Herodotus (?), Theopompus, and Aristotle in their visits to Macedonia. Wartown-Saintsburg, on the other hand, is Theopompus' addition for moral or allegorical purposes.[15] If all that is so, it reinforces the argument made in the next chapter that the long diatribe is not just an attack on Philip but also a denunciation of the Macedonian policy of conquest.

On the surface, the lives of the Saintsburgers would seem scarcely distinguishable from those of uncontrolled degenerates in the known world. They do no work and spend all their time laughing and (no doubt) observing festivals. Their only apparent distinction is their piety. Even the gods feel comfortable in their presence. How they avoid pressure from the evil Wartowners is not clear. Perhaps the information has been eliminated by whoever epitomized Theopompus' text. Divine protection is an obvious guess, however. Perhaps the message was that the dedicated pursuit of piety is the most effective way of conducting politics and war.

Diogenes Laertius said that Theopompus praised "only Antisthenes of all the Socratics" (F295 = D.L. 6.14). As a result of his remark, some scholars have seen in Theopompus an adherent of the moralizing Cynic school of philosophy. E. Rohde was not convinced.[16] For him the moral views of Theopompus all find parallels in Isocrates. He also points out that the line of praise attributed to the historian by Diogenes is equivocal: "he says that [Antisthenes] was clever and able to convert anyone at all by means of a harmonious discourse." Rohde argues that there is nothing in the quoted passage to suggest that Theopompus admired Antisthenes' doctrines, only his ability to interest and persuade. Despite Rohde's argument, it seems to me that Diogenes' remark is quite unequivocal. It suggest that Theopompus had things to say about the Socratics (the major ones like Plato and Speusippus, not necessarily all of them) and that Antisthenes came off best. This is not surprising. The author of the fragments cited above (and below!) has much in common spiritually with a philosopher to whom Diogenes Laertius, at least, attributes such sayings as (D.L. 6.1.3, 6, 9):

"I'd rather go insane than feel pleasure;" and "May the sons of our enemies live in luxury;" and "It is odd that we weed out our corn, debar the useless from warfare, but do not excuse villains from politics."

However, the idea that Theopompus might have been a converted Cynic philosopher who wrote history lacks evidence and is, in my view, just about impossible. No, as Professor Murray says:

Had Theopompus been a true Cynic he could never have ploughed his way on through forty-eight [sic] books describing the solemn follies of mankind. But he was not altogether a philosopher; only a man of letters, oppressed by the ill fortunes of his country, and his whole age, and fascinated by a particular philosopher of strong character and great powers of persuasion.[17]

The Cynics tended to scorn politics and pageantry, favourite topics of ancient historians. This was especially true of Diogenes, the most famous Cynic of all.

In book 50, where Theopompus was apparently describing Philip's activities in Thrace just before his final showdown with southern Greece (FF226, 228), a digression took him across the water to the island of Lesbos and the town of Methymna (F227). The Methymnaeans are described as sumptuaries, "conducting their daily business lavishly, reclining and drinking." The word *akrasia* is not used of their condition, but would have been appropriate. "They did no work (ἔργον) worthy of their expenditures." However, they came to be ruled by a curmudgeon who put a stop to their extravagance by having the procuresses and "three or four of the most flagrant whores" bound up in sacks and dropped into the ocean. The tyrant's personal war on immorality is likely to have won applause from Theopompus. However, if he approved of his summary methods, his morality has a brutal side similar to much of the barbarity that he condemns in Philip.

Dedication and industry are his ideal attributes, therefore. But he seems not to approve of "aimless diligence." That is a contradiction in terms. Aimless living is a form of *akrasia* for which diligence is an antidote. Therefore, a person is good at that activity in which the most experience has been gained. By implication, no one should undertake any important responsibility without first acquiring training from an expert. This was a teaching of Socrates with which the historian would likely have agreed,[18] and I shall return to it. What was the full range of *akrasia's* meaning? Were some people more uncontrolled than others? These are the shades of grey.

"Grey tones" can be differentiated in two ways: by an analysis of Theopompus' language and by the substantial type or intensity of the *akrasia* that he attributes to this or that character. For many descriptions of debauchery he uses rather colourless language. Debauchery is a state of enervation; it is the *ennui* or indolent boredom of pampered aristocrats. At times Phaedra exhibits this characteristic. She lies on her bed indifferent to life. She does not eat because her emotions distress her too much. By contrast, most of Theopompus' debauchees have no trouble with their appetites. For Aristotle softness is the sister condition of *akrasia*. However, there is another side to the state characterized by crazed utterances and destructive deeds. Phaedra falsely accuses Hippolytus of rape and commits suicide, sealing Hippolytus' doom at the hands of her enraged husband, Theseus, by means of her own self-destruction; and Aristotelian *akrasia* is occasionally on the level of bestiality — a life of mindless sensuality. Theopompus has some crazed individuals in his history. When he turns to these extreme cases, his language loses its own somewhat "acratic" colourlessness and takes on the turgidity of which Dionysius of Halicarnassus speaks: Aristotle would probably have recognized his bestial man in Theopompus' portrait of Philip.

First, there is what might be called the unexceptional case of *akrasia*. In F49 the Thessalians are described in generally rather bland terms. They "live (ζῶσιν) some spending time [dallying?] (διατρίβοντες) with girls" who play musical instruments at parties. Others wile away the days (διημερεύοντες) at dice, boozing, and similar undisciplined activity." They are not altogether lethargic. They show zeal (σπουδή), to be sure, but "more to ensure that their tables are laden with a rich variety of delicacies than in making their own lives as well ordered as possible." This description has much in common with many other fragments in language and substance.[19]

There is a small group of super debauchees, and Philip is among them. In the descriptions of these people superlatives are reinforced by colourful verbs and extremely abusive nouns and adjectives. Straton provides a good paradigm (F114). He excelled all humans in addiction to pleasure (ἡδυπαθεία). He "had got into a state of frenzied agitation" toward pleasure (παρεκεκινήκει πρὸς τὰς ἡδονάς). He rejoiced in that sort of existence (χαίρων τῷ βίῳ τοιούτῳ), being by nature a slave of pleasures. Precisely how this rejoicing differed from the laughter of the just, healthy, and happy (ἡδόμενοι) Saintsburgers is not made clear. It is interesting that the only other use of "rejoicing" in the fragments describes Philip getting drunk and rejoicing in the inanities of his flatterers in a fragment that begins with merciless language (F162). Philip was a natural buffoon (φύσει βωμολόχος), "dancing, revelling and submitting to every incontinence (ὀρχούμενος καὶ κωμάζων καὶ πᾶσαν ἀκολασίαν ὑπομένων)." However, unlike the more normal victims of *akrasia*, he was able to use his incontinence as a means of conquest. "He conquered more of the Thessalians who associated with him more by parties than bribes."[20]

Lack of self-discipline and self-control can be regarded as relatively passive afflictions compared to the wanton, even brutal extravagance (ἀσελγεία) introduced by Philip and schemers of his ilk. On their level debauchery gains a kind of missionary fervour (F121 = Athen. 10.444E–5A):

Theopompus ... says the following in book 16 of his *Histories*: "Hegesilochus of Rhodes rendered himself worthless because of his heavy drinking and gambling and had altogether no esteem (ἀξίωμα) among the Rhodians, but was a scandal both to his friends and the rest of the citizenry owing to the desperate corruption of his lifestyle (διὰ τὴν ἀσωτίαν τὴν τοῦ βίου)."

Athenaeus continues:

He goes on right away to speak of the oligarchy which he set up with his friends and says: "and many well-born wives even of the first citizens he debauched, and corrupted many lads and young boys. Indeed, they went to such a degree of debauchery that they cajoled each other into throwing dice for respectable women. They agreed in advance that those who threw the lower numbers on the dice would have to bring a certain of the citizen women to have intercourse with the winner. They let no one off for any reason, they made him bring her however he could, whether by persuasion or by force. To be sure, other Rhodians played this same dicing game, but Hegesilochus himself did it the most openly and the most frequently, he who presumed to be head of the state (ὁ προστατεῖν τῆς πόλεως ἀξιῶν)."

In this fragment, debauchery and corruption seem to be more extravagant, more aggressive states of moral incontinence than the more passive *akrasia* and *akolasia*. Indeed, the charge that a corrupt ruler spreads corruption in his house, amongst his fellow citizens, and, at times, to other nations is not levelled at Hegesilochus alone but also at Philip (F162, the corruption of the Thessalians, and FF224, 225, 81, where Philip all but destroys his own household and attracts the desperate from everywhere and aids and abets their further debauchery). In Sicily, Dionysius the tyrant wanted everyone around him to be corrupt fops (F134).

A person who loses all control of his lustful appetites enslaves himself to them. He is afflicted with "pleasure-addiction" (ἡδυπαθεία, F114) and becomes a slave of pleasures (δοῦλος ἡδονῶν, F210) or, like Straton, king of Sidon (but, to judge from his name, a Greek nonetheless), a natural slave of pleasure (δοῦλος φύσει τῶν ἡδονῶν, F114). And, when this person is an absolute monarch like Straton, his *akrasia* unavoidably blends with the life of the state over which he exercises political power (κράτος). His international business becomes concerned with the voracious acquisition of foreign delicacies, and his use of them echoes the shamelessness of the barbarian Etruscans:

Straton adorned his banquets with flute-girls, harpists and lyre-players. He acquired many prostitutes from the Peloponnese, many female musicians from Ionia, and other little girls from all parts of Greece, some to sing songs, and some to be dancers. With his friends he would set them contests, and he spent his time having intercourse with them.

Like Straton, Philip is maniacally "hyperactive." In different passages his actions are described in frenzied terms. Most specifically, he is no model general. Far from being industrious and dedicated, Philip "was a regular boozer and frequently went drunk into battle" (F282). In the same fragment he is "partly by nature maniacal (μανικός) and inclined to rush headlong into danger (προπετὴς ἐπὶ τῶν κινδύνων) and partly through drink." In a way that calls to mind the [Ardiaeans] and their *prospeletai*, Theopompus says that Philip got control of a vast sum of money (ἐγκρατὴς πολλῶν ἐγένετο χρημάτων) and then proceeded not to spend it but "throw and toss it away." Philip was "of all humans the worst manager." His friends were the same; not one of whom "knew how to live rightly nor manage his own estate sensibly." The spendthrift Philip was the cause of that, "doing everything compulsively (προχείρως ἅπαντα ποιῶν) whether acquiring or spending. Though he was a soldier, he was incapable of calculating (οὐκ ἠδύνατο λογίζεσθαι) at leisure his revenues and expenses." Philip attracted the vilest of humans from all parts of Europe, and if some came with innocence, they quickly lost it under his influence and that of his court. Philip actively spurned the habitually orderly (τοὺς ... κοσμίους τοῖς ἤθεσι). An enemy of diligence, he rejected men who were "diligent about their private lives" (τῶν ἰδίων βίων ἐπιμελουμένους) and honoured drunkards and gamblers instead. He did not just cultivate (παρασκευάζειν) this behaviour in them, he even set them contests in "injustice and brutality." They practised a flagrant and un-Greek form of homosexuality and were murderers. Again the reader is reminded that they were drunkards who were eager for killing; and as if getting his second wind, Theopompus finds even more corruption on which to expatiate. They were liars and disloyally foreswearing and sacrilegious. Careless of their present fortunes, though fabulously wealthy, they "lusted for what was not theirs (τῶν ἀπόντων ἐπεθύμουν)." At last his fury is nearly spent, and he decides to bring his diatribe to a close. As a parting shot, he compares the Macedonians to disadvantage with such legendary savages as the Centaurs and Laestrygonians.

While most voluptuaries simply pass time in a state of sumptuous indolence (for example, the Thessalians, F49; the Athenians, F213), Philip is mad and Straton is caught up in an agitated frenzy (παρακίνησις). Philip is the most abused character in the fragments, but not enough of the *Philippica* survives to prove conclusively whether he excelled all others in corruption or was just a "member of a select club" of super debauchees. Nonetheless, the attack on Philip from book 49 deserves to be recognized as a masterpiece of rhetorical vitriol, combing Plato's archfiend, the tyrannical man, with Aristotle's bestial *akratic*. In his long treatise on "justice," *The Republic*, Plato sketched in cameo some of the worst humans. For him, the worst of the worst is the tyrannical man who must purge his own city of the best citizens, the theory goes, and leave it peopled by the vilest. Next, like Philip, he draws the dregs of humanity to his court just as a corpse attracts vultures!

"Blessed, then, is the necessity that binds him," said I, "which bids him dwell for the most part with base companions who hate him, or else forfeit his life." "Such it is," he said. "And would he not, the more he offends the citizens by such conduct, have the greater need of more and more trustworthy bodyguards?" "Of course." "Whom, then, may he trust, and whence shall he fetch them?" "Unbidden," he said, "they will wing their way to him in great numbers if he furnish their wage." "Drones, by the dog," I said, "I think you are talking again, of an alien and motley crew." "You think rightly," he said. (567 B–D, Paul Shorey, tr., L.C.L.)

For Aristotle, senseless and undisciplined action taken to excess (ὑπερβάλλουσα ἀφροσύνη ... καὶ ἀκολασία) is a sign of bestiality or a morbid disease. Certain barbarian tribes are bestial because they are by nature unreasoning and live solely on the level of sensation. The Laestrygonians and Centaurs illustrate well the destructive frenzy Theopompus seems to associate with his more advanced degenerates. In possession of great physical power, the Laestrygonians, apparently panicstricken, destroy Odysseus' ships, which they dwarf and by which they might rationally have felt quite unthreatened, and gobble up of his men, while the Centaurs were notorious for their drunken brawling at the wedding of Hippodamea. The destructive violence of the Laestrygonians and the socially disruptive acts of the Centaurs make them excellent parallels for the abandon attributed to Philip and his entourage. Perhaps Theopompus' claim that the historical humans outshone the mythical beasts in monstrous behaviour is purely rhetorical exaggeration. However that may be, he has succeeded consciously or not in taking two classic extremes of corruption, political as described by Plato and moral as delineated by Aristotle, and blending them in to one superb outburst against Philip.

Perhaps it would be useful to pause and sum up some of Theopompus' more negative views. In the aphorism in F57 Theopompus described the results of overeating: "Excessive eating and the consumption of meat deprive souls of the ability to calculate logically (τοὺς λογισμούς) and makes them sluggish; otherwise it fills them with anger, harshness and much awkwardness." If food had that effect, alcohol was far worse. Nevertheless, to Theopompus a controlled private life was not necessarily the key to political effectiveness. Some leaders were personal ascetics (Agesilaus, Lysander), but despite their distinguished military careers, they were probably not seen as effective governors; others were good officials, their private lives of debauchery notwithstanding (Callistratus, Alcibiades). However, personal *akrasia* more usually undermined political effectiveness (the [Ardiaeans], Charidemus, Archidamus, Straton, and others) because politics involve the exercise of power and the debauchee is powerless: Lysander was κρείττων τῶν ἡδονῶν ἁπασῶν (lit. was more powerful – had more κράτος than – pleasures), but the corrupt were so under the control of pleasure they were its slaves (δοῦλοι τῶν ἡδονῶν, Straton and Timolaus, F210). Obviously, when pleasures corrupt (literally "destroy," διαφθείρω, F62) people, they have become powerless to resist. Generally, *akrasia* seemed to be a state of indolence, time wasted by inactivity or in unproductive and self-indulgent pursuits. Sometimes, however, it became maniacal or, as Aristotle might have put it, bestial. Philip and perhaps Straton and Hegesilochus were examples of the extreme. On the positive side, Theopompus praised two Spartan kings (Lysander and Agesilaus), three Athenian statesmen (Alcibiades, Callistratus, Eubulus), an Athenian philosopher (Antisthenes), most likely a tyrant from Lesbos (Cleommis), and Clearchus of Arcadia. He also had some kind words for Demosthenes, another Athenian statesman, who is treated in the next chapter. In the following discussion the Illyrians will be added to this list. In general, if a theme of the critical fragments is lack of control, it is some form of control exercised through diligence and industry that unifies the laudatory ones.

So far the conclusions are not likely to generate much controversy. They raise their own questions, however, one of which is probably unanswerable. First, if Theopompus really did see Philip as an uncontrolled and relatively mindless monster, how did he maintain this picture through many pages of narrative? Even if only sixteen books of the *Philippica* were devoted to Philip, in them he will have gone on many long marches, successfully prosecuted sieges, and won perhaps scores of pitched battles. Was there no industry or dedication to be seen in all this success? Next to nothing is known about this very important facet of the work. Polybius found the battle narratives artificial and unreal (T32), but that is scarcely a useful piece of information. The second question is closely related and may be more answerable: how was Philip's incredible success explained? Was Philip, like Alcibiades or Callistratus, privately corrupt but publicly diligent? Or was he more like the majority, and if he was a corrupt politician and inept general, why was he so successful?

The next chapter shows how variously the ancients explained Philip's greatness. In brief anticipation, the three answers were: Philip was a model general and a friendly and affable politician (for example, Diodorus); Philip was an energetic tyrant who took advantage of his ability to make quick decisions and impose his will on his followers, while Athens, his major opponent, was a democracy and prone to take too long debating issues (Demosthenes); Philip was a bad general who invaded a Greece too enfeebled by the Peloponnesian War (431–404) to offer meaningful resistance (Pausanias). These are all reasonably coherent lines of argument. Which, if any, is Theopompus likely to have followed?

Diodorus' is out of the question, but the other two deserve closer scrutiny. Demosthenes' is spelled out elegantly in the *First Philippic* (40–41):

But you, Athenians, possessing unsurpassed resources – fleet, infantry, calvary, revenues – have never to this very day employed them aright, and yet you carry on war with Philip exactly as a barbarian boxes. The barbarian, when struck, always clutches the place; hit him on the other side and there go his hands. He neither knows nor cares how to parry a blow or how to watch his adversary. So you, if you hear of Philip in the Chersonese, vote an expedition there; if at Thermopylae, you vote one there; if somewhere else, you still keep pace with him to and fro. You take your marching orders from him; you have never framed any plan of campaign for yourselves, never foreseen any event, until you learn that something has happened or is happening. (J.H. Vince, tr., L.C.L.)

According to this speech Philip attacks when the winds make it difficult for the Athenian fleet to reach the trouble spot (31) and schemes with Athens' neighbours, the Euboeans (37), while the Athenians enjoy their ease and leisure (8), ordering festivals with more care and thoroughness than any military campaign (36). The attribution of indolence to the Athenians suits the express view of Theopompus, but Demosthenes' Philip is too good a planner. Perhaps Pausanias' idea of an enfeebled Greece is closer to Theopompus'. Indeed, it could easily be derived from the *Philippica*. So what was the nature of Greek resistance to Philip? Since Athens was the main centre of opposition to Philip in southern Greece, why did Theopompus attack the Athenians?

Some four or five answers to this question were considered at the beginning of this chapter: the Athenians were senselessly opposing the healthy march of Panhellenism (Momigliano); they were corrupt because they were a democracy (von Fritz); their vilification is part of the explanation of Philip's success (Connor, Shrimpton, Flower with differences, particularly with reference to the part played by Demosthenes). Sorting out the last three views is one of the tasks reserved for the last chapter. Momigliano's notion of an Isocratean Panhellenism was considered in chapter 1, where it was concluded that the thesis was unacceptable. As for von Fritz's thesis, it relies in part on the story that identified Theopompus' father as a Spartophile and, by implication, an aristocrat, and, by further implication, the son had the same political views as the father. However, chapter 1 showed that the historian's political affiliation on Chios was likely with the democratic faction. Nor is it clear that he always exhibited the wealthy man's contempt for the mob. In F248 from *On the Treasure Plundered from Delphi* it was the mob (πλῆθος) that stopped the tyrants from profaning the Pythian ceremonies. Their intervention would certainly have won the historian's approval considering his regard for the sacred. Otherwise, von Fritz's argument hangs on F213, the fragment in question regarding the Athenians, and F62. As for this last fragment, despite its apparent denigration of democracy, it is equally arguable that it illustrates the enervation that the assumption of power and the acquisition of wealth can produce. This first part, concerning the Byzantians, can be momentarily set aside. The second part, which speaks of the Calchedonians, reads:

The Calchedonians, before they gained a share in the constitution (πολιτεία), all used to spend their time at their business and living the better life (ἐν βίῳ βελτίονι ὄντες). However, when they got a taste of the democracy of the Byzantians, they were corrupted (διεφθάρησαν) [turning] to luxury, and in their daily lives they changed from being very sensible and moderate into boozers and profligates (ἐκ σωφρονεστάτων καὶ μετριωτάτων φιλοπόται καὶ πολυτελεῖς γενόμενοι).

Wealth and political power have a corrupting influence. Philip, the [Ardiaeans], and Straton go mad or lose control after gaining mastery over much power and wealth. Riches alone destroyed the well-being of the Colophonians (F117). Their lucrative trade in purple garments elevated a thousand of them to the status of plutocrats. But "by reason of this way of life" they fell into tyranny and political disorder and so, with their city, were destroyed. F62 fits the same scheme: democracy is one of several ways whereby people achieve power and, sometimes, money and expose themselves to corruption. This interpretation appears to be supported by the first part of F62, which characterizes the Byzantian democracy:

The Byzantians, because they had a democracy for a long time, had maintained their city as an emporium, and all the people spent their time about the market-place and the harbour, were undisciplined (ἀκόλαστοι) and were accustomed to holding get-togethers and drinking bouts (συνουσιάζειν καὶ πίνειν) in taverns.

As in the case of the Calchedonians, this is mild abuse coming from Theopompus. There is no hint of any Hegesilochan frenzy or Philippic mania. Furthermore, trading and the leisure of marketplace and harbour are as much to blame for the corruption as the Byzantians' democratic constitution. Moreover, in the case of Athens, two fragments suggest that he saw her corruption as much in terms of her daily economic life as of her politics. F281 speaks of the "economic," judicial, and "cultural" activities centred at or near the market-square (ἀγορά): "Athens was full of shyster-actors, sailors and pickpockets, also false-witnesses, swindlers, and false accusers." Again, her harbour, the Piraeus, was a centre of timeconsuming pleasure and moral corruption. In it were (F290): "flute-girls, brothels, flute-players, singers, and dancers." Democracy is bad because it makes power, wealth, and their opportunities for time-wasting and corruption available to a very great number of people. In an oligarchy or tyranny, the power is more concentrated among fewer people, and the debauchery associated with those political organizations looks to have been correspondingly worse.

Again, F62 does not speak of the relative merits of constitutions. No type of government other than democracy is mentioned in the fragment. Therefore, the assumption that democracy is being compared implicitly or explicitly with another specific constitution is gratuitous. Finally, from all appearances, Theopompus attacks politicians for their corruption regardless of their politics. Hegesilochus of Rhodes, who set up an oligarchy, is assaulted for his profligacy. Thessaly seems generally to have had tyrannies or oligarchic regimes, and they too, especially the oligarchies (see D.S. 16.14.1–2), are denigrated for their corruption, which, indeed, Philip used to conquer them. The moral, if violent, actions of Cleommis of Methymna were made possible by virtue of his tyrannical power, it is true, but there is no hint that being a tyrant made him moral. Not all tyrants were corrupted by their power, to be sure. The Lyceum in Athens was a gymnasium, a place which the Athenians could go to exercise their minds and bodies, an alternative to gambling-halls, brothels, and taverns. The building was a gift of the tyrant Pisistratus (F136), who is otherwise described as a generous man not given to excessive pleasure (F135). However, the fragments contain references to tyrants from Sicily and other places too numerous to list (but see, for example, FF134, 181), and with the exceptions of Pisistratus and Cleommis, they are desperately corrupt sots to a man. The denunciations of democratic peoples is "noise," therefore, not information about the historian's political views. Theopompus' political preferences are beyond recovery.

A few years ago I made a somewhat different attempt to read some political meaning into the moral pronouncements of Theopompus. I put known agents and enemies of Philip on a scale and observed that the moral denunciation seems to increase the closer the individuals were to Philip. Timolaus of Thebes is singled out as a politician and vehemently attacked. The only political decision he is known to have made was to join the Macedonian cause (F210). Much the same could be said of the Thessalian Thrasydaeus (F209). Equally, the Pharsalians of Thessaly actively supported Philip and he them. They too are savaged in violent terms (F49). Other Thessalians neither resisted nor actively supported Philip, and a rather unspectacular form of *akrasia* was attributed to them. They were lazy and preoccupied with self-gratification. These fragments all come from sections of the *Philippica* wherein the respective nations or individuals were having dealings with Philip. In the case of people who opposed Philip, the criticism is not excessive. The Olynthians who first joined Philip then resisted him to the death are described as "generally devoted to drink, laziness and much licentiousness." The remark is from F139 from book 22 where the context was Philip's invasion of Olynthian territory. The Athenian general Chares and the Athenians themselves offered sporadic, ineffective resistance. Significantly again in the context of Athens' opposition to Macedonia, Chares was "sluggish and slow," and the Athenians are more preoccupied with festivals than the proper running of their state. Theopompus seems disappointed with their effort. Various Illyrian tribes gave Philip a great deal of trouble throughout his reign. They went to parties, certainly, but cinched their belts ever tighter as they drank (F39). This must have clamped a serious restriction on their appetites. The apparent approval of Cleommis in book 50 was not included in my "spectrum," but it should be added now, for it is most suggestive. Book 49 had ended with the diatribe against the Macedonians. It is not known how soon Theopompus turned to Cleommis in the next book, but it is very tempting to assume a direct connection, for he had apparently been instrumental in helping Athenians resist Macedonian piratical raids on their shipping. An inscription honours him for helping ransom Athenians captured no doubt by the Macedonian pirates. In sum, FF224–5 (book 49) contain scarcely disguised denunciations of Macedonian piracy against Athens. F227 from book 50 applauds the morals of this tyrant from Lesbos known to have voluntarily helped Athens against these pirates.[21] The tendency of the narrative looks to have been sympathetic to Athens, hostile to Macedonia, and generally approving of voluntary Aegean cooperation with Athens against Philip. Where the ideal spirit, the theory of the Second Athenian Confederacy lived on, Theopompus apparently warmed to the subject. Finally, Demosthenes was Philip's most implacable enemy. He was generously treated, it was argued, for an Athenian politician. Only when he failed at Chaeronea was he subjected to criticism (F328).

Michael Flower claimed to see a few anomalies in this list. To him the Byzantians are more severely attacked than the Olynthians (F62), despite their more stubborn resistance to Philip. Neither of Flower's evaluations is secure, however. The Byzantians are really not treated as savagely as many, nor is there any way of determining their relative stubbornness of the two states' resistance to Philip's besieging efforts. To be sure, Philip did not take Byzantium, unlike Olynthus, but the sources make it his own decision to raise the siege.[22] Further, F62 is from book 7 of the *Philippica* and is, therefore, not likely to be a comment on the Byzantians' ability to resist Philip since it is far removed from the context of Philip's siege, which must have been narrated much later, book 47 or 48. Another alleged anomaly is the [Ardiaeans]. F40 celebrated their *akrasia*, but they were stubbornly resisting Philip by the end of his reign. On the other hand, Theopompus also says that they fell into the clutches of the Celts as a result of their incontinence. Clearly, then, the fragment, coming as it does from book 2, does not relate to the period of their opposition to Philip, which must have found its place in book 37 or 38. Had they still been under Celtic control when Philip confronted them, they would have been in no position to offer resistance. Finally, Flower assumes that Ardiaeans is the correct reading in F40. However, that assumption is most uncertain. If the more probable "Autariatae" is read, Philip had no known contact with them at all.

Nonetheless, this "sliding scale" of opposition is not without its problems. The approach is statistical and subjective. Statistically, the "sample" is too small to mean very much, and Flower's remarks do serve as a reminder that the decision that person A is more severely attacked than person B is a subjective evaluation. Further, it is not clear that resistance to Philip is necessarily the overriding criterion of Theopompus' approval (or lack of it) rather than some other, more general consideration, such as industriousness. It took energy and dedication to resist Philip. Once people departed from their innate or acquired lethargy to do so, they are likely to have won some sort of recognition from Theopompus. Finally, the claim that Demosthenes was treated generously has not won universal acceptance. Therefore, the treatment of Demosthenes and his policies emerges as the single most important problem in the interpretation of Theopompus' fragments. If Demosthenes met with no approval, then the sliding scale will have to be abandoned, and the *Philippica* will indeed be "history without heroes." If he was praised, it will be necessary to pay careful attention to what things were applauded and how. If the remarks seem to focus on his industry, then the work will seem to be little more than an enormous moral tract; but if his policies are approved, then, without denying the moral tendencies, there is an anti-Macedonian, political theme in the *Philippica*.

The Treatment of Philip and Demosthenes

When Philip II became king of Macedon, he was in his early twenties. The kingdom to which he laid claim was fragmented and tributary to an Illyrian, and the succession was disputed. When a certain Pausanias assassinated him nearly two and a half decades later in 336, he left an organized kingdom rich in revenues and master over all its neighbours. One of his last acts had been to declare war on Persia.[1] His Hellenic neighbours to the south, notably Thebes, Athens, and Sparta, had been slow to appreciate the growing threat to their independence. Until 352 Philip must have seemed to them no different from any number of northern potentates who had exercised power for a time only to disappear: Bardylis of Illyria, Cotys of Thrace, Archelaus of Macedonia, and Jason of Pherae (in Thessaly) are a few examples.[2] However, after 352 Philip was not to be ignored, for he began to menace and then subjugate regions of grave importance to the traditional Greek city-states: the Chalcidic peninsula, the Thracian Chersonese, and the heart of central Greece, Delphi itself. In the scant fourteen years between 352 and the Macedonian victory over the Hellenic allies at the battle of Chaeronea, the Greek world changed with a brutal swiftness that makes the permanence of the new order seem miraculous. The southern Greeks did not really have much time to change their ingrained habits of internecine squabbling and either unite to resist the new power or find terms on which to prepare themselves for submission. Was Philip a barbarian or a Greek? It mattered if he was to rule Greeks, if he was to dominate that most sacred and most Greek of all shrines, the Delphic oracle, if he was to lead Greeks against Persia in a war of revenge for Xerxes' invasion of 480 B.C. It was hardly for a barbarian to avenge a sacred Greek cause.[3]

Philip's military and diplomatic offensives have been well studied and will continue to receive attention. Inevitably, a story like Philip's struggle with Greece is a litany of bloodshed, manipulation, and lies. It is the lies that are of interest here. People need to give and hear explanations of what they do and what happens around them. In service or opposition to a program of conquest, the explanations become propaganda. Propaganda appeal superficially to reason, but feed most heavily on emotional issues. When Philip moved against southern Greece, he stirred up a hornet's nest of ethnic, religious, and patriotic disputes. To understand Theopompus, his place in the complex spectrum of the age's propaganda must be found.

When he settled the Sacred War in 346, Philip took for himself a seat on the Amphictionic Council and assumed the two votes of the Phocians, forfeit by virtue of their plundering the oracle's treasures. A sketch of the history of the Amphictionic League (league of "neighbours") helps explain the significance of these acts. It is not known when the League first began. In origin, it was apparently a sacred affiliation of twelve north-central Greek tribes located near Thermopylae. It included Thessalians, Phocians, Dorians, Ionians, Thebans, and seven others from the immediate region, but no Macedonians. By classical times Athens and Sparta were members, no doubt because they were recognized as the most powerful representatives of the Ionian and Dorian tribes respectively. The Macedonian and Thessalian concern to settle the affairs of the Council in their interest in 346 may seem puzzling at first. For much of its history the League was scarcely more than an exclusive sacred club that came to be charged with organizing the quadrennial games in honour of Apollo at Delphi, the so-called Pythian Games. However, earlier in the fourth century ambitious men had begun to realize the potential for political influence that lay in the oath of membership. Ehrenberg reconstructs and translates:

[They swore] not to destroy any Polis of the Amphictyones, or starve it out, or cut off its running water, either in war or in peace; if anyone transgresses these rules, to take the field against him and call up[?] the Poleis, and if anyone plunders the property of the god or is privy to such robbery or has any designs against the sanctuary, to take vengeance for it with hand and foot and voice and all one's power.[4]

It takes little imagination to see how this oath could be used to transform the Amphictiony into a military alliance prosecuting "holy wars" for Apollo.

Perhaps that was the dream of the energetic Jason of Pherae. In the late 370s this Thessalian tyrant organized his country under his personal control and spoke of invading Persia. He showed great interest in the Amphictiony, and his reign no doubt marks the beginnings of its historical importance in the fourth century. In 370 he called up a general levy of Thessalian armed forces, intimated that he would celebrate the Pythian Games with unprecedented splendour (from his seat on the Council, of course), and make an announcement of great import to the Greek world. A gang of assassins forestalled his arrival at Delphi. Afterwards, there was plenty of time for the Greeks to speculate about the announcement that was never made. Some modern scholars think that Jason was going to declare war on Persia; perhaps some of the ancients thought so as well.[5]

A scant year before Jason's murder the Thebans had stunned the Greek world by destroying a Spartan army in a pitched battle on the plains of Leuctra. When Jason died, Thebes was unquestionably the power in central Greece. She was not slow to dominate the Amphictiony, and soon Pelopidas, one of her most able generals, was campaigning in Thessaly. Theban fortunes were varied, but domination of the Amphictiony had not changed by 356, when the Theban representatives pushed a motion through the Council condemning Thebes' old enemy, Phocis. The Phocians, it was alleged, had tilled sacred ground, and a heavy fine was imposed. Delphi is in Phocis, so Theban stupidity must be blamed for not foreseeing and forestalling what happened next. Naturally, the Phocians refused to pay the fine. To anticipate the inevitable declaration of a Sacred War, they seized the shrine from the defenceless township of Delphi and began to negotiate loans from Apollo to finance their resistance to the other Amphictions. The main source (D.S. 16.23–27) indicates that Apollo's treasures, if not his devotees, were first used with as much moderation, even reverence, as was possible. But the Phocians were poor in silver and manpower. Against the might of Thebes, supported sporadically by Thessaly, they needed allies or mercenaries. Their allies, the Athenians and Spartans, gave little help. They exerted themselves only when Philip threatened to pass Thermopylae into southern Greece. For most of the war, therefore, Phocis needed money for mercenaries. The war lasted for ten years, but moderation did not. In desperation, the Phocians eventually turned to unrestrained plundering of the Delphic treasures to coin money. Significantly, the tide of war, first favouring Phocis, was turned by Macedonian soldiers fighting with laurel wreaths on their heads (Just. 8.2.3). They were Apollo's avengers. Their victory was won at the so-called crocus-field near the gulf of Pagasae in 352. The end was still six years off, but there was little doubt what it would be. When it came, the Council expelled the Phocians and Spartans from the Amphictiony, imposed a tax on Phocis to repay the shrine, and took away the Athenians' priority of access to the oracle, προμαντεία (a kind of prearranged priority in "pecking order" of the regular users of the oracle). Philip was given the two votes of the Phocians and made president over the impending Pythian Games.[6]

The expulsion of Phocis made a reorganization of the Council necessary. A number of possible approaches lay before Philip. He could have chosen simply to redistribute the vote among the surviving members, perhaps adding new representatives from two of the old tribes. Obviously, he regarded the League as too important for such an arrangement. He would not permit himself to be excluded. Three or four years later, in c. 343/2, he was to solidify his control of Thessaly by reorganizing the country more firmly under his control.[7] Had he chosen the time of the settlement of the Sacred War to do this, he might have claimed the Thessalian votes as his right *ex officio* as archon of the country. Such a pretence might have reduced the risk of offending the southern Greek city-states, but it would certainly have strained his relations with Thessaly whose friendship he wanted and whose cavalry he needed. His decision reveals his priorities. He gave Thessaly permanent pride-of-place in the Council, making himself second only to them. History records no attempt by Philip to justify this unprecedented assumption of two votes on the sacred Council by one man who had not even a tribal connection to the oracle. He probably made none. As for Athens and Sparta, they had been allied to the Phocian temple-robbers. The Council will scarcely have been concerned to appease those two states; and if Theban religious scruples were offended by Philip's action, their silence was purchased with gifts of Phocian territory and Macedonian support for their control over Boeotia.

In response the Spartans could do nothing. The Athenians protested with a murmur by passing a decree against the settlement and silently by boycotting the proceedings and the games.[8] They were too nervous to do more. Isolated, they certainly feared the possibility that the Council might invoke the oath of membership to declare war on them. In hope of forestalling such action, they had just concluded a treaty of peace and alliance with Philip, the Peace of Philocrates. Philip's long-awaited, but, finally, astonishingly swift resolution of the war must have shocked many. With Philip in Delphi, the delicacy of Athens' position called for guarded speech, if not silence. Demosthenes' contemporary observation characterizes the situation well (*On the Peace* 13–14). He calls for two precautions. The first was to consider strengthening Athens' position only insofar as the newly signed Peace would not be threatened. "The second precaution, men of Athens, is to avoid giving *the self-styled Amphictyons now assembled* any call or excuse for a crusade (πρόφασιν κοινοῦ πολέμου) against us" (J.H. Vince, tr., L.C.L., my emphasis)·. Demosthenes was not merely lamenting the Athenians' inability to help their old allies, the Phocians; by describing the assembly as one of "self-styled Amphictyons," he was questioning the legitimacy of Philip's inclusion and all of the subsequent decisions of the Council, but that was as far as he, the anti-Macedonian "hawk," felt that he could go under the circumstances.

It cannot be said categorically that Athenians questioned Philip's inclusion in the Council on the grounds that he was not a Hellene. Demosthenes' veiled remark is all the evidence that exists. However, it may be no coincidence that the authenticity of Philip's Hellenic credentials came under scrutiny in the literature at this very time and in the years immediately following 346. Isocrates' address to Philip, the *Philippus*, is instructive. Internal references leave little doubt that the address was written during the months immediately following the settlement of the Sacred War. Philip is urged to unite the Greeks by declaring war on Persia and inviting them to participate as his partners, thus directing his expansionist ambitions away from Greece. The example of Jason of Pherae is specifically cited. As for the leadership, the Greeks will not be ruled by Macedonians, the argument goes, for they are not racially the same. Isocrates shrinks from calling them "barbarians," but he certainly means that Greeks would refuse to be ruled by men of whose "Greekness" they were uncertain. However, fortunately for all, the argument continues, Philip is not a Macedonian, but a Hellene – a descendant of Heracles.[9] Isocrates was not inventing this argument. Herodotus makes it plain that the Greeks at Olympia had heard and been convinced by it in the early fifth century. At that time Alexander, the so-called Philhellene, Philip's ancestor, had come forward to compete in the Olympic Games. At first his right to do so was questioned on the grounds that he was Macedonian and not Greek. He proved to everyone's satisfaction, Herodotus says, that his lineage was in truth Greek, indeed, Argive in origin. He must have traced his descent through Temenus of Argos, the grandson (or great-grandson) of Heracles, the famous Argive hero. Philip himself had already reasserted his family's claim to Hellenic status by sending a horse to compete at Olympia in 356 (and winning).[10] Arguably, therefore, the question of Philip's Greekness was beyond dispute in 346.

Philip's detractors, however, of whom the chief spokesman was Demosthenes, were not convinced. To Demothenes, Philip was a Macedonian, a barbarian, and not even related to the Greeks. Many Greeks thought of barbarians as fit only for slavery. To Demosthenes,

Macedonians did not even make good slaves.[11] For him, to recognize Philip as a Greek was traitorous, proof of Macedonian agency. There is a famous anecdote told to an Athenian audience by Demosthenes in 343 that illustrates this point. In that year, Demosthenes brought his most famous political enemy, Aeschines, to trial on a charge of mishandling one of the embassies and other matters connected with negotiating and concluding the Peace. One of the things Demosthenes was anxious to prove was that Aeschines was really a Macedonian agent betraying the cause of Athens in exchange for bribes from Philip. Toward the end of the speech that he gave in prosecution, Demosthenes addresses the circumstances of Aeschines' alleged conversion. In the years before 346, before he had gone to Macedonia and encountered Philip on the embassies for peace, Aeschines had agitated vigorously against Philip. He had urged the sending of embassies "almost as far as the Red Sea" to call for Greek unity against the Macedonian threat. He himself went on a speaking tour of the Peloponnese. He came home and began to denounce Philip as a barbarian and a brigand frequently in public speeches.[12]

But after he had visited Macedonia, and beheld his own enemy and the enemy of all Greece, did his language bear the slightest resemblance to those utterances? Not in the least: he bade you not to remember your forefathers, not to talk about trophies, not to carry succour to anybody. As for the people who recommended you to consult the Greeks on the terms of peace with Philip, he was amazed at the suggestion that it was necessary that any foreigner should be convinced when the questions were purely domestic. And as for Philip, – why, good Heavens, he was a Greek of the Greeks, the finest orator and the most thorough-going friend of Athens you could find in the whole world. And yet there were some queer, ill-conditioned fellows in Athens who did not blush to abuse him, and even to call him a barbarian! (J.H. Vince, tr., L.C.L.)

Demosthenes' Greek exhibits some fine touches of irony. He coins a word (ἑλληνικώτατος = the Greekest) translated as "Greek of the Greeks"; and his oath (translated "good Heavens") is really Heracles ('Ηράκλεις)! Demosthenes is certainly well aware of the arguments about Philip's Hellenic descent. Most significantly, Demosthenes expected his audience of 1501 (?) jurymen (not to mention interested bystanders)[13] to take the point – the people like Demosthenes himself who made Philip a barbarian were his enemies; his friends and flatterers defended his alleged Greekness.

What was Theopompus' position? The opening sentence of his history has an allusion of sorts to Philip's birth and origins (F27 =

Polyb. 8.11[13].1): Theopompus declared that he had "turned to this subject because Europe had never born such a man at all as Philip, son of Amyntas." Is this a careful introduction of Philip, the Greek, or a rejection of his Hellenic claims – Philip, the European barbarian? An advocate of Philip like Isocrates would not hesitate to clarify. Born in Europe, yes, but of Hellenic stock. Did Theopompus immediately produce a royal genealogy? F393, from Syncellus (an eight–ninth century Byzantine scholar) leaves little doubt that Theopompus reproduced a genealogy that made Philip a descendant of Heracles. But Syncellus did not cite the context of the fragment, and its location in the *Philippica* must be inferred. In the first century B.C. the historian Trogus Pompeius introduced the Macedonian section of his universal history by tracing Philip's descent, and Hammond believes that he must have got his information from Theopompus.[14] Trogus probably did know Theopompus, but he did not use him slavishly or exclusively. His summing up of Philip's career, for example, drew heavily on comparisons with Alexander, the information for which came from sources other than Theopompus.[15] Therefore, Trogus could arrange his material to suit his own purposes. Even for his less creative moments Theopompus was not necessarily his only source. Anaximenes also wrote a *Philippica*, which may have been used by Trogus.[16] Therefore, it seems unwise to conclude that Theopompus introduced Philip with a genealogy just because Trogus did so. The only description of the introduction to the *Philippica* is Polybius', and there are remarks in it that can be interpreted in conflicting ways. After giving the opening line, Polybius says that "immediately, in his introduction and through the entire history," Theopompus went on to make Philip out to be a most incontinent man in his relations with women and in the handling of his domestic affairs. "Immediately" (παρὰ πόδας) may leave no time or space for a genealogy. Therefore, if the genealogy was placed in a negative context elsewhere in the history, then perhaps Theopompus rejected it or held it up to ridicule. However, "immediately" is perhaps too vague a term to support a firm conclusion, and when Polybius returns to the introduction a little later (8.10[12].12), he provides more information. Now he is complaining about the inconsistency between the promise of noble things implied by the introduction and the scurrility of the rest of the work: "For having set forth in his introduction the subject of a king most nobly born for the path of manliness (εὐφυεστάτου πρὸς ἀρετὴν γεγονότος) he omits nothing shameful or outrageous." I once argued that this remark refers to a mock eulogy that began the *Philippica* the ambivalence of which escaped the notice of the humourless Polybius.[17] That was a lot to read into Polybius, but without some such assumption Polybius himself was reading a lot into "Europe has never born such (τοιοῦτος) a man as Philip." Neither the English word "such" nor its Greek equivalent necessarily suggests dignity of birth or any disposition to the manly virtues. On the other hand, a genealogy tracing a king's descent to Heracles says everything about both subjects. On balance, therefore, the assumption that the genealogy was in the introduction makes the best sense of Polybius.

To recapitulate, Polybius found in Theopompus' introduction: a sentence explaining why the subject had been taken up followed by something that, he felt, credited Philip with excellent birth and a disposition to manliness, quite likely Syncellus' genealogy; the heroizing effect of all that was then undermined by some scurrilous references to his corruption and womanizing. If that is correct, then Theopompus began like a good Isocratean. Philip was a European, fine, but a shoot from the very heroic and very Greek stump of Heracles growing, no doubt, in a forest of somewhat alien Macedonians. Polybius was scandalized by the contradiction he found between this flattering introduction and the savage hostility toward Philip that permeated the rest of the introduction and the work. The contrast is indeed puzzling, if not scandalous, for Polybius' claims of scurrility seem to be confirmed by the surviving fragments. Perhaps Theopompus did discredit the genealogy after going to the trouble of recording it, for elsewhere (F81 and, less certainly F280, also F289 of Philip's father, Amyntas), he refers to Philip as "the Macedonian," sounding more like Demosthenes than Isocrates; and the manners of the Macedonian court were not just debauched but un-Greek, at least in the way it accepted an unrefined form of homosexuality. Theopompus' view of Philip's Hellenic credentials is therefore unclear. His court, however, even if led by a Hellene, was not very Hellenized. He was a Greek by birth, but a reckless barbarian to the point of "bestiality" in his choice of lifestyle.

Philip projected his own view of himself. It is mirrored in contemporary speeches and subsequent historical narrative. Diodorus of Sicily preserves it in a statement summarizing Philip's career (D.S. 16.95.2):

He increased his empire not so much through military bravado as through friendly communication and comradeship. Philip boasted about his strategic cunning and accommodations made through friendship more than his bravery on the battlefield. For everyone on an expedition shared in the successes won by military encounter, but he alone got the glory from the arrangements arising from his friendships.

These words were for Greek ears. Amongst his Macedonian generals and soldiers Philip will scarcely have belittled soldiering. Indeed, Theopompus caught and caricatured the Macedonian side of his image from the much closer standpoint of an eyewitness. Unfortunately Diodorus' source for this passage remains unidentified. One of his main sources had been Ephorus, a contemporary of Theopompus, but his *Hellenica* was interrupted by his death, and despite the addition of a book by his son Demophilus, it did not reach the end of Philip's career. Nevertheless, the source was someone close to the age, for the information has an authentic ring.[18] Demosthenes himself was an eyewitness to Philip's "friendships," describing them with jaundice. In *Second Olynthiac* (18) delivered in 349, Philip is described as being jealous of the military glory of his lieutenants. In *On the Embassy* (259), delivered in 343, Demosthenes dwells on Philip's camaraderie:

A strange and distressing epidemic, men of Athens, has invaded all Greece, calling for extraordinary good fortune, and for the most anxious treatment on your part. The magnates of the several cities, who are entrusted with political authority, are betraying their own independence, unhappy men! They are imposing on themselves a servitude of their own choosing, disguising it by specious names, as the friendship of Philip, fraternity, good-fellowship, and such flummery. (C.A. Vince and J.H. Vince, trs. L.C.L.)

Coincidentally, Theopompus was at the Macedonian court just at this time. His own description of Philip's "friendship" is long and lurid. He included it in book 49, which covered the period shortly after 343. Despite the length of the passage, it is worth quoting in full. It must be pieced together from three quotations in two sources, Polybius (8.11.5–13 = F225a) and Athenaeus (4.166F–7C = F224; 6.260D–1A = F225b):

After Philip had become possessor of a large fortune he did not spend it fast. No! he threw it outdoors and cast it away, being the worst manager in the world. This was true of his companions as well as himself. For to put it unqualifiedly, not one of them knew how to live uprightly or to manage an estate discreetly. He himself was to blame for this; being insatiable and extravagant, he did everything in a reckless manner, whether he was acquiring or giving. For as a soldier he had no time to count up revenues and expenditures. Add to this also that his companions were men who had rushed to his side from very many quarters; some were from the land to which he himself belonged, others were from Thessaly, still others were from all the rest of Greece, selected not for their supreme merit; on the contrary, nearly every man in the Greek or barbarian world of a lecherous, loathsome, or ruffianly character flocked to Macedonia and won the title of "companions of Philip." And even supposing that one of them was not of this sort when he came, he soon became like all the rest, under the influence of the Macedonian life and habits. It was partly the wars and campaigns, partly also the extravagances of living that incited them to be ruffians, and live, not in a law-abiding spirit, but prodigally and like highwaymen. (C.B. Gulick, tr., L.C.L.)

For Philip in general showed no favour to men of good repute who were careful of their property, but those he honoured and promoted were spend-thrifts who passed their time drinking and gambling. In consequence he not only encouraged them in their vices, but made them past masters in every kind of wickedness and lewdness. Was there anything indeed disgraceful and shocking that they did not practise, and was there anything good and credit-able that they did not leave undone? Some of them used to shave their bodies and make them smooth although they were men, and others actually practised lewdness with each other though bearded. While carrying about two or three minions with them they served others in the same capacity, so that we would be justified in calling them not courtiers but courtesans and not soldiers but strumpets. For being by nature man-slayers they became by their practices man-whores. (W.R. Paton, tr., L.C.L.)

In addition, they loved drunkenness instead of soberness, they were eager to plunder and murder instead of living decent lives. Truth-telling and keeping promises they regarded as no part of their duty, whereas they readily assumed the odium of perjury and cheating in the most august sanctuary. Careless of what they had, they itched for what they had not, though they owned a whole section of Europe. For I believe that though these com-panions numbered at that time not more than eight hundred, yet they enjoyed the profits of as much land as any ten thousand Greeks possessing the richest and most extensive territory. (C.B. Gulick, tr., L.C.L.)

In a word, not to be prolix, and especially as I am beset by such a deluge of other matters, my opinion is that those who were called Philip's friends and companions were worse brutes and of a more beastly disposition than the Centaurs who established themselves on Pelion, or those Laestrygones who dwelt in the plain of Leontini, or any other monsters. (W.R. Paton, tr., L.C.L.)

Much of this is self-explanatory. The prolonged attack on Philip's vaunted style of "friendship" is unmistakable, but it would be a shame to miss the implications of the sentence: "For as a solider he had no time to count up revenues and expenditures." This is not the Philip of Dio-dorus' source, who prides himself in strategic cunning. Theopompus does not even honour him with the word "general." He is a mere "sol-dier" who has no time for planning even such basic things as finances.

The homosexuality of Philip's friends is described with evident disgust; and yet the meaning of the description may not be immediately obvious. Theopompus is not necessarily reacting to the homosexuality *per se* but, more likely to its un-Greek crudeness. Homosexuality or, more properly, pederasty, had become highly conventionalized in the classical Greek states. It was a sort of avuncular relationship of an older, bearded man with an unbearded youth. The attraction was erotic, but the youth was expected to be coy and play "hard-to-get," and in the most famous case known of such a relationship, that between Socrates and Alcibiades, there was physical contact without sexual gratification.[19] Clearly the Macedonians lacked Greek manners. Two bearded men might have a relationship quite openly, and some would shave their bodies, supposedly to simulate youthful smoothness. There was no coyness; a man would take several minions with him wherever he went. This is a picture of a court lacking any semblance of Greek refinement; the sexual practices parallel the Etruscans' and make Philip and his court barbarian by habit, regardless of any claim some might have made to Hellenic birth and lineage. The closing lines attributing "bestiality" to the court are unmistakable. Theopompus probably recorded approvingly the *bon mot* of a certain Arcadion the Achaean. According to the story (F280) Arcadion went into voluntary exile because of his hatred for Philip. Philip did not exercise control over Achaea until after Chaeronea. Therefore, this is likely a precious fragment from books 55 to 58, wherein the short period of Philip's absolute control over Greece was described. The two met by chance at Delphi, and when "the Macedonian" saw Arcadion, he cried to him "How far will you flee, Arcadion?" and the other replied: "Until I come to people who do not know Philip."

Was this description of Philip's court in book 49 an isolated outburst or was it a summation, a pulling together of themes that permeated and somehow unified this enormous work? The evidence is insufficient for a definite answer, but which way does it point? Polybius had quoted the passage as the prime example of what he saw as malicious bias that plagued the entire *Philippica*. However, another ancient critic, Dionysius of Halicarnassus, was more charitable. For him, Theopompus was an energetic, "truthloving" historian given to sporadic outbursts of vehement denunciation of peoples and their leaders (T20). Which view is more likely?

At an early state in the *Philippica* Theopompus narrated Philip's first intrusions into Thessaly. It took him more than a decade to acquire the country. At the end of his reign he had won the loyalty of its entire military, especially its renowned calvary.[20] Thessaly was the first great test of Philip's strategic diplomacy, to use a modern term, his method of conquest by "friendship," to evoke the ancient expression. Neither Diodorus' source nor Trogus Pompeius missed this point. Diodorus makes Philip Thessaly's ally against the Phocians, who invaded Thessaly from time to time during the Sacred War. Otherwise, he enters the country by invitation in support of various factions. Trogus was more explicit: Philip moved against Thessaly because he wanted to add the strength of her cavalry to his army. In both versions, he wins Thessalian loyalty by virtue of his persistence and ultimate success in helping them fight their battles. Polyaenus (a second-century A.D. rhetorician and collector of military stratagems) is the clearest of all. Philip entered Thessaly only on the invitation of at least one side in the civil wars: "in victory he did not destroy the cities of the vanquished, nor disarm them, nor dismantle their walls ... their class war in the cities he encouraged rather than ended, he supported the weak and put down the strong, he was a friend of the populace in the cities, and he cultivated their leaders. It was by these stratagems that Philip won Thessaly, not by arms."[21] Unfortunately, Theopompus' narrative cannot be compared with that of Trogus and Diodorus, but his summation can be compared with Polyaenus. It comes from Athenaeus (F162 = Athen. 6.260B–C):

Theopompus, again, in the twenty-sixth book of the *Histories,* says that "Philip, knowing that the Thessalians were licentious and wanton in their mode of life, got up parties for them and tried to amuse them in every way, dancing and rioting and submitting to every kind of licentiousness; he was himself naturally vulgar, getting drunk every day and delighting in those pursuits which tended in that direction and in those men, the so-called gallants, who said and did laughable things. And so he won most Thessalians who consorted with him by parties rather than by presents." (C.B. Gulick, tr., L.C.L.)

Therefore, by at least book 26, when the subject was the events of 347, which led to the Peace of Philocrates and the settlement of the Sacred War, the idea of Philip's conquest by "friendship" was recognized, and Theopompus' caricature of it, well developed.

A slightly different variation on essentially the same theme is found in F81 (= Athen. 6.259F–260A), from book 9. A certain Agathocles, formerly a Thessalian slave, had advanced himself at Philip's court by flattery and by telling jokes and dancing at his parties. For this Philip commissioned him to destroy the Perrhaebians and put him in charge of their affairs. "The Macedonian," as Theopompus calls him, "always kept such people about him; and he spent very much the greater part of his time holding meetings and pondering the gravest matters with them, because of their love of boozing and buffoonery." Indeed, if the caricature was not developed even earlier, in book 4 (F49 = Athen. 12.527A), the groundwork for it was at least being laid. There Theopompus must have been turning to Philip's first communications with the Thessalians (as early as 356?). They are introduced as inveterate party-goers, gamblers, and drinkers, more worried about loading their tables with a variety of foods than with ordering their lives properly. Ready soil, it seems, for the seeds of Philip's "friendship." Of the Thessalians, the Pharsalians are singled out for special mention. He calls them "of all mankind the most useless and profligate." In their dealings with Philip, once won over, they were staunchly loyal. When Philip was besieging Olynthus (349), Demosthenes had apparently heard rumours of unrest in Thessaly (*First Olynthiac* 22). However, the Thessalians remained loyal to Philip, and at the end of this all too obscure period in Thessalian history, Philip was treating the Pharsalians most generously. No doubt, they were being well rewarded.[22]

Was this true of other claims made in the diatribe that began book 49? There are two further allegations that call for attention. One is that Philip was a soldier too distracted to make plans like a real general, and the other is that he and his court attracted the corrupt and, if possible, corrupted them further.

The previous chapter concluded that Philip's friends were generally given very harsh treatment, while his enemies, though usually corrupt as well, are frequently treated more softly. However, it was not possible to show conclusively whether support for or hostility to Philip was the overriding criterion for the awarding of blame or an even more general moral consideration: the exhibition of diligence and industry associated with a recognition of one's own limitations. The great problem with Philip and his henchmen was indolence and a lack of self-discipline. It took considerable industry to resist Philip. Therefore, arguably people who did so received some recognition for their industry, however grudging.

On the subject of Philip's generalship the case is clearer. Later sources still reverberate with an echo of a bitter controversy over Philip's military leadership. The second-century A.D. traveller Pausanias, who wrote an extensively annotated guidebook to Greece, digresses on Philip in some five widely scattered passages, all critical.[23] He regarded Philip as a bad general, a womanizer, a swindler, and foreswearer who sowed seeds of dissension in previously well-ordered states. The Greece he conquered, Pausanias believed, had been enfeebled by the Peloponnesian War. In other words, Philip was lucky to have marched against Greece at a time when she was too weak to resist. This characterization sounds as if it originated with Theopompus. Diodorus was at pains to reject this view (16.1.3–6). Philip established his kingdom "not by the favour of Fortune, but by his own valour. For king Philip excelled in shrewdness in the art of war, courage, and brilliance of personality." However, in the fragments of Theopompus, from an unspecified book, there is a brief notice that (F282) Philip frequently went into battle intoxicated. Elsewhere (F237), most probably as part of the explanation for Philip's success at Chaeronea, Theopompus describes him as miraculously lucky. He would have to be if he never planned his campaigns and frequently went into battle drunk.

Demosthenes had a similar view of Philip's success. When he delivered *On the Crown* in 330, a speech given to justify his whole program of resisting Philip, he blamed Athens' ultimate defeat on Fortune. She had frowned on Athens and, implicitly, smiled on Philip. Elsewhere, Demosthenes had argued that Athenian indolence had done more to aid Philip than Macedonian superiority.[24] Theopompus, too, had characterized the Athenians as lazy, preoccupied with self-gratification through sex and gambling (F213). They "squandered more money on the public banquets and distributions of meat than on the administration of the state." The location of this fragment in the *Philippica* adds significance. Athenaeus (12.532B–D) says it comes from book 45, where the subject was the events of 344–342, the breakdown of the Peace of Philocrates and the opening of the hostilities between Athens and Philip that would lead to Chaeronea. It is difficult not to see the fragment as a comment on Athens' inept prosecution of the war, as I argued in chapter 4. The comparison with Demosthenes is, therefore, highly appropriate. Both Demosthenes (by clear implication) and Theopompus attacked Chares, a general who served Athens frequently through the Macedonian wars, as a lazy manipulator.[25] Theopompus claimed that the administration of Eubulus – dominant immediately before Demosthenes – had enervated the Athenian people because it had distributed to them the vast financial resources that it had accumulated. This is surely an attack on Demosthenes' favourite target, the Theoric Fund: a state fund distributed to the people to enable them to attend and participate in public festivals. Demosthenes would have rather seen the money spent on prosecuting the war.[26] Cases of agreement between the historian and politician abound, therefore, but possibly the most thought-provoking example comes from Demosthenes' *Second Olynthiac* (17–19) delivered in 349. There, the orator gives a description of

Philip's court. He had not yet been there himself. So he quoted an unnamed informant who had lived there, a man "incapable of falsehood." According to this source Philip was insatiably ambitious and jealous of every successful man in his entourage. He lived a life of incontinence (ἀκρασία) and intoxication. He spurns the just and sensible and promotes the dregs of humanity who drink with him and perform disgusting dances. Demosthenes finds this account very plausible because the scum of Athens, as he saw it, had all fled to Philip's court. Theopompus was the only person "committed to truth" who is known to have described Philip's entourage and courtly manners in these terms. He was with Philip in 343, but he was already known to the Athenian Speusippus and had probably spent some time with Isocrates in Athens if the interpretation of Speusippus' letter in chapter 1 is correct. After the funeral celebrations for Mausolus, he might have gone to Macedonia (c. 350) and thence to Athens to become Demosthenes' informant, but certainty is impossible.

Wherever Demosthenes got his information, the extensive agreement between him and Theopompus on Philip's nature and the way the two sides, Macedonia and Athens, were waging the war is undeniable. However, Theopompus' treatment of Demosthenes is disputed, and the points of agreement between the two do not prove that the historian's account of the events was necessarily sympathetic to the orator. Indeed, in the discussion of Theopompus' moral views in the preceding chapter, the treatment of Demosthenes and his cause was identified as the single most important question for a full and clear understanding of Theopompus' historiography.

Theopompus' digression "On the Demagogues" was inserted into book 10 of the *Philippica* and refers to Athenian political leaders from Themistocles to Eubulus. It was the subject of a valuable study by W.R. Connor whose conclusions are generally followed in the present discussion. Whether it included individuals from before Themistocles' time is not known. It seems to have ended with Eubulus, which means that it probably did not include Demosthenes. By book 10 Theopompus had reached the years c. 353–352. The precise chronology of the main events of this period is not certain. Nevertheless, the historical context of the digression can be described in general terms; at this time Eubulus had emerged as a main force in Athenian politics, probably as the result of some changes to the Theoric Fund or its administration that he persuaded a by-no-means reluctant assembly to approve; Philip had not yet appeared to be Athens' single most formidable enemy in the north, but he was soon to do so; and Demosthenes was a fledgling politician just testing or about to test his wings on the policies of importance both to his own mature career and to Theopompus: the collection and husbanding of Athens' financial resources and their concentration on prosecuting the war against Philip.[27]

Connor believes that the main theme of the digression is the pandering to the *demos* by self-seeking politicians who use their own money, or misappropriate public funds, to curry favour. The scant fragments suggest the digression may well have culminated with a condemnation of Eubulus' administration. He is accused of enervating the Athenians and mishandling their funds: "the indictment of Eubulus is clear," says Connor. "His policy, according to Theopompus, although successful in some respects, weakened Athens and helped bring about her ineffectiveness in opposing Macedonia."[28]

Therefore, if it was pandering to the *demos*, the dissipation of public resources, and personal incontinence that Theopompus deplored, personal self-control along with the actions of amassing resources, their careful preservation (except for the war) once amassed, and the expenditure of effort to strengthen the state by securing its revenues and forging suitable alliances were no doubt reported with approval in the digression. Now Demosthenes was famous for a personal self-control that failed him only now and then and for advocating the abolition of all "needless" effort and expenditure that detracted from the war effort.[29] In short, if the themes of the digression have been correctly identified, its insertion at the beginning of book 10 paved the way for a sympathetic treatment of Demosthenes' opposition to the Theoric Fund and, ultimately, Philip.

Demosthenes' apparent exclusion from the digression does not permit the conclusion that the term "demagogue" was not used of him in the *Philippica*. However, his political style was not described as pandering. F327 looks like a reflection on his leadership, and I can see no way to construe it as a criticism. The Athenians wanted him to prosecute a case and he refused. They raised an outcry (θορυβούντων), but Theopompus makes him say, with a display of Socratic courage (*Dem*. 14.3–4), "Men of Athens, I will serve you as a counsellor, even though you do not wish it; but not as a false accuser (συκοφάντῃ) even though you wish it" (B. Perrin, tr., L.C.L.).[30]

As a politician, therefore, Demosthenes was somewhat above average for a demagogue if he was characterized by that term at all. Again, as a man he was presented as at least somewhat better than the baser political leaders. Connor has pointed out that Theopompus accepted or invented stories about the base or foreign birth of certain of the demagogues.[31] Demosthenes' father, however, was described as well-born (F325 = Plut. *Dem*. 4.1). It is worth a moment to appreciate this point. In political trials the two would-be leaders, Demosthenes and Aeschines, invested time and ink smearing each other's parenthood. According to Demosthenes, Aeschines' mother was a priestess in the gaudy cult of a foreign divinity, and his father a casual labourer doing menial tasks around a schoolhouse. Aeschines' own birth was so low and shady that his claim to citizenship was doubtful, but he got himself enrolled in the citizen registry, "I won't say how." From the opposite rostrum Demosthenes' father was a knife-maker, no slave "for there is no need to lie." This man married a Scythian woman illegally. (By law, Athenian men could not formally "marry" foreign women. If they consorted with them, any children could not be citizens.) The illegitimate outcome of this improper union was Demosthenes.[32] Theopompus, no prude when it came to reporting scurrility, obviously sided with Demosthenes on this issue.

However, Plutarch discovered some less complimentary remarks about Demosthenes in the pages of Theopompus. He reported them in his "Life" of the orator. He says that he cannot understand how Theopompus could find Demosthenes unstable in character and "unable to abide with the same people or policies for very long" (F326 = Plut. *Dem* 13.1). Plutarch sketched a Demosthenes courageously and implacably resisting Philip. Typically, he selected episodes and reported them in a drastically truncated narrative with the sole purpose of delineating character. On the other hand, Theopompus, as historian, had undertaken to narrate the events of Philip's expansion and, presumably, Athens' resistance in much greater detail. Anyone who tries to record Demosthenes' activities through this period will observe how he began on friendly terms with Philocrates and even Aeschines, only to be led by his hawkish policies into attacking these men. And even the hawk had to don dove's feathers when he recognized the necessity of peace and alliance with Philip in 346. However, he quickly shed his peaceful disguise to lead the way in attacking the Peace soon after it had been signed. The remark about inconstancy is, therefore, either a sign of hostility to Demosthenes or simply narrative thoroughness on Theopompus' part, and there is no way to decide which it is without reference to other evidence.[33] Plutarch could abbreviate a narrative to the extent that difficult things like the inconstancy of a hero disappear from view,[34] but a historian who undertook a comprehensive account of Demosthenes' attempts to lead Athens against Philip would have to deal with apparent inconsistencies. Faced by them, Theopompus will not have been kind, but insofar as inconstancy is a generally acknowledged fact of Demosthenes' career, it has to be reported somehow by both admirers and detractors. Therefore, no conclusion about Theopompus' attitude to Demosthenes can be drawn from F326. The remark is not of the same order as the criticisms of Philip. Theopompus' view of Philip was extreme – idiosyncratic even. Others looked at Philip and did not see what he saw. His characterization of Philip is a choice, a rejection of reasonable alternatives. Even the language makes this abundantly plain. Men whom others saw and described as the king's "friends," Theopompus described as his "boyfriends," coining a grotesque word to make a ghastly pun. And in another crude pun, the warriors, self-styled "menslayers" (ἀνδρόφονοι), were dubbed "menlayers" (ἀνδρόπορνοι). Much can be learned about a historian when he stretches or distorts the truth or takes an extreme position; much less can be learned when he simply reports or comments on things in a way that could be agreed on by both sides of a controversy.

The second and last fragment concerning Demosthenes unquestionably includes a criticism of his management of Greek business in the preliminaries to the battle of Chaeronea. It has been seen as irrefutable proof that Theopompus condemned Demosthenes.[35] It must be examined carefully, first in its context. Luckily, two useful forensic speeches survive. In 336, a scant two years after Chaeronea, a certain Ctesiphon had proposed to the Athenian Council that Demosthenes be publicly honoured with a golden crown in recognition of his service to the state. Before the democratic assembly could ratify the Council's decision to do this, Aeschines brought legal action against Ctesiphon effectively stalling the award – indeed, in an attempt to block it completely. For some reason the case waited six years before coming to trial in 330. Aeschines, of course, spoke in prosecution. His speech, *Against Ctesiphon*, was published, probably altered and improved after the event. Demosthenes replied in behalf of Ctesiphon. It was not illegal for a friend to speak in another's behalf, and the supporting speech could (and in this case did) turn into the main statement for the defence. Demosthenes' speech, *On the Crown*, also survives, again no doubt revised with the advantage of hindsight. These two speeches give the modern scholar a rare opportunity to see the age through the eyes of two observers, leading participants, who held antagonistic views of the major events. Fortunately, it does not matter who is telling the truth at any given moment. How the story was told now from one side, now from the other, is the only concern. Then clues from the actual fragments of Theopompus can be compared to each line of argument. In Demosthenes' version of the crucial events (*On the Crown* 211–14), Philip had suddenly appeared with an army at Elatea on the Boeotian border. The Athenians, with some justice, saw the move as a threat; Philip was moving to settle southern Greek affairs in this own interest. Boeotia was a sovereign ally of Macedonia whom Philip did not wish to drive into the Athenian camp. He therefore sent ambassadors respectfully requesting permission to pass through the country and asking for support, if Thebes wished to give it, in an attack on Athens. The Athenians decided to try to win Thebes as an ally against Philip, and they sent Demosthenes as one of the ambassadors to negotiate the alliance if the Thebans could be persuaded. When the Thebans assembled to hear the arguments, Demosthenes reports that the Macedonian ambassadors were permitted to speak first since they were the present allies.

They came forward and made their speech, full of eulogy of Philip, and of incrimination of Athens, and recalled everything you had ever done in antagonism to Thebes. The gist of the speech was that they were to show gratitude to Philip for every good turn he had done them, and to punish you for the injuries they had suffered, in whichever of two ways they chose — either by giving him a free passage, or by joining in the invasion of Attica. They proved, as they thought, that, if their advice were taken, cattle, slaves and other loot from Attica would come into Boeotia, whereas the result of the proposals they expected from us would be that Boeotia would be ravaged by the war. (C.A. Vince and J.H. Vince, trs., L.C.L.)

Plutarch's description of Demosthenes' mission to Thebes was written centuries later. His account is an abbreviation of narrative taken from two historians, but it reflects the details cited above. He gave the names of the Macedonian ambassadors on the authority of Marsyas of Pella, who wrote a Macedonian history (now lost) in the third century B.C., but his description of how the Thebans decided to join Athens cites Theopompus (F328 = Plut. *Dem.* 18.2.3):

Well, then, the Thebans in their calculations, were not blind to their own interests, but each of them had before his eyes the terrors of war, since their losses in the Phocian war were still fresh; however, the power of the orator, as Theopompus says, fanned up their courage and inflamed their honourable ambition and obscured all other considerations, so that, casting away fear and calculation and feelings of obligation, they were rapt away by his words into the path of honour. (B. Perrin, tr., L.C.L.)

This account of the effects of Demosthenes' speech requires explanation. What is meant by "casting away fear and calculation and feelings of obligation (χάρις)?" Generally, gratitude and (rational) calculation are thought to be good things, while, on the other hand, fear is bad for a would-be army, and an orator is behaving appropriately if he tries to overcome it by fanning up the soldiers' courage. Did Theopompus sympathize with Demosthenes' cause? It is true that Plutarch says that he goaded the Thebans "into the path of honour" (πρὸς τὸ καλόν), but these could be Plutarch's own words, not necessarily Theopompus'.

Plutarch's sources, Marsyas and Theopompus, no doubt gave much fuller versions. Probably it would be easier to understand Plutarch if we had more of the context. While the sources are gone, what they should have said is clear from Demosthenes, manifestly an eyewitness, and there is no reason to suppose that he invented the details he reports. Demosthenes' task had been to refute the arguments of the Macedonians, who, he says, made three central points: Thebes owed a debt of gratitude (χάρις) to Philip, she could reckon the chances of gaining plunder from an invasion of Attica (a calculation, λογισμός), and the alternative was to be plundered herself (a threat, intended to induce fear, φόβος). One of Plutarch's sources pointed out how vulnerable the Thebans were to the force of these arguments, as the opening sentence of the last quotation shows. The Macedonian speakers will scarcely have missed the opportunity to point out that Thebes had lost men and suffered much in the Phocian (Sacred) War. Their claim on Thebes' gratitude was based on the favourable treatment she received from Philip at the conclusion of that war. Theopompus, the expert on the subject, will scarcely have ignored the point. What he had to describe, therefore, was a rhetorical contest in which the Macedonians clearly began with the advantage over Demosthenes.

Demosthenes won that day as Theopompus duly reported. His rhetorical power made Thebans forget, as the historian put it, fear, calculations, and obligation and choose the path of ... The path of what is indeed the question. If Theopompus said πρὸς τὸ κακόν (the path of evil), or words to that effect, then Plutarch has done some violence to his source, "adjusting" the quotation to make it say the exact opposite of what had been intended by the original author. This is not his usual practice. When he disagrees with a source, he generally quotes the offending statement and expresses his differing view. It would seem more likely that his πρὸς τὸ καλόν (in the path of honour) was more in keeping with Theopompus' actual remarks. This, of course, means that the historian approved of Demosthenes' initial strategy of resisting Philip by forging the alliance with Thebes.[36]

Once the probability of this idea is accepted, there is much to be said for it in retrospect. The last chapter showed how Theopompus generally softened his criticisms of people who got a grip on the management of their states and exerted themselves – usually in resistance to Philip's military aggression. Framing the alliance,

Demosthenes was exerting himself, employing his rhetorical powers to defeat the insinuations of Philip's envoys. This sounds like ἐπιμέλεια (diligence) and φιλοπονία (industry) in service to the state, things which Theopompus usually praised. Further, and finally, Demosthenes was not overreaching the skills he had developed through a lifetime of oratory. Not insignificantly, it was the "power of the orator," in Theopompus' own pregnant phrase, that won the day. He was doing what he had trained himself to do through a whole lifetime, and Athens was winning.

Unfortunately, things went wrong, and the allies eventually lost. How was the historian to explain that loss? How did others do it? Demosthenes makes scattered allusions to the events after the conclusion of the alliance. This fact alone suggests that a continuous narration of the story was not in his best interests. When he is not claiming bad luck, he hints at incompetent generals,[37] but only two isolated passages suggest the level of his own involvement. In *On the Crown* (178) he describes the mandate he sought from the Athenians when the peril first became known and he felt called upon to propose a response to the crisis. He asked and, presumably, received agreement that ambassadors be appointed who would, among other things, "determine the time of the march to Thebes and the conduct of the campaign ... in consultation with the generals." He was appointed chief ambassador, of course. A little later in the same speech (179), he is at pains to show that he saw the whole business through, devoting himself to the service of Athens "in face of the perils that encompassed our city."

Aeschines told a different story (*Against Ctesiphon* 145–6). In his view, the Thebans had been driven into the arms of Athens because they feared Philip. He made no mention of Macedonian ambassadors and their honied appeals to the Theban people. His Demosthenes has the audacity to "look" the Athenians "in the face" and claim "that the Thebans made the alliance ... not because of the crisis, not because of the fear surrounding them, not because of your [Athenian] reputation, but thanks to the harangues of Demosthenes" (C.D. Adams, tr., L.C.L.). That was indeed Demosthenes' claim, though harangues was not his word. Theopompus agreed with Demosthenes, and harangues does not seem to have been his word either.

So far Aeschines can only make Demosthenes look bad by suppressing information: the presence of the Macedonian ambassadors and the force of their arguments, which Demosthenes successfully resisted. However, on subsequent events, where Demosthenes falls silent or makes brief, scattered allusions, he becomes more circumstantial. Some of his allegations are unprovable and were probably false: he alleges that Demosthenes drew state pay for fictitious units of mercenaries. Demosthenes had been audited and not convicted of any such thing. However, the really sensitive point seems to have been Demosthenes' "managerial style." He transferred the seat of Athenian government to Thebes, in Aeschines' description, and assumed authority (δυναστεία) for himself, making other Athenian officers his slaves. The generals were not to oppose his diplomatic initiatives; the war office (τὸ στρατήγιον) was to give way to his rostrum (τὸ βῆμα).

Aeschines' motive in reporting things that way was to secure a final political (or judicial) victory over Demosthenes. Theopompus, for his part, had to explain the Macedonian success at Chaeronea. It was not necessarily open to him to claim that the allies had been outgeneralled, especially if he was to maintain his picture of Philip as a soldier who could not even plan his finances and was a maniacal sot when going into battle. There had to be corruption in the allied camp, and Demosthenes, who did not deny his involvement, was implicated. Not one to be soft on human frailty when he thought he saw it, Theopompus described Demosthenes' handling of Athenian and Theban affairs preparatory to Chaeronea in very critical terms (F328.3 = Plut. *Dem.* 18.3 with Jacoby's comment): He was "exercising supreme power (δυναστεύων) illegally (ἀδίκως) and unworthily (παρ' ἀξίαν)."

Precisely what it was that Theopompus deplored is beyond certain recovery without new evidence, but suggestions can be made. Once the alliance was solemnized, Plutarch tells us, generals were subjected to Demosthenes and accepted his orders (ὑπηρετεῖν ... τοὺς στρατηγοὺς τῷ Δημοσθένει ποιοῦντας τὸ προσταττόμενον). He became, then, *de facto* supreme commander with no known *de jure* appointment, a rhetorician with no practical military experience leading a grand alliance into possibly the most crucial battle in Athenian history. Demosthenes (*On the Crown* 18.178) himself claims that he recommended that the Athenian ambassadors be appointed in charge, along with the generals, over when to march out to Thebes and over the expedition (κυρίους μετὰ τῶν στρατηγῶν καὶ τοῦ πότε δεῖ βαδίζειν ἐκεῖσε καὶ τῆς ἐξόδου). Plutarch's words, however, suggest that he went beyond acting in concert with the generals and other ambassadors – they were "subjected" to him. On the reasonable assumption that *On the Crown* 178 is the orator's recollection not just of what he recommended, but of what the *demos* actually approved, Plutarch's version, perhaps based on Theopompus, had him going beyond the strict terms of his mandate. If Theopompus told the same story, it would not be surprising to find him condemning the orator's conduct of the business as unjust and unworthy: unjust because Demosthenes' elevation was unconstitutional and his exercise of military power was legally *ultra vires* and unworthy because Demosthenes lacked the experience for such an important command. He was generalling beyond his capacity ([στρατηγῶν] παρ' ἀξίαν).

The conclusion that Theopompus sympathized with Demosthenes' policy of resistance to Philip seems difficult to avoid. The digression "On the Demagogues" deplored a form of demagoguery that Demosthenes made a show of rejecting. It brought the reader down to the period of Demosthenes' political career, and one of its effects must have been to illustrate Athens' need for his policies. When the statesman was introduced, his parentage and political style was characterized as superior to the average demagogue. Finally, when the moment came for his final test, the crafting of an alliance with Thebes with a view to risking all in battle against Philip, information about how this effort was reported by the historian exists. Theopompus emphasized Demosthenes' rhetoric as the means of accomplishing a voluntary alliance with Thebes. But Theopompus seems generally to have favoured voluntary alliances if the interpretation of the clues about the Second Athenian Confederacy and Cleommis of Methymna is correct. He would also be able to report that Demosthenes was using his rhetorical experience with diligence and industry to effect the alliance. Considering his distaste for Philip, it seems difficult to imagine how he could have attacked Demosthenes for any of that. Indeed, Plutarch, paraphrasing Theopompus, shows how the Thebans were persuaded to reject the overtures of the Macedonians "into the path of honour." That must have been more or less how Theopompus saw it, as an honorable thing, not an evil one. Closer to the showdown at Chaeronea, however, attacks on Demosthenes begin. Perhaps Demosthenes' excessive exercise of authority reminded the historian of past Athenian behaviour, a tendency to turn erstwhile voluntary allies into subordinates and tributaries. This behaviour called for and received scathing denunciation. In particular, Theopompus' disappointment over the allied failure at Chaeronea seems to shine through. Someone had to take the blame for making the right idea go wrong, and that had to be the man who was, by all reports including his own, in charge: Demosthenes. As in the Sacred War, history was indeed to produce no untarnished heroes, but that is not to say that Theopompus had no political sympathies. Perhaps his *Epitome of Herodotus* made him dream of a Greece that could unite to repel a powerful invader. The Spartans of his *Hellenica* were not the tough, simple, law-abiding stalwarts of Herodotus. They offered freedom to the Hellenes only to snatch it away when in control with a more self-seeking authoritarianism than had been exercised by the Athenians. Even his Demosthenes, after seeing the path of honour, had fallen into the same trap. His Greeks, too self-seeking or lethargic to effect anything good for themselves, deserved the evil that they got: conquest by Philip, Macedonian domination.

Epilogue

Theopompus was writing at a critical moment in the history of Greece and her literature. If he saw the issues of the age in simplistic, moral terms, he may be forgiven, for who really understands momentous events when they are actually stirring. Hindsight always seems to provide the clearest vantage point. He was a creature of his age who probably lacked the genius to transcend it. I like Lentz' formulation of Isocrates' significance. The shift in which Theopompus was perhaps unwittingly involved was away from orality in the direction of the literary transmission of ideas.[1] The needs of the writer predominated with an effect well illustrated by Vivienne Gray. She has shown how battle-narratives that probably originated with Ephorus were structured according to pre-set formulas.[2] Apparently the need to compose literature overrides any requirement to mirror the true events in all their particular diversity. The convenience of the writer proves more important than accuracy in detail. Simplistic morality aside, Theopompus seems to have worked this way too as I shall explain below. Nothing can be said about his battle-narratives; and his word-play and other verbal excesses do not of themselves speak of an inept historian. His main narrations were probably substantially reliable as F103 shows, but his willingness to create scenes of sordid debauchery, mostly, I suspect, from his own imagination, strikes me as excessive. His account of Evagoras' death at the hands of an emasculated erstwhile Elean democrat after some sordid harem intrigue in which both Evagoras and his son Pnytagoras debauched the wife of a Cypriot exile unbeknownst to each other seems to me to be a wild exercise of a lurid imagination. All indications are that the facts were not publicly known until some twenty years later when Theopompus somehow "discovered" and reported them.[3]

However, the main similarity I see between Ephorus' formulaic battles and Theopompus' material lies in what could be called a tendency to adopt a form or caricature of something without verification and to use the notion so established to inform, even create the subsequent narrative. The two best examples of this are the account of the geography north of Olynthus in book 21 and the characterization of Philip. In the introduction to the *Philippica*, Theopompus had boasted of his extensive travels to impress his prestige and authority upon the reader. He knew of Issa, a Syracusan colony on the Adriatic, but it seems hard to believe that he visited it in light of how seriously he misconceived its geography. It looks as if he was prepared to interrupt the important account of the attack on Olynthus and devote a very substantial part of a book to the advancement of a geographical theory that a visit would have exposed as imaginary. He seems to have accepted a theoretical demythologizing of the Jason story in combination with a slanted interpretation of confused hearsay information as sufficient basis for the development of a major geographic theory. In this he was little different from most people of his time and many from any other period. More serious is his picture of Philip. It was based on autopsy, but it looks twisted by the torturing force of hatred. His Philip was a grotesque caricature which no amount of positive information was going to erase. I suggested reasons for this hostility in chapter 1.

However, it is not necessary to rely on Philip alone as the sole explanation for Theopompus' melancholy. The shocking fate of Delphi seems to have disgusted him more than any other writer of the time. In fact, it is astonishing to see how little space the ransacking of the oracle gets in the literature surviving from the fourth century. It seems to me that Theopompus' veneration of Delphi, which I suspect was heavily infused into the *Philippica*, had the effect of bringing sharply into focus the spiritual bankruptcy of the mainland powers. If they could not unite under their sacred vow to save the integrity of their most ancient and venerable shrine, what chance had they against the archfiend Philip of Macedon?

Who Wrote the
Hellenica Oxyrhynchia?

The search for the identity of P (papyrus historian) is now eighty years old at least, and no general consensus has been reached. The bibliography on the subject is enormous.[1] A reopening of the issue without new evidence would be questionable, but new pieces of this historian continue to appear. Most recently, the so-called Cairo fragments were published in 1976. Their publication was followed in 1980 by an article by Eberhard Ruschenbusch, who advanced an ingenious new argument in favour of Theopompus. My own more reserved view is reflected in the text of this book; there is no conclusive case for this identification. Nevertheless, the Cairo fragments and Ruschenbusch's argument change the nature of the debate in ways that the many previous discussions could not anticipate. Papyrologists date the Cairo fragments to the late first century A.D. on the basis of such considerations as letter-forms. Therefore, P's "popularity" (if that is the right word) in Egypt must now be dated approximately to the period from the late first century A.D. to the late second, for all previously known fragments (the London fragments [found 1906, published 1908] and the Florence fragments [found 1934, published 1949]) were assigned to the late second century. Without the Cairo fragments, scholars like Herbert Bloch could argue for the anonymity of P, a short-lived "flash-in-the-pan," a historian whose importance was far from assured. Now, however, it is clear the work was being read in Egypt for a century or more. Is it likely that we do not have a name without a history to which we can attach this history without a name?

Fortunately, some matters are now conceded by all sides on this question and can be taken as given (barring some startling new discovery). These points of consensus help narrow the field of search.

There is general agreement that P was a continuator of Thucydides. Most scholars believed this even when the London fragments were the only ones available, but the Florence and Cairo fragments have removed all doubt. The Cairo fragments include events from 409. The Florence fragments seem to finish 409 and get to the battle of Notium in 407. The London fragments are quite substantial, providing extended pieces of a very detailed narrative of the years 397/6 and 396/5. As a continuation of Thucydides, the work must have begun in earnest in 411 (a few preliminaries to make a good connection cannot be ruled out). If it carried on with the same detail for many decades past 395, the work would have been enormous, and it should have got more notice if only for its size. There is some reason to believe that it went no further than the King's Peace (387/6), if it went that far. This is the first criterion: the candidate should be a known or demonstrable continuator of Thucydides.

On one other point there is something approaching a consensus: the author was mined as a source by Ephorus. Again, the scholarship is extensive. In brief, the argument goes like this: Diodorus of Sicily is known to have relied extensively and apparently exclusively on Ephorus for mainland and Aegean history for the years in question (Sicilian history may be another matter); however, the details and underlying structure of his narrative derive demonstrably from P. P wrote year-by-year, Ephorus wrote by subject, Diodorus reverted to a year-by-year style, but he tends to group too many events in a single year and so misdates many of them. He is obviously summarizing a source who wrote by subject (Ephorus) without being able to check it against the one who wrote year-by-year (P). Therefore, though Diodorus derives ultimately from P, he cannot have had P in front of him, only Ephorus.

Known continuations of Thucydides are the *Hellenica*s of Theopompus, Xenophon, and, evidently, Cratippus. Known sources of Ephorus are Callisthenes, Anaximenes, and Daemachus of Plataea. Xenophon's work is not P. Callisthenes' and Anaximenes' *Hellenica*s could not be continuations of Thucydides by the wildest stretch of imagination. This leaves Theopompus and Daemachus. Perhaps Cratippus should be added to this list on the basis of evidence to be considered below.

He is a most shadowy figure whom Jacoby (1950) regarded as a figment, a Hellenistic forgery. However, Gomme (1954), Pédech (1970), and Lehmann (1976) seem to have nullified the thin evidence on which that argument was based. Dionysius of Halicarnassus (Jacoby no. 64, Fl = D.H. *Th.* 16) says that Cratippus "shared his 'acme' with Thucydides" and "collected together the things omitted [by Thucydides] and wrote them up" but that he rejected his method of including speeches because they interrupt the action and are tedious to the readers (a point to which I shall return). Plutarch gives an indication of the glorious Athenian achievements to be found in Cratippus (*Mor.* 345C–E = T2):

411–408 Take away Alcibiades' spirited exploits in the
    409 Hellespontine region, and those of Thrasyllus
    411 by Lesbos, and the overthrow by Theramenes of
         the oligarchy, Thrasybulus and Archinus and
    403 the uprising of the seventy from Phyle against
         the Spartan hegemony, and Conon's restoration
394–392 of Athens to her power on the sea — take these
(or   away and Cratippus is no more. (F.C. Babbitt, tr., L.C.L.)
later?)

This is, of course, a deliberate selection of glorious Athenian achievements in Cratippus, not a dispassionate table of contents. One need only look at the highly selective summary of Thucydides immediately preceding to see that. Plutarch claims that if certain items are taken away from Thucydides, he too "is no more." Few would agree. Consider the list:

Item	Date	Reference in Thuc.
Pericles' statesmanship	c. 450–429	1 – early 2.
Phormio at Rhium	429	2.84–92.
Nicias at Corcyra	424	4.53–57.
Nicias against Megara, Corinth	427	3.51.
Demosthenes' Pylos	425	4.2–23.
Cleon's 400 captives	425	4.26–41
Tolmides' *periplous*	457	1.108.5.
Victory at Oenophyta	457	1.108.2–3.

Nothing from Thucydides' last four books is even mentioned, and as a summary of the first four it is disorderly and trivial (except for Pericles' statesmanship). On the other hand, Plutarch's summary does suggest that Cratippus continued Thucydides. Only the overthrow of the oligarchy had been narrated by Thucydides (8.90–4), but he had not made Theramenes an untarnished hero of the democracy (8.68.4). Perhaps Cratippus went back to "correct" Thucydides when he described Theramenes' death in 403, but, obviously, it is not certain that Plutarch's summary reflects Cratippus' narrative order. One scholar thought that "Conon's restoring Athens to her sea-power" meant that Cratippus ended with the battle of Cnidus, like Theopompus, but that seems doubtful to me.[2] Cratippus recorded the "restoration of sea-power to Athens," but Cnidus restored sea-power to Persia, not Athens. Conon began the transferral to Athens in 393, and Thrasybulus took it up and continued it until 389. In fact, Athenian claims to sea-power were ended, or at least drastically curtailed, by the King's Peace, the only natural stopping place once a narrative had gone beyond Cnidus and got involved with the Corinthian War. The scope of Cratippus' history was, therefore, c. 411–the late 390s. Indeed, Plutarch attributes nothing after 393 to Cratippus, but he is no guide on this matter. The latest event he cites from Thucydides belongs to 424.

The distribution of the papyrus fragments eliminates the candidacy of neither Theopompus nor Cratippus, and there is no evidence to indicate P's actual stopping point. I should think it surprising if he did not intend to continue to 387/6, however. His detailed account of the outbreak of the Corinthian War, which ended with the King's Peace, suggests more than a casual interest. Is it really possible that he had no thought of telling the whole story? Again the meticulous description of the organization of Boeotia hangs as an isolated curiosity without the narration of its dissolution by the Spartans in 387/6. Despite P's dullness, he is not an antiquarian. He is careful to provide explanation by means of his monotonous progression of circumstantial subordinate clauses and connects his narrative to previous material in his (or even Thucydides') work (2; 7.4). Looked at the other way, this makes him conscious of the principle that a present narrative prepares for something to be related in a later year.

On the criterion of "continuator of Thucydides," therefore, it is hard to see who has a clear edge for nomination as the author. P probably intended to go beyond 394, and Cratippus seems to have done so, but it is not known whether P fulfilled his apparent intention, and the scope of the fragments of P suits the scope of Theopompus a little more snugly. On the criterion of being a source for Ephorus, both begin the contest with points against. If P was Theopompus, it is necessary to assert that Ephorus mined Theopompus' *Hellenica*, a sensational thesis to which the total absence of any evidence from antiquity is very damaging. There were stories about these two "pupils of Isocrates" oft-repeated in antiquity. Theopompus needed the master's rein, it is said, and Ephorus the spur. There was a market for this sort of story: someone must have noticed the close structural and substantive relationship between the two histories that this thesis requires and sought to explain it. The substantial difference between the writers' accounts of Lysander's political activity and death (chapter 2) proves nothing, but it does little to help Theopompus' cause. Most damning of all is Porphyry's discussion of the "plagiarisms" of Ephorus and Theopompus. Of course, Porphyry's list of sources for the two may not be complete, but it is worthwhile to recall the context wherein the accusations of plagiarism were made (Theop. T27, FF21, 102 = Porph. in Euseb. *PE* 464–5). The ostensible circumstance is a dinner of sophists at which a dispute over the alleged superiority of Ephorus over Theopompus arises. Ephorus is inferior, it is alleged, because he has stolen "up to three thousand entire lines *verbatim* from Daemachus, Callisthenes and Anaximenes." The response to this is that Theopompus is just as bad, and a series of alleged plagiarisms from Isocrates and a certain Andron is listed off from the *Philippica*. Then Nicagoras, one of the banqueters, joins the fray with information about the *Hellenica*. He claims to have caught Theopompus transposing "much" from Xenophon's *Hellenica* into his own and cites as a specific instance a meeting between Agesilaus and Pharnabazus arranged under truce by the mediation "of Apollophanes of Cyzicus." Nicagoras also insists that both the circumstances of the visit and "their conversation with each other" were transposed from Xenophon's fourth book (*HG* 4.1.29–40) to Theopompus' eleventh. In this case as in all others, Nicagoras alleges, Theopompus changes everything for the worse.[3]

This is a lengthy and extraordinarily learned discussion. Daemachus and Andron are little more than names today, and they were scarcely "household names" in antiquity. Further, Nicagoras' discussion of the *Hellenica* is detailed and informative. Apollophanes' mediation is indeed recorded by Xenophon as the key to the meeting's occurrence. After Nicagoras' speech, another banqueter, Apollonius, dismisses both historians as lazy plagiarists, and one must wonder how this discussion could have been held if Ephorus had plundered Theopompus' *Hellenica* to the extent required by the identification of P with Theopompus. Did not all the banqueters know that Ephorus himself had established Theopompus' superiority by stealing his material? There is more to be done with Porphyry's information, but the conclusion that Ephorus did not draw on Theopompus seems inescapable. The fact would have been obvious and noteworthy, and there were too many missed opportunities for its mention in ancient literature, the debate in Porphyry being the most prolonged and significant. The silence of the ancient sources is too loud to ignore.

However, if the use of Theopompus by Ephorus can only be advanced over grave difficulties, Cratippus' claim at first suffers from a similar shortcoming. Porphyry mentions the obscure Daemachus but is silent on Ephorus' possible use of the equally obscure Cratippus. It could be that it is possible to say so much against Theopompus' claim because there is so much more information about him and his work.

It will be worthwhile to search a little further, but a brief procedural comment seems in order before beginning. The temptation to narrow the range of choices to Theopompus and Cratippus should be resisted despite its obvious pull. Intrinsically, it seems too much to believe that there could be yet a third continuation of Thucydides of just about exactly the same scope as Cratippus and Theopompus. If there are only two candidates, however, one author could "win by default." Points against X in such a closed system raise the chances of Y. Thus there is a danger that Y could win the nomination through no special merit, but only because there are too many problems with X. Therefore, Daemachus or Anonymous must remain in the field of vision as potential candidates.

When the London fragments were first published, Theopompus won some influential advocates in Eduard Meyer and Ulrich von Wilamowitz-Moellendorff. The case hinged on the assumed importance of P; he was important enough to be preserved and read ahead of all others in Roman Egypt. The author ought to have a name and an important one. It was found that Agesilaus' intrusion into Pharnabazus' satrapy was indeed reported somewhat less vigorously than in Xenophon. If that could have been book 11 of Theopompus, it was then found in F19 that Carpaseans (as opposed to the alternative "Carpaseotes") were mentioned in book 10. Sure enough, in P, in a preceding section, a Carpasean is found leading a revolt against Conon. A further ransacking of Byzantine grammarians produced a verb "swoop-down" (κατᾶραι, F265) meaning "to go" (ἐλθεῖν). Just such a usage can be paralleled in P, not once, but twice.[4] Meyer also found a description of the valley of the Meander in Strabo (13.4.12), attributed by him to Theopompus (F391); a similar description is found in P with verbal parallels. This seemed to be a great number of coincidences for such a few pages of papyrus. Nor did the coincidences cease with the discovery of more fragments. The Florence fragments revealed that P had included a flashback digression on Pedaritus, the Spartan harmost on Chios who died there in 412 and whose death had already been reported by Thucydides. Theopompus must have done much the same thing in his second book (F8, Meyer 160). If Theopompus is not P, he mirrors him closely. Either Theopompus is the author, or some theory must be provided to explain these persistent coincidences.

Chronological arguments have been raised against Theopompus' candidacy. However, my own views on the evidence for the historian's life are clear from chapter 1. The dates we usually give for his birth and the writing of the *Hellenica* are not firm and cannot be used to argue dogmatically, for example, that P was written too early to be Theopompus. However, a difficulty of more substance that has generally been ignored involves the question of the historian's native dialect: East Ionic.[5] Theopompus writes in Attic in all his fragments except for a Dorian-looking infinitive, if it is cited correctly (F265), and, more significantly, his place names are consistently Attic except for one (Dorian! See F82) exception that I have noticed. The texts could conceivably have been Atticized by anthologists, but the place-names are cited expressly for their orthography. The obliteration of his native accent and orthography must have gone hand in hand with his education in Athens, his "Isocrateanization." Here is the dilemma: P's style exhibits at best only modest exposure to the refinements of Isocrates. His avoidance of hiatus stands out rather mechanically as one exception. He makes inflexible use of a type of Isocratean period but exhibits vestiges of the older paratactic style.[6] Laqueur, a Theopompus lobbyist, noticed this and suggested that the *Hellenica* was written at an early stage in the development of the historian's style. P, then, was a blossoming author from Chios. But the papyrus fragments lend no support to this claim. P's interest in Chios never takes him beyond the necessary to the gratuitous,[7] and his dialect and nomenclature show no traces of East Ionic.

In fact, Cratippus' claim looks a little better than Theopompus'. It has long been recognized that P avoids giving his characters speeches. The London fragments include a full account of the beginnings of the Corinthian War, Conon's attempt to quell a mutiny amongst Cypriot Greeks in the King's fleet, and Agesilaus' intrusion into Pharnabazus' satrapy. Opportunities for speechmaking are not absent, but P takes none. One of the few things known about Cratippus is that he criticized the use of set speeches because they "do not just interfere with the facts, but they are also a nuisance to the reader." Of course, scholars were wisely reluctant to make too much of this. With only the London fragments, there was perhaps insufficient material for a generalization. Today the discoveries of the Florence and Cairo fragments have changed nothing except to reinforce somewhat the impression that P consistently avoided speeches. Cratippus was an Athenian, and P's content and Attic dialect are both suitable. Despite Meyer's early doubts, the case that P could well have been written by an Athenian has often been recognized but was perhaps most forcefully stated by Underhill:[8]

P seems to show a more intimate acquaintance with Athenian than with Boeotian or even Spartan affairs. In cols. i.1–24, ii.35–iii.9 he enters into minute details about the unimportant expedition of Demaenetus; in cols. i.25–ii.1 and ii.10–14 he professes full knowledge of the motives of the Athenian democrats; and in col. xiii.15–40 he gives curious particulars about the furnishing of Attic houses. Moreover ... his account of the exploits of the Athenian Conon seems to be fuller and more enthusiastic than that of the campaigns of the Spartan Agesilaus.

P's heroization of Conon is unmistakable. Cratippus attributed the restoration of Athenian sea-power to Conon, apparently making his accomplishments heroic in a similar fashion.

Arguments have been advanced against Cratippus, however. Lehmann pointed out that Plutarch's *De Gloria Atheniensium* seems to imply that Cratippus must have included the Athenian politician Archinus in his account of the outbreak of the Corinthian War, and P does not mention him. However, all that is known from Plutarch, who certainly seems to be using Cratippus, is that Archinus was associated with the expulsion of the Thirty Tyrants. This point is made twice, and Archinus is not otherwise mentioned. It is never clear just why ancient historians include or suppress the names of political agents. Without more direct knowledge of Cratippus the point is far too speculative to carry conviction.

Somewhat more forceful is the argument by Bloch that seems to eliminate both candidates.[9] He notices Dionysius' claim that after Thucydides no historian had written year-by-year. This means that Dionysius is ignorant of P, but since he goes on to quote Cratippus, he knew him, and there is no doubt that he knew Theopompus. If Dionysius knew that Theopompus and Cratippus had written year-by-year, the remark would not be possible. Therefore, they did not. But P did. Therefore, neither can be P. This looks clever until one remembers that Xenophon continued Thucydides year-by-year, and Dionysus can scarcely have ignored him. To me it seems better to try to appreciate the main thrust of Dionysius' argument, which is that year-by-year historiography died out after Thucydides: "that this style [year-by-year] is not correct and is unsuitable to history is clear. For not one of the historians who came after divided his history by summers and winters." Bloch assumes that Dionysius is being as precise and meticulous in his language as a trained scholar of the twentieth century. To the contrary, the fact that Thucydides spawned a few slavish imitations need not detain Dionysius and does nothing to undermine his main point: the style quickly died out. "Thucydides" in this passage, and in Aelius Theon,[10] I take to mean "the historian and his school." Dionysius (and Aelius) attacks the style by attacking its main practitioner; the blow is aimed at the "serpent's" head. These objections, therefore, are not prohibitive, and the key still remains the question of Ephorus' possible use of Cratippus as a source.

Now that Ruschenbusch's article has reopened the Theopompus theory, it is necessary to recall why the thesis had died. Some of the scholarship that effectively squelched the notion seems to have been forgotten by some writers. P's style was examined minutely at a very early stage and compared with that of Ephorus and Theopompus in the fragments and the differences were found to be extensive. These were not the general notion of Isocrateanism but the use of particles and small expressions that introduce clauses of explanation. Of course, the substantive examples of Theopompus' style come mostly from the *Philippica*, but there is no scrap of evidence for a belief that his style changed in any way between the writing of the two histories. This was shown succinctly by Maas, who also explored the problems raised by Porphyry's description of Theopompus' use of Xenophon. McKechnie and Kern downplay this information, but it is clear and damning. Porphyry says that Theopompus took the speeches of Agesilaus and Pharnabazus out of Xenophon and changed them for the worse. But P omits these speeches altogether! Porphyry insists that "many things" beside this scene were taken by Theopompus from Xenophon. However, the independence of the two accounts P-Xenophon is notorious. There are no identifiable borrowings from Xenophon in P.

The conclusion that P was not Theopompus seems difficult to avoid. There are too many problems: the source relationship (Ephorus can scarcely have mined Theopompus); the dilemma of the non-Isocratean style vs. the dialect; Maas' stylistic minutiae; the demonstrable non-use of Xenophon by P; the absence of the speeches of Agesilaus-Pharnabazus. In addition to these traditional objections, some new ones have emerged as a result of my own general examination of Theopompus. There is circumstantial reason to believe that Theopompus maintained a strand of Sicilian narrative through the *Hellenica*. P has none. P does not seem to know Theopompus' two favourite moral words φιλοπονία and ἐπιμέλεια and uses προθυμία instead, a word attested to only once in Theopompus (F344). Of greater significance is P's clear failure to discriminate between Greeks and barbarians. Both Cyrus the Persian and Conon the Athenian display προθυμία (19.2, 20.6). Racial outlooks are generally deeply ingrained, and the clear shifts in language evidenct in the *Philippica* when the subject became a non-Greek are not traceable in P.

Therefore, the verbal similarities must be explained as borrowings from P by Theopompus. The Pedaritus coincidence must mean that Theopompus knew and answered P in a place where he had stepped onto the "hallowed ground" of Chian history. Theopompus' *Hellenica* looks to have been written as a work hostile to P with the intention of displacing him as the "official" (that is, generally accepted) continuation of Thucydides. That assumption explains the evidence better than using a few verbal echoes against a mass of overwhelming circumstantial obstacles to identify P with Theopompus.

Now Ruschenbusch's attempt to reverse the established trend by means of inferences from word-distributions must be examined. He begins from the Byzantine allegation (F261) that Theopompus used the word *antipoliteuesthai* in the special sense of "to oppose a fellow-citizen in domestic politics." His claim is that the word used in this sense enjoyed limited success and that it is frequently found in contexts where Theopompus may be suspected as the source; moreover, others who use it this way are known to have read Theopompus. It is used five times by Diodorus, allegedly, four times in contexts where Theopompus is a possible source and once where Duris, who knew Theopompus, is a likely source. Its alleged infrequent use is proof that it was not part of Diodorus' vocabulary; therefore, it must come from his source. Diodorus' source was Ephorus who used P, but the usage is not Ephorus' but Theopompus'. Therefore, Ephorus must have got it from Theopompus; he must have used Theopompus, but, in fact, he used P. Therefore, P must be Theopompus.

I was able to find not five but eight uses of the word in the desired sense in Diodorus. After three uses in book 13 its occurrence once each in books 17 (15.2), 18 (66.4), 20 (62.2), 27 (4.5), and 30 (5) suggest to me the opposite of Ruschenbusch's claim. It is in fact part of Diodorus' vocabulary or was far too generalized in his source material to be used as a "trademark" of any single source. Further, its frequent (fourteen times) use by Polybius in a variety of contexts, its appearance even in a letter to Atticus (7.8.5) by Cicero, and a couple of examples (3.5.1, 2) in Dionysius' *Roman Antiquities* (not to mention the eight uses distributed throughout Diodorus) all suggest that it was in vogue for about a century from Polybius' to Diodorus' time. Moreover, a few of Ruschenbusch's allegedly Theopompan uses of the word are extremely difficult. When the word is used of Solon by Aristotle (*Politics* 1247a) and of Cleisthenes and Isagoras by a Scholiast (Schol. Aristid. *Pan.* 3.118), both references to the sixth century, a new phase develops in the argument. Now, instead of using *antipoliteuesthai* to confirm a suspicion that Theopompus could be the source, Ruschenbusch uses the word to reconstruct Theopompus; and one is left to wonder which is the hypothesis and which is the evidence. If sixth-century demagoguery cannot be fitted into book 10 ("On the Demagogues") as chapter 3 showed, book 21 (the other suggestion) is not much happier. That book contains the "reconstruction" of Adriatic-Euxine geography and ends with a mention of Syracusan and Athenian tyrants. It is hard to see how a digression on Solon and the dispute between Cleisthenes and Isagoras would fit in here. Theopompus had covered all that in his "Epitome of Herodotus," a work that no one seems to have read. It would be more likely that the word was employed by the chroniclers of local Athenian history, the Atthidographers.[11] This would explain its association with Solon and Cleisthenes.

Most problematic of all is P's failure to use *antipoliteuesthai* despite several excellent opportunities. London fragments 6.1–7.2 give a lengthy description of Athenian factions, and 7.3 changes to Corinth where Timolaus opposes the anti-Spartans "on private grounds." Particularly, there is P's description of politicking in Thebes. A Scholiast (Schol. Aristid. *Pan.* 3.83) says that Ismenias and Leontiades "opposed each other politically in Thebes" (*antepoliteuonto*), and Ruschenbusch makes Theopompus the source for this information. Now P gives a detailed account of the early phases of this very struggle. He introduces it in 16.1 and elaborates on it in 17.1 and 2, and there is no hint of *antipoliteuesthai*. Accordingly, Ruschenbusch argues that the reference belongs to a later context, the garrisoning of the Cadmea in 382, but that puts it in what Polybius calls the *Leuktrikoi kairoi*, a period deliberately omitted by Theopompus. It seems best to assign a period of limited use to the word among the Atthidographers, Aristotle, and other lost authors of the fourth century. If Theopompus really did coin the usage, it looks as if it quickly became a commonplace. It was perhaps known to Ephorus as well, but Diodorus' use of it need not have come from him. The word enjoyed a second period of limited popularity in his day, and it appears to have been part of his vocabulary.

That is the main part of Ruschenbusch's argument. Somewhat less substantial but still important is his attempt to link Theopompus F103 with Plutarch's *Artaxerxes* (21.4). The connection is made through another word, also used metaphorically, *brabeuein*. This word means "to act as umpire" basically, but it was extended somewhat metaphorically to mean "to arbitrate" or "settle" (of a legal or international dispute), probably in the fourth century. Theopompus used the word in F103 to describe the King's intervention in Greek disputes in 387, imposing the terms of the King's Peace. Plutarch used the same verb to describe the same event:

But after Artaxerxes, by the sea-fight which Pharnabazus and Conon won for him off Cnidus, had stripped the Lacedaemonians of their power on the sea, he brought the whole of Greece into dependence upon him, so that he dictated [*brabeuein*] to the Greeks the celebrated Peace of Antalcidas. (F.C. Babbitt, tr., L.C.L.)

Furthermore, *brabeuein* is used by Diodorus in a similar sense in 13.53.2 where the situation in Athens in 410 is the topic, obviously a section in which P could be the ultimate source through Ephorus. In the same sentence there is another metaphorical usage: *meteorizein* ("elevate, raise in height" basically, "buoy up [a person's] spirits" metaphorically). This strongly suggests that Diodorus can reflect quite closely the language of his fourth-century sources, for it was probably in that century that the development of these metaphors took place. This much looks reasonable, but the metaphors do not point to Theopompus specifically. Diodorus uses *meteorizein* metaphorically in 11.32.4 (the battle of Plataea) where the ultimate source can have been neither P nor Theopompus. Nor is it likely that Theopompus is the source for Plutarch's *Artaxerxes* (21.4). His version (F103) seems to have made little or nothing of Conon and Pharnabazus at Cnidus. For him the Peace was "arbitrated" simply to make it possible for Artaxerxes to attack and reduce Cyprus and end Evagoras' revolt.

In the present state of the evidence I doubt that anyone can give an identification of P that will meet with universal satisfaction. The above discussion should make clear my reasons for not using the papyrus fragments in my treatment of Theopompus' *Hellenica* in chapter 2. Further, there is some reason for favouring Cratippus' candidacy. If he could be identified as a source for Ephorus, he would have to be regarded as a very strong candidate indeed. Harding recently advanced just such a view. Dionysius reported Cratippus' rejection of speeches "because they do not just interfere with the facts, but they are also a nuisance to the reader." Diodorus expresses a similar sentiment in 20.1.1. Now book 20 covers events from 307 B.C. and after, and Ephorus was not the source, for he did not live to that year, but the passage in Diodorus is an introduction, a *Prooimion*, of which there are several in Diodorus, and Bloch believed that this and other *prooimia* in Diodorus came from Ephorus. But the sentiment reflects the view of Cratippus so closely that borrowing has to be suspected. If it were certain that this *prooimion* was taken from Ephorus, then Ephorus could justifiably be suspected of plundering Cratippus. Unfortunately, the attribution of this passage to Ephorus is nothing more than an attractive guess. Somewhat more substantial is the observation that Diodorus, certainly following Ephorus, attributes the overthrow of the oligarchy to Theramenes (13.38.1–2) as did Cratippus (see Plutarch's summary).[12] This certainly establishes the possibility that Ephorus mined Cratippus' history. It would be nice to have more evidence, but the identification of P with Cratippus looks like not a bad guess to me. He suits the bill linguistically and temporally, for P was probably an Athenian as was Cratippus, and both must be assigned to the first half of the fourth century; Dionysius is explicit about Cratippus' "acme," and P's description of events is too circumstantial to have been written many decades after. Cratippus continued Thucydides, as did P; and he could have been a source for Ephorus as P certainly was.

The Testimonia
and Fragments[1]

Generally speaking the *testimonia* and fragments are translated exactly as they are in Jacoby. In those cases the source-references must be found there, for I do not wish to have this translation replace his work, but rather make it more accessible. In some cases, however, particularly in the *testimonia*, I have made some changes. Many of them read better when kept intact rather than separated from associated fragments. As a result, some of the fragments are found in the context of a *testimonium*. For others, the reader is referred to the text of this book.

Similarly, some of Jacoby's *testimonia* are included in the full text of a *testimonium* as I give it. In those cases the beginning is indicated by the insertion of the T or F number in brackets; and "T" or "F" "ends," with the number of the fragment or *testimonium* all in brackets, marks the termination. T2 is a good example. In Jacoby T2 is the first few lines of Photius' assemblage of biographical information about Theopompus. I have simply reproduced the entire assemblage which Jacoby had dissected along thematic lines into TT2, 3(a), 31, 34, and F25, permitting a few lines of text to fall away completely and re-using the first line or two of F25 as T3(a).

I have frequently given a *testimonium* in full or in a fuller form than Jacoby's. In those cases references are supplied. I have also added some supplementary texts that seemed useful to illustrate or expand the context of a *testimonium* or fragment. These supplements are supplied with source-references and are identifiable by the absence of a T or F number (see, for example, the list starting with Zosimus after T5b). In a few cases I have borrowed a translation from another scholar. These are as noted.

Generally, explanatory insertions of my own and information about the text or variant translations are in square brackets [ ].

References to other fragmentary historians in Jacoby's collection are given in parentheses ( ). For example (no. 124, F4) is a reference to the fourth fragment of historian number 124 (who is Callisthenes). Parenthetical expressions in the text itself are set off with a dash −.

TESTIMONIA

T1   Theopompus. Chian, orator. Son of Damasistratus. Born [flourished?] round the time when no archon was elected in Athens [404/3], in the 93rd Olympiad [408/5], contemporary of Ephorus. Pupil of Isocrates with Ephorus. Wrote an *Epitome of Herodotus* in two books, a *Philippica* in 72 [*sic*, 58] books, and a *Hellenic History*, continuing the work of Thucydides and Xenophon [*sic*, like Xenophon's?], in 11 [*sic*, 12] books; it contained events after the Peloponnesian War, etc. [He also wrote a great many other things.]

T2   Photius' Life of Theopompus. (Westermann, *Vitarum Scriptores*, 204–6): Theopompus was a Chian by birth, the son of Damostratus. It is said that he went into exile with his father when his father was convicted of "Spartanizing," that he was restored to his native country after his father died, and that his return was arranged by Alexander of Macedon through a letter to the Chians [334]. At that time Theopompus is said to have been forty-five years old. After the death of Alexander, driven out everywhere, he came to Egypt, and Ptolemy, king of Egypt, did not accept him but wanted to do away with him as a meddler had not some of his friends interceded and saved him. (T2 ends) (T3 [a], F25) and he himself says that he was in his prime at the same time as Isocrates, the Athenian, Theodectes of Phaselis, and Naucrates of Erythrae, (T3 [a] ends) and that these men, along with himself, were foremost in rhetorical learning among the Greeks. He says that Isocrates wrote speeches and gave instruction for want of an income, and Theodectes also for pay; both gave young men instruction and reaped benefit therefrom. However, he claimed that he himself and Naucrates were the self-sufficient ones and spent their whole time in the pursuit of wisdom and knowledge. And [he says] that it would not seem unreasonable for him to claim pre-eminence, since he has written epideictic speeches of no less than 2,000 lines and more than 150,000 lines [in total?] in which it is possible to learn of the doings of Greeks and barbarians that are still being reported even to the present day and, moreover, because there is no important place or eminent city of the Greeks that he did not visit to put on a rhetorical display nor in which he did not leave a great fame and lasting memory of his rhetorical prowess. So he speaks about himself, and he declared the pre-eminent authors of former time to be greatly inferior even to the second-rate authors of his own day. He claims that this is clear both from their best-wrought works and from their neglected ones; for, according to him, literary knowledge made great progress in his genera-tion. But who he means by "the authors of former time," I cannot rightly guess. I do not suppose that he has the effrontery to rail at Herodotus and Thucydides, for in many respects he is far inferior to those men. Perhaps he is alluding to Hellanicus and Philistus, the historians, or perhaps he is making veiled allusion to Gorgias and Lysias and men like that, born before his time but very near it, but even they are not such inferior authors. (F25 ends) Well, so says Theopompus. (T5 [a]) They say that he and Ephorus were students of Isocrates. His manner of expression proves that for, by imitation, there is much of the form of Isocrates' speech in the expression of Theopompus, even if there is lacking something of his accuracy in execution. (T5 [a] ends) The master is said to have set them their historical subjects. The study of ancient times went to Ephorus, and to Theopompus went the Hellenic history after Thucydides. So he fitted the task to the nature of each. Wherefore their respective introductions are very similar in thought and in other respects as though they were each issuing from the same starting gate onto the race-course of history. (T31) Theopompus extends his historical narrations with a great many digressions on miscellaneous historical subjects. Wherefore, Philip – who made war against the Romans – [Philip V of Macedon] extracted the digressions and put together the activities of Philip [Theopompus' subject] into a mere sixteen books. He fitted it all together adding nothing of his own, nor, as the story goes, did he subtract anything but the digressions. (T31 ends) (T34) Duris of Samos, in Book 1 of his *Histories* says, "Ephorus and Theopompus gave very inadequate accounts of happenings, for they give neither a sense of emotion nor pleasure in the narrative. Their concern was with style only." (T34 ends) In spite of this, Duris is in many respects worse than they, committing the very errors of composition of which he accuses them. However, whether he aimed his remark at Theo-pompus' arrogant claim that the ancients were not up to second-rate standard, I cannot say, except that neither understood the ancients properly; on this I would most strongly insist. Kleo-chares of Myrlea, speaking, I think, about all of Isocrates' speeches – for that is what I take him to mean in his comparison with Demosthenes when he warns against citing irrelevant parallels–says that the speeches of Demosthenes are like the bodies of soldiers, while those of Isocrates are like the bodies of athletes. It is clear that Theopompus is inferior to none of the Isocrateans as a stylist.

T3(a) See T2.
T3(b) Theopompus was born sometime after Alcibiades.
T4 the Chian orator Caucalus, the brother of the historian Theopompus.
T5(a) See T2.
T5(b) Demosthenes studied rhetoric together with Aesion the Athenian and Theopompus the Chian philosopher.

Zos.? *Vit. Isoc.* (Westermann, *Vitarum Scriptores*, 256), see after T8.

Men. *On the Epidictics* (Walz, *Rhetores Graeci*, 9: 262): Even as Ephorus and Theopompus, students of Isocrates, were crowned as distinguished above the others.

Cic. *De Or.* 2.13 (57): After that, [that is, after the time of Philistus of Syracuse], a very famous rhetorical factory–so to speak–produced two highly talented men, Theopompus and Ephorus, who turned to history on the encouragement of their teacher, Isocrates. They never touched a case. (Russell and Winterbottom, trs., *Ancient Literary Criticism*, 254).

Cic. *De Or.* 2.22–23 (94): And lo! There arose Isocrates, master of all orators, from whose school, like the Trojan horse, only leaders came forth, but some of them sought distinction in rhetorical display, others on the battlefield. Indeed, the former sort were the Theopompuses, the Ephoruses, the Philistuses, and the Naucrateses.

Cic. *De Or.* 3.9 (36) = Quint. 2.8.11: Isocrates, the eminent teacher, used to say that he normally used the spur on Ephorus but the rein on Theopompus.

T6(a) Theodectes of Phaselis in Lycia, son of Aristandrus, orator turned to writing tragedies ... he, Naucrates of Erythrae, Isocrates the orator from Apollonia, and Theopompus delivered funerary encomia over Mausolus in the 106th Olympiad [356–352]. Artemisia, Mausolus' wife, promoted the competition. Theodectes won with great distinction because he spoke in tragic verse. Others say that Theopompus took first prize.

T6(b) To contend for these prizes, they say, came men of eminence in wit and exalted speech: Theopompus, Theodectes, and Naucrates. Some have even recorded that Isocrates himself contended with them. But in this contest Theopompus was adjudged the winner. He was a student of Isocrates.

(*The Suda*) "Isocrates, son of Amyclas": Isocrates of Apollonia on the Pontus or of Heraclea according to Callistratus, son of Amyclas the philosopher, orator, pupil, and successor to the great Isocrates. Attended lectures given by Plato the philosopher. This Isocrates contended with Theodectes the orator and tragic poet, Theopompus the Chian, and Naucrates of Erythrae in the funerary speech-making competition for Mausolus, king of Halicarnassus.

T7   (Bickermann and Sycutris, "Speusipps Brief," 7–12): (Speusippus to Philip). The bearer of this letter, Antipater, is a Magnesian by birth, but for a long time now he has been writing his *Hellenica* in Athens. He says that he is being wronged by a person in Magnesia. Hear the business out and help him as eagerly as you are able. It would be right for you to help him for many reasons but especially because when we read in the school the address sent to you by Isocrates, he approved of its main argument but found fault with his omission of your good services to Greece. I shall try to speak of a few of them, for Isocrates did not make clear the good services of yourself and your forebears to Greece, nor did he dispel the slanders that some have raised against you, nor has he spared Plato in his letters already sent to you.

And yet in the first place he should not have overlooked your present friendliness to our city, but made it clear for your offspring. When Heracles wanted to be initiated into the mysteries, though it was a custom with us in olden days never to initiate a foreigner, he became adoptive son of Pylius. This being the case, it was open to Isocrates to address you as a fellow-citizen, since your family is descended from Heracles. After that he could have reported the good services to Greece of Alexander your ancestor and of the others. As it is, he has kept them hushed as if they were unmentionable disasters. For example, when Xerxes sent ambassadors to Greece demanding earth and water, Alexander killed the ambassadors. Later, when the barbarians had begun their invasion, the Greeks opposed them at your Heracleion, and when Alexander reported the treachery of Aleuas and the Thessalians, the Greeks withdrew and were saved thanks to Alexander. Yet it were fitting that not just Herodotus and Damastes make mention of these services, but also the one who vaunts [Isoc. *Address to Philip* 77) himself in his arty phrases [text corrupt] ... well-disposed students ought to be towards you. He should have mentioned also his kindness at the time of

Mardonius at Plataea and the many subsequent services of your forebears. So written, his speech about you would have represented aright the Greeks' goodwill for you rather than saying nothing good about your kingdom. Moreover, the discussion of ancient history belonged to Isocrates' advanced years, and, as he himself said, to do it stylishly [Isoc. *Address to Philip* 10] would require "the full blossom of his intellectual powers."

Moreover, he could have dispelled the slanders that arise for the most part from the Olynthians. For who would think you so foolish that, with the Illyrians and Thracians making war on you, also the Athenians and Lacedaemonians and other Greeks and barbarians, you would initiate a war against the Olynthians? However, a letter is not the appropriate place for an expatiation on these matters. Rather I should like to speak of things that no one who encounters them is prevented from reporting but that have been kept hushed up for a long time by everyone, although it is to your advantage to hear them, and I think I can ask the messenger's reward for this good news, just recompense from you to Antipater. You see, concerning the land that came to the Olynthians, the bearer of this letter is the first and indeed the only writer to report trustworthy stories to the effect that it belonged in ancient days to the Heraclids and not to the Chalcideans. He says that in just the same way Neleus in Messene and Syleus in the land of Amphipolis were killed by Heracles, both of them as criminals: Messene was given to Nestor, the son of Neleus, to keep in trust; and the land of Phyllis was given to Dicaeus the brother of Syleus. Many generations later Cresphontes acquired Messene, but the Athenians and Chalcidians seized Amphipolis, though it belonged to the Heraclids. In the same way other malicious and lawless men were done away with by Heracles: Hippocoön, tyrant in Sparta, and Alcyoneus in Pallene [the region of Amphipolis]. Sparta was turned over to Tyandareus, Potidaea and the rest of Pallene to Sithon the son of Poseidon. The sons of Aristodemus took the land of Laconia at the time of the return of the Heraclids, but Eretrians, Corinthians and Achaeans from Troy took Pallene, though it belonged to the Heraclids. He reports how Heracles put down in similar fashion the tyrant sons of Proteus, Tmolus and Telegonus in the region of Torone and how on killing Cleides and his sons in Ambracia, he assigned to Aristomachus the son of Sithon Torone to guard, but the Chalcidians occupied it, though it is yours. He also entrusted Ambracia to Ladices and Charattes, enjoining upon them to pass on these entrusted territories to his descen-

dants. Again, all the Macedonians know of the most recent
acquisitions of Alexander from the land of the Edones. Now
these are not the protestations of Isocrates nor a mere noise of
names, but reports that are able to benefit your rule.

Moreover, since you are clearly concerned about the Amphic-
tyony ([that is at Delphi], I wanted to tell you an old story from
Antipater of how first the Amphictyons were established and
how, as Amphictyons, the Phlegyae, were removed by Apollo,
the Dryopes by Heracles, and the Crisaei by the Amphictyons. All
of these, though they were Amphictyons, were deprived of their
votes, and others took their votes and joined the Amphictyonic
union. Some of them he says you have copied, even to take as
your prize in the Pythian Games for your invasion of Delphi the
two Phocian votes from the Amphictyons. About these histories
the professor who claims to teach how "to say old things in a new
way, and new things in an old one" [Isoc. *Panegyricus* 8] in the
present case has related neither the ancient deeds nor your most
recent victories nor anything that happened in the times between
them. Indeed, he seems not to have heard of some of them, to be
ignorant of others, and to have forgotten the rest.

In addition, the man of wisdom calls you to acts of justice.
He describes approvingly the exile and return of Alcibiades
by way of example [*Address to Philip* 58–61], but omits the
greater and finer achievements of your father. Alcibiades was
exiled on a charge of impiety and returned after doing a great
deal of damage to his own homeland; but Amyntas, after being
worsted in a struggle for the throne, withdrew for a short time
and afterwards ruled Macedonia again. Later, Alcibiades was
exiled again and ended his life shamefully, but your father
grew old on his throne. Again, he sets before you the monarchy
of Dionysius (65), as though it were fitting for you to imitate
the most impious rather than the most outstanding men and
emulate the vilest rather than the most just. He claims in his
arty phrases that it is appropriate to apply domestic paradigms
and well known examples (113), but then, in contempt of his
craft, he makes use of examples that are outlandish, most
shameful, and as opposed to his argument as possible. Yet the
most ridiculous of all the things he writes is this: he claims to
have fended off skilfully those of his students who criticized
his endeavour (22). The defeated ones from among his students,
because they were at the height of their rhetorical power and
had nothing to say against his remarks, praised his speech so

warmly that they have awarded the first prize to this one of his speeches (23). But you can quickly learn the worth of Isocrates' historical work and teaching from the fact that he makes Cyreneans, people who are known by all to be Therans, colonists of the Lacedaemonians (5) and from the fact that he has appointed his Pontic student [Isocrates] as successor to his school. Now you have seen many sophists but none more of a blackguard than this one.

Moreover, I hear that Theopompus is with you and is being very insipid and that he is slandering Plato, as though it were not Plato who prepared the beginning of your reign in the time of Perdiccas and who became thoroughly distressed if any violence or lack of harmony arose in your palace. So in order to stop Theopompus from being so difficult, order Antipater to read from his *Hellenica* to him; and Theopompus will learn that he is justly ignored by all and unjustly receives your patronage.

Similarly, when Isocrates was a young man, he and Timotheus wrote shameful letters against you to the people of Athens. And, now that he is old, he has ignored your success as though out of hatred or envy. He has sent you the address that first he wrote to Agesilaus. Later, he made a few alterations and peddled it to Dionysius, tyrant of Sicily. Thirdly, he took a bit out here and added a bit there and went wooing Alexander of Thessaly. Finally, he has thrown it greedily at you. However, I should like my scroll to return to a recollection of the protestations sent to you by him in his address. On the subject of Amphipolis he says that the peace treaty hinders him from writing at length (6-8), that he will speak to you in future on the subject of Heracles' immortality (33), he claims your pardon on account of his great age, agreeing that he has dealt with some matters rather inadequately (149), and not to be surprised if his Pontic student makes the letter seem rather too putrid and inferior when he reads it (25–27), and he says that you know how you will outgeneral the King of Persia (105). Alas, my scroll is not sufficient for me to write about his remaining pretexts. What a shortage of papyrus the King has created by capturing Egypt.

Farewell. Take care of Antipater quickly and send him back to us.

T8 *The Suda*, "Ephorus" (Westermann, *Vitarum Scriptores*, 213): Ephorus of Cyme and Theopompus the Chian, son of Damasistratus, both students of Isocrates, were opposite in character and turned to literature for different reasons. Ephorus was uncom-

plicated in character, and his historiographical style was dull and
sluggish and lacked all intensity. (T28 [b]) Theopompus, however, was sharp and malicious in character, and his style was full,
dense, and elaborate. He was fond of frankness in his manner of
speech. (T28 [b] ends) Wherefore Isocrates said that he needed
the rein, but Ephorus the spur. (T8 begins) When Theopompus
was in exile, he became a suppliant of the Ephesian Artemis. He
sent many letters to Alexander against the Chians, and, moreover, he wrote many encomia of Alexander himself. It is also said
that he wrote a diatribe against Alexander, but it does not
survive.

Zos. *Vit. Isoc.* 3.90–105 (Westermann, *Vitarum Scriptores,*
256–7): He [Isocrates] had many disciples. These are the ones
who have won fame and distinction: Theopompus and Ephorus,
whose histories survive, Hypereides, Isaeus, and Lycurgus, who
are judged and acknowledged to be among the ten orators,
Philiscus and Isocrates, his namesake, Theodectes and Androtion, who wrote the Atthis and against whom Demosthenes wrote
a speech, and Python of Byzantium, Philip's orator. Concerning
Ephorus and Theopompus there is a story that nicely typifies
Isocrates. When he saw Theopompus taking a small subject and
stretching it out and greatly expanding on it, as he did in the
Philippica, and Ephorus taking one that was large and required
many words, yet treating it in few and scantily, he said, "I have
two students, one of whom needs the whip and the other the
rein." The whip he meant for Ephorus because of his natural
sluggishness and brevity. The rein was for Theopompus because
of his uncontrolled garrulity.

T9   Theocritus. Chian orator ... was a political opponent of Theopompus the historian.

T10   Anaximenes seems to have dealt with an enemy in no dull-
witted, but in a most vindictive way. He was a natural writer and
could imitate the style of others. There arose a quarrel between
him and Theopompus, the son of Damasistratus. Anaximenes
wrote a derisive pamphlet against the Athenians, Spartans, and
Thebans alike (that is, the *Tricaranos*). It was a most accurate
imitation of Theopompus. He wrote Theopompus' name on
the pamphlet and sent it around to the cities. So, although Anaximenes was the author, hatred for Theopompus grew up throughout all Greece.

Lucianus *The Mistaken Critic* 293: To say, judging Theopompus for his *Tricaranos,* that he razed the foremost cities with a
three-pronged speech, and, again, to say that he skewered Greece
with a trident, and that he is a Cerberus of a speech-maker.

T11   Demetrius said that no one touched the writing up of these laws because it is a sacred practice and holy. He claimed that some had already suffered harm from the divinity after attempting them; for example, Theopompus was troubled in mind for more than thirty days when he went to write a history about them, and only in so far as he relaxed his intention could he propitiate the god, whence came his derangement of mind. Moreover, he even saw a dream to the effect that this would happen to him should he persist in meddling with holy things and in wanting to vulgarize them. When he left off, he regained his sanity.

T12   Like him [Ephorus no. 70, T8] Callisthenes [no. 124, T24] and Theopompus, who belonged to the same generation, refrained from the ancient mythological stories.

T13   Of the historians, Thucydides ended his history here [411/10], and Xenophon and Theopompus took it up where he left off. Xenophon covered forty-eight years, but Theopompus ended his history with the battle of Cnidus [394], covering the Hellenic activities of seventeen years in twelve books.

T14   [394/3] Theopompus of Chios ended his work, the *Hellenica*, with this year, that is, with the battle of Cnidus. He wrote twelve books. This historian began from the battle of Cynossema [the point where Thucydides left off writing] and wrote, covering seventeen years.

T15   [Thucydides] died after the Peloponnesian War ... He wrote up the events of the twenty-first year ... Theopompus and Xenophon filled out the remaining six years, to which they added their *Hellenicas*.

T16   That [the eighth book of Thucydides] is not by Xenophon its character fairly shouts out ... and it is certainly not by Theopompus either, as some have thought.

T17   Of the historians, Theopompus of Chios made this year [360/59] the beginning of his history *About Philip*. He wrote fifty-eight books, of which five are lost.

T18   The historical books of Theopompus were read, of which fifty-three survive. Some of the ancients said that the sixth, seventh, and eleventh, twenty-ninth, and thirtieth were lost. And of these I have no knowledge. A certain Menophanes – one of the ancients and no despicable fellow – writing some things about Theopompus says that the twelfth also was lost. However, I read it, along with the others. (F103 follows)

T19   Polyb. 8.8 (10).2-11 (13).8. I went on in the present case and in the previous book to elaborate more clearly on this subject not just for the above-mentioned reasons but also because some writers have omitted the events in Messenia entirely; and others, because of their goodwill toward the kings or the opposite, their fear of them, argued us the case that Philip's disregard of divine propriety and human law against the Messenians could not at all have been in error; quite the contrary, they were praiseworthy and wholly proper. One can see that this has been done by the historians of Philip not just in the Messenian affair but in other cases too. Whence it happens that their works do not at all have the form of history so much as panegyric. My own belief is that one should neither castigate nor extol the kings falsely, as has been done in the past to many, but that one should always harmonize the account to what has previously been written, suitable to the reputation of each individual. However, perhaps this is far easier said than done, because many and varied are the situations and circumstances, in yielding to which throughout their lives men were unable to speak or write the obvious thing. Wherefore to some of them a pardon must be granted, but not to others.

On this score one might especially rebuke (F27) Theopompus, who, in the beginning of his history of Philip, says that there was a special reason why he felt impelled toward this work, namely that "Europe had never born such a man at all as Philip, the son of Amyntas." Immediately after that, in his proem and throughout the entire history, he depicts him as a most uncontrolled woman-chaser, to the point of destroying his own household, as far as he could, through his impulsive predilection for that sort of thing; and, moreover, as a most unjust man and thorough mischief-maker in the manipulation of friends and allies; as the enslaver of a great number of cities, deceiving them with treachery and force; and as an impassioned alcoholic, so as frequently to be seen by his friends obviously drunk even in the day-time. (F27 ends, F225 [a]) If any one should wish to read the beginning of his forty-ninth book, the absurdity of this author would be a wonder to all. Apart from other outrages, he has dared to write as follows – I have set it down in his very own words –: (see p. 166, above [Paton]), (F225 [a] ends)

Who would not condemn this bitter blabbering of the writer? For he merits censure not just because he contradicts the intent of his opening statement, but also because he has lied against the king and his companions and especially because he lies so shame-fully and unseemly. If a person were writing about Sardanapal-lus or one of his associates, one would scarcely dare to use such vindictive language. *His* life-style and debauchery we know of from the inscription on his tomb. The writing reads as follows:

"As much as I have eaten, all my excesses, and the joys of love,
They are yet mine." (10 [12].11) ... And after the death of
Alexander, when they (the friends) disputed over most parts of
the inhabited world, they established their own fame which was
handed down in a great many memoirs. So the bitterness of
Timaeus the historian, with which he inveighs against Agathocles
the ruler of Sicily, though apparently extreme, is nevertheless
reasonable, because he levels his tirade against a vile and inimical
tyrant. However, the bitterness of Theopompus is quite beyond
reason. For setting out as if to speak of a king born with all
natural disposition for manly quality, there is nothing shameful
or horrendous that he has not omitted. Thus, the historian must
seem either to be a liar and flatterer in his preface at the start of
his work or as entirely senseless and childish in his judgments on
particular subjects; as if he thought that by unreasonable and
irrelevant vitriol he himself would seem more trustworthy and
that his encomiastic judgments of Philip would be considered
more worthy of acceptance.

Moreover, no one would approve the overall scheme of the
above-mentioned author. He undertook to write the *Hellenica*
from the point where Thucydides left off, but when he got near
the times of Leuctra and the most brilliant deeds of the Greeks,
he abandoned the subject of Greece and related matters abruptly
and took up as his subject and began to write on the activities of
Philip. Surely it would have been far more dignified and just to
have included the actions of Philip under the heading of Greece
rather than Greek affairs under Philip. For not even a man
preoccupied with royalty would have refrained from changing
the name and character to Greece if he had the power and the
opportunity. And once he had started on that subject and got
well into it, no one in the world would have been so simpleminded
as to exchange it for the ornament of a king's biography.
Whatever was it that forced Theopompus to overlook such great
contrarieties? Unless it was that in the first work his object was
quality, but in the second, his own advantage. All the same,
perhaps he would have had something to say about the one error,
the change of subject, if anyone had asked him about it; but as for
his shameful speech about "The friends" [that is, F225 (a)], I
think he would not be able to give an explanation, but he would
concede that he had far exceeded the bounds of propriety.

T20(a)   Theopompus of Chios is the most famous of all the students of Isocrates. He wrote many panegyrics, many hortatory
speeches, Chian Letters – as they were entitled –, and other

themes worthy of note. He deserves praise as an historian first
for the subjects of his histories (both are good, the one embraces
the remainder of the Peloponnesian War, the other the activities
of Philip); second for management (both are easy to follow and
clear); and especially for his tireless care in composition. (F26)
Obviously, even if he had never written [a word?], he was
extremely well equipped for the work. He spent huge sums
collecting his material. In addition, he was eyewitness to much.
He further came into association with many important men of
the time, generals, demagogues, and philosophers, for the sake
of his history. He did not make of the writing of history a mere
pastime like some but the most important of all his activities. (F26
ends) Consider the many facets of his work, and you will
recognize the toil that has gone into it. Accordingly, he speaks of
the settlements of peoples and has included the foundation-
stories of cities, lives of monarchs and their intimate habits he
reveals, and if there is anything remarkable or peculiar about
each land or sea, he has embraced it in his work. Let no one
consider this mere entertainment. Not at all, it comprises the
totality of usefulness, as one might say. To say nothing of all the
other things, who will not agree with the lovers of learned
discourse that it is essential to gain thorough knowledge of many
customs of foreigners and Greeks, to hear about many laws and
structures of constitutions, and of the lives of men, their deeds,
their ends, and their turns of fortune? To these matters he has
devoted an abundance wholly involved in and not detached from
the matters discussed. All these accomplishments of the historian
are enviable, as are also, moreover, all his wise judgments
throughout the entire history, for he expands on the subjects of
justice, propriety, and the other virtues in many fine passages.
The crowning and most characteristic of his achievements is
something never accomplished with such precision and power by
any other historian either before or after his time. And what is
that? It is the ability not just to see and report what was obvious to
all in each event, but to scrutinize both the hidden reasons for
deeds and of their doers and their inner feelings, things not
easily seen by the many, and to bring to light all the mysteries of
apparent virtue and undetected vice. I should think that the
mythical scrutiny of bodiless souls in Hades before the infernal
judges is about as keen as that throughout the writings of
Theopompus. Therefore, he has seemed to be even a slanderer,
because he takes up certain needless charges against important
persons over and above the essential ones, acting somewhat like

the doctors who cut and cauterize body wounds, cauterizing and cutting so very deeply, aiming at parts that are healthy and normal. Of some such quality is the nature of Theopompus in action.

His style is most like Isocrates'. It is pure, colloquial, and clear, also lofty, magnificent, and full of solemnity. It falls into the "mixed" classification of styles, flowing sweetly and gently. It differs from the style of Isocrates for its bitterness and tension on some subjects whenever he discusses feelings and especially when he denounces cities or generals for bad plans and wicked practices – he is heavy on those subjects –. Then it does not much differ from the severity of Demosthenes, as you might see from many passages, but especially from his Chian Letters, written with all of his inborn spirit. If in these letters, over which he has been especially zealous, had he spurned the interweaving of letter-sounds, the circular and regular ordering of his periods, and the uniformity of mannerism, he would have far excelled himself in stylistics.

There are certain places in the mainstream of his narrative where he errs, and especially in his digressions. Some of them are neither necessary nor opportune and seem altogether childish. Included here would be (F74 [b]) the story of Silenus' appearance in Macedonia, the story of the dragon who fought against the trireme, and many other yarns like that. (F74 [b] ends)

These historians who have been considered in turn will be sufficient to provide suitable starting points for examples of every form to all who take pleasure in political discourse.

T20(b)   I should not have thought it necessary to present an argument for Isocrates' superiority amongst all of these orators, these nor any who lived in Isocrates' day and imitated the quality of his style. I mean Theodectes, Theopompus, Naucrates, Ephorus, Philiscus, Cephisodorus and countless others. For those men are not worthy to be ranked beside the power of Isocrates.

T21   Theopompus ranks next to these [Herodotus and Thucydides], inferior to them as an historian, but more like an orator than either – and an orator indeed he was for a long time before he was persuaded to enter this new field. (D.A. Russell and M. Winterbottom, trs. *Ancient Literary Criticism*)

T22   I hear that he [Theopompus] was a very eloquent man in Greece.

T23   About Theopompus, Ephorus, Hellanicus, Philistus, and the others like them it seemed to me superfluous to write anything.

T24 The most eloquent [of Isocrates' students] was Hypereides, the orator; but if it were Theopompus the Chian or Ephorus of Cyme I would not discredit it, nor be surprised.

T25(a) Encomia and invectives should be sparing, circumspect, honest, well-argued, rapid, and opportune. After all, your characters are not in court. You don't want to find yourself liable to the same criticism as Theopompus, who condemns most of his personages with real malice and makes a regular business of it, acting as prosecutor rather than historian. (Russell and Winterbottom, trs. *Ancient Literary Criticism*)

T25(b) [Antium, April 59 B.C.] Here, doubtless I should play the politician. For there [in Romè] I am not only debarred from the game, but am fed up with it. Therefore I shall write some secret memoranda, which we shall read together, in the style of Theopompus or even much bitterer.

T26(a) Wherefore, Quintus, <on the whole> the test of history is truth, and in Theopompus there are countless fables.

T26(b) He seems to me to be a great yarn-spinner both in the preceding story [F75] and in other places.

T27 Euseb. *PE* 10.3.1–12 = Porph. *On the Greeks as Plagiarists*, from book 1 of *The Study of Philology* (Mras, ed.): Longinus, celebrating the Platoneia in Athens, invited me to a feast along with several others, particularly Nicagoras the Sophist and Elder, Apollonius the Grammarian, Demetrius the Geometrician, Prosenes the Peripatetic, Callietes the Stoic, and he himself made the seventh. When the dinner was under way, there arose a discussion among the others about Ephorus. "Let us hear," said he, "what this tumult is over Ephorus." The disputants were Caÿstrius and Maximus. Now Maximus was ranking Ephorus above Theopompus even, but Caÿstrius was calling him a plagiarist. "And what is the distinctive mark of Ephorus," he asked, "seeing that he has transposed *verbatim* three thousand entire lines from the works of Daïmachus, Callisthenes, and Anaximenes?" To which Apollonius the Grammarian replied, "Did you not know that Theopompus also, whom you prefer, contracted this disease. (F102) For in the eleventh book of his *About Philip* he transcribed in the exact words that part of Isocrates' *Areopagiticus* that begins: 'Of good and evil nothing befalls men unmixed' and so forth. (F102 ends) (F345) 'Nevertheless, he is scornful of Isocrates and claims that the master was worsted by him in the contest over Mausolus. (F345 ends) (F70) He has also pilfered stories, assigning anecdotes to the wrong people; wherefore he can be exposed as a plagiarist in this way also. Andron in his *Tripos* – about

Pythagoras the philosopher – investigated the question of his prophetic powers and wrote: 'Once in Metapontum he got thirsty, and when he had drawn water from a cistern and drunk it, he foretold an earthquake on the third day.'" He [Porphyry?] brings in other examples and adds: All these things that Andron recorded about Pythagoras were purloined by Theopompus. Now if he had told them about Pythagoras, then others would have quickly understood that they were about him and said, "Ah, these are the Master's words." As it is, the switching of the names has exposed the theft, for Theopompus has used the same stories but assigned them to a different person. He says, you see, that Pherecydes of Syros made these prophecies. Not only has he concealed his thievery by this name-change, but he has altered the locations as well. The prediction of the earthquake that Andron located in Metapontum, Theopompus placed on Syros. In addition, in the story of the boat, he does not say it was seen from Megara in Sicily, but Samos; again, he altered the capture of Sybaris to that of Messene; and in order to seem to have something beyond the usual to report, he has added the name of the stranger. He was called, he claims, Perilaus. (F70 ends) "I too," said Nicagoras (F21), "when I read his and Xenophon's *Hellenica*s, discovered that he had transposed a great deal from Xenophon's work. What is particularly shocking is that he degrades the stolen passages. A good example is the meeting between Pharnabazus and Agesilaus held at the request of Apollophanes of Cyzicus and their conversation with each other held under truce. Xenophon wrote them up in his fourth [X. *HG* 4.1.29–40] in a charming way and suitable to the dignity of each; but Theopompus transposed them into the elventh of his *Hellenica,* making them sluggish, lifeless, and inconsequential. He is anxious to add and put on a display of force of language and – through plagiarism – stylistic polish. But he proves to be dull and lazy like a procrastinator, destroying Xenophon's animation and vividness." (F21 ends) When Nicagoras had said this, Apollonius said: "Why do we wonder that Ephorus and Theopompus caught the disease of plagiarism? Both are such lazy men."

T28(a)   See F181(a).

T28(b)   (See *Suda*, "Ephorus") = T8.

T29   And this, I think, is why the most thoughtful of ancient writers were in the habit of giving their readers a rest in the way I say, some of them employing digressions dealing with myth or story and others digressions on matters of fact; so that not only do they shift the scene from one part of Greece to another, but include doings abroad. (F28) For instance, when dealing with Thessalian affairs and the exploits of Alexander of Pherae, they interrupt the narrative to tell us of the projects of the Lacedaemonians in the Peloponnese or of those of the Athenians and of what happened in Macedonia or Illyria, and after entertaining us so tell us of the expedition of Iphicrates to Egypt and the excesses committed by Clearchus in Pontus. So that you will find that all historians have resorted to this device but have done so irregularly, while I myself resort to it regularly. For the authors I allude to, after mentioning how Bardyllis, the king of Illyria, and Cersobleptes, the king of Thrace, acquired their kingdoms (F28 ends), do not give us the continuation or carry us on to what proved to be the sequel after a certain lapse of time, but after inserting these matters as a sort of patch, return to their original subject. But I myself, keeping distinct all the most important parts of the world and the events that took place in each, and adhering always to a uniform conception of how each matter should be treated, and again definitely relating under each year the contemporary events that then took place, leave obviously full liberty to students to carry back their minds to the continuous narrative and the several points at which I interrupted it, so that those who wish to learn may find none of the matters I have mentioned imperfect and deficient. This is all I have to say on the subject. (W.R. Paton, tr., L.C.L.)

T30   It is imperative to avoid the insertion of long digressions in the middle of one's discourse. No, it is not necessary to avoid digressions altogether as Philistus does, for they rest the readers' concentration. Only avoid the digression that is of such length that it causes the reader to lose the chain of thought with the result that he is unable to recall the thread of the story. Theopompus is like that in the *Philippica*. For there we find about two, even three, and more entire histories in the form of digression; and in them there is no mention of Philip nor even the name of a Macedonian.

T31   See T2.

T32   Polyb. 12.25f. What I mean will be yet clearer from the following references, as, for example, what has befallen Ephorus in certain parts of his history. For, in battles, that historian seems to me to have a certain understanding of sea actions, but he is altogether ignorant of land battles. Consequently, when we examine the battles of Cyprus and Cnidus, which the King's generals fought against Evagoras of Salamis and again against the Lacedaemonians, we marvel at the author for his prowess and experience, and we take away much useful information for similar circumstances. But when he describes the battle of Leuctra, between the Thebans and Lacedaemonians or again the one at Mantinea between the same antagonists – in which Epamimondas lost his life —, if we take them point by point and examine the formations and reformations during the actual battles, he does seem ridiculous, entirely inexperienced, and ignorant of such things. Granted, the battle of Leuctra was a unified action involving one segment of the force; and so it does not completely reveal the author's lack of experience. However, the battle of Mantinea gets an ornate, "field marshal's" description, but it is unfounded and not the least understood by the historian. This will be clear if you examine the terrain and accurately measure out the movements described by him. The same thing is found in Theopompus and especially Timaeus, the present subject of our discussion. For in whatever of such actions they give a summary description, they go unnoticed, but whenever they choose to elaborate and clarify something in them in particular, this is how they appear, just like Ephorus.

T33   Plut. *Mor.* 803A–B. Political oratory, more than judicial, is suitable for maxims, historical anecdotes, myths, and changes of subject [or metaphors], by using which in moderation and at the proper moment speakers move their audiences greatly ... But as for the orations and periods of Ephorus, Theopompus, and Anaximenes, which they declaim after arming and arraying their forces, it is possible to say: "No one near the steel prates thus."

T34   See T2.

T35   See T27.

T36   Cic. *Brut.* 66. [Cato] lacks admirers, just as many centuries ago did Philistus of Syracuse and Thucydides himself. For just as Theopompus' lofty, elevated rhetoric overshadowed their sentences clipped as they were and sometimes even obscured by brevity or excessive pungency – as Demosthenes' did to Lysias – so did this modern overconstructed rhetoric of subsequent writers hide Cato's from the light.

T37   Cic. *Or.* 207. Therefore, putting aside other forms of oratory, we have selected for our discussion that used in law-court and public assembly. In the other forms, that is in history and epideictic oratory, as it is called, it is desirable to have everything done in the periodical style of Isocrates and Theopompus, so that the language runs on as if enclosed in a circle until it comes to an end with each phrase complete and perfect. (H.M. Hubbell, tr., L.C.L.)

D.H. *Comp.* 23. The smooth type of arrangement, which I placed second, has the following characteristics. It does not seek "all-round visibility" for every individual word, or a broad secure base for them all, or long intervals between them. Any effect of slowness or stability is alien. The aim is words in motion, words bearing down on one another, carried along on the stability afforded by their support of one another, like a perpetually flowing stream. This style likes the individual parts to merge into one another, to be woven together so as to appear as far as possible like one continuous utterance. This is achieved by exactly fitting joints which leave the intervals between the words imperceptible. It is like cloth finely woven together or pictures in which the light merges into the shade. All the words are expected to be euphonious, smooth, soft, virginal; it hates rough, recalcitrant syllables, and has a cautious attitude towards anything at all bold or risky.

Not satisfied with suitable joins and smooth connections between words, this manner aims also at a close interweaving of cola, the whole building up to a period. It limits the length of the colon – not too short, not unduly long – and of the period, which should be such that an adult man's breath can control it. It cannot tolerate non-periodic writing, a period not divided into cola, or a colon out of proportion. It employs rhythms that are not very long but medium or quite short. The ends of its periods must be rhythmical and precisely based. Connections between periods here are formed on the opposite principle from those between words: this type of writing merges words but distinguishes periods and tries to make *them* visible all round, as it were. Its favourite figures are not the more archaic or such as produce an impression of solemnity or weight or tension, but the luxurious and blandishing kind, full of deceptive and theatrical qualities. To put it more generally, this manner has in all important respects the opposite characteristics to the former; no more need be said.

It remains to enumerate its distinguished practitioners. Of epic writers, the finest exponent of this manner is, I think, Hesiod; of lyric poets Sappho, and then Anacreon and Simonides; among the tragic poets there is only Euripides; strictly speaking there is no historian, though Ephorus and Theopompus are nearer than most. Among orators, we have Isocrates. (D.A. Russell and M. Winterbottom, trs. *Ancient Literary Criticism*)

T38 Cic. *Or.* 151. This [the natural order of words] the Latin language so carefully observes that no one is so illiterate as to avoid the juxtaposition of vowels. On this score some criticize even Theopompus for going to great lengths to avoid such vowel positions, though the same is true of his master. Quint. *Inst.* 9.4.35. On the other hand, hiatus is not so horrendous a crime. I hardly know if it is worse to neglect it or to make a great fuss over it. Of necessity, the fear of it inhibits the flow of language and diverts us from more forceful expressions. Wherefore, it is negligent to allow it everywhere but slavish always to shun it. It is generally agreed with good cause that Isocrates and his followers, especially Theopompus, went too far in avoiding it.

T39   Isocrates ... used to restrain him [Theopompus] from vainglorying in stylistic boldness.

T40   What can you find more pleasant than Herodotus, more serious than Thucydides, more clipped than Philistus, more bitter than Theopompus, more gentle than Ephorus?

T41   Similarly, that phrase of Theopompus seems to me to be most expressive because of the analogy. I do not know how Caecilius can find fault with it. (F262) "Philip was formidable," he says, "at stomaching facts." (F262 ends) There are times when a colloquial expression is far more emphatic than adornment. For inasmuch as it is from every day life itself, the familiar idea is that much easier to believe. Therefore, of the man who overcomes hardships and squalor with patience, and pleasure even, for the sake of advancement, "stomaching facts" is a very apt turn of phrase.

T42   See pp. 22–3, above (F263).

T43   Demetr. *Eloc.* 240. We now come to forcefulness and it will be clear from what has already been said that it too springs from the same three sources as all the preceding styles. There are some subjects which have an inherent forcefulness which makes even writers whose style is feeble seem forceful. (F290) When Theopompus, for example, speaks of the flute-girls of the Piraeus, the brothels, and the men playing the flute, singing, and dancing (F290 ends), all these ideas have such a forceful effect that his feeble style is overlooked and he is thought forceful. (D. A. Russell and M. Winterbottom, trs., *Ancient Literary Criticism*)

T44   Demetr. *Eloc.* 247. We avoid antithesis and homonyms in our periods because they are bombastic and lack forcefulness. They are more frigid than forceful. Theopompus provides an example of this when he attacks the "Friends of Philip." He destroys the forcefulness with the antithesis: (F225 [c]) "Men-killers they were by nature; men-kissers were they by habit." (F225 [c] ends) When the reader must apply himself to too much style, rather than to bad style, he loses contact with all feeling.

T45   D. Chr. 18.10. Now in the case of Herodotus, if you ever need some real enjoyment, read him when you have plenty of time. The leisurely and pleasing aspect of his reporting will convey the impression that his work is more of story-telling than history. Thucydides is in the first rank of historians, in my opinion, and Theopompus in the second. There is a rhetorical influence in the narrative parts of *his* works. Stylistically, he does not lack forcefulness, nor is he negligent. The moments of frivolousness in his diction are not as despicable as to cause you grief. Ephorus, on the other hand, has transmitted a lot of history, but you should not imitate the supine leisure of his narrative style.

T46   See F339.

T47   See F341.

T48   Th[eopompu]s' [Theodectes'?] *Laconicus*, one [scroll]; [*Corin*]*th*[*ia*]*cus*, one; [*Mauso*]*llus*, one; [*Olym*]*picus*, one; [*Philip*]*pus*, one; [*Alexand*]*er Encomium*, one; *About* [vacat], one; [vacat], one; *To Evagoras* [vacat]; *Lette*[*r*] *to* [vacat], one; *Advi*[*ce to*] *Alexander*, [vacat]; *Panathenaïcu*[*s*, one]; *Attack on th*[*e*] *Teachin*[*g of Plato*]. Of another Theopompus: *About Kingship.*

T49   See FF68, 316-20.

T50   Ten historians: Thucydides, Herodotus, Xenophon, Philistus, Theopompus, Ephorus, Anaximenes, Callisthenes, Hellanicus, Polybius.

T51   (Charax of Pergamon, no. 103, T2 = Evagrius *HE* 5.24): all the things that happened, whether fabulous or truthful – wars of Hellenes and ancient barbarians amongst themselves and against others – or if anything else was done by anyone, the historians have reported that they were humans. This is recorded by Charax, Ephorus, Theopompus, and countless others.

THE HISTORICAL FRAGMENTS OF THEOPOMPUS

Epitome of the Histories of Herodotus

F1   "Surmount [ἀναβῆναι] your horse," instead of "mount" [ἐπιβῆναι]. Theopompus in the *Epitome of Herodotus.*

F2   "poverty-stricken." Theopompus in the *Epitome of Herodotus.*

F3   "Fugitize" = "to drive into exile." Theopompus in the *Epitome of Herodotus.*

F4   "Be eager" ... in place of "urge on." Theopompus in the *Epitome of the Works of Herodotus*; and in place of "want to," the same in the *Epitome.*

Hellenic Histories (Hellenica)

F5   [Thucydides] ceased from his history in the sea-fight near Cynossema ... He left the events thereafter for others to write, Xenophon and Theopompus. There were other battles following that one. [He included] neither the second sea-fight near Cynossema, of which Theopompus spoke, nor the one near Cyzicus in which Thrasybulus, Theramenes, and Alcibiades were victorious, nor the battle of Arginusae where the Athenians defeated the Lacedaemonians, nor the crowning Athenian disaster, the sea-fight at Aegospotami where the Athenians lost their ships and subsequent hopes. Their defensive wall was dismantled and the tyranny of the thirty was established and many misfortunes befell the city, which Theopompus accurately recorded.

Book One
F6   Cardia ... is situated, as Theopompus says in the first book of the *Hellenica*, on the Chersonese by the so-called Black Sea.
F7   Chrysopolis, in Bithynia near Chalcedon ... Ephorus book, 23 ... and Theopompus in book 1 of the *Hellenica*: "They set sail for Chalcedon and Byzantium with the rest of the armament aiming to put in at Chrysopolis."

Book Two
F8   Pedaritus. Isocrates in the *Archidamus* [53]. He was one of those sent out from Lacedaemon, a harmost, one of the well-born as Theopompus says in the second book of the *Hellenica*.

Book Four
F9   Aspendus, a city of Pamphylia ... Theopompus in the fourth book of the *Hellenica*: "having got away from the Aspendians." The feminine is the same, Aspendia; also Aspendis and Aspendid territory [Aspendia and Aspendis – same author].
F10   Trinessa, a place [river?] in Phrygia. Theopompus *Hellenica* 4.
F11   Sellasia, a city of Laconia. Theopompus *Hellenica* 4.

Book Six
F12   Oropus ... also Theopompus in *Hellenica* 6. "[Some] of the Oropians communicated with Telephus and the men of his company who wanted Oropus to belong to them."

Book Seven
F13   Theopompus in *Hellenica* 7 [or: and Hellanicus], speaking

about the Helots that they were also called heleatae, writes as follows: "The race of Helots is in a thoroughly harsh condition and bitter. They have been in a state of enslavement by the Spartans for a long time. Some of them are from Messene, but the heleatae in former time used to occupy the place in Laconia called Helos.

Book Eight

F14   Embatum, a place in Erythraea. Theopompus *Hellenica* 8.

F15   Calpe, a city of the Bithynians. Theopompus *Hellenica* 8.

F16   Ladepsi and Tranipsi, tribes of the Thynians. Theopompus *Hellenica* 8 [mss: 50, *ergo Philippica*?].

F17   Cytonium, a city between Mysia and Lydia. Theopompus *Hellenica* 8.

Book Nine

F18   Theopompus in the ninth book of the *Hellenica* says that Athenaeus the Eretrian became a flatterer and a minion of Sisyphus of Pharsalia.

Book Ten

F19   Carpasia, a city of Cyprus ... the citizen is a Carpaseot ... Theopompus in book 10 calls them Carpasians.

F20   Nearly everyone records that Pausanias and Lysander were notorious for luxurious living; but Theopompus in the tenth book of the *Hellenica* says the opposite about Lysander, "he was industrious and capable of cultivating both private men and kings. He was moderate and in control of all pleasures. Indeed, though he had become lord of nearly all Hellas, he will not be shown to have been an addict of sexual pleasure in any of the cities nor given to intoxication nor unseasonable tippling.

Book Eleven

F21   See T27.

F22   Of fatted geese and calves Theopompus in *Philippica* 13 [F106] and *Hellenica* 11 – in which he exhibits the Spartans' self-control in matters of the belly – writes thus: The Thasians also sent to Agesilaus as he approached sheep of all kinds and well-nurtured cattle, and besides these there were also cakes and every kind of dessert item. Agesilaus accepted the sheep and cattle, but at first he did not even notice the cakes and desserts – for they had been out of sight —. However, when he saw them, he ordered the men to take them away, declaring that it was not lawful for Lacedaemonians to eat such foods. When the Thasians insisted, he said, "Take and give them to those men – pointing to the Helots –." He continued: "It were far more appropriate that they be corrupted than myself and the Lacedaemonians here."

Unnumbered

F23   He means Hypoplacian Thebes in Asia ... Moreover, Phileas says that there is a Thebes in the Phthiotic region of Thessaly; and Theopompus in the *Hellenica* [book 3?] says that there is another one near Mycale and the Milesians surrendered it to the Samians.

Philippic Histories (Philippica)

Prooemium

F24   I am forced to begin with a few words about myself, though I am most reluctant to repeat the speeches that are customary in the introductions of histories. Neither do I intend to elaborate on my own merits ... nor am I determined to calumniate other historians, as Anaximenes [Anaxilaus] and Theopompus did in the introductions to their histories.

F25   See T2.

F26   See T20(a).

F27   See T19.

Book One

F28   See T29.

F29   Argaeus ... Concerning this man Theopompus also speaks in book 1 of the *Philippica*: "They call Archelaus [or: Argaeus and Pausanias sons of Archelaus?] both Argaeus and Pausanias." (?)

F30(a)   What is "that once much discussed secret" in Demosthenes' *Philippica* [2.6]? Theopompus has explained it in book [thirty-?] 1. He says: "He also sent Antiphon and Charidemus as ambassadors to Philip to treat for friendship. When they arrived, they tried to persuade him to make a secret bargain with the Athenians, promising Pydna in order that they get Amphipolis. The Athenian ambassadors reported nothing of this to the people because they did not want the Pydnaeans to know that they were going to turn them over but arranged it secretly with the council.

F30(b)   Why in secret? In order that neither the Potidaeans nor the Pydnaeans would know and be on guard; but Theopompus says that it only concerned Pydna and Philip in order that he himself give Amphipolis to the Athenians and receive Pydna from them for his own. It was secret in order that the Pydnaeans should not know about it and be on guard, for they did not want to be under Philip.

F31   In the first book of the *Philippica* Theopompus says the following of Philip: "On the third day he arrived at Onocarsis, a district of Thrace that has an exceptionally well-planted grove and pleasurable to dwell in at other times but especially in the summer season. It was one of Cotys' select places. He of all the kings who ever lived in Thrace was the most given to pleasure addiction and luxury. He used to go about his country and wherever he saw places shaded by trees and watered by streams had them prepared as banqueting spots. He would frequent each of them whenever he happened to be nearby and would make sacrifices to the gods and keep company with his subordinate officers. He continued happy and blessed until he set about to blaspheme and offend against Athena." The historian goes on to relate how he got up a dinner as though he was about to marry Athena preparing a bridal chamber and awaiting the goddess intoxicated. When he had got quite out of his wits, he sent one of his spear-bearers to see if the goddess had come into the chamber. When the messenger returned with the report that there was no one in the chamber, he shot and killed him and a second messenger also for the same reason. Finally, the third one realized and reported that the goddess had arrived a long time ago and was waiting for him. This king once, in a fit of jealousy, cut up his own wife with his own hands starting from her genitals.

   Harp., Cotys. He ruled Thrace for twenty-four years. At first he lived in luxury and pleasure-addiction, but later, as success increased for him, he fell into extreme savagery and rage, even to the point of cutting his wife, with whom he had got children, through the middle with his own hands, starting from her genitals.

F32   Mocarsus, a region of Thrace. Theopompus, *Philippica* 1.

F33   Allante, a city of Macedonia [and Arcadia]. Theopompus in *Philippica* 1 called it Allantium.

F34   Chalce ... There is another Chalce also, a city of Larissaea. It is also given in plural form, Chalcae: Theopompus *Philippica* 1 [vacat?] and 3: "he still prosecuted the war setting out from Chalcae of Larissaea" [F48].

F35   Cineas ... It is agreed amongst the historians that Cineas was one of those who surrendered Thessalian affairs to Philip – especially by Theopompus in book 1 when he details the man's activities.

F36   See p. 113, above.

F37 "have reason," instead of "ponder," Theopompus *Philippica* 1.

Book Two

F38 In *Philippica* 2 Theopompus says that the kings of the Paeonians, since the cattle raised in their land grow large horns with a capacity of three and four choae, make drinking cups from them, decorating their rims with silver and gold.

F39 And in the second book of the *Philippica* [Theopompus] says, "The Illyrians dine and drink sitting down. They take their wives to their parties, and it is a good thing for the women to drink to whichever men of the company they encounter. They lead their husbands home from their drinking parties. They all lead harsh lives and gird their bellies with wide belts whenever they drink. At first they do this moderately, but whenever they drink more excessively, they draw the belt progressively tighter."

F40 And he says, "The [Ardiaeans] [Autariatae] have acquired three hundred thousand Prospeletae, who are just like Helots. Each day they get drunk, hold parties, and dispose themselves to eating and uncontrolled tippling. Wherefore, when the Celts were at war with them, since they knew about their lack of self-control, they gave orders to all their soldiers to prepare the most lavish dinner possible in their tents and put a herbal drug into the food that had the power to devastate the bowels and cause diarrhoea. When this happened, some of them were caught by the Celts and destroyed; others threw themselves into the rivers having no control over their bellies."

F41 Neon, Demosthenes in *For Ctesiphon* [*on the Crown* 295]. Concerning his friendship with Philip, Theopompus writes the history in *Philippica* 2? [32?, 52?]; [and see F235].

Book Three

F42 Hierax ... Hierax was one of the ambassadors sent by the Amphipolitans to Athens when they were desirous of turning their city and territory over to the Athenians, as Theopompus has recorded in *Philippica* 3.

F43 Datus, a city of Thrace richly blest. From this city arose a saying: "a Datus of good things." They explain about it and its surrounding land sometimes using it in the neuter, Datum; sometimes feminine, Datus, as Ephorus always does in book 4 (no. 70, F37). There is one instance of Datus; masculine: Theopompus *Philippica* 3. However, the city of the Datenes had its name changed [to Philippi] when Philip, king of Macedon, conquered it, as Ephorus says, and Philochorus in book 5.

F44   Zirenia, a city of Thrace. Theopompus *Philippica* 3.
F45   Hippace, a food of the Scythians made from horses' milk. Some call it horse-whey; it is used by the Scythians. They drink it or eat it curdled according to Theopompus in book 3 of the same [his?] work.
F46   Sesonchosis, king of all Egypt after Horus, son of Isis and Osiris, attacked Asia and subdued it all, similarly the most part of Europe. There is a more accurate account of his exploits in Herodotus [2.102ff.]. Theopompus in book 3 calls him Sesostris.
F47   Thapsacus, a city of Syria by the Euphrates. Theopompus in *Philippica* 3.
F48   See F34.

Book Four
F49   Speaking of the Thessalians in his fourth book, he says: "They wile away their lives in the presence of dancing girls and flute-girls. Some waste their days at dice, drinking, and similar incontinence. They are more concerned to furnish themselves with tables full of every sort of delicacy than to have their own lives well ordered. [deest aliquid?] Pharsalians of all mankind," he goes on, "are the laziest and most profligate."
F50   Halonnesus ... Theopompus mentions the dispute over Halonnesus in book 4, Anaximenes also in his *Philippica* 4 (no. 72, F7).
F51   Eion ... Theopompus in the fourth book says that the Athenians expelled the Amphipolitans from Eion and devastated the city.
F52   During the siege of Methone he [Philip] lost his right eye when he was struck by an arrow while he was inspecting the siege machines and sheds as they are called. This is what Theopompus relates in book 4, of his history about him. Marsyas the Macedonian agrees (no. 135–6, F16). However, Duris (no. 76, F36) ...

Book Five
F53   Pagasae, Demosthenes in *Philippica* [1.9]. It is a harbour of the Pheraeans, Pagasae, as Theopompus in *Philippica* 5 [some mss omit "5"] makes clear.
F54   Amphanae, a city of Doris. Hecataeus in *Genealogies* 1 (no. 1, F3). Theopompus calls it Amphanaea in *Philippica* 5. There is a district of Thessaly with the same name.
F55   Maccarae, a region above Pharsalus. Theopompus, *Philippica* 5.
F56   Olyca, a city of Macedonia. Theopompus, *Philippica* 5.
F57   See pp. 113–14, above.
F58   Nonetheless, according to many people, asses' packsaddles are to be found in book 5 of the *Philippica*.

Book Six

F59   Pygela ... Pygela is a city in Ionia, which Theopompus says in
book 6 got its name when some of Agamemnon's crew remained
there on account of an affliction of their buttocks [Gr. *pygae*].

F60   Eua, a city in Arcadia. Theopompus book 6.

F61   Euaemon, a city of the Orchomenians. Theopompus book 6.

Book Eight

F62   Of certain of the people who live beside the ocean Theopompus in *Philippica* 8 says that they became accustomed to soft
living. Concerning the Byzantians and Chalcedonians the same
Theopompus says the following: "The Byzantians were undisciplined and accustomed to holding get-togethers and drinking in
their shops. The reason was that they had been a democracy for a
long time, they had their city organized for trade, and the entire
populace spent its time around the market-place and harbour.
The Chalcedonians, before joining with their constitution, all
pursued better habits and lifestyles. However, when they got a
taste of the democracy of the Byzantians, they were corrupted
[deest aliquid] to luxury, and they changed their daily mode of
living from the most sensible and moderate of pursuits,
becoming tipplers and profligates.

F63   Amphictyon, a Hellenic assembly that met at Thermopylae. By
one account it got its name from Amphictyon, son of Deucalion,
because he drew the tribes together during his reign as Theopompus says in book 8. There were twelve tribes: Ionians,
Dorians, Perrhaebians, Boeotians, Magnesians, Achaeans,
Phthiotians, Melieis, Dolopians, Aenianes, Delphians, Phocians.
By another account [the name] derived from the fact that the
assembled were all neighbours of the Delphians, as Anaximenes
says in *Hellenica* 1.

Marvels

F64(a)   Aristotle in the first book of *On Philosophy* says that [the Magi]
were even older than the Egyptians, and they hold that there are
two supreme powers: a good spirit and an evil one. The name of
the one is Zeus and Oromasdes [Ahura Mazda], the other is
Hades and Ahriman. Hermippus says this too in *On the Magi*
book 1, and Eudoxus in his *Circuit-tour*, also Theopompus in
Philippica 8. He also says that the Magi believe in resurrection,
that humans will be immortal and existing things continue
thanks to their imprecations. Eudemus of Rhodes also records
this.

F64(b)   Zoroaster predicted that there will come a time when there will be a resurrection of all the dead. Theopompus knows what I mean, and others learned it from him.

F65   See p. 16, above.

F66   Zopyrus' talents, Cratinus in *Pylaeae*. In book 8 of *About Philip* Theopompus says that he was a Persian who, out of an ambition to ingratiate himself with the King, whipped himself and had his nose and ears cut off. He entered Babylon and, winning their confidence thanks to his wretched condition, took the city. He uses "talents" and "yokes" metaphorically for "deeds" and "accomplishments."

F67(a)   According to the report of Theopompus and a great many others, Epimenides was son of Phaestius, but some say of Dosiadas, and others of Agesarchus. By birth he was a Cretan from Cnossus, and he would change his appearance by letting down his hair. Once he was sent to the field for the sheep by his father. On the way he rested in a cave at mid-day and slept for fifty-seven years. Afterwards he got up and went looking for the sheep, thinking that he had slept for a short time. But seeing that he was not finding them, he went into the field. He perceived that everything had changed and that it was in the possession of another. So he travelled back and came to the city. There, when he entered his own house, he encountered people who were asking him who he was until he discovered that his younger brother was now an old man. Thus he learned the whole truth from him.

F67(b)   Epimenides of Crete is said to have been sent by his father and brothers to the field to bring the sheep to the city. When night overtook him, he rested from his journey and fell asleep for fifty-seven years as many others have said and especially Theopompus when he goes through the *Marvels* place by place. Then, the story goes, it happened that Epimenides' family died, but he awoke from his sleep and went looking for the sheep for which he had been sent. When he did not find them he came to the field – he supposed that he had awakened on the same day he thought he had gone to sleep – but when he perceived that the field had been sold and the out-building bartered away, he returned to the city. When he entered his house, from there he learned everything, including the time when he had disappeared. According to Theopompus the Cretans say that he lived for one hundred and fifty [-seven] years and died. Not a few other remarkable stories are told about this man.

F68(a)   This man [Epimenides] lived for 157 years according to Theopompus. For [fifty-] seven of those years he was asleep.

F68(b)   Epimenides of Cnossus, whom Theopompus claims to have
lived 157 years.

F68(c)   Theopompus [attributes] 157 [years] to Epimenides of
Cnossus.

F69   In the *Marvels* Theopompus [says that] when he [Epimenides]
was building the temple for the Nymphs, there broke a voice
from heaven: "Epimenides, not for the Nymphs, but Zeus." [He
says that] he predicted to the Cretans the defeat of the Lacedaemonians by the Arcadians as I mentioned above [see section
114]; and, to be sure, they were defeated near Orchomenus. He
became old in as days as many he slept years. This too is recorded
by Theopompus.

F70   See T27.

F71   Pherecydes of Syros, son of Babys ... Theopompus says that he
was the first to write on nature and the gods. Moreover, many
marvels are told about him. Indeed, when he was strolling by the
shore of Samos [of the sand?] and saw a ship running with a fair
wind, he said that it would sink in a little while; and it sank before
his eyes. Once, when he had drunk some water drawn from a
well, he predicted an earthquake on the third day, and it
happened. As he was going up from Olympia to Messene, he
advised his friend Perilaus to move house with all his possessions.
He did not comply, and Messene fell. He also said to the
Lacedaemonians not to honour gold and silver, as Theopompus
says in the *Marvels*. This instruction is said to have been given him
in a dream by Heracles, who, that very same night, commanded
the kings to obey Pherecydes. Some assign these exploits to
Pythagoras.

F72   As for Pythagoras, he was a Samian, son of Mnesarchus, as
Hippobotus says; but according to Aristoxemis, Aristotle, and
Theopompus he was a Tyrrhenian. Neanthes (no. 84, F29) says
that he was from Syros or Tyre.

F73   [Athenion gets himself put in command of the Athenian
forces.] Not many days later this "philosopher" appointed
himself dictator, illustrating the teaching of Pythagoras concerning treachery and the import to them of the philosophy that the
noble Pythagoras introduced according to the record of Theopompus in the eighth book of the *Philippica*, also Hermippus the
Callimachean. Straightaway this rascal ... did away with the
better-minded citizens.

F74(a)   The finest examples of the recounting of mythical stories
would be ... From Theopompus in *Philippica* 8 the story of
Silenus.

F74(b)   See T20(a).

F75(a)   Heliodorus says that Antiochus Epiphanes, whom Polybius [26.1] calls Epimanes [the deranged] because of his actions, mixed the fountain in Antioch with wine in just the same way as Theopompus says Midas of Phrygia did when he wanted to catch Silenus under the influence of alcohol. According to Bion (no. 14, F3) this fountain, called Inna, was between the Maedi and the Paeonians.

F75(b)   Of course, it is not thought that this story about Silenus was Vergil's fiction but translated from Theopompus; for he says that Silenus was captured besotted with overdrinking and asleep because of it by shepherds of King Midas. They approached him while asleep and subdued him by treachery. Afterwards, when the chains slipped off by themselves and he was freed, he discussed natural and ancient topics in response to Midas' questions. All these things concerning Silenus are recorded by Theopompus in the book called the *Marvels*.

F75(c)   Theopompus describes a meeting of Midas the Phrygian and Silenus. This Silenus was child of a nymph, by nature more obscure than a god, but more powerful than a human, since, of course, he was immortal. They discussed many things with each other, and, in particular, Silenus told the following story to Midas. He said that Europe, Asia, and Libya were islands around which Ocean flows in a circle. The only continent is the one outside of this world. He described its size as immeasurable. It supports other living creatures of great size and humans twice as large as here. Their lifespan is not the same as ours, but it too is double. They have many large cities and peculiar ways of living. The laws that have been arranged for them are opposite to the ones to which we are accustomed. He said that there were two cities great in size not like each other at all. The one is called War-town and the other Saintsbury. The Saintsburgers live in peace and great abundance. They continue healthy and without disease and die laughing a great deal and enjoying themselves. They are so unambiguously just that not even the gods disdain from visiting them frequently. But the Wartowners are extremely warlike. Born fully armed, they subjugate their neighbours. This one city controls many peoples. Their inhabitants are no less than two million. They die after being ill for the rest of their lives but rarely; most are struck down by stones or clubs. They are not wounded by iron weapons. They have an abundance of gold and silver such that gold is cheaper to them than iron is to us. He said that these [Wartowners] once set out to cross over to these islands of ours. They crossed Ocean with myriads of thousands of men until they came to the Hyperboreans. When they found out that these were the happiest of all the peoples in our world, they scorned us as pettifogging low-life and for that reason disdained to go any further. And he added a yet more remarkable thing. Certain people, Meropes as they are called, live among them in many large cities, and in the furthest part of their land is a place called No Return (see p. 18, above). Let that be believed if the Chian is to be trusted at all when he tells stories. I think he is a clever story-teller in this and other things besides.

F75(d) From these (Apollodorus, no. 244, F157) goes on to the historians who talk about the Rhipaean mountains, mount Ogyium, the settlement of the Gorgons and Hesperides, and the land of Meropis in Theopompus.

F75(e) ... unless one is to believe the famous Silenus at the court of King Midas, who made earnest assertion about another world, as Theopompus claims.

F76 Theopompus [says] in the *Marvels* that in the Olympic contest, though there were many kites hovering overhead and screeching during the sacred festival, the meat portions from the sacrifices that were distributed around remained untouched.

Book Nine

F77 There are three Bacises [according to Philetas of Ephesus]: the eldest was from Eleon of Boeotia, the second was an Athenian, the third was an Arcadian from the city of Caphye. According to Philetas of Ephesus he is also called Cydas and Aletes. In book 9 of the *Philippica* Theopompus records many other remarkable things about this Bacis and particularly that he once purified the wives of the Lacedaemonians after they had gone mad. Apollo gave this man as a purifier for them.

F78 Many things are reported among the ancients ... In particular we have in the ninth book of Theopompus' *Philippica* Thessalian Tempe, which lies between two great mountains, Ossa and Olympus. Between these two mountains flows the Peneus into which flow all the rivers throughout Thessaly.

F79 The Attic [stylists] say "about so much" using both accusative and dative cases. Theopompus, *Philippica* 9: "the length is about forty stades" [using accusative].

F80 See pp. 110–11.

F81 In *Philippica* 9 Theopompus says: "Philip sent Agathocles, a born slave, one of the Thessalian Penestae, a man of great influence with him through flattery and because he accompanied

him in his drinking bouts, dancing and making jokes, to destroy
the Perrhaebians and take care of their affairs. The Macedonian
always kept men of that sort about him, who, even taking counsel
over the most serious matters, generally wasted the greater part
of their time in hard drinking and buffoonery.

F82   Pharcedon, a city of Thessaly. Theopompus, *Philippica* 9 [says],
Pharcadon, keeping the long a.

F83   Drongilum, a region of Thrace [mss. Thessaly]. Theopompus
Philippica 9.

F84   Cobrys, a city of Thrace. Theopompus *Philippica* 9.

Book Ten

On the Demagogues

F85   Immediately after these accomplishments he [Themistocles]
undertook to rebuild the city and to fortify it – as Theopompus
says, inducing the Ephors by bribes not to oppose the plan but, as
most say, duping them.

F86   Much of his [Themistocles'] property was secretly conveyed
over the sea to Asia by his friends, but the sum of what was found
and gathered into the exchequer Theopompus says was a hundred talents, while Theophrastus says eighty, though he wasn't
worth even three talents before he started a political career.
(W.R. Connor, tr., *Theopompus and Fifth-Century Athens*)

F87   For not wandering about Asia, as Theopompus says, but
dwelling in Magnesia and enjoying great gifts and being honored
like the best of the Persians, he [Themistocles] lived without fear
for a long time, because the King paid not the least attention to
Hellenic matters because he was busy with inland affairs. (Ibid.)

F88   Theopompus in the tenth book of the *Philippica* says about
Cimon: "When five years had not yet gone by, a war having
broken out with the Lacedaemonians, the people sent for Cimon
thinking that by his proxeny he would make the quickest peace.
When he arrived at the city, he ended the war." (Ibid.)

F89   Pisistratus used pleasures with moderation. So much so that, as
Theopompus reports in the twenty-first book [F135], he posted
no guards on his estate or in his gardens, but allowed anyone who
wanted to come in and enjoy and take away what he needed.
Cimon later did the same thing in imitation of him. Concerning
him in his turn Theopompus says in the tenth book of the
Philippica: "Cimon the Athenian stationed no guard over the
produce in his fields or gardens so that any citizen who wished
might go in and harvest and help himself if he needed anything
on the estate. Furthermore, he threw his house open to all so that

he regularly supplied an inexpensive meal to many men, and the poor Athenians approached him and dined. And he tended also to those who day by day asked something of him. And they say that he always took around with him two or three youths who had some small change and ordered them to make a contribution whenever someone approached and asked him. And they say that he helped out with burial expenses. Many times he also did this: whenever he saw one of the citizens ill-clothed, he would order one of the youths who accompanied him to change clothes with him. From all these things he won his reputation and was the first of the citizens." (Ibid.)

F90   But Theopompus writes concerning him [Cimon] that he was both a most thievish sort of person and was convicted more than once of yielding to opportunities for shameful profit-making. And the lesson of bribery from him first of all seems to have dawned on the generals at Athens. (Ibid.)

F91   "which Thucydides also experienced once when he was being prosecuted": ... The fact that an ostracism took place indicates [that Thucydides was] the son of Melesias and the one who was ostracized. Theopompus the historian, however, says that it was the son of Pantaenus who was Pericles' rival. But not Androtion, who also says (no.324, F37) that it was the son of Melesias. (Ibid.)

F92   Cleon was a demagogue of the Athenians and was their leader for seven years. He was the first while addressing the *demos* to shout on the *bema* and revile. He was a bold man, so bold in fact that, according to Theopompus, when the Athenians had assembled, he came into the *ecclesia* wearing a wreath and ordered them to postpone their meeting – for he happened to be sacrificing and was about to entertain guests from abroad – and to adjourn the *ecclesia*. (Ibid.)

F93   "hating him": Theopompus in the tenth book of the *Philippica* says that the knights hated him [Cleon]. For after he had been insulted and provoked by them, he applied himself to the *politeia*, and he kept devising troubles for them. For he denounced them on a charge of refusing to fulfil their military duties. (Ibid.)

F94   "The five talents that Cleon coughed up": ... Cleon received five talents from the islanders so that he would persuade the Athenians to lighten their payments. When the knights got wind of this, they spoke in opposition and demanded he return them. Theopompus mentions it. (Ibid.)

F95   This Hyperbolus, as Androtion (no. 324, F42) says, was the son of Antiphanes of the *deme* Perithoidae ... Andocides wants him to be a foreigner and a barbarian ... In Demotyndareus (F5,

Edmonds, *Fragments*) Polyzelus says he's a Phrygian ... Plato, the
comic poet, says he's a Lydian of the race of Midas in his play
Hyperbolus (F170, ibid.). Others have other stories. But in truth
he is the son of Chremes, as Theopompus says in his work *On the
Demagogues*. (Ibid.)

F96(a)   And again Theopompus in the tenth book of the *Philippica*
says that a plot was made against him [Hyperbolus] on Samos by
his enemies from Athens, and he was killed and his corpse was
thrown in a sack and hurled into the sea. (Ibid.)

F96(b)   Theopompus says that they even threw his body into the sea,
writing that they ostracized Hyperbolus for six years [*sic*], but
after he sailed to Samos and took up residence there, he died.
Forcing his corpse into a wine skin, they hurled it into the sea.
(Ibid.)

Schol. Aristoph. *Peace* 681: "Hyperbolus now": Because he
enjoyed political prominence after Cleon. Hyperbolus was the
son of Chremes [see F95] and the brother of Charon; he was a
lamp-seller and morally reprehensible. After the dominance of
Cleon, he took over the leadership of the *demos*. Beginning with
him the Athenians entrusted the city and the leadership of the
demos to a worthless sort of man, though formerly quite prominent citizens had led the *demos*. The *demos* chose men of this
stamp because the war with the Lacedaemonians had broken
their confidence in the more distinguished of the citizens and
brought the fear that they might overthrow the democracy. He
was ostracized not on account of any fear of his power or position
but because of his bad conduct and the city's feeling of embarrassment. While residing on Samos, he became the object of a
plot arranged by his Athenian enemies and died. Throwing his
body into a sack, they hurled it into the sea [see F96]. (Ibid.)

F97   And he [Theopompus] says that Callistratus, the son of
Callicrates the demagogue, lacked self-control in pursuit of
pleasure but was diligent in political business.

F98   Assessed contribution ... They called the tribute "assessed contributions" since the Hellenes resented the word "tribute." Callistratus gave it that name as Theopompus says in *Philippica* 10.

F99   "Eubulus ... Theopompus in the tenth book of the *Philippica*
gave an elaborate account that he was a most eminent leader of
the *demos*, both painstaking and hard-working, and he raised a
good deal of money, which he distributed among the Athenians,
in consequence of which during the political career of this man
the city became less courageous and more lax." (Ibid.)

F100   Theopompus in *Philippica* book 10, from which some people

231 Testimonia and Fragments

separate the last section in which is the account of the Athenian [demagogues], says that Eubulus the demagogue became a profligate. These are his words: "So far did [Eubulus?, the Athenian people?] exceed the people of Tarentum in profligacy and greed that while the latter only displayed profligacy in public festivals, the Athenian people thoroughly squandered their state revenues on them.

Book Eleven

F101   Amadocus ... There were two of them, father and son. The son went to Philip in order to become his ally in the war against Cersobleptes. Theopompus mentions both in *Philippica* 11.

F102   See T27.

Book Twelve

F103   The twelfth book includes: concerning Acoris King of Egypt how he made treaty with the Barcaeans [barbarians?] and acted on behalf of Evagoras of Cyprus in resistance to the King of Persia; how Evagoras came into the rule of Cyprus unexpectedly, putting down Abdymon of Citium who was ruling then; how the Hellenes with Agamemnon drove out the followers of Cinyras, the remnant of whom are the Amathusians, and took Cyprus; how the King was persuaded to make war on Evagoras and appointed Autophradates to the generalship and Hecatomnos to be admiral; also concerning the peace that he arbitrated for the Hellenes; how he prosecuted the war more vigorously against Evagoras, and concerning the sea-fight off Cyprus; also how the city of the Athenians tried to abide by the terms of the agreement with the King, but the Lacedaemonians arrogantly transgressed them; how they established the Peace of Antalcidas; how Tiribazus made war, how he plotted against Evagoras and how Evagoras denounced him to the King and got him arrested [fought against him?] with the help of Orontus; also how, when Nectenibis had inherited the Egyptian throne, Evagoras sent ambassadors to the Lacedaemonians; how the war of Cyprus was settled by him; also concerning Nicocreon how he hatched a plot and was unexpectedly discovered, how he fled leaving behind his daughter, how Evagoras and his son Pnytagoras unbeknownst to each other slept with her. Thrasydaeus the half-man [eunuch], an Elean by birth, arranging the incontinence with the girl for each man in turn, how this became the cause of their deaths when Thrasydaeus engineered their undoing. Then how Acoris the Egyptian made alliance with the Pisidians, and concerning their country and that of Aspendus; concerning the doctors of Cos and Cnidus, how they were Asclepiads, and how they came from Syrnos, the first offspring of Podalirius; also concerning Mopsus the seer and his daughters, Rhode, Melias [Rhodia, Mallos?, Milyae?] and Pamphylia, from whom Mopsuhestia, the Rhodia in Lycia, and Pamphylia were colonized by Hellenes and the war [that broke out] against each other; and how the Lycians fought against the Telmisseis who were under the leadership of their king, Pericles, and did not relax from the war until, having shut them up in their walls, they came to terms of agreement; this is what Menophanes' "lost" twelfth book contains.[2]

F104   "I am pleased with the Chians" (Aristophanes, *Birds* (1.)880), he [Aristoxenus] got this too from history. The Athenians in their public festivals used to pray in community for both themselves and the Chians, since the Chians would send allies to Athens when a need of war was upon them, as Theopompus says in *Philippica* 12: "but most refused to do this, and so they used to make common prayers both for the Chians and themselves and likewise when they made libations at the state-paid sacrifices, they prayed for the gods to give good things both to the Chians and themselves." Eupolis also talks about Chios in *Cities*, "This is Chios, a fine city: she sends us warships and men whenever there is need." Thrasymachus says the same thing as Theopompus in *Great Skill*. Hyperides in *Chian Discourse* makes clear that the Chians also pray for the Athenians.

Book Thirteen

F105   In *Philippica* 13 [Theopompus] records the following about Chabrias [general] of the Athenians: "Unable to live in the city partly because of his licentiousness and the extravagance of his lifestyle and partly because of the Athenians. They are harsh with all their [eminent citizens]. Wherefore [nearly? all] their prominent citizens chose to live outside the city: Iphicrates in Thrace, Conon in Cyprus, Timotheus on Lesbos, Chares in Sigeum, and Chabrias himself in Egypt."

F106(a)   Theopompus of Chios in his *Hellenica* (F22) and in the thirteenth book of the *Philippica* [says that], when Agesilaus the Laconian arrived in Egypt, the Egyptians sent him geese and fatted cows.

F106(b)   Ridiculous also are the people who say that the Naucratic wreath is the one made from the papyrus called "wreathy" by the Egyptians. They cite Theopompus from the thir[teenth of the *Philippica* and the eleven]th of the *Hellenica* [mss. third of the

Hellenica], who says that the Egyptians sent some other gifts to Agesilaus when he arrived in Egypt and in particular the "wreathy" papyrus.

F107   Having assembled his [Agesilaus'] mercenaries with the money that Tachos had sent him ... after he had arrived in Egypt by ship, immediately the foremost of the king's officers and administrators came up on board ship to attend to him. Amongst the other Egyptians too there was much enthusiasm and anticipation because of the name and reputation of Agesilaus. They all ran together to get a look. But when they saw no splendour nor furnishings but an old man lying down in some grass by the sea, paltry and small in stature, wrapped in a rough, ordinary cloak, they scoffed at them, and it came about that they made jokes and said: "This was the old story: 'The mountain groaned and brought forth a mouse.'" They marvelled at his absurdity all the more when after the mercenaries had been conveyed and brought to them, he took barley-meal, cows, and geese but spurned the delicacies, cakes, and myrrh. And when they insisted and begged, he ordered them to give them to the Helots. However, Theophrastus [*sic*, Theopompus] says that he was pleased with the "wreathy" papyrus. Because of the smoothness [and neatness] of the wreaths, he asked for and received some from the king when he sailed away.

F108   Even Tachos, the king of the Egyptians, scoffed at Agesilaus ... when he came to join him as an ally – he was short in stature – and he became a private citizen when the king renounced the alliance. The jest went as follows: "A mountain groaned, Zeus was terrified, but it brought forth a mouse." Agesilaus heard the comment and responded angrily: "There'll be a time when I'll seem to you a lion." Later, after the Egyptians had gone into revolt, as Theopompus says and Lyceas of Naucratis in his *Egyptian History*, he cooperated with him in nothing, lost his kingdom, and fled to Persia.

Nep. *Ages.* 8: While nature had been kind in endowing him with great mental ability, she was less generous in physical endowments. He was very short and had a limp. Those who did not know him, mocked his deformed appearance [see F108]; people acquainted with his fine qualities could not praise him enough. There is an interesting story told about the undistinguished looking Agesilaus. In his eightieth year on a trip to Egypt to aid Tachus, he made camp out in the open on the beach with his men. For a table, he threw straw on the ground and covered it with a skin. The soldiers followed his lead and lay down in their simple, badly worn garments. Such attire indicated that these were all poor men, and would never have suggested that a king was one of them. When news of his approach reached the Egyptian king's attendants, they rushed gifts of every description to him. Although they could hardly believe Agesilaus was one of those camping there, they presented gifts to him with the king's compliments. Agesilaus refused to take any of the presents except the veal, bread, and fish, which he and his men needed for that moment. The perfumes, wreaths, and sweet things he distributed to his servants, and then ordered all the rest to be returned. This action made the king's attendants despise him even more, because they felt he had chosen what he had out of ignorance of what was valuable [see F107]. (G. Schmelling, tr.)

F109   Angaroi [means] ambassadors. Theopompus in his thirteenth book: "He sent down ambassadors whom they [the Persians] call angaroi."

Nep. *Chabrias* 3: In consequence of such actions Persian officials sent a delegation to Athens [see F109?] to complain that, contrary to their understanding, Chabrias was fighting with the Egyptians against the Persians. The leaders at Athens responded by setting a date for Chabrias, on or before which he had to return home. Should he not return by that date, he would be sentenced to death in absentia. Chabrias dutifully returned to Athens as soon as he heard the order, but did not stay longer than was absolutely necessary. It was not his plan to live a life open to public scrutiny, especially that of Athenian citizens: it was his wont to indulge himself more freely than would meet their approval. It is the common fault of large, free states that envy rides close to glory, that the envious slander any who excel, and that the poor cannot objectively consider the good fortune of the rich. Although Chabrias frequently left Athens for extended visits, he was not alone in this: all the leaders of Athens did the same thing. They thought they could be free of jealousy only as long as they stayed away from their own people. Conon lived on Cyprus, Iphicrates in Thrace, Timotheus on Lesbos, Chares at Sigeum. Because of his deeds and habits Chares was unlike the others; still he was honored and powerful in Athens [see F105]. (G. Schmelling, tr.)

F110   Slaveston, in Libya. Ephorus, 5 (no. 70, F50), There is another Slaveton in Crete, of slaves to the god according to Sosicrates in his *Cretica*. Also in Thrace there is a Degenerateville, which, they say, Philip founded. He collected together there people accused of [or: who make accusations for degenerate purposes?] degeneracy, sycophants, false-witnesses, and professional prosecutors, and other degenerates to the number of two thousand, as Theopompus says in *Philippica* 13.

F111   Cillicon is infamous for his degeneracy. Some say that he betrayed Samos or Miletus to the Prienians, but Theopompus in his *Histories* 13 says that he betrayed the island of Syros to the Samians. When people repeatedly enquired of him what he would do, he replied: "Nothing but good." Thus the speaker says he is doing all for the best as Cillicon put it. However, his treachery was punished in the following way. [See p. 118, above.]

F112   Andira, a city [of the Troad]. It is neuter. There is a kind of stone there which turns to iron when exposed to fire: then, when it is mixed with some earth and heated in a furnace, false silver trickles off. Finally, mixed with copper, it becomes orichalcum [that is, mountain, or yellow copper].

Book Fourteen
F113   See p. 116, above.

Book Fifteen
F114   In the fifteenth book of the *Philippic Histories* Theopompus says that Straton, king of Sidon, surpassed all humans in pleasure-addiction and sumptuous living. Just as the Phaeacians did, according to Homer's fable, banqueting, drinking, and listening to lyre-players and singers of stories; in such pursuits Straton continued for a great length of time. Indeed, he so far exceeded them in his frenzy for pleasures that while the Phaeacians, as Homer says, held their drinking sessions in the company of their own wives and daughters, Straton planned his parties with flute-girls and women who entertained with harp and lyre. He sent for many courtesans from the Peloponnese, many female musicians from Ionia, other young girls from all of Hellas, some singers, some dancers. In the company of his friends he would set them competitions and would spend his time consorting with them. He rejoiced in that sort of life and was [himself] by nature a slave of pleasure – even more when he began competing with Nicocles. They happened to be in excessive rivalry with each other, each one being eager to make his own life the more pleasant and light-hearted. They went to such an extent of rivalry, as we hear, that they would enquire from people who arrived about the furnishings of each other's houses, their extravagance in the sacrifices that took place in each other's courts, and strove to outdo each other in such things. They

exerted themselves to create an appearance of being fortunate and very blessed. However, they did not remain lucky until the ends of their lives, but both were put to death violently.

F115   Dionia, a city catalogued by Theopompus among the Cypriot cities: *Philippica* 15.

F116   Cresium, a city of Cyprus. Theopompus, *Philippica* 15.

F117   In *Histories* 15 Theopompus says that a thousand of them [Colophonians] used to go about the city wearing purple cloaks, something that was rare and much sought after at that time even for kings. Purple dye was considered of value equal to silver. For that very reason on account of such behaviour they fell into tyranny and faction and were destroyed state and all. Diogenes the Babylonian says the same thing about them in book 1 of the *Laws*.

F118   Notium, this is a region situated before the city of the Colophonians according to Theopompus in book 15.

F119   Cercidas, Demosthenes in *For Ctesiphon* [*On the Crown* 295] listing the traitors gives Cercidas the Arcadian; and Theopompus says that he was [a slave?] of the Macedonian sympathizers in *Philippica* 15 [5?].

F120   After the dissolution of the Four Hundred he was impeached with Archeptolemus, one of the Four Hundred. He [Antiphon] was convicted and subjected to the traitors' punishments: expulsion with loss of burial rights and registration as an outcast along with his descendants. But some record that he was done away with by the Thirty, as Lysias says in his speech for Antiphon's daughter ... That he was put to death by the Thirty Theopompus records in *Philippica* 15. However, this would have been another man whose father was Lysidonidas of whom Cratinus makes mention as a degenerate in *Pytine*.

Book Sixteen

F121   In the sixteenth of his *Histories* Theopompus says the following about another Rhodian: [see p. 147, above].

Book Seventeen

F122(a)   The first Greeks I know to have made use of bought slaves were the Chians, as Theopompus records in the seventeenth book of his *Histories*. "The Chians were the first of the Hellenes, after the Thessalians and Lacedaemonians, to make use of slaves. However, their acquisition was not [made] in the same way by them. The Lacedaemonians and Thessalians will be shown to have arranged the enslavement of the Hellenes who formerly occupied the territory that they now have: the former of Achaeans and the Thessalians of Perrhaebians and Magnesians. They called their enslaved populations Helots in the one case and Penestae in the other. However, the Chians acquired barbarians for domestics by paying a price for them.

F122(b)   Theopompus says that the slaves of the free born are called Penestae among the Thessalians and among the Lacedaemonians, Helots.

F123   Assessus, a city of the land of Milesia. Theopompus *Philippica* 15 [24?].

Book Eighteen

F124   In the eighteenth book of the *Histories* Theopompus, speaking about Nicostratus of Argos, says that he was a flatterer of the Persian King. He writes: "How should one not consider Nicostratus of Argos to be a petty man? He was born foremost man in the city of the Argives; and though he inherited good birth, money, and a considerable estate from his forebears, he surpassed all men in flattery and servility: not just all the men who were also on the expedition at the time, but those who had gone before as well. In the first place, he fell so in love with being honoured by the barbarian that, in his desire to be pleasing and win greater trust, he took his son to the King's court, something that not one of the others will ever be shown to have done. Then, each day whenever he was about to dine, he would set a separate table invoking the spirit of the King. He would fill it with corn and other daily needs, for he had heard that the Persians who wait at [the King's] gates do this, and he thought that he would be rewarded the more with money from the King on account of this servility. He was sordidly greedy and I do not know if any other man was more susceptible to the allure of money."

Book Twenty

F125   Sirrha, a city of Thrace. Theopompus *Philippica* 20.

F126(a)   And Theopompus in the twentieth book of the *Histories* says that around Bisaltia hares are born with two livers.

F126(b)   Bisaltia, a city and territory of Macedonia ... around it nearly all the hares that are caught have two livers; Theopompus records it, and Favorinus.

F127   [Good examples] of story-telling are the story of the aulos-player in Herodotus (1.141), about the horse in Philistus, and the one in the twentieth book of Theopompus' *Philippica* about War and Hybris, which Philip told to the rulers of Chalcidice.

Book Twenty-One

F128(a)   The Ionian Sea of Italy into which the Adriatic issues,
wherefore some call it too the Adriatic. It got its name from an
Ionius, an Illyrian by birth as Theopompus says in the twenty-
first ... Some [derive it] from the wandering that befell Io.

F128(b)   The Ionian Sea around Sicily got its name from Io as some
say. However, Theopompus says it was from Ionius, a man of
Illyria. Archemachus [derives it] from some Ionians who drowned
in it.

F128(c)   Also Lycophron named it from Io. Theopompus and many
others [derive it] from Ionius, an Illyrian by race, who was king of
the regions there, a son of Adrias who founded a city, Adrias as it
is called, on this sea. Others say that this Adrias was founded by
Dionysius the Elder.

F129   The mouth is common to both seas, but the Ionian sea is
different because that used to be the name of the first part of the
sea, and the Adriatic of the inner part towards the gulf, but now
of the entire body of water. Theopompus says about the names
that the one [the Ionian] came from a man who was ruler of the
regions [there], his family was from Isse, and that the Adriatic
was a name derived from a river. The distance from the
Liburnides to the Ceraunian mountains is a little more than two
thousand stades. Theopompus makes their distance from the
gulf six-days' sail and thirty on foot for the length of Illyria – too
long, in my estimation. Moreover, he says some incredible things:
that the two seas are connected by a channel, inferred from the
discovery of Chian and Thasian pottery at the mouth of the
Naro; that the two seas are visible from a certain mountain; [that
some of] the Liburnides islands [are so great in size, or having set
down one of the ...] as to have [or: as having] a circumference of
five hundred stades; and that the Ister issues by one of its mouths
into the Adriatic. There are some similar false notions and
popular assertions in Eratosthenes, as Polybius says in his
remarks on him and some others.

F130   Next there is the so-called Adrian sea. Theopemptus [*sic*,
Theopompus] describes its position. He claims that it shares an
isthmus with the Pontic sea and has islands very like the Cyclades,
some of which are called Apsyrtides, some Electrides, and some
the Libyrnides. They record that a host of barbarians dwell
around the Adriatic gulf, nearly a hundred and fifty myriads,
cultivating a rich and fertile soil. They say the animals bear
double offspring. Their climate is different from that by the
Pontic sea, close though the two seas are. It is not snowy nor

excessively chilly. Persistent rain predominates throughout; and it is always prone to sharp and violent change. Especially during summer it undergoes typhoons as they are called with hurricanes and lightning bolts. Approximately fifty cities of the Venetians are situated there on the extremity of the gulf. They say that they came from the land of the Paphlagonians to colonize the shores of the Adriatic.

F131 Ladesta or Ladestum, one of the Liburnides islands. Theopompus *Philippica* 21.

F132 And in the twenty-first book of the *Philippica* he says that the Umbrian nation – it is situated on the Adriatic – enjoys a reasonably soft lifestyle similar to the Lydians, and their country is fertile; this contributes to their happiness.

F133 [prickly evergreens and Christ's thorns] Theopompus mentions these plants in *Philippica* 21.

F134 And he records much the same [as about Philip, F225] about Dionysius in his twenty-first book: Dionysius tyrant of Sicily [preferred] men who threw away their fortunes on drinking, gambling, and that sort of uncontrolled behaviour. He wanted them all to be corrupt fops, and he described them euphemistically [as ... ?]

F135 To be sure, their father Pisistratus was moderate in his enjoyment of pleasure. He did not even place guards on his orchards nor his fields, as Theopompus records in his twenty-first, but permitted anyone who wanted to enter and drive off or take what he needed. Later, Cimon did the very same thing in imitation of him (F89).

F136 Lyceum ... One of the Athenian gymnasia is the Lyceum. Theopompus in book 21 says that Pisistratus built it, but Philochorus in book 4 says that it was put up during Pericles' ascendancy.

Book Twenty-Two

F137 Omarium, a city of Thessaly. Theopompus *Philippica* 22. Zeus is honoured there and Athena.

F138 Symaetha, a city of Thessaly. The citizen is called a Symaetheus, according to Theopompus *Philippica* 22.

F139 In his twenty-second book Theopompus writes about the Chalcideans in Thrace and says: "They happened to be contemptuous of the best pursuits and were moderately inclined to drinking, easy living, and considerable incontinence."

F140 Therma ... this is a small Thracian town, as Theopompus says in book 22.

F141   Chytropolis, a region of Thrace. Theopompus *Philippica* 22: "He came to Chytropolis, a region colonized from Aphytis." The ethnic follows next: "The Chytropolitans admitted him."

F142   Thestorus, a city of Thrace. Theopompus 22.

Book Twenty-Three

F143   In the twenty-third book, talking about Charidemus of Oreus, to whom the Athenians gave citizenship, he [Theopompus] says: "He used to provide for himself a daily mode of living that was wanton and so arranged as to be at drinking and getting intoxicated always, and he even dared to corrupt respectable women. He went to such a point of incontinence that he undertook to ask for a young lad from the council of the Olynthians. The lad was good-looking and graceful in appearance. He happened to have been one of the prisoners of war with Derdas the Macedonian.

F144   Aeoleum [Aeolium], a city of the Thracian Chersonese. Theopompus *Philippica* 23: "I [*sic*, they? he?] went to a city of Attica [*sic*, Bottica], Aeoleum, whose constitution was shared with the Chalcideans.

F145   Brea, a city [of Thrace] that the Athenians fitted out as a colony. The ethnic ought to be Breate, but it is "Breaean" in Theopompus 23.

Book Twenty-Four

F146   Baetium, a city of Macedonia. Theopompus 24.

F147   Assera, neuter, a city of the Chalcidians. Theopompus 24.

F148   Ares – genitive: Aretos – ... a region of Euboea. Theopompus twenty-fourth *Philippica*.

F149   Dystus, a city of Euboea. Theopompus in *Philippica* 24: "When he had caused the people in the actual vicinity of the Eretrians to revolt, he marched against a city, Dystus."

F150   Ocolum, a region of the Eretrians. Theopompus *Philippica* 24.

F151   Scabala, a region [country?] of the Eretrians. Theopompus *Philippica* 24.

Book Twenty-Five

F152   Milcorus [Miacorus], a Chalcidic city in Thrace. The citizen is "Milcorian" [Miacorian]. Theopompus 25 *Philippica*.

F153   From Theopompus in the twenty-fifth book of the *Philippica*: [see p. 80, above].

F154   "In Attic letters," in the twenty-fifth book of the *Philippica*, Theopompus says that the treaty with the barbarian is a forgery; it is not "in Attic letters" on the stele, but in Ionian.

F155   "The people of Samos," Archinus [the Athenian?] persuaded the Athenians to use Ionian letters in the archonship of Euclides [403/2] ... Theopompus writes about him who persuaded them.

F156   [The war] is called Sacred because it arose over the shrine at Delphi. Thucydides [1.112–5] writes about it, Eratosthenes in book 9 (no. 241, F38), and Theopompus in book 25.

F157   Hedyleum ... There is a mountain in Boeotia, Hedyleum, as Theopompus says in book 25.

F158   They say that orichalcum has the appearance of copper and was named after its discoverer, a man called Orius. Aristotle in *Mystery Initiation Rites* says that the name and form of this substance does not even exist, but some reply that the name is used, though the substance is nonexistent. However, others say that it is the name of a sculptor. So says Socrates, also Theopompus in his twenty-fifth. So it was in the mixed speech of the comic stage.

Book Twenty-Six

F159   "Sacred Objects" ... also "wooden statues." Theopompus in the twenty-sixth.

F160   Apros, feminine, a city of Thrace. Theopompus 26: "while Antipater was waiting near Apros."

F161   Drys [Drison?], a city in Epirus. There is another one in Thrace. This one Theopompus in his twenty-sixth says was founded by Iphicrates.

F162   In the twenty-sixth of his *Histories* Theopompus says: "Philip knew that the Thessalians were undisciplined also in their mode of living. So he prepared them debauched parties and tried to be ingratiating to them in every way. Indeed, he would dance and revel and submit to every undisciplined act – he was a buffoon by nature –; each day he would set about getting drunk, finding joy in the habits that strive for that end and in the so-called 'wits' who say and do funny things [and] he [won over?] more of the Thessalians who came over to him more by parties than bribes."

F163   Also Philip, Alexander's father, was a tippler, as Theopompus records in the twenty-sixth of his *Histories*.

F164   He called the Megarians abominable because they and the Boeotians were not friendly to the Athenians according to what Theopompus testifies in the speech in which Philocrates the demagogue introduces it for him, saying as follows: [see p. 84, above].

F165 Ag[ain he (Demosthenes, *On the Crown* 28) did not report] the names of the ambassadors from Philip. They were [Antipater], Parmenio, a[nd Eurylochus?], according to Theopom[pus in the twenty-] sixth of the *Philippica*.

Book Twenty-Seven

F166   Theopompus gives testimony in the twenty-seventh *About Philip* concerning the Athenians' income of four hundred talents during Philip's time in the speech in which the demagogue Antiphon introduces it for him, saying as follows: [see p. 84, above].

Book Thirty

F167   Corisae ... A city of Boeotia is Corisae. Theopompus 30.

F168   Pylae ... that there was a meeting-place of Amphictions at Pylae is reported by both Hyperides in his *Funeral Oration* [6.18] and by Theopompus in 30.

F169   "Sacred representatives" ... magistrates sent to the Council of the Amphictions from each city of the peoples participating in the assembly are given this title. Theopompus makes this clear in 30.

F170   Wherefore the Thessalians did well to raze the city called Flattery, which the Melieis used to inhabit. Theopompus in the thirtieth.

Book Thirty-Two

F171   Theopompus explains clearly about the Epeunacti as they are called amongst the Spartans – they too are slaves – in the thirty-second book of his *Histories*. He says: "When many Lacedaemonians had fallen in the war with the Messenians, the survivors took precautions not to become extinct as a result of being desolated by their enemies. They assigned certain of their Helots to each bed of their fallen comrades. Later, they even made them citizens calling them Epeunacti [bed-detail] because they were assigned to the bridal beds in place of their fallen comrades.

F172   Thalamae, a city of Messenia. Theopompus *Philippica* 32.

F173   Asae, a village of Corinth. Theopompus 32 of the *Philippica*: "Asae and Mausus are large and populous villages."

F174   Mausus, a village of Corinth. Theopompus 32.

F175   Nostia, a village of Arcadia. Theopompus *Philippica* 32.

Book Thirty-Three

F176   The same [Theopompus] records in book 33 of his *Histories* also that among the Sicyonians certain people similar to the Epeunacti are called Catonacophori ["wearers of a rough, sheepskin, or hairy, animal-skin garment"]. Menaechmus records a similar thing in his *Sicyoniaca* (no. 131, F1).

F177   Melandia, a region of Sithonia (?) [Sicyonia?]. Theopompus
    Philippica 13 (?), [33].
F178   About the Lacedaemonian expulsions of foreigners Theo-
    pompus speaks in 33: "When there is a shortage of food in their
    country, an expulsion of foreigners takes place." Theopompus in
    the thirty-sixth.

Book Thirty-Five
F179   In the thirty-fifth of his *Histories* Theopompus says that Thys,
    the king of the Paphlagonians, provided his table with a hundred
    of everything, starting from cattle, when he dined. When he was
    captured and taken up to the King, though under guard, he
    again provided himself with the same things and lived in
    splendour. Wherefore, when Artaxerxes heard it, he said that he
    seemed to him to be living like a man who would soon be dead.
F180   Catanira, neuter, a city [of ?]. Theopompus *Philippica* 35.

Book Thirty-Six
See F178.

Book Thirty-Eight
F181(a)   If anyone doubts this, let him learn from Theopompus of
    Chios, a truthful man who spent a lot of money on the precise
    investigation of his history. Concerning Clearchus, tyrant of
    Heraclea Pontica, he says in the thirty-eighth of his *Histories* that
    he violently did away with many people, giving most of them
    hemlock to drink. He says: "But when all got to know about this
    'loving cup' of poison, they did not go out of doors without first
    eating rue." People who eat this beforehand suffer no ill effects
    from drinking aconite. They say that it gets its name from the fact
    that it grows at a place called Aconae, which is near Heraclea.
F181(b)   Theopompus the historian says that the drug called aconite
    grows at a place called Aconae near the Heraclea on the Pontic
    sea, whence it has won its appellation. It is ineffective and
    incapable of doing harm if a person drinks rue the very same day.
    Clearchus the tyrant had put many people to death by poison and
    tried to keep the fact concealed, but when it came out, most of the
    Heracleots would not go out before eating rue. He records the
    reason and the cause of his being discovered at very great length.
    Wherefore I have left it out.
F181(c)   Aconite grows in Aconae. There is a ridge in Heraclea
    called by this name, Aconae, as Theopompus records and
    Euphorion in *The Guest*.

F182   Oedantium, a city of the Illyrians. Theopompus *Philippica* 38.

Book Thirty-Nine

F183   Aethicia ... Theopompus *Philippica* 39.

F184   Of the historians Theopompus of Chios in his *History of the Philippica* devoted three books to embrace Sicilian affairs. Beginning from the tyranny of Dionysius the Elder and covering fifty years, he ended with the expulsion of Dionysius the Younger [344/3]. [The three books are from the forty-first (?) to the forty-third (?).] The books are five in number from the forty-first [*sic*, thirty-ninth] to the forty-third.

F185   [Theopompus] says in book 39: "Apollocrates the son of the tyrant Dionysius was undisciplined and a tippler. Some of his flatterers manipulated him into an attitude of extreme alienation from his father."

F186   He also says that Hipparinus, the son of Dionysius, became tyrant [was an alcoholic?] and had his throat slit while intoxicated.

F187   And this is what he says about Nysaeus: "Nysaeus, the son of Dionysius the Elder, after becoming master of affairs in Syracuse, prepared himself a four-horse chariot and more broidered garments. He also put on gluttony and besottedness and the violation of children and women and whatever naturally goes with those things. And that is how he conducted his daily life."

F188   See book 40, below.

F189   Merusium, a region [of Sicily]. Theopompus *Philippica* 39 [31?]. The founders were similarly called Merusians. There is also Artemis Meroessa. The place is seventy stades distant from Syracuse. Some say they are from Meroe in Ethiopia.

F190   Xiphonia, a city of Sicily. Theopompus *Philippica* 39.

F191   Hydrous, a fort, it is masculine. Theopompus *Philippica* 39.

Book Forty

F188   Nysaeus, the tyrant of the Syracusans, and Apollocrates drank very heavily. They were sons of Dionysius the Elder as Theopompus records in his fortieth and subsequent part of his *Histories*. About Nysaeus he writes: 'Later, when Nysaeus became tyrant of the Syracusans, he lived in gluttony and intoxication like a man served with a sentence of death and knowing that he had but a few months in which to live."

F192   Pharax the Lacedaemonian was a man of luxury as Theopompus records in his fortieth. He indulged in pleasures so wantonly and promiscuously that he was far more likely to be taken for a Siceliot because of his lifestyle than a Spartan because of his place of birth.

F193   The silver and gold offerings were first dedicated by Gyges, king of the Lydians. Before the reign of this king, the Pythian had no silver nor yet any gold, as Phaenias the Ephesian says and Theopompus in *Philippica* 40. These historians write that the Pythian shrine was adorned by Gyges and by the king who came after him, Croesus, and after them by Gelon and Hieron of Sicily. Gelon dedicated a tripod and a Victory made of gold at the time of Xerxes' invasion of Greece; the gifts of Hieron were similar. This is what Theopompus says: "In the olden days the shrine was adorned with bronze dedications, not statues but cauldrons and tripods made of bronze. Now, when the Lacedaemonians wanted to cover the face of the Apollo at Amyclae with gold and not finding any gold in Hellas, they sent to the oracle of the god and asked the god from whom should they buy gold. He answered that they should go to Croesus the Lydian and buy gold from him; and they went and bought some. When Hieron of Syracuse wanted to dedicate to the god his tripod and Victory of refined gold, for a long time he could obtain no gold, but later he sent investigators to Hellas. They had scarcely got to Corinth and begun their search when they found it at the home of Architeles the Corinthian. He had been buying it up for over a considerable time and little by little had acquired substantial stores of it. He sold to Hieron's agents as much as they wanted. After that he filled his own hand with as much as he could hold and gave it to them for good measure. For this Hieron sent a shipload of grain and many other gifts from Sicily.

F194   Dyme, a city of Achaea ... the citizen is a Dymaean ... Theopompus 40: "The leaders from the city were Athenis and Heraclides and of the mercenaries Archelaus the Dymaean."

F195   Eleutheris, a city of Boeotia close to Oropus [a foundation], of Cothus and Aïclus. Theopompus 40 [43?].

F196   Talaria, a city of the Syracusans. Theopompus 40.

Book Forty-Two

F197   Hippus, an island of Eretria[?] [Erythraea?]. Theopompus 42. It is also a city in Sicily.

F198   Miscera, a city of Sicania. Theopompus *Philippica* 42.

Book Forty-Three

F199   Xera, a city near the Pillars of Heracles. Theopompus 43.

F200   Massia, a country adjacent to Tartessus. The ethnic is "Massian." Theopompus 43.

F201   Tletes [*sic*, Gletes – no. 31, F2], an Iberian tribe living near Tartessus. Theopompus 43.

F202   Drilonius, a large city, furthest of the Celtic cities. The ethnic is Drilonian. Theopompus 43.

F203(a)   Ipsicuri, a Ligurian nation. Theopompus 43: "which former-ly the Ipsicuri, Arbaxani, and Eubii cultivated, Ligyes by birth."

F203(b)   Arbaxani, a Ligurian nation. [Theopompus 43]: "They sailed by the first uninhabited country, which [formerly] the Ipsicuri and Arbaxani cultivated."

F204   In the forty-third book of his *Histories* Theopompus says there is a custom among the Etruscans that wives are common property. The women take great care over their bodies and often exercise naked with the men, and sometimes by themselves. [See pp. 104–5, above].

F205   Yes indeed! Theopompus records in the forty-third of his *Philippica* that Homer was born four hundred years after the expedition to Ilium [the Trojan War]. Euphorion in *On the Aleuadae* reckons his birth at about the time of Gyges, who began to rule from the time of the eighteenth Olympiad. He says that Gyges was the first to be called tyrant.

F206   Elatea: Demosthenes *For Ctesiphon* (*On the Crown* 143). It was the largest of the cities in Phocis. From the orator [Demosthenes] again in the seventh Philippic [*On Halonnesus* 32], if genuine, the following words: "In Cassopia three cities: Pandosia, Bucheta, and Elatea." It must be said that it is better spelled by some authors with an "r": Elatrea. Theopompus, for example, in 43 says that there were four cities of the Cassopaeans ... Elatrea, Pandosia, Bitia, and Bucheta.

F207   Pandosia: Demosthenes in the *Philippics* [*On Halonnesus* 32]. Theopompus wrote the history of the capture of the cities in Cassopia, one of which is Pandosia, in his [forty-]third.

Book Forty-Four

F208   Tetrarchy: Demosthenes in the *Philippics* (*Third Philippic* 26). There were four districts of Thessaly, and each part was called a quarter [tetrad] according to Hellanicus in his *Thessalica* (no. 4, F52) ... Aristotle in his *On the Communal Constitution of the Thessalians* says that Thessaly was divided up into four parts at the time of Aleuas the red ... Theopompus in his forty-fourth shows how Philip established a governor over each of these parts.

F209   In the forty-fourth of *The Histories* Theopompus says that Philip set up Thrasydaeus the Thessalian as tyrant of his country-men. He was an intellectual pygmy but a gigantic flatterer.

Book Forty-Five

F210   The same historian says this about Timolaus of Thebes in his forty-fifth book: "Not a few people have become wanton in their daily lives and drinking habits, but I know of no one in public life more uncontrolled, more greedy, or who became more of a slave to pleasures, if not, as I said before, Timolaus."

F211   Chalia, a city of Boeotia. Theopompus 45: "Chalia and Hyria, as it is called, which is right next to it in Boeotia."

F212   Chalia ... The ethnic is Chalian. The same author: "later the Chalcideans made war on the Aeolians who held the mainland: namely, the Chalians, Boeotians, Orchomenians, and Thebans."

F213   And about Chares he says in his forty-fifth: "Chares was sluggish and slow, living, moreover, a life of luxury. On his campaigns he took flute-girls with him, and girls who played the harp, and 'foot-girl-friends.' Of the monies that came in for the war, some he would spend on that sort of outrage, and some he would leave behind in Athens with the speakers and movers of decrees, and defenders of his private business in the law-courts. The Athenian people never got upset at this, but on account of it they loved him more than the [other] citizens. And rightly so, for they themselves lived in this fashion: the young men dallied over prostitutes in the little flute-girl establishments, men slightly older than they over drinking [and] dice and similar debauchery, and the entire citizenry spent more on public festivals and sacrifices than on the management of the war."

F214   Zeranii, a nation of Thrace. Theopompus 45 [25?].

Book Forty-Six

F215   Theopompus says in his forty-sixth: "The Arcadians entertain masters and slaves at their festivals and prepare a single table for all. They set the same food in the midst for all and mix the same mixing-bowl for all."

F216   In the forty-sixth of the *Histories* Theopompus says: "The Getae carry lyres and play them while conducting their embassies."

Book Forty-Seven

F217   [The following things are includ]ed in the seven[th and fortie]th of Theopom[pus' Philip]pica: [the] war [against Phili]p, its beginning [for the Athenian]s; [the seige of] Perin[thus and Byza]ntium; ... of Thracians, the so-called Tetr[achorites]; the capture b[y storm b]y Antipater of the Thracian [city] of Angissus; [what] Philip [wrote] to Antipater and Par[menio who were] among the Tetrachor[ites].

F218   Agessus [*sic*, Angissus?], a city of Thrace. Theopompus 47.

F219   Astacus, a city of Bithynia ... it is also a region of the Byzantians. Theopompus 47.

F220   Cabyle: Demosthenes in the eighth *Philippic* [*On the Chersonese* 44]. It is a district of Thrace according to Theopompus 47 and Anaximenes *Philippica* 8.

Book Forty-Eight

F221   Danthalitae, a Thracian nation. Theopompus 48.

F222   There are two Aristomedeses. [The one] was from Pherae. He allied himself to the generals of the [King] against Philip. Philip himself [among] oth[ers] had written about [him] in his letter to the Athenians; also Theo[pompus] in the forty-eighth of his *About Philip*. He was arrayed against Alexander with Darius in Cilicia and fled to Cyprus according to Anaximenes in the ninth[?] [fifth? second?] of *About Alexander*.

Book Forty-Nine

F223   Melinophagi, a nation of Thrace. Xenophon *Anabasis* 5 [5.7] and Theopompus in the forty-ninth.

F224   See pp. 165–6, above.

F225   See p. 166, above.

Book Fifty

F226   Caroscepi [Head gardens], a district of Thrace. Theopompus 50. The ethnic is Carocepite. Same citation.

F227   Theopompus in the fiftieth says the following about the Methymnaeans: "They conducted their daily business extravagantly, reclining and drinking, and accomplishing nothing worth their expenditures. Cleomenes the tyrant put a stop to that. He tied up in sacks the procuresses who were in the habit of acquiring free-born women [for prostitution] [and] three or four of the most flagrant harlots and instructed some people to dump them into the sea."

F228   "sciraphia" [scirapheum] ... they used to call gambling houses "sciraphia" since gamblers used to spend time on Sciros, as Theopompus explains in 50.

Book Fifty-One

F229   Cranea, a district of the Ambracians. Theopompus 51.

F230   Hieronymus: ... A second Hieronymus was the Megalopolitan. Demosthenes mentions him in *Against Aeschines* [*On the False Embassy* 11). Theopompus also records in 51 that he was very much with the Macedonian faction.

F231   Myrtis: Demosthenes in *For Ctesiphon* [*On the Crown* 295] gives a list of the traitors to each city "the Argives: Myrtis, Teledamus,

Mnaseas." In 51 [1??] Theopompus names Paseas and Amyr-
taeus as Macedonian agents from the Argives. One ought to see if
these are spelling errors.

Book Fifty-Two

F232   In 52 he [Theopompus] says that Archidamus the Laconian
accustomed himself to luxury like a foreigner when away from
the regimen of his home country. For that reason he was unable
to endure life at home but was always anxious to spend time away
because of his lack of self-control. When the Tarentines sent an
embassy seeking alliance, he was eager to go out to their aid.
When he got there and was killed in the war, he did not even
merit a burial and that even though the Tarentines offered a
considerable sum of money to the enemy to get back his body!

F233   And in the fifty-second of his *Histories* he writes the following
about the Tarentines: "Just about every month [*sic*, every day?]
the city of the Tarentines slaughters an ox and holds public
festivities. The mob of private citizens is always involved in
get-togethers and drinking. Indeed, the Tarentines have a
saying, 'Others, by their dedication to toil and by persevering at
their work, are preparing for life, but they, thanks to their parties
and diversions, are not putting it off but living already.'"

F234   Baretium, a district on the Adriatic. Theopompus 52 [42?].

F235(a)   "Tha'lt keep watch in Naupactus." The garrison of Naupactus was paid little, but their provisions were costly; hence the
proverb. However, some say the proverb arose because Philip
took Naupactus and slaughtered its entire garrison of Achaeans
[?] [on the recommendation? of (the) Achaeans?]. Theopompus
records this in book 2 [?] [52, 42?].

F235(b)   "Keep watch in Naupactus." When Philip took Naupactus
[the] Achaeans [*sic*] slit the guards' throats and killed Pausanias,
the captain of the guard [or: he slit the throats of the garrison of
Achaeans and ... killed ... ?]. So says Theopompus.[3]

Book Fifty-Three

F236   In the fifty-third he [Theopompus] speaks about the events in
Chaeronea, how he [Philip] invited the ambassadors who had
come to him to a dinner: "As soon as they had withdrawn, Philip
sent for some of his Companions and he gave the order to call the
flute-girls, Aristonicus the lyre-player, Dorion the aulos-player,
and the men who were accustomed to drink with him. Philip used
to lead around such sorts with him everywhere and was prepared
with a lot of equipment for drinking-bouts and parties. He was a

tippler and undisciplined in character, and he used to keep himself surrounded with a host of buffoons, musicians, and jesters. He drank the whole night through and became intoxicated having quaffed a great deal (?); he permitted all the others to depart; when it was already near daybreak, he went revelling to the ambassadors of the Athenians [but the text is corrupt or Theopompus' Greek has been subjected to careless epitomization].

Book Fifty-Four

F237(a)   In 54 of *The Histories* Theopompus says that in Philip's kingdom around Bisaltia, Amphipolis, and Graestonia of Macedonia in the middle of spring the fig trees bear figs, the vines grapes, and the olive-trees olives at the time you would expect them to be sprouting, and Philip was lucky in everything.

F237(b)   Gastronia [*sic*], a region of Macedonia. Theopompus 54.

Book Fifty-Five

F238   Carya, a district of Laconia Theopompus 55.

F239   Tricaranum, a fort in Phliasia. Theopompus 55.

Books Fifty-Six and Fifty-Seven

F240   In book 56 of *The Histories* Theopompus describes Xenopithea, the mother of Lysandridas, as more beautiful than all the women in the Peloponnese. However, the Lacedaemonians murdered her and her sister Chryse when Agesilaus the king routed Lysandridas, his political enemy, and had him exiled by the Lacedaemonians.

F241   Aegirussa, a city of the Megarid. Strabo [9.1.10]. It is otherwise spelled Aegirus. Theopompus 56.

F242   Alea, a city of Arcadia. Theopompus 56.

F243   Eugea, a district of Arcadia. Theopompus 56.

F244   Lycaea, a city of Arcadia. Theopompus 56. In Menelaus "Lycaetha" with a "th."

F245   Messapeae, a district of Laconia. The ethnic is Messapean. Zeus is honoured there. Theopompus 57.

F246   "Crowning the victors": Demosthenes in his speech against Aeschines [uses it] instead of "honouring"; also in other authors with the sense of "to crown." So Theopompus in 57 and Menander in *He Mourns for Himself*.

Fragments with No Book-number

On the Treasures Plundered from Delphi (TPD)

F247   Theopompus in *TPD* says that Asopichus, Epaminondas' lover, had the trophy at Leuctra emblazoned on his shield, that he used to run incredible risks, and that this shield is dedicated at Delphi in the stoa.

F248   In the same work Theopompus says that Phaÿllus the tyrant of the Phocians was a womanizer, and that Onomarchus preferred boys, and that Onomarchus had intercourse with [deest], the good-looking son of Pythodorus of Sicyon, who had come to Delphi to dedicate his locks, and gave him favours from the god's treasures, namely, four golden tiaras, dedications of the Sybarites. Phaÿllus gave to Bromias, the flute-girl and daughter of Diniades, a silver drinking cup of the Phocians, and a g[olden crow]n of ivy, gift of the Peparethians. "She was even going to play in the Pythian Games," he says, "had she not been prevented by the crowd." "Onomarchus gave the pretty-boy Physcidas," he adds, "the son of the Trichonean, Lycolas, a [golden] crown of laurel, a dedication of the Ephesians." This lad was taken by his father to Philip, and though he served there as prostitute, he was sent away empty-handed. Onomarchus gave Damippus, the pretty-boy and son of Epilycus the Amphipolitan, an offering of Plisthenes [*sic*, Clisthenes?]. Philomelus gave Pharsalia, a Thessalian dancing girl, a golden crown of laurel, a dedication of the Lampsacenes. This Pharsalia was in Metapontum, and when there came a voice from a bronze laurel-tree that the Metapontines had set up at the time of the visit of Ariseas of Proconnesus, when he said that he had arrived from the Hyperboreans, was torn apart by maddened seers in the market-place the moment she was seen entering it. Later, when people sought the explanation, she was found to have been killed because of the god's crown.

F249   In the work of Theopompus entitled *TPD* "To Chares," it says, "the Athenian sixty talents from Lysander. With them he dined the Athenians in the market-place when he made the victory-sacrifice after the battle against Philip's mercenaries. Their leader was Adaeus, nicknamed Alectryon [the Rooster].

FF250–9   Miscellaneous works. See after F396.

Fragments without Book-title or Book-numbers

F260   but why the town [Pessinus] was called by that name, historians are not agreed. Some derive the city's name from *pesein* [Gr. "fall"] since the image of the goddess fell from the sky; others say that Ilus, son of Tros, king of Dardania, in the war with [deest] named it thus; however, Theopompus avers that it was Midas, the once very powerful king of Phrygia, not Ius, who did it.

F261   *diapoliteuesthai* and *antipoliteuesthai* are different. They use *diapoliteuesthai* of people from the same city and *antipoliteusthai* for political opponents from one city in another one. However, Theopompus uses *antipoliteuesthai* of people striving with each other in a single city.

F262   See p. 117, above, and T41.

F263   See pp. 22–3, above.

F264   *geitonia* [an adjacent region], instead of geitnia. Theopompus Philippica, also *geitonein* [be near].

F265   *katarai* [swoop down], instead of "go." Theopompus.

F266   Theopompus says that in Thracian Chalcidice there is the following sort of place: when any animal enters it, it departs unharmed, but no scarab-beetle escapes from it, they just go round in circles and die there. For this reason the place is called Cantharolethron (Scarabeetledoom).

F267(a)   They say that there are only two ravens in Crannon of Thessaly. That is why the emblem of the city on all inscribed proxeny decrees [public decrees of formal friendship] – as it is the custom for all states to add an emblem – is a depiction of two ravens on a bronze chariot because more than that are never seen there. The chariot is added for the following reason – for it too would seem to be an oddity: they have a bronze [chariot] dedicated that they shake whenever there is a drought and ask the god for rain; and they say it comes. Theopompus adds a more peculiar thing than this, for he says that they remain in Crannon for only as long as it takes to hatch their young. When they have done this, they leave their young and go away.

F267(b)   Crannon ... a city of Athamania [?], from Crannon the son of Pelasgus. They say that there are only two ravens in this place, so Callisthenes in *The Marvels* and Theopompus. Whenever they hatch their young, they leave them behind, an equal number [to themselves], and go away.

F268(a)   [Callimachus says that Theopompus reports] that in the country of the Agrean Thracians a river called Pontus washes down coal-like stones. They burn but behave in the exact opposite way to charcoal. They go out when fanned by a bellows but burn better when sprinkled with water. No animal can endure the smell of them.

F268(b)   Agriae ... a nation of Paeonia between Haemus and Rhodope. In Polybius (18.5.8) they are spelled tetrasyllabically with a long "a" ... Agriaei, and Agrieis according to Theopompus.

F269   According to a story in circulation at Lampsacus, the spring at Lusa has in it [field-]mice similar to house mice. Theopompus records this.

F270(a)   [Callimachus] says that Theopompus writes that anyone who drinks from the spring among the Thracian Cinchropes dies immediately.

F270(b)   Theopompus says that there is a spring in Thrace, and when people wash themselves in water from it they quit [life].

F270(c)   Theopompus says that in Thrace also, among the Cychri, you can be killed by the water.

F271(a)   In Scotussa there is a small spring that has the power to cure wounds not just of humans but cattle also. Even if you cut off or smash a piece of wood and throw it in, it sprouts.

F271(b)   Theopompus says there is a lake at Scotusa that heals wounds.

F272   And from the spring near Chaonia, whenever the water is boiled off, salt forms.

F273   Also [Callimachus] says that Theopompus records that near Thesprotia coals are dug from the ground that can be set on fire.

F274(a)   [Callimachus] also says that Theopompus reports that the Venetians who live on the Adriatic send gifts to the jackdaws; these are cakes of ground and coarse barley. When they have laid them out, the people who take them withdraw. The flock of birds remains congregated on the borders of the country while two or three fly forward, examine the gifts, and fly back again" just like ambassadors or scouts. Whenever the flo[ck deest].

F274(b)   Theopompus says that the Venetians who live on the Adriatic send gifts to the jackdaws at the season of ploughing and seeding. The gifts would be some ground barley cakes and coarse barley cakes well and thoroughly kneaded. The intent of this offering of gifts is to be an appeasement to the jackdaws by agreement under truce that they do not scratch up the grain harvest scattered on the ground nor peck it up. Lycus agrees with this but adds the following [deest? or: but (says that) the following things are added to the gifts] also ribbons, red in colour. After they have set out these gifts, they then withdraw. The clouds of jackdaws wait beyond the borders. Then two or three are chosen out like ambassadors who are sent from cities to scout out the number of gifts. Accordingly, when they have had a look, they return and call them in the manner in which it is their nature, some to call and others to obey. So they come in clouds. If they taste the aforementioned, the Venetians know that they have a treaty with the aforementioned birds. However, if they scorn them, dishonouring them as skimpy and do not taste them, the inhabitants believe that their hunger is the price of the birds' scorn. For if the aforementioned go untasting and, so to speak, unbribed, they fly onto the corn fields and strip off most of the sown seed; with a most savage fury they dig it up and ferret it out.

F275   What deceives the many is just what deceives Theopompus the orator in the passage where he charges Plato with wanting to define each thing. What does he say? "Did none of us say anything good or just before you? Or, unless we pay [paid] minute attention to what each of these things is, do [did] we utter sounds emptily and without meaning?"

F276   Theopompus says that red wine was first developed by the Chians; and the Chians were the first to learn the propagation and care of the vine from Oenopion, the son of Dionysus, who colonized the island with them. They then shared their knowledge with other people.

F277   Theopompus of Chios records that the vine was discovered in Olympia beside the Alpheus. He also says that there is a place in Elis five stades distant in which the inhabitants close and seal up three empty bronze cauldrons during the Dionysia in the presence of the festival's attendants. Later, when they open them, they find them full of wine.

F278(a)   Theopompus says that the water by the river Erigo is harsh and that when people drink it, they become intoxicated just like people drinking wine.

F278(b)   And he says that Theopompus claims that in Lyncestae there is [a source of] harsh water, and people who drink from it are changed as if from drinking wine. Very many others bear witness to this.

F278(c)   Theopompus says that there is harsh water in Lyncestae which intoxicates its drinkers.

F278(d)   Theopompus says that in Lyncestum [sic, Lyncestae] there is a spring that tastes like vinegar and makes people who drink it intoxicated as if from wine.

F278(e)   but Theopompus claims that one can get drunk from the springs I mentioned above – that is, the somewhat acidic water called Lyncestis makes people intoxicated like wine. The same is found in Paphlagonia and in the region of Cales [see Plin. N.H. 2.230].

F279   Perdiccas reigned before Archelaus for forty-one years according to Nicomedes of Acanthus, thirty-five according to Theopompus, forty according to Anaximenes (no. 72, F27), twenty-eight according to Hieronymus (no. 154, F1), twenty-three according to Marsyas (no. 135–6, F15) and Philochorus.

F280   Arcadion of Achaea was not a flatterer. Theopompus writes about him, and Duris in his *Macedonica* (no. 76, F3). This

Arcadion fled into voluntary exile from his homeland out of hatred for Philip. He was very witty and a great many of his rejoinders are recorded. Once it so happened that Arcadion was in Delphi when Philip was visiting. When the Macedonian saw him, he called to him and said, "How far will you flee, Arcadion?" "Until I find people," he replied, "who do not know Philip."

F281   See p. 52, above.

F282   And in another part of his history he writes: [see p. 148, above].

F283(a)   Theopompus gives a list of tipplers and alcoholics and includes Dionysius the Younger, tyrant of Sicily, who, he says, damaged his eyesight from drinking wine.

F283(b)   Theopompus says that he damaged his eyesight from his excessive uncontrolled drinking so as to see very dimly and that he used to sit idly in the barber shops and make funny remarks.

F284   They record that in Molossis the cattle have very large horns. Theopompus writes about their treatment.

F285(a)   As Chamaeleon of Heraclea records in his *On Pindar*, there is an ancient custom in Corinth. Whenever the city prays to Aphrodite about something important, a very great number of the prostitutes join in the supplication. They pray to the goddess and later attend the sacred rites. When the Persian invaded Hellas, as Theopompus records and Timaeus in his seventh book, the Corinthian prostitutes prayed for the safety of Hellas going into the temple of Aphrodite. Wherefore, when the Corinthians dedicated a tablet to the goddess – it survives to this very day – and inscribed separately the prostitutes who performed the supplication at that time and later attended the rites, Simonides composed the following epigram:

> These women stood forth to pray
> To our lady Cypris on behalf
> Of Hellas and her straight-fighting citizens.
> For goddess Aphrodite did not wish
> To hand over the citadel
> Of the Hellenes to the Persian bowmen.

F285(b)   Theopompus says that the [Corinthian] women prayed to Aphrodite to inspire a passion in their husbands to fight against the Medes on behalf of Hellas. They went into the temple of Aphrodite, which they say Medea founded on instructions from Hera. Even now, says he [Theopompus] there is an inscribed elegiac poem to the left as you enter the temple:

> These women stand and
> Pray to our lady Cypris for
> The Hellenes and her close-fighting
> Citizens. For Goddess Aphrodite
> Did not want to give the citadel
> of the Hellenes to the Median bowmen.

F286   Similarly, on account of the fair division of booty Bardylis the Illyrian brigand – about whom you can read in Theopompus – had great wealth.

F287   See p. 114, above.

F288   Most historians malign Alcibiades. I, however, follow three serious historians who do not: Thucydides, his contemporary, Theopompus, born a little later, and Timaeus. Although the latter two seldom have a kind word for anyone, they both agree in praising him. Permit me to add just a few more notes from them about Alcibiades. He was born at Athens, the most magnificent city of the time, and still managed to surpass all men in sumptuous living and grandeur. After he had been exiled and had taken residence in Thebes, he devoted himself so entirely to the propensities of those people, that he excelled all in the manly arts. (Boeotians attached much more importance to physical fitness than quickness of the mind.) For his stay among the Spartans, who place utmost stress on physical endurance, he practiced such physical austerity that he outdid the Spartans in frugality of both food and clothes. While he lived among the Thracians, who are given over to excessive drinking and licentiousness, he surpassed them in their own national customs. The Persians, who are noted for their hunting and luxurious living, were forced to admire his hunting ability and style of living. Because of such things, he was held in the highest respect wherever he went.

But enough of this. I must go on to others (G. Schmelling, tr.).

F289   Iphicrates was of large stature, physically and mentally, and his imposing size helped him look the part of a general. His size alone made an impression on all who met him. Theopompus tells us that although he was a good and trustworthy citizen, he was lacking in perseverance. He displayed exceptionally fine qualities in his treatment of the children of the Macedonian Amyntas: after Amyntas had died, his wife Eurydice took their two children, Perdiccas and Philip, and fled to Iphicrates where she found protection. (Ibid.)

F290   See T43.

F291   See pp. 125–6, above.

F292   The Athenians' war against the Macedonian was provoked both [because] of other offences that Philip committed [against] (?) the Athenians while pretending to be at peace, and his expedition against Byzantium and Perinthus especially [exasperated them. These] cities he strove to win over for two reasons: to take away the grain-route from the Athenians and so that with their naval superiority they would not have coastal cities offering bases for a fleet or havens in the war against him. At that time, indeed, he committed his most lawless act when he diverted the merchants' vessels at Hierum, 230 ships according to Philochorus, 180 according to Theopompus. From them he acquired seven hundred talents.

F293   [Concerning the flooding of the Nile] Ephorus and Theopompus, who above all others devote special attention to these causes, are furthest from the truth.

F294   [Plato] died in the way I said in the thirteenth year of Philip's reign as Favorinus says in his *Memorabilia* 3. Theopompus says that he was held in honour by Philip [or, was honoured by Philip at his funeral].

F295   [Antisthenes] alone of all the Socratics Theopompus praises and says that he was both very skilful and could lead anyone along with his elegant conversation.

F296   The story of the serpent that fought against the trireme.

F297   Artemisia ... The younger – (mentioned) by Demosthenes – [*For the Freedom of the Rhodians* 11] was daughter of Hecatomnos, wife and sister of Mausolus. Theopompus says that she died when seized by a wasting illness through grieving for her husband and brother, Mausolus.

F298   Thronium: Aeschines in *On the False Embassy* [132]. There is a city in Locris, Thronium, Theopompus in book [deest, 8?].

F299   Mausolus ... Ruler of the Carians. Theopompus says that there is nothing he would not do for money.

F300   (Homereuein) "Being hostage:" ... Hostages are people surrendered on agreement. [Homerein] "to join" is to make agreement. Homer [*Odyssey* 16.468] "He joined me having come as a messenger from your companions." Theopompus says that *homerein* used to mean "be a follower" among the ancients. Thence, he says, those who were surrendered on condition of conformity with the agreement came to be called "homeri" [that is, "joiners" or hostages].

F301   Tilphossaeum: Demosthenes in *Against Aeschines* [*On the False Embassy* 48]. It is a mountain not far from Lake Copais. Theopompus in *Philippica*.

F302   Bisyras, a Thracian hero. Theopompus calls him Bisyras of the Chersonnese.

F303   Donactas, Apollo. Theopompus.

F304   Zira: some regard it as a form of tunic, others as a belt. It is better taken as an overcloak worn from the shoulders similar to an ephod. Herodotus mentions them in book 7 (69, 75) and Theopompus of Chios.

F305   We, observing the authors who wrote about the [war over] Melia and the division of its territory, though all the others say that [the Samians were allotted] Phygela in the division – four Samians, namely: Uliades, Olympichus, Duris (no. 76, F25), and Euagon; two Ephesians: Creophylus and Eualces; the Chian Theopompus all record in their histories that the [Samians] received Phygela as their portion ...

F306   To be sure, some have launched attacks on the dignity of nations and of the most famous cities and hurled abuse on their constitutions. Theopompus did it to Athens and Polycrates to Sparta.

F307   That [Miltocythes] revolt[ed from Coty]s Philochorus showed in the fifth of his A[tthis. That], captured by Cersobleptes, Milocy[thes die[d Theopompus sa[ys in the ? of the *Philippica*, writing as follows:] "Setting out from the city [vacat] he raised mercenaries with the help of Heraclides [and P]yth[on], sons of Archelaus. [At] fi[rst] he triumphed in the war, [took one of the (cities?) in Thrace?] (or) ['penned up' some of the peoples on the sea (coast)?], and overran the country dama[ging and] ravaging all of it [vacat] soldiers of [Smi]cythion [vacat] against Cersobleptes."

F308   Th[eo]p[ompus also in ? records something] very simi[lar to this. Xenophon, however ... [The context is lost. The subject is the division of the Spartan soldiery.]

F309   "Just with a shout," that is the abrupt resolution of a military dispute, as right after or simultaneous with the raising of the war-cry. So Thucydides [2.8.3; 3.113.6]. In Theopompus it means "by storm."

F310   Teres, King of the Odrysians, died at age ninety-two according to Theopompus.

F311   "Catonace:" When people went into exile for a time, when they returned, a bit of fleece [*nakos*] was sown onto their cloaks. As Theopompus says: "In order that they should not return into the city, they were forced by the tyrants to wear a catonace [that is, a hairy or fleecy garment]."

F312   When Archidamus, the son of Agesilaus, was king, the

Phocians seized the shrine at Delphi. Mercenary allies came privately to the Phocians to fight against the Thebans, and the Lacedaemonians and Athenians aided them openly. The Athenians did so in memory of an ancient favour from the Phocians, the Lacedaemonians too on the pretext of friendship, but I think it was out of hatred for the Thebans. Moreover. Theopompus, the son of Damasistratus, says that he [Archidamus] obtained some of the money himself [or: participated in their activities?] and that Dinicha, wife of Archidamus, received a bribe from the men in control in Phocis to make Archidamus more amenable to their alliance. Now I do not approve ... of the taking of sacred money. This much, however, I find praiseworthy in him. When the Phocians were about to dare to slaughter the grown men of Delphi, sell the women and children into slavery, and raze the city itself to the ground, Archidamus interceded for them not to be treated thus by the Phocians. Later he crossed to Italy and waged war with the Tarentines against some barbarians who were their neighbours. He was killed there by the barbarians, and his body received no burial, for the wrath of Apollo hindered it.

F313   "Disputable" [that is, *amphisbetesimon*], Plato [*Sophist* 231E] and Theopompus. "Disputatable" [that is, *amphisbeteton*], Thucydides [6.6].

F314   "cilicism:" Theopompus the historian uses it for killing in transgression of the law [or: murder committed under the influence of alcohol?; killing as a result of some lewdness?].

F315   "To be today" drags out "to be," Theopompus.

F316   For if that agreeable Bowl of Nymphaeus, which does not scorch the foliage of the thick wood above it and though near a cold stream is always glowing hot, ceases to flow, it portends horrors to its neighbours in the town of Apollonia, as Theopompus has recorded. It is augmented by rain, and sends forth asphalt to mingle with that unappetizing stream, which even without this is more liquid than ordinary asphalt. (H. Rackham, tr., L.C.L.)

F317   Theophrastus, the first foreigner to write with special care about the Romans – for Theopompus, before whom nobody mentioned them, merely states that Rome was taken by the Gauls, and Clitarchus (no. 137, F3), the next after him, only that an embassy was sent to Alexander. (H. Rackham tr., L.C.L.)

F318   Mandonia (?) [Mardonia, Pandosia, Manduria, Mandonium ?] was a city of the Lucanians, according to Theopompus, in which Alexander of Epirus met death.

F319   Molossians in whose country is a temple of Zeus Dodonaeus
with its famed oracle, and Mount Tmarus [Talarus, Tabarus,
Tiliarus, Tiliarum, Tomarus ?], celebrated by Theopompus,
with its hundred springs at its base.

F320   Theopompus recorded that in the land of the Apolloniates
one finds a pitch in the earth that is not inferior to the
Macedonian variety.

F321   And while he was journeying [to Phrygia] he received a scytale
[a baton with an inscribed strip of leather on which Spartans
would send their dispatches] from the officials at home ordering
him to assume command of the fleet as well. This promotion fell
to Agesilaus alone of all men. And he was by general agreement
the greatest of the men living at that time and the most illustrious,
as Theopompus said somewhere. Indeed, he won himself the
reputation for good sense more through his virtue than his
leadership.

F322   [Epaminondas] invaded Sparta ... and they ravaged the
country up to the river and the city, and no one went out against
them, for Agesilaus would not permit the Spartans "to fight
against so great a torrent and billow of war," as Theopompus put
it.

F323   The Thebans withdrew from Laconia because winter was
coming on and the Arcadians were beginning to leave, dispersing
in disorderly fashion, as most reports have it. They had stayed
there for three months in all and had ravaged most of the
country. However, Theopompus says that, when the Boeotarchs had already determined to withdraw, there came to them
a Spartiate, Phrixus, bringing ten talents from Agesilaus as a
bribe for their withdrawal, so they got an extra "travel allowance"
from their enemies for doing what they had long since decided
upon. But I know not how the others overlooked this and
Theopompus alone spotted it. All agree that Agesilaus was
responsible for saving Laconia on that occasion, he did not
succumb to his natural impulses to seek honour and victory but
made things safe.

F324   What Duris adds to this (no. 76, F70) [concerning Alcibiades'
return to Athens] not Theopompus, nor Ephorus, nor Xenophon records.

F325   Demosthenes, the father of Demosthenes, was one of the
Athenian nobility, as Theopompus records, and was called a
knifemaker because he had a large factory and slaves skilled in
that work.

F326   I do not know whence it came to Theopompus to say that he

[Demosthenes] was of an inconstant character and unable to remain steadfast in the same policies or toward the same people for a long time. To the contrary, it is apparent from the beginning into what division on policies and station of the government he placed himself; and he kept it right to the end. Not only did he not change it in his lifetime, but he gave up his life to avoid changing.

F327   Theopompus [Theophrastus?] records that when the Athenians were urging him [Demosthenes] to prosecute someone, and he would not obey, they became tumultuous, but he arose and said: "You shall have the use of me, men of Athens, as adviser, though you do not wish it, but not as a sycophant, though you do."

F328   Indeed, when Philip, buoyed up by his good fortune at Amphissa, suddenly invaded as far as Elatea and siezed Phocis, the Athenians were panic-stricken, and no one dared go up on the rostrum or knew what he should say. But with perplexity and silence in their midst, Demosthenes alone came forward and advised them to get the Thebans as allies. He encouraged the people and buoyed up their hopes, as was his custom; and was sent with others as ambassador to Thebes. Philip sent Amyntas and Clearchus [Cleander and Casander ??] of Macedonia, Daochus of Thessaly, and Thrasydaeus, as Marsyas says (no. 135–6, F20), to speak against him. The advantage did not escape the Thebans in their calculations, but each had before his eyes the terrors of war. Their losses in the Phocian War were still recent, but the orator's power, as Theopompus puts it, stirred their courage, inflamed their love of honour, and cast all other thoughts in shadow. So, inspired by his words, they rejected fear, reckoning, and gratitude [to Philip] for the noble cause. The orator's accomplishment was seen to be so great and illustrious that Philip at once sent heralds asking for peace. Hellas, however, was confident and aroused for the oncoming conflict. Not only were the generals [of the Athenians] placed in this service to do his bidding, but also the Boeotarchs. All the assemblies were managed by him at that time, those of the Thebans no less than those of the Athenians. He was much sought after in both cities and he wielded power not unjustly or unworthily as Theopompus alleges, but with complete propriety.

F329   When the catastrophe [at Chaeronea] befell the Hellenes, then Demosthenes' political opponents attacked him and prepared audits and indictments to his discredit. However, the people not only acquitted him, but continued honouring him

and recalled him to public life as a man of goodwill. So, when the
bones were carried from Chaeronea and were being laid to rest,
they gave him the honour of speaking the eulogy over the men.
They did not take their misfortune "all grovelling and mean," as
Theopompus writes theatrically, but they made it clear, especially by honouring and decorating their counsellor, they were
not disavowing his advice.

F330   At that time [the Athenians] sent Harpalus away from the city
in fear lest they be called to account for the monies that the
politicians had snatched. They began a frenzied enquiry after
them, entering the houses and searching them, except Callicles,
the son of Arrhenides. They did not permit his house to be
searched because he had just got married and his bride was
within, as Theopompus records.

F331   But after the libations and the customary prayers, the moon
was eclipsed. Now, to Dion this was nothing astonishing, for he
knew that eclipses recurred at regular intervals, and that the
shadow projected on the moon was caused by the interposition of
the earth between her and the sun. But since the soldiers, who
were greatly disturbed, needed some encouragement, Miltas the
seer stood up amongst them and bade them be of good cheer,
and expect the best results; for the divine powers indicated an
eclipse of something that was now resplendent; but nothing was
more resplendent than the tyranny of Dionysius, and it was the
radiance of this which they would extinguish as soon as they
reached Sicily. This interpretation, then, Miltas made public for
all to know; but that of the bees, which were seen settling in
swarms upon the sterns of Dion's transports, he told privately to
him and his friends, expressing a fear that his undertakings
would thrive at the outset, but after a short season of flowering
would wither away. It is said that Dionysius also had many
portentous signs from Heaven. An eagle snatched a lance from
one of his body-guards, carried it aloft, and then let it drop into
the sea. Furthermore, the water of the sea which washed the base
of the acropolis was sweet and potable for a whole day, as all who
tasted it could see. Again, pigs were littered for him which were
perfect in their other parts, but had no ears. This the seers
declared to be a sign of disobedience and rebellion, since, as they
said, the citizens would no longer listen to the commands of the
tyrant; the sweetness of the sea-water indicated for the Syracusans a change from grievous and oppressive times to comfortable circumstances; an eagle, moreover, was servant of Zeus, and
a spear, an emblem of authority and power, wherefore this

prodigy showed that the greatest of the gods desired the utter dissolution of the tyranny. Such, at all events, is the account which Theopompus has given. (B. Perrin, tr., L.C.L.)

F332   For this reason especially [Gylippus' embezzlement of money from Lysander], the most sensible Spartans came to fear the power of money as a corrupter of not just their fortunate citizens. They reproached Lysander and insisted to the ephors that all the silver and gold be exorcised as curses from without, and they agreed. Theopompus names Sciraphidas and Ephorus names Phlogidas (no. 70, F205), who advanced the view that gold and silver coin not be received in the city, but they should use their traditional means of exchange.

F333   The poverty of Lysander that came to light when he died made his virtue the more evident. From the vast sums of money, power, and such great attention from cities and the King, he had not even spent a little money to aggrandize his home. So records Theopompus, whom one would rather trust when he praises than when he blames, for he blames more readily than he praises. A little later, Ephorus says (no. 70, F207) ...

F334(a)   [Timoleon] ... taking with him one of his relatives, Aeschylus the brother of Timophanes' wife, and from among his friends, the seer, Satyrus according to Theopompus, but Ephorus (no.70, F221) and Timaeus call him Orthagoras ... [the context is Timoleon's resistance to the tyranny of his brother, Timophanes].

F334(b)   Theopompus, Ephorus, and Timaeus write about a certain seer called Orthagoras.

F335   Theopompus records that people who live in the West believe that winter is Cronus, summer Aphrodite, and spring Persephone and that they call the seasons by those names. They also believe that everything was born from Cronus and Aphrodite.

F336   The most important example is the Rhetrae by which Lycurgus organized the constitution of the Spartans. They were given to him in prose. Indeed, while Herodotus, Philochorus, and Istrus have very assiduously collected oracles in verse, they have also recorded myriads [?] unversified. However, Theopompus, who is second to no one in attention to the oracle excoriated the writers who think that the Pythia did not give verse responses at that time; but then, when he wanted to prove his point, he was altogether at a loss with just a few oracles as proof. This shows that even in his time they were already being given in prose.

F337   Who would not take greater pleasure from actually sleeping with the loveliest of women than just sitting up late with what

Xenophon wrote about Panthea (*Cyr.* 5.1.2–3) or Aristobulus (no. 139, F2) about Timoclea, or Theopompus about Thebe.

F338   Execrable expressions of Theopompus the historian are: outcitizens, outfriends, and outathenians [for ostracized or exiled people].

F339   The noun banishee [*apokeryctos* = "outheralded"] is not in ancient usage. Theopompus uses it, but he is not reliable for discriminating style.

F340   Famed is the Epirot Cerberus and Alexander's Peritas [?], the "beast of India." He overcame a lion and was purchased for one hundred minas. Theopompus says that Alexander founded a city for him when he died.

F341   He [Timaeus] finds fault with Theopompus because when Dionysius made his crossing from Sicily to Corinth in a warship, Theopompus says that Dionysius crossed over in a merchant vessel.

F342   See p. 115, above.

F343   To claim that some bodies do not cast a shadow when put in the light is the product of a sick mind. Theopompus did it when he said that people who enter Zeus' holy-of-holies in Arcadia lose their shadows.

F344   See pp. 134–5, above.

F345   See T27.

F346   Clarus, a place in Colophon sacred to Apollo, an oracle of the god. It was founded by Manto, the daughter of Tiresias, or by a certain hero called Clarus according to Theopompus. However, Nearchus (no. 133, F29) ...

F347(a)   Chytri [the Pots, a festival]. Theopompus says that the survivors of the deluge boiled an earthen pot [*chytra*] with all types of seeds in it, whence the name of the festival, "and [th]ey make it [a custom] to sacrifice to Hermes Chthonius" [or so they have a custom to make offerings to ?]. No one tastes from the pot. The survivors did this beseeching Hermes on behalf of the dead. The festival is held on the thirteenth of Anthesterion according to Philochorus.

F347(b)   Chytri is a festival for the Athenians. It is held for the reason that Theopompus puts forth. He says: "Therefore the people who survived called the entire festival by the name of the day on which they recovered." And, "They make it a custom to sacrifice to no one at all of the Olympian gods, but to Hermes Chthonius. From the earthen pot which everyone in the city boils no priest tastes. This they do on the day." Also, "The survivors at that time besought Hermes on behalf of the dead." Games were held on the occasion, the so-called Chytrini, as Philochorus says.

F348   Theopompus says that the largest and strongest of all the Macedonians were chosen to be spear-bearers for the king and were called foot-companions (*pezetairoi*).

F349   "For there is no one so simple as to suppose that Philip covets shabby little places in Thrace – for how else would one describe Drongilum [F83], Cabyle [F220], and Mastira ... – and not the harbours of the Athenians, but that he will permit you to retain these things while he goes to perdition for the millet and barley in Thracian storage pits" (Demosthenes *On the Chersonese* 44–45). In storage pits, that is, cellars. Theopompus and Sophocles in *Inachus*: "storage pits of barleycorns."

F350   "And holy Cilla" [Homer *Il.* 1.38], here is the history: Pelops the son of Tantalus and [deest?] in payment for his boyish favours received from Posidon some untamed horses, and with his chariot he hastened to Pisa in the Peloponnese to wed Hippodamea, for he wanted to defeat her suitor-murdering father, Oenomaus. When he was near Lesbos, Cillus his driver died. And in a dream he stood over Pelops, who was in great distress over him, and lamented his own death and made requests about a funeral. Therefore, when he awoke, he reduced his corpse to ashes in a fire. Next he buried the ashes of Cillus magnificently, raising a mound over him. Beside the mound he founded a temple which he called the temple of Apollo Cillaeus because of the suddenness of Cillus' death. What is more, he also founded a city and called it Cilla. Cillus, however, even after death appears to have helped Pelops' cause in order for him to defeat Oenomaus in the race. The history is in Theopompus.

F351   "The planks of the ships have rotted and the cables frayed" [Homer *Il.* 2.135]: these words suit two meanings: one is to depart before the ships become completely useless, and the other is to stay because they have rotted in the meantime and cannot sail. Theopompus says that this is the reason for the shipwreck; and so Calchas and Amphilochus and their men returned on foot.

F352   Theopompus says that Alexander of Pherae used to reverence Dionysus of Pagasae, surnamed Pelagius, very greatly. And when Alexander was drowned at sea [*sic*, his body was thrown into the sea?], Dionysus stood over one of the fishermen in a dream and ordered him to take up "the basket of bones." He went back to Crannon and gave them to the relatives, and they buried them.

F353   However, *anenenkein* [bring back] is worth a little more consideration. That *anenenkein* has the sense of both to lead back and return is made clear by the quotation: "They bore up to the

Corycian [that is, cave]" (Hdt. 8.36). That is to say, they returned
... That it stands in place of "he recovered his breath," as
Pausanias [second century A.D. Atticist] says, Theopompus
shows: "he became speechless, but then he was brought back
again." Also Herodotus: "He was astonished at this and was
speechless for a time, but scarcely was he brought back when he
spoke" [1.116], and again [1.86].

F354   In Gortynia; Theopompus says that after Odysseus had come
home and found out all that had happened to Penelope, he
departed and came to Tyrrhenia where he founded Gortynia.
He died there and was greatly honoured by the people.

F355   Olympias his mother [Alexander's] traced her lineage back to
Pyrrhus, the son of Achilles, and Helenus, the son of Priam, as
Theopompus says and Pyrander. Pyrrhus goes back to Aeacus
and Helenus to Dardanus.

F356(a)   Theopompus says that Medea fell in love with Sisyphus.

F356(b)   Theopompus of Chios (?) reports what Eumelus, the
Corinthian historical poet, says about the division of the Kingdom of Helios between his sons Aeëtes and Aloeus: "But when
Aeëtes and Aloeus were born of Heëlios and Antiope, then did
the glorious son of Hyperion divide the land asunder for his
sons. One part Asopus held, and this he gave to godlike Aloeus.
The other Ephyre possessed, and he gave it all to Aeëtes.
However, Aeëtes willingly gave it to Bunus to guard until he
return or someone from him, whether son or grandson; and he
went to the land of Colchis."

F357   The festival of the Carnea is celebrated to Apollo Carneus in
the Peloponnese. It originates from a seer, Carneus, who gave
oracles to the Heraclids. From him they call Apollo "Carneus."
The history is in Theopompus. The Argives call the same god
both Zeus and Hegetor [leader] because they believe that he leads
their army. The Heraclids murdered Carnus when they were
entering the Peloponnese because they suspected that he was
spying out their army. Later they began to honour him when
they were being wasted away by a plague.

F358   "From the river Gela" [Chuckle] [Th. 6.4.3]: Someone says it
comes from a laughing-fit of Antiphemus – it was Theopompus
– "When he learned from an oracle that he would found a city, he
laughed thinking this was a hopeless thing, from this he gave the
name Gela [Chuckle] to the city."

F359   Theopompus says that for these reasons a sweet substance has
been shown to exist but not sweetness.

F360   Adrane, a city of Thrace that is situated a little above Berenice.
Theopompus.

F361   Aegys, according to Euphorion, The citizens are Aegytae according to Pausanias [3.2.5; 8.27.4]. But Lycophron makes the ethnic Aegyan, using it in the feminine: "You will endure everything for an Aegyan bitch ... Theopompus calls them Aegyeans.

F362   Acraephia, a city of Boeotia. Some call it Acraephium. Pausanius [9.23.5] calls it [Acraephnium] in the neuter ... The ethnic is Acreaphiaean and Acraephian – Apollo is honoured by this surname – also [Acraepheus and] Acraephias ... Ephorus (no. 70, F229) uses Acraephnian and Acraephneot. Theopompus talks about Acraephnia and used the ethnic Acraephneus.

F363   Acylina, an Illyrian city. Theopompus.

F364   Acyphas, one city in the Dorian tetrapolis. Theopompus.

F365   Halicyae, a city of Sicily. Theopompus.

F366   Halisarna, a city in the country of the Troad. Theopompus. The ethnic is Halisarnaean.

F367   Achani, a nation near Scythia. They are also called Acharni in Theopompus.

F368   Bubastus, a city of Egypt ... and the Bubastite province. It is also called Bubastian in Theopompus.

F369   Buthia, a city in Ionia. Theopompus calls it a region.

F370   Hermonassa, an island with a small city on it in the Cimmerian Bosporus, colonized by the Ionians according to The Periegete ... Menippus calls it a region of Trapezeon in his *Circuit-tour of the Two Seas*. Hecataeus (no. 1, F208) and Theopompus call it a city.

F371   Indara, a city of the Sicanians. Theopompus.

F372   Meliboea, a city of Thessaly. Strabo [5.16.22]. The ethnic is Melibean. Theopompus.

F373   Melitaea, a city of Thessaly. Alexander in *Asia*. Theopompus calls it Melitea ... Ephorus in 30 (no. 70, F95): "The tyrants of Pherae and their Melitaean friends being formerly ..."

F374   Neandrea, a city of the Troad on the Hellespont ... Neandreum, neuter, in Theopompus.

F375   Scithae [?], a city of Thrace near Potidaea. The ethnic is Sciathian [Scithaean?]. Theopompus.

F376   Scybrus, a region of Macedonia. Theopompus.

F377   Trallia [Tralles?], a province of Illyria. They are called Tralli; also Tralleis in Theopompus.

F378   Trerus, a region of Thrace. The Treres are a Thracian nation. Theopompus calls them Trares.

F379   Hyperesia, a city of Achaea. The ethnic is Hyperesian. Theopompus calls them Hyperasians with a long "a."

F380   See p. 114, above.

F381   Theopompus confesses, saying that he will relate mythical

stories, and this is better than what Herodotus, Ctesias, Hellanicus (no. 4), and the authors of *Indica* do.

F382   Theopompus says the nations of Epirus are fourteen in
number. The most famous of them are: Chaones and Molossians. This is because the Chaones once ruled all of Epirus; but
later the Molossians did. They increased in power thanks to their
close relationship to the royal family – they were of the clan of
Aeacides – and because the oracle of Dodona (F319) is in their
district ... The Chaones, Thesprotians, and next after them the
Cassopaeans – these too are Thesprotians – occupy the sea-coast
from the Ceraunian Mountains to the Ambracian Gulf. Their
country is productive ... Near Cichyrus is a small town of the
Cassopaeans, Buchaetium [*sic*, Buchetium]. It is situated slightly
inland. Further inland are Elatria, Pandosia, and Batiae. Their
territory reaches as far as the gulf.

F383   The people of A[sine, which is] a village of the Argolid near
Naupl[ia, by the L]acedaemonians to Messenia were transp[osed
where], there is another villa[ge] with the same name as the
Argolic Asine. Theopompus says that the Lacedaemonians,
having acquired a great deal of external territory, settled on it
such people as they accepted who came to them as fugitives.
[Also] the people from Nauplia moved there.

F384   Between Troezen and Epidaurus there is a fortified place,
Methana, and a peninsula with the same name. In some texts of
Thucydides [4.45.2] it is called Methone, the same as the
Macedonian city in which Philip lost his eye during the siege
[F52]. That is why Demetrius of Scepsis supposes that some
authors have been deceived into thinking that it was the Methone
in Troezen against which it is said that the men sent by
Agamemnon to collect sailors uttered the curse that they should
have no rest from building its walls. It was not these but the
Macedonians who refused, as Theopompus says, for they [the
people near Troezen] are not likely to have disobeyed, being so
near.

F385   Parapotamii is a settlement established on the Cephissus near
Phanoteus, Chaeronea, and Elatea. Theopompus says that the
place is about forty stades distant from Chaeronea; that it forms a
boundary between the Ambryseans, the Panopeans, and the
Daulians; that it is situated in the pass from Boeotia into Phocis
on a moderately high hill and between Parnassus and [Hadyl-
ium] mountains which leave a pla[in between them] of nearly five
stades. This plain is divided by the Cephissus, which affords a
narrow approach from either side. The Cephissus rises near

Lilaea, a Phocian city, as Homer says: "They held Lilaea, fountainhead for the Cephissus" [*Il.* 2.523]. It issues into Lake Copaïs. The Hadylium [Hedylium?] massif stretches for sixty stades as far as [Hyphanteum?] Acontius [?], on which Orchomenus is situated. Hesiod says more about the river and its flow, how it flows through the whole of Phocis winding and twisting snake-fashion. "By Panopeus, across fortified Glychon and through Orchomenos it goes coiling like a snake" [F38]. The narrows near Parapotamii or Parapotamia – both spellings are used – were fiercely contested in the [Phocian war], for they provide the only entrance [into Phocis].

F386   and in the Peloponnese the Argive heights and the Larisus river that separates Elis from Dyme. Theopompus says there was also a city, Larisa, situated on the same border.

F387   The Ellopians moved to Histiaea and increased the size of the city when they were forced to do so after the battle of Leuctra by Philistides the tyrant. Demosthenes [*Third Philippic* 32] says that Philip made Philistides tyrant of Oreus also. Later they were called Histiaeans and the city Oreus instead of Histiaea. Some say that Histiaea was colonized from Athens, from the deme of Histiaeans, like Eretria from that of Eretrians. Theopompus says that when Pericles was subduing Euboea, he resettled the Histiaeans in Macedonia under an agreement and two thousand Athenians went and occupied Oreus. They were formerly the deme of Histiaeans.

F388   There is no information about who they [the Mariandyni] are and where they came from. Neither the dialect nor any other ethnic distinction [of theirs?] is found among [other] people. They are most similar to the Bithynians. So they are probably a Thracian tribe. Theopompus says that Mariandynus once ruled a part of Paphlagonia, a country governed by many dynasts. He attacked and subdued the Bebryci, but left his name on the country which he abandoned.

F389   Amisus ... Theopompus says that Milesians first colonized it, [deest] ruler of the Cappadocians, thirdly it was recolonized by Athenocles and some Athenians and its name was changed to Piraeus.

F390   I have already described Sestos and the entire Chersonese in my section on the places in Thrace. Theopompus says that Sestos is a small but well-fortified place connected to its harbour by a wall two plethra [thick? two hundred feet]. For these reasons and because of the current it controls the sea-lanes.

F391   The Tmolus is sufficiently confined, has a moderate circumference, and is completely enclosed by parts of Lydia. The Mesogis is opposite and reaches as far as Mycale, starting from Celaenae according to Theopompus. As a result, the Phrygians possess part of it, those regions toward Celaenae and Apamea; the Mysians and Lydians, another part; and the Carians and Ionians, a third part.

F392   Phormio. Theopompus writes about him in the *Philippica*. He was from Croton and was wounded in the battle of Sagra. When the wound proved slow to heal, he received an oracle to go to Sparta. It said that a man would be his doctor who should first invite him to dinner. When he had arrived in Sparta and had stepped down from his chariot, a young man invited him to dinner. After dinner he asked the purpose of his visit. When he heard about the oracle, he scraped [a bit?] of the spear and covered it [he scraped off the wound and put it on the spear?]. When they got up from dinner, he, thinking he was mounting his chariot, took hold of the door of his own house in Croton. Moreover, as he was celebrating the Theoxenia [a festival to the Dioscuri], the Dioscuri [Castor and Pollux] summoned him to Battus in Cyrene, and he arose holding a stalk of silphium [thought to be a variety of fennel grown near Cyrene].

F393   This Caranus was the eleventh from Heracles and ... the seventh from Temenus. His genealogy is given by Diodorus and most of the historians – of whom one is Theopompus – as follows: Caranus, son of Phidon, son of Aristodamides, son of Merops, son of Thestius, son of Cissius, son of Temenus, son of Aristomachus, son of Cleadates, son of Hyllus, son of Heracles.

F394   Suetonius [*Nero* 46] says that Nero never dreamed, and Theopompus said the same of Thrasymedes.

F395   See p. 114, above.

F396   "May a stranger come who will buy you." This proverb was first uttered by Philip, according to Theopompus. When Philip destroyed a city of the Thessalians and sold the strangers in it into slavery, he said scoffing, "May a stranger come who will buy you."

FF250-259. Miscellaneous Works

Letters, Advice to Alexander

F250   The s[ame author in his l]etter [t]o Phi[lip] also writes about the reputation [he (Hermeas) had cultivated with t]he Greeks. [Though he was a eunuch, he behaved like] a man of innate cul[tivati]on and grace. [Barb]arian though he is, he philoso-phizes with the P[lat]onists; and though he has become a slave in bonds of gluttony, he competes at the sacred festivals. He has acquired some headlands [and] tiny [regions] and has won the esteem of [the] bodily fit. So he persuaded (?) the city of Elis to an[nounce the] cessation of hostilities [with him] ... [presumably with a view to competing in the Olympic games].

F251   I often attempt a *Symbouleutikon* [a letter or essay giving advice]; but I find nothing despite having with me books *To Alexander* by both Aristotle and Theopompus. But where is the similarity? They were writing what was honourable for themselves and pleasing to Alexander.

F252   Theopompus of Chios in his advice to Alexander embarks on a discussion of his [fellow-] citizen Theocritus saying: "He drinks from silver plate [?] [silver drinking cups?] and even gold ones, and he uses other similar utensils on his table, he who formerly lacked the wherewithal to drink from silver plate or even bronze but from ceramic cups, and they were sometimes chipped.

F253   In the letter to Alexander Theopompus attacks Harpalus' lack of self-control, "Consider and learn clearly from sources in Babylon the way he attended to the dead Pythionice. She was a slave-girl of Bacchis the flute-girl and she, in turn, of the Thracian harlot Sinope, who moved her 'house' from Aegina to Athens. Therefore, she was not just thrice slave but thrice whore. At a price of more than two hundred talents he built two monuments to her. What astonishes everyone is that no one, neither he nor any other of the governors, has organized a memorial for the soldiers who died in Cilicia for your kingdom and the freedom of the Greeks. However, the memorial for Pythionice the harlot, the one in Athens and the other in Babylon, will be shown to have been completed for some considerable time now. She was commonly available to those who wanted, as everyone knew, for a modest price; for her the man who claims to be your friend has dared to establish a temple and sacred enclosure and call it the shrine and altar of Aphrodite Pythionice in contempt of divine reverence and besmirching your own honour also.

F254(a)   Theopompus in his *On the Chian Letters* [letters about Chios?] says that Harpalus sent for Glycera from Athens after the death of Pythionice. When she arrived, she lived in the royal residences at Tarsus, and the people prostrated themselves before her and called her queen. He also forbade people to crown Harpalus unless they also crowned Glycera. In Rhossus he even dared to set up a bronze statue of her beside [that of Alexander and?] his own.

F254(b)   After the death of Pythionice Harpalus sent for Glycera, she too a courtesan, and, as Theopompus records, Harpalus forbade people to crown himself unless they crowned the prostitute also: "He set up a bronze statue of Glycera in Rhossus of Syria in the very place where he is going to erect a statue to you [the letter is addressed to Alexander] and himself. He permitted her to live in the royal residences at Tarsus, and he watches her receiving obeisance from the people, being addressed as queen, and being honoured with other favours that befit your own mother or your consort."

Encomium of Philip

F255   We have encomia from Isocrates, funeral speeches from Plato, Thucydides, Hyperides, and Lysias, and encomia of Philip and of Alexander from Theopompus, also the *Agesilaus* of Xenophon.

F256   It is useful to project the future from past events ... as Theopompus does in his *Encomium of Philip*, saying, "If Philip should wish to remain in the same pursuits, he will rule all of Europe."

Encomium of Alexander

F257   See F255.

Criticism of Alexander

F258   See T8.

Attack on the Teaching of Plato

F259   Theopompus of Chios, moreover, in his *Attack on the Teaching of Plato*, says, "One would find that many of his dialogues are worthless and fake. Most are plagiarized from the teachings of Aristippus, some even from those of Antisthenes, and many also from those of Bryson of Heraclea."

Dubious Fragments

(Perhaps assignable to Theopompus, the comic poet or some other)

F397   Theopompus says that the mother of the poet Euripides made a living by selling country vegetables.

F398   Acatus, a broad, flat bowl [*phiale*] because it resembles a merchant vessel. Theopompus.

F399   *alypos* [unsorrowing], one who never sorrows. *alypetos* is also used. Theopompus.

F400   *anthelios* [sun-reflection], the moon, also the shadow of the sun's image. Sometimes it also means imitation or something given in exchange. Theopompus.

F401   In this speech the orator advises the Athenians to suspect Philip as an enemy ... for he alleges that Philip is plotting against the Athenians and all the Greeks, and he says that his deeds prove him guilty in this regard. He proclaims that he will give answers to certain ambassadors who had arrived, for the Athenians were perplexed about how they should reply. Whence they had come and for what reason is not revealed in the speech, but is possible to learn it from the *Philippic Histories*. At this time Philip sent ambassadors to the Athenians to lay complaints that they were slandering him to the Greeks, alleging that though he was promising them many great things, he was really a liar. He insists that he had promised nothing and had not lied. He demands proofs concerning the matters of dispute. Also the Argives and Messenians sent ambassadors to Athens in support of Philip. They also accused the people of Athens alleging that they were well disposed to the Spartans and applauded them though they were enslaving the Peloponnese, but opposing them [the Argives and Messenians] in their fight for freedom.

F402   labda [the Greek letter lambda], the Spartans inscribed it on their shields as the Messenians did an "M." Eupolis, "He was dumbstruck seeing the labdas gleaming." Theopompus the same.

F403   "It has happened," about the same as "it turned out ... However, "he has written it" in Theopompus and others is a barbarism.

F404   Next, he went on embassies, communicating with the Greeks and urging them. So he caused all but a few to join the alliance against Philip. The result was an array of fifteen thousand infantry and two thousand cavalry apart from the forces of the cities. Money also came in eagerly for mercenaries. And when the allies demanded that the revenues be put in separate accounts, as Theophrastus [Theopompus?] says, Crobylus the demagogue replied that war does not feed on arrangements.

F405   Theopompus says that *amphiphoreis* are called *metretai* [a liquid measure] by some people. Lysanias says that the amphiphoreus is called the *amphoreus* by the Athenians.

F406   There was a custom, whenever the table was to be removed, to have an extra swallow for the good spirit. So says Theopompus. However, Apollodorus (no. 244, F215) ...

F407   Chaeronea ... named after Chaeron ... the mythographers call him son of Apollo and There, Hellanicus in book 2 of *Sacred Things* (4, F81) says Hera. [Theopompus?], "The Athenians and their supporters attacked the 'Orchomenizers' and took Chaeronea, a city of Orchomenus."

F408(a)   *lopas* [a flat dish], among the Syracusans a frying pan. In Theopompus it is a cinerary urn, and in the comic poets.

F408(b) *lopada* [accusative, a flat dish], the [goddess?]. Theopompus.

F409   "Counted as nothing"; this is used in place of "scorned," "swindled": "Having trampled on the treaty and counted his oaths as nothing, Alexander imprisoned Pelopidas and put him under guard."

F410 and 411 are spurious.

Notes

ABBREVIATIONS

Periodicals and annuals are abbreviated according to the system in *American Journal of Archaeology* (*AJA*) 74 (1970): 1–8; otherwise see the list of abbreviations at the front of any volume of *L'Année Philologique* (Paris 1924/26–   ).

Ancient authors. Lists of ancient authors and their abbreviations can be found in: H.G. Liddell, R. Scott, H.S. Jones, R. McKenzie, *A Greek English Lexicon* (LSJ) Oxford, 1968 xvi–xlv; and P.G.W. Glare, ed., *Oxford Latin Dictionary*. Oxford, 1982 ix–xxi.

Reference works are cited as follows.

Ditt., *Syll.*	W. Dittenberger, *Sylloge Inscriptionum Graecarum.*[3] 4 vols. Leipzig, 1915–24. Reprint. Hildesheim, 1982.
FGrHist	F. Jacoby, *Die Fragmente der Griechischen Historiker.* Berlin, 1923–30, Leiden 1940–
I G II²	J. Kirchner, ed., *Inscriptiones Graecae*, II–III, *Inscriptiones Atticae Euclidis anno posteriores.* Editio minor.
I G V	Friedrich Hiller von Gaertringen, ed. *Inscriptiones Graecae*, V, *Inscriptiones Arcadiae.*
Jacoby	F. Jacoby, *Die Fragmente der Griechischen Historiker.* Berlin, 1923–30. Leiden 1940– .
RE	*Paulys Real-Encyclopädie der Classischen Altertumswissenschaft*, G. Wissowa, W. Kroll, W. Witte, K. Mittelhaus, K. Ziegler, eds. Stuttgart, 1894– .

| Suda | *Suide Lexicon*, A. Adler, ed. 1886. Reprint. Stuttgart, 1967. |

Series Titles

APA (Monographs)	(Monographs of the) American Philological Association.
L.C.L.	The Loeb Classical Library.
OCT	Oxford Classical Texts.
TDGR 1	Translated Documents of Greece and Rome. C.W. Fornara, ed. and tr. *Archaic Times to the End of the Peloponnesian War*. Vol. 1. Baltimore and London, 1977.
TDGR 2	Translated Documents of Greece and Rome. P. Harding, ed. and tr. *From the End of the Peloponnesian War to the Battle of Ipsus*. Vol. 2. London, New York, New Rochelle, Melbourne, Sydney, 1985.

INTRODUCTION

1 Fragments and *testimonia* were first collected by Wickers, *Theopompi Chii Fragmenta*, then by Müller, *Fragmenta Historicorum Graecorum* (*FHG*). These works were superseded by Jacoby, *Die Fragmente der Griechischen Historiker* (*FGrHist*). Theopompus is no. 115 found in vol. 2B in two parts: one is the text and the other the commentary.

2 The standard English texts on the subject are Hall, *Companion to Classical Texts*, and Kenyon, *Books and Readers in Ancient Greece and Rome*.

3 Hall, *Companion to Classical Texts*, 40.

4 Wachsmuth, "Pentadenbände der klassischer Schriftseller," 329–31; Phot. *Bibl.* 176, p.120a; Henry, *Photius*, 172 translates, "le neuvième livre, le vingtième et le trentième," but this cannot be correct for καὶ δὴ καὶ τὴν ἐνάτην καὶ εἰκοστὴν καὶ τὴν τριακοστήν.

5 This comes from a *testimonium* not in Jacoby but "discovered" by Lane Fox, "Theopompus of Chios,' 107 and note 14.

6 For a critical appraisal of the tradition of Theopompus' affiliation with the school of Isocrates, see Reed, "Theopompus of Chios," 7–50.

7 Harding, "Authorship of the *Hellenica Oxyrhynchia*," 101–4; and *Appendix* A (below).

CHAPTER ONE

1 T2. Photius' *Life* of Theopompus is found in Westermann, *Vitarum Scriptores*, 204–6. Alexander issued a general amnesty decree in 324,

but it has long been held that Theopompus' restoration to Chios took
place at an earlier date. From Chios there survives the inscribed text
of a letter to the Chians instructing them to receive back "all their ex-
iles." Ditt. *Syll.*, Vol. 1, no. 283, gives the text and a commentary.
He argued that the letter from Alexander to the Chians was sent in
winter 333 or spring 332. However, 334 was persuasively advocated
by Heisserer, "Alexander's Letter to the Chians," 191–204. The connection of this decree with the restoration of Theopompus had already
been made by Rohde in an important note: "Theopomp," 623–4. If
Theopompus was not restored to Chios in 334, it would have to be
assumed that he returned home in the general amnesty of 324. But if he
was only forty-five in 324, then his birth year would be 369, and he
would have been too young (16) to compete in the funeral games of
Mausolus in 353. See also Laqueur, "Theopompos," col. 2181.
Brown, *Greek Historians*, 116, argues that Alexander would have written
a special and, therefore, undatable letter on behalf of Theopompus
alone. His reasoning is that Alexander's general restoration decree of
333/2 (334) was issued on behalf of exiled democrats, and Brown sub-
scribes to a widespread (but to me doubtful) view that makes Theopompus anything but a democrat. For a recent text and discussion of the
letter, see Heisserer, *Alexander the Great and the Greeks*, 83–95; see also
Harding, *TDGR* 2, no. 107.

2 T1 = *Suda*, formerly known as *Suidae Lexikon*, ed. Adler, see Θεόπομπος
Χῖος ῥήτωρ.

3 T3b = Nep. 7 (*Alcibiades*) 11.1: Theopompus, post (Alcibiadis aetatem)
aliquanto natus.

4 The ancients worked out the lives and careers of many early philosophers with pupils following masters at intervals of forty years. See
Kirk, Raven, Schofield, *The Presocratic Philosophers*[2], 143, 181, and especially 240. Herodotus went on the colony to Thuria (444/3). His birth
date is usually given as c. 484.

5 Wormell, "Hermias of Atarneus," 63–9. See also Jacoby, comment on
T2; D.S. 16.77.2. The alliance was anti-Macedonian but not initially
pro-Athenian if Demosthenes' *De Corona* 87–94, and Plut. *Phoc.* 14 are
to be trusted. There is a papyrus document that is part of a commentary on Demosthenes' *Philippics* by the Alexandrian scholar, Didymus
(nicknamed "bronzeguts") c. 80–10 B.C. See F292 = Did. *In D.* 10.34.
Didymus gave a strongly anti-Macedonian account of Philip's attacks on
Byzantium and Perinthus, events which occasioned the alliance. He
names as his sources: Philochorus (Jacoby no. 328, F162) and Theopompus (F292).

6 T1, FF1–4. Another possibility is that the *Epitome* was written for Philip
(or the young Alexander?) after the *Hellenica* but before the *Philip-*

pica; see Lane Fox, "Theopompus of Chios," 111. Nothing is known of this work. The four "fragments" are one-word entries from ancient and Byzantine lexica.

7 Speusippus (c. 407–339) was nephew to Plato and his successor in the leadership of the Academy. In a collection of Socratic letters, Hercher, *Epistolographi Graeci*, 632 ([Socr. *Ep.* 30.12 = T7]), there is one addressed to Philip attributable to Speusippus (see Athen. 11.506 E–F). A great many ancient letters from important literary figures are clearly forgeries. Consequently, they must all be used cautiously. Nevertheless, the good forgeries are full of circumstantial information about the people and the times in question that may be perfectly reliable. Strong arguments for the letter's authenticity are found in Bickermann and Sykutris. According to the letter in question Theopompus was visiting Philip's court maligning Plato. It is suggested that Philip have Antipater's *Hellenica* read to him "and Theopompus will learn that he is rightly ignored by all, and that he undeservedly enjoys your support." This letter implies a comparison between Antipater's *Hellenica* and Theopompus'. Therefore, Theopompus visited Philip's court after publishing the *Hellenica*, which is not unlikely. Most likely it was not yet generally known how bitterly Theopompus would malign Philip in the *Philippica*.

8 Despite the fact that Philip had been steadily increasing his power through the late 350s and that he had been allied with Olynthus since 357/6, Demosthenes ignored the Macedonian king until 352. That year, in *For the Megalopolitans*, he was urging the Athenians to begin meddling in the Peloponnese, and later Philip seems no more important than Cersobleptes and his lieutenant Charidemus as a threat to Athenian security in *Against Aristocrates*.

9 The *Philippus* or *Address to Philip* advocated a major expedition against Persia with all of Greece united under Macedonian leadership. It was written shortly after Philip and Athens had made peace in the so-called Peace of Philocrates of 346.

10 Markle, "Support of Athenian Intellectuals," 80–99, especially 92–7.

11 Porph. in Eus. *PE* 10.3 (465 B–C) = F21.

12 Markle, "Support of Athenian Intellectuals," 93, n42.

13 Wormell, "Hermias of Atarneus," 69–71.

14 Flower, "Theopompus of Chios," 49–50.

15 Schwartz, "Kallisthenes' Hellenika," 106–30, especially 109. Brown, *Greek Historians*, 119–20.

16 From various literary sources and one inscription the following titles survive: *Laconicus* (Address to Sparta?), *Corinthiacus, Olympicus, Panathenaicus, Mausolus*, [??] to *Evagoras, Attack on the Teaching of Plato, Philippus, On the Treasures Plundered from Delphi, Encomium of Philip, Letter*

to Philip, Encomium of Alexander, Censure of Alexander, Letter to [*Alexander?*], *Symboulae to Alexander, Symbouleuticus to Alexander, Chian Letters,* two others inscribed but illegible. Some of these titles could be spurious, some are probably variants of one title (for example, *Letter to* [*Alexander?*] and the *Symboulae* and *Symbouleuticus* come from three different *testimonia* and so might be different authors' ways of referring to the same work), and some might be passages extracted from larger works, particularly the histories, and separately titled. It is possible that *On the Treasures Plundered from Delphi* is a digression excised from book 7 or 8 of the *Philippica.* For more on the list of minor works, see Reed, "Theopompus of Chios," 55–7, who overlooks *On the Treasures Plundered from Delphi.*

17 D.S. 16.42–3, 46.

18 T6a = *Suda,* See Θεοδέκτης Ἀριστάνδρου Φασηλίτης ἐκ Λυκίας; T6b = Gell. 10.18. His competitors were said to have been Theodectes, Naucrates, and Isocrates. However T6a identifies the Isocrates who competed as the orator from Apollonia and not the Athenian. Blass, *Attische Beredsamkeit*[2], 2:449–50, finds chronological difficulties with this and argues (75–6) that Theopompus' opponent was Isocrates of Athens.

19 This is implicit in the speech itself; *Panath.* (12) 3, 267–70.

20 T8 = *Suda,* see Ἔφορος; which records that Theopompus became a suppliant of the Ephesian Artemis while in exile and that he sent many letters "against the Chians" to Alexander and many eulogies of Alexander. See also D.H. *Pomp.* 6.10 = T20. A third source might be Athen. 13.50 (586C) as emended by Scheighaüser.

21 Phot. *Bibl.* 176, 120b; D.H. *Pomp.* 6.2–3 = T20. On the expulsion of the harmosts: Andrewes, "Two Notes on Lysander," 206–17.

22 Blass, *Attische Beredsamkeit,*[2] 2:404; Connor, *Theopompus and Fifth-Century Athens,* 3.

23 See Introduction, note 6, above.

24 Classic statements in favour of the view: Kalischek, *De Ephoro et Theopompo Isocratis Discipulis,* and Laqueur, "Theopompos," cols. 2188–93; recent criticisms: Reed, "Theopompus of Chios," 10, and Flower, "Theopompus of Chios," 12–30.

25 It appears that Theopompus included a digression on Athenian lies and historical exaggerations in book 25 of the *Philippica,* FF153–5. He impugned certain inscribed Athenian public documents because their letter forms were Ionic and, therefore, anachronistic: F154 = Harpocration, see Ἀττικοῖς γράμμασιν.

26 Westermann, *Vitarum Scriptores,* 248, from the *Lives of the Ten Orators* of [Plutarch].

27 F102 = Porph. in Eus. *PE* 10.3 (464D).

28 Flower, "Theopompus of Chios," 20–3.
29 Merlan, "Zur Biographie des Speusippus," 194–214, especially 206–10.
30 A proposal specifically advocated in the *Philippus*.
31 FF255, 256 = Theon. *Prog.* 2.8; Schranz, "Theopomps Philippica," 26; Shrimpton, "Theopompus' Treatment of Philip," 124 where my suggestion that the *Eulogy* was part of the introduction to the *Philippica* is probably best rejected.
32 See Shrimpton, "Theopompus on the Death of Evagoras 1," 105–11, especially 108; see also F114.
33 Isoc. *Antidosis* 274–77.
34 F275 = Arr. *Epict.* 2.17.5–6.
35 Hirzel, "Zur Characteristik Theopomps," 359–89; Murray, "Theopompus or the Cynic as Historian," 149–70.
36 Rahn, "The Date of Xenophon's Exile," 103–19.
37 Schwartz, "Ephoros" = *Griechische Geshichtschreiber*, 3–26, especially 3–5; Barber, *The Historian Ephorus*, 1–3.
38 Schultze, "Dionysius of Halicarnassus and His Audience," 128–29.
39 Schwartz, "Daimachos" = *Grieschische Geschichtschreiber*, 200–1; Jacoby, "The Authorship of the Hellenica of Oxyrhynchus," 1–8.
40 Stiewe, *Kleine Pauly*, "Anaximenes, 2"; also Jacoby's comment (no. 72).
41 Pearson, *The Lost Histories of Alexander the Great*, 22–33.
42 Bruce, *Historical Commentary on the 'Hellenica Oxyrhnchia,'* 3–4.
43 Accame, *Ricerche intorno alla guerra corinzia*, 433–4.
44 Bruce, *Historical Commentary on the 'Hellenica Oxyrhynchia,'* 7–8, 17nl.
45 Bartoletti, *Hellenica Oxyrhynchia*, xxi–v; Gomme, "Who Was Kratippos?" 53–5.
46 Harding, "Authorship of the *Hellenika Oxyrhynchia*."
47 Pearson, *The Greek Historians of the West*, 19–30.
48 There is a most valuable study of the way the accident of preservation through fragments can distort our impression of an ancient work: Thompson, "Fragments of the Preserved Historians," 119–39. For Theopompus specifically, see the end of this chapter.
49 The digression concluded book 10, FF85–100. It has been studied extensively by Connor, *Theopompus and Fifth-Century Athens*.
50 FF64–77; Reed, "Theopompus of Chios," 74–5.
51 The *Philippica* began with Philip's accession. Apart from the struggles with his dynastic competitors, his first ventures had involved wars with the Illyrians and interference in the internal affairs of Thessaly. The fragments from the first five books contain a high frequency of references to the Illyrians and the Thessalians or include place-names from those and nearby regions. See FF28–58, also Jacoby's comment p. 359 and Schranz, "Theopomps Philippika," 27–34.
52 F64 = D.L. 1.8–9. There seems no reason to suspect that the idea of

resurrection has intruded from Christian teaching into the text of Diogenes.

53 F65 = Plut. *Mor.* 370 B–C. For a history of early Zoroastrianism, see Boyce, *Zoroastrians*, 1–100. The same scholar has edited and translated the ancient texts: see Boyce, *Textual Sources for the Study of Zoroastrianism.*

54 F66 = Phot. *Lex.* See Ζωπύρου τάλαντα. See also T41 with F262 = [Longinus], *On the Sublime* 31.1; F338? = Pollux 3.58; F339 = Pollux 4.93; and T44 with F225c = Demetr. *Eloc.* 27.

55 Kirk, Raven, Schofield, *The Presocratic Philosophers*, 52.

56 Burkert, *Lore and Science in Ancient Pythagoreanism*, tr. Minar, 118–9.

57 F75a–e = Athen. 2.23 (45C); Serv. Dan. *Verg. Buc.* 6.13, 26; Aelian *VH* 3.18; Strab. 7.3.6; Tert. *Adv. Hermog.* 25. The quotation is from Aelian *VH* 18.7–9; also F74. Was this story the invention of Theopompus (Shrimpton, "Theopompus' Treatment of Philip," 128–9), or was it already current in the fourth century and known also to Aristotle (Reed, "Theopompus of Chios," 74–5)?

58 F77 = Schol. Ar. *Peace* 1071, and *Suda*, see Βάκις = Schol. Ar. *Birds* 962.

59 Boyce, *Zoroastrians*, 48–9.

60 T31 = Phot. *Bibl.* 176 (121a 35); T30 = Theon. *Prog.* 4 (2.80.27); T20 = D. H. *Pomp.* 6.2–11, see especially 6.2.11.

61 F127 = Theon. *Prog.* 2 (2.66.9); T26b = Aelian *VH* 3.18.1; T26a = Cic. *Legg.* 1.5.

62 F225a = Polyb. 8.11.5–13; F225c = Demetr. *Eloc.* 27. See also F225b.

63 F263 = [Longinus] *On the Sublime* 43.2–3, tr. D.C. Innes in Russell and Winterbottom, *Ancient Literary Criticism*, 500. See also Shrimpton, "Theopompus' Treatment of Philip," 127, and Connor, "History without Heroes," 139. Jean de Joinville gives a similar description of Louis' stockpiles of supplies on Cyprus before the descent on Egypt (1248 A.D.) (Shaw, tr., *Joinville and Villehardouin*, 197.

64 See T25b. Memoranda written to attack powerful political opponents sound like the *Chian Letters* of Theopompus intended for Alexander and described by Dionysius of Halicarnassus as very bitter. They could be the model about which Cicero is thinking in this passage. See also T40 = Cic. *Hortens.* F18, "What can you find . . . more bitter than Theopomus?" For a different interpretation, see Hirzel "Zur Characteristik Theopomps," 369 nl.

65 T25a = Lucian *How to Write History* 59.

66 Arist. *Rh.* 3.16.1–2 (1416b) tr. Russell and Winterbottom, *Ancient Literary Criticism*, 163.

67 Woodman, *Rhetoric in Classical Historiography*, 117–59.

68 T33 = Plut. *Mor.* 803B. The aphorism is from Euripides' *Autolycus* (Nauck, *Tragicorum Graecorum Fragmenta*, 441, l. 22).

69 T32 = Polyb. 12.25f 6. Ephorus' battle descriptions are probably reflected in Diodorus. They have been studied by Gray, "The Value of
Diodorus Siculus," 72–89.
70 Gorg. *Hel.* 11, tr. Guthrie, *The Sophists*, 273 and nl.
71 Pl. *Grg.* 456A–7C.
72 Cf. Shrimpton, "Greek Views of Reality," 135–43.
73 Thuc. 1.22.4, tr. Raubitschek, "Andocides and Thucydides," 121.
74 Demetr. *Eloc.* 11–12, tr. Russell and Winterbottom, *Ancient Literary Criticism*, 176.
75 See Reed, "Theopompus of Chios," 84–94.
76 Phot. *Bibl.* 176, 20–5 (Westermann, *Vitarum Scriptores*, 205). The calculations represented in the text are based on the following assumptions:
ἔπος in this context means line not word (see Turner, *Greek Papyri*, 95,
103, and LSJ, s.v. ἔπος IV d); the average line was twenty to twenty-five
letters (see Hall, *Companion to Classical Texts* 9, and especially 11–12). An
average book of Theopompus would have been about the right length
for a normal scroll of papyrus: Kenyon, *Books and Readers in Ancient
Greece and Rome*, 50–64.

CHAPTER TWO

1 Pearson, *Greek Historians of the West*, vii, recommends a different method: identifying a later continuous narrative that is derived from the
historian in question and reading the earlier source through the later
one. Unfortunately, it is not possible to identify such a later source
that is clearly derived exclusively from Theopompus. This is not to deny
his *Hellenica*'s influence on Plutarch's "Lives" of Alcibiades, Lysander,
and Agesilaus. Special studies of the sources of these lives include:
Smets, "A propos du chapitre XVII, de la 'Vie de Lysandre' de
Plutarque," 168ff.; Burn, "A Biographical Source on Phaiax and
Alcibiades?" 138–42; Van der Meuhl, "Direkte Benützung des Ephoros
und des Theopomp bei Plutarch," 243–4; Herbert, "Ephorus in Plutarch's Lives"; Sasone, "Lysander and Dionysius," 202–6. Busolt, *Griechische Geschichte bis zur Schlacht bei Chaeroneia* 3.2: 742, considered part of
the *Alcibiades* to have been based on Xenophon with "Zusätze" from
Ephorus and Theopompus. This is a likely view which could also apply to
large parts of the *Agesilaus*, but see Uxkull-Gyllenband, *Plutarch und
die Griechische Biographie*, 76–88. For Lysander, Xenophon's narrative is
insufficient to provide a narrative backbone for a biography. Significantly, quotations form Ephorus and Theopompus abound in the *Lysander*. Lane Fox, "Theopompus of Chios," (110n46), argues for Plutarch's use of Theopompus in later sections of the *Alcibiades*. General
studies of Plutarch and his aims and methods include: Ziegler, *Plu-

tarchos von Chaironeia; Russell, *Plutarch*. The chapter on the *Alcibiades* (117–29) is of special interest. Wardman, *Plutarch's Lives*, especially 153–96. Pelling, "Plutarch's Method of Work," 127–40 focuses on the Roman lives, but comparisons with the Greek biographies are implicit.

2   Martin, *Tacitus*, 105.

3   Ferretto, *La citta dissipatrice*, 12–13.

4   Meyer, *Theopomps Hellenika*, 160 believed that the mention of Pedaritos will have come during the report of Cratesippidas' overthrow of the Chian democracy in 409/8. I see nothing to support that view, but neither is there much to be said against it. Either Theopompus made a sort of second beginning in book 2, or he continued chronologically and "flashed back" to connect his narrative with Thucydides. Either way, Theopompus went back to 412/11 and recovered ground already charted by Thucydides. Ruschenbusch, "Theopompea," 81–90 follows Meyer's thesis on this fragment and on the wider view that the author of the *Hellenica Oxyrhynchia* was Theopompus. *Pace* Ruschenbusch (see *Appendix A*), there are insufficient grounds for reviving this thesis over the long-established objections of Roberts, "Theopompus in the Greek Literary Critics," 118–22, restated more recently by Bruce, *An Historical Commentary on the 'Hellenica Oxyrhynchia,'* 22–7.

5   Jacoby, comment to FF5–23; Bruce, "Theopompus, Lysander and the Spartan Empire," 4–5; Meyer, *Theopomps Hellenika*, 143; Walbank, *A Commentary on Polybius* 2, 80, 84, 87; Lane Fox, "Theopompus of Chios," 109–10.

6   143.

7   Bruce, "Theopompus, Lysander, and the Spartan Empire," 3.

8   It is generally recognized that the ancient judgment of Lysander's organization of the empire was wholly negative, see Cartledge, *Agesilaos and the Crisis of Sparta*, 78, with bibliography. However, there were two approaches: one, attributed to Ephorus by Cartledge (93; and see D.S. 14.13.1, *pace* Bruce, "Theopompus, Lysander and the Spartan Empire," 3) made Lysander the obedient servant of the ephors; the other seems to have ignored the ephors and allegedly held Lysander solely responsible. It is represented by Nep. *Lys.* 1.5 (also 1.4) and Plut. *Lys.* 13. It is natural to suspect that this was Theopompus' version.

9   Lane Fox, "Theopompus of Chios," 110, concludes that Theopompus took Xenophon's account and "tried to make it more forceful and showy." His alterations "lengthened and slowed the original, we learn: its contrast between Spartan austerity and Persian luxury offered ample scope for Theopompus' talents. So, too, did the scene between Agesilaus and a Persian boy, concluding with a note on Agesilaus' homosexual loves." Lane Fox argues indirectly and, seemingly, reluctantly that Agesilaus will scarcely have emerged unscathed after

being exposed for so long to "Theopompus' talents." But these talents inclined notoriously towards the malicious: see Plutarch's "he criticises more readily than praises" (*Lys*. 30.2) and Nepos (*Alc*. 11.1) – about Theopompus and Timaeus who praised Alcibiades – "I know not how these two most malicious historians agreed in their laudations of the same person" (qui quidem duo maledicentissimi nescio quo modo in illo uno laudando consensuerunt); see also TT19, 20, 25.

10 Unfortunately, even this is not certain. Without knowing the structure of the *Hellenica*, it is not possible to tell where the surrender of Messenian Pylos (409) would have been narrated, but if Theopompus saved his narration of this struggle in the southern Peloponnese until after the surrender of Athens and the ensuing civil war, then book 5 would not be an impossible place to locate that story (X. *HG* 1.2.18).

11 Even the generally admiring Xenophon recognized that the Spartans made terrible administrators (*Constitution of the Lacedaemonians* 14.2–7) despite their enviable knowledge of warfare (11–13). The fragments do not permit the belief that Theopompus was more of a Spartophile than Xenophon. Whitewashing Spartan governmental ineptitude was no aim of his.

12 Plutarch said that no one was more knowledgeable about Delphi than Theopompus (Plut. *Mor*. 403E–F = F336). Andrewes, "Two Notes on Lysander," 212, suggests that Put. *Lys*. 15.5 could be based on Theopompus' account of the destruction of Athens' walls. It seems to echo Xenophon (*HG* 2.2.23), and Theopompus used Xenophon, but there is no reason why it could not be Plutarch's direct paraphrase of Xenophon.

13 A few moments of fancy were probably indulged in the early 380s, however, if Stylianou is right: "How Many Naval Squadrons Did Athens Send to Evagoras?" 463–71.

14 *IG* II^2.34; Tod 118, 50–2; Harding, *TDGR* 2, no. 31. See also Cawkwell, "Foundation of the Second Athenian Confederacy," 47–60. I cannot agree that the Athenians regarded the King's Peace "null and void" after Sphodrias' raid. They decided only that the Spartans had broken it (D.S. 15.29.7) and, probably, that they could begin to interpret it as the Spartans did with greater (and more self-interested) latitude from that time on.

15 Harding, *TDGR* 2, no. 35 = *IG* II^2. 43; Tod 123, 59–70; see also no. 33 = *IG* II^2.40.

16 Griffith, "Athens in the Fourth Century," 127–44, especially 143–4.

17 Ibid., 135.

18 Sealey, "Athens after the Social War," 75–81, questions the traditional view that Eubulus was the founder and advocate of an anti-imperialist policy. His argument must be largely accepted, but with modification.

Cawkwell, "Eubulus," 47–67, shows how Eubulus began the most important part of his political career in about 355, and it entailed a significant restructuring of Athenian finances involving the so-called Theoric Fund. Even Sealey admits that the fund as administered by Eubulan policy would inhibit spending on prolonged military adventures (of the sort, I might add, required by aggressive imperialism). Perhaps the most important modification to Sealey's position, however, is Cawkwell's dating of Xenophon's *Ways and Means* to c. 355 with all its implications (63nn89, 90). See also Montgomery, *The Way to Chaeronea*, 36–7, 68.

19 See Ferretto, *La citta dissapatrice*, with whose observations and conclusions (109–13) I am in general agreement.

CHAPTER THREE

1 Compare FF185–7 (= Athen. 10.435F–436B) with Aelian *VH* 2.41.
2 Kennedy, *The Art of Rhetoric*, 536.
3 It is quite possible that Theopompus was a source for, e.g., Strabo 1.3.21; 9.5.8, 16; and compare 7.30 with F266; 14.1.20 with F59; and see note 29 below on [Aristotle].
4 He probably was claiming a superiority over Herodotus and Thucydides. Perhaps more pointedly, however, he was vaunting his own enterprise over the *Hellenica Oxyrynchia*. His style was more energetic than that of P, and his boast of having visited many places could be read as a claim to a broader historical perspective than P's. This would be necessary if his *Hellenica* was to replace P's earlier work as *the* generally accepted continuation of Thucydides. As regards Anaximenes, it is not known how many of his forerunners he attacked, but Theopompus was sure to be one of them, at the head of the list, no doubt.
5 There are two other fragments that look assignable to the introduction, but solid evidence is lacking: F36 from book 1, and F342 from a passage in which Polybius is comparing the methods of various historians perhaps as they described them themselves in their introductions. F40 belongs to book 2 but looks to be somewhat programmatic.
6 Heckel, "Philip and Olympias," 51–7.
7 On Machaon: Homer *Il.* 2.732, 4.200–208; Strabo (9.5.18) speaks of an Ormenium (or Orminium) at the foot of Mt. Pelium on Pegasae and makes Euaemon son of Ormenus. Eustathius makes him his grandson (on *Il.* 2.754). See also *Il.* 2.734. On the synoecism, *IG* 5(2). 343 11. 80–83.
8 When no book name is given, a reference to the *Philippica* is presumed. Meyer (*Theopomps*, 164–5) considered assigning this fragment to the *Hellenica* but ended up leaning more toward the *Philippica* and the con-

text of the Social War, a view that I (obviously) find more persuasive. To judge from Xenophon (*HG* 1.2.2), Pygela was probably mentioned in Theopompus' *Hellenica* but in connection with the events of 409, far too early for *Hellenica* 6.

9 Pearson, *Lost Histories*, 23–5.

10 S. Hornblower, *Mausolus*, 204–9.

11 Another reason for the exclusion of Alcibiades and Thrasybulus might be their inevitable inclusion in the *Hellenica*. Alcibiades was described in a laudatory fashion, unlike the other fifth-century demagogues so perhaps he does not belong in the digression anyway.

12 Wallace, "Isocrates' *Areopagitikos*," 77–84.

13 S. Hornblower, *Mausolus*, 127, 204–9, on Assessus, see Jacoby's comment to F123.

14 Beloch, *Griechische Geschichte*, 3.^{2} 1: 535.

15 *FGrHist* 2B, 359. In other words, I believe that Momigliano's old thesis, recently revived by Walbank, *Polybius*, 2, that Theopompus was at pains "to restore Persia to her due place of prominence in the historical scene" lacks evidence.

16 Luzzatto and La Penna, eds., *Babrius Mythiambi Aesopei*.

17 For an outline of the history with source bibliography, see Bengston, *History of Greece*, tr., Bloedow, 167, 193.

18 Connor, "History without Heroes," 94–96, also includes F156 on the Sacred War in this digression, but this is less certain. There had been another Sacred War in the fifth century (448 and after) in which the Athenians had supported Phocian claims for control of Delphi against the Delphians, who were backed by the Spartans, and the some-what vague implication of F156 is that it was this event of the fifth century that was mentioned by Theopompus in book 25. However, there is no need to assume that the context of F156 was the digression on fifth-century Athenian foreign policy. FF164 (from book 26) and, probably, 166 (from book 27) are from the debate in Athens over whether to agree to Philip's offer of a peace treaty in 346, and book 24 told of the fall of Olynthus (348). This leaves the momentous events of 347 for book 25, and its main burden must have been the final events of the fourth-century Sacred War. It is natural to regard the description of the earlier Sacred War as background to the main subject. Certainty is unobtainable, but an attractive suggestion would be that Theopompus' narrative of the closing events of the fourth-century Sacred War followed the same general pattern as the one in Diodorus (16.56–7) covering the years 347–346. From very early in the war, which broke out in 357, the Phocians had made some use of Delphic treasures to finance their operations, but in the last years, under Phalaecus, the mercenary general, the plundering had been greatly intensified.

Diodorus is careful to point out that such venerable Greek states as
Athens and Sparta did not scruple to accept the sacred treasures (or
money coined from it), and he digresses for a moment on the historic
Spartan association with the oracle. Greed was one of Theopompus'
favourite topics. Perhaps he too digressed at this moment, adding to or
substituting for the Spartan history a digression on past Athenian
dealings with the oracle. This would include the war in the fifth century,
which, in turn, would lead to the consideration of Athenian policy in
general during the same period.

19 Emendations of the text discussed at length by Connor, "History without
Heroes," 78–81, are unnecessary.
20 Tod, *Selection of Greek Historical Inscriptions* 2, no. 204; Fornara, *TDGR* 1,
no. 204.
21 Badian, "Peace of Callias," 1–39.
22 Markle, "Peace of Philocrates" 45–7. Markle points out the probable
relationship between *Philippica* 25 and these embassies (46nl); Ellis,
Philip II and Macedonian Imperialism, 105.
23 Davies, *Athenian Propertied Families*, no. 2108.
24 Buckler, *Theban Hegemony*, 107–9.
25 Shrimpton, "Theban Supremacy," 310–18.
26 Talbert, *Timoleon and the Revival of Greek Sicily*, 35–7; Westlake, "The
Sicilian Books of Theopompus' *Philippica*," 288–307; Pearson, *Historians of the West*, 35.
27 X. *HG* 1.1.18–31, 1.2.8–14, 3.4.1, 3.5.14.
28 H. Bunbury, *History of Ancient Geography*, 1: 384, 388–9.
29 Compare F267b with 126, F268 with 115, F269 with 125, F271 with 117,
F274 with 119, F277 with 123, F316 with 127.
30 On the relationship of ethnography to ancient historical writing:
Fornara, *History of Ancient Greece and Rome*, 12–16; for a brilliant
structuralist analysis of an ancient ethnographic discourse: Hartog,
Mirror of Herodotus, tr. Lloyd; for a similar study of Ammianus with
further bibliography: Weidemann, "Between Men and Beasts," 189–
201; for a fascinating account of how white scientists of modern times
have structured their descriptions of non-whites to the point of
making their prejudices (which parallel those of Theopompus
remarkably) masquerade as scientific discourse: Gould, "Flaws in a
Victorian Veil," 169–76. I am grateful to my student Richard Ross for
calling my attention to this book.
31 For a discussion: Smith, "Aristotle's Theory of Natural Slavery," 109–
22; Aristotle, *Politics* 2152b 9, 1327b 23–38.
32 Assuming one hundred ships, two hundred men per ship paid at 4 obols
a day, see X. *HG* 1.4.4–7.
33 Pairault, *Recherches sur l'art et l'artisanat étrusco-italiques*, 5–6, sketches the

complex structure of Etruscan society as organized for the produc-
tion of art; Cristofani, *Saggi d'istoria etrusca-arcaica*, 107–25, where the
observations about Etruscan nomenclature clearly invalidate Theopompus' claims.

34 To mention but a few of its functions and characteristics, see Lacey, *The
Family in Classical Greece*.

35 Gardiner-Garden, "Ateas and Theopompus," 29–40, tries to fill the
vacuum somewhat at least as far as the Scythians are concerned. He
argues that Theopompus is the only fourth-century historian known to
have reported Philip's invasion of Ateas' Scythia in 339 after the
abortive attempts on Perinthus and Byzantium. This makes him the
most likely source for the stories concerning Ateas and Philip
reported in the later anecdotal literature. This takes no account of
Anaximenes' *Philippica*, however, which might have included a brief and
quotable version of the story, and Gardiner-Garden himself allows that
Duris of Samos (c. 340–c. 260, *FGrHist* no. 76) reported at least part
of the story (30n2). Now Anaximenes was Theopompus' enemy and
Duris had his own definite ideas about how to tell a story (see Fornara,
History in Ancient Greece and Rome, 124–30). In the absence of any substantial fragments of this story from any of those three historians,
even tentative conclusions seem premature to me.

36 von Fritz, "The Historian Theopompus," 777–8.

37 Wormell, "Hermias of Atarneus," 57–92.

38 On Theopompus' approach to nature: Lana, "L'utopia di Teopompo,"
3–22, and a brief response in my "Philip in the *Philippica*," 129n13; on
escape and marvel literature in general: Rohde, "Zum Griechischen Roman," 9–25 = *Rh Mus* 48 (1894): 110ff.; Brown, "Some Hellenistic
Utopias," 57–62; J. Hornblower, *Hieronymus of Cardia*, 43–4.

39 Powell, "Puns in Herodotus," 103–5; Th. 1.110.2; and for discussion
and bibliography on the so-called Gorgianic figures: Kennedy, *The Art
of Persuasion in Greece*, 64–6.

40 Hammond and Griffith, *History of Macedonia*, 2: 704n4.

41 J. Hornblower, *Hieronymus of Cardia*, 2, and on Justin in general 26,
65–7.

42 Pearson, *Historians of the West*, 208.

43 Watson, tr., *Justin, Cornelius Nepos, and Eutropius*, 172–3, 175.

44 Pearson and Stephens, eds., *Didymi in Demosthenem Commenta*.

45 *TDGR* 2, no. 90A.

CHAPTER FOUR

1 There was much to admire in Philip. Theopompus' bitterly negative treatment of him is likely to have resulted in the repression of his impulse

to admire, but a personal conflict is apparent from the author's extended preoccupation with a subject he professes to hate. For a discussion
of the principle of internal conflict and how it can produce violent contradictions in an author, see Jung, *Answer to Job*, 73–89.

2 Pearson, *Greek Historians of the West*, vii.

3 Iustini, *Epitoma Historirarum Philippicarum*, ed. Seel. On Trogus' use of
Theopompus, see Hammond and Griffith, *History of Macedonia*, 2: 225,
2, and, generally, chapter 3, note 41, above.

4 Momigliano, "Teopompo," 230–42, 335–53 = *Terzo contributo alla
storia degli studi classici e del mondo antico* 1: 367–92; von Fritz, "The
Historian Theopompus," 765–87; Shrimpton, "Theopompus' Treatment of Philip," 133–6; Flower, "Theopompus of Chios," 106–94;
Connor, "History without Heroes, 133–54.

5 Campbell, *Grammatical Man*, 34.

6 Hirzel, "Zur Characteristic Theopomps," 359–89; Blass, *Attische Beredsamkeit*[2], 414–27; Roberts, "Theopompus in the Greek Literary Critics,"
118; Murray, "Theopompus," 149–70; see also Connor, *Theopompus
and Fifth-Century Athens*, 13–16; and, for a very useful recent general
survey Lane Fox, "Theopompus of Chios," 105–20.

7 FF247–9 with comment. It seems natural to wonder whether the treatise
was really an excerpt from *Philippica* like *On the Demagogues* and *Marvels*, but Athenaeus, who seems to have had generally good bibliographi-
cal information, always refers to it as a separate work.

8 See Andocides 1.42; Lysias 22.13.

9 Flower, "Theopompus of Chios," 108.

10 Murray, "Theopompus," 149–70, especially 155.

11 On Ardiaeans and Philip's campaign against them, see Hammond and
Griffith, *History of Macedonia*, 1: 271–4; in general, Dell, "Origin and
Nature of Illyrian Piracy," 344–58, especially 348–54. However, Mócsy,
"Zu Theopompos Frg. 39–40," 13–14, argues persuasively that F40
really refers to the Autariatae, see note 12 following.

12 The problem is with the name of the people under consideration.
Athenaeus gave the name of the people on two separate occasions:
here (10.443 B–C) and in a brief allusion (6.271E). In book 6 they are
called Arcadians, and in 10, Ariaeans. "Arcadians" is an impossible
reading. The citation is from book 2 of the *Philippica* where the subject
was Illyria and, perhaps, Epirus; there is no likely river for the
Arcadians to hurl themselves into in great numbers; and, most convinc-
ingly, there can scarcely have been a Celtic invasion of Arcadia for
Theopompus to report. "Ariaeans," for its part, is unintelligible.
Casaubon emended Ariaeans to Ardiaeans long ago, and that emendation has held the field, but Mócsy pointed out that Polyaenus (7.42)
tells the same story of the Autariatae. This was an important tribe in

northern Illyria that had probably had much experience of Celtic invasions. There is no known case of those Autariatae having come into contact with Philip. Because the text is uncertain, the standard reading Ardiaeans is used, but it is put in square brackets to show that it is doubtful.

13 See especially Walsh, *Aristotle's Concept of Moral Weakness*, particularly the first chapter, "The Socratic Denial of Akrasia."

14 Arist. *EN* 7.1–10. See also Rorty, "Akrasia and Pleasure."

15 Reed, "Theopompus of Chios," For Aristotle's version, see Rose, ed., *Aristotelis Fragmenta*, F44 = W.D. Ross, ed., *OCT* "Eudemus" F6 = Plut, *Mor.* 115 B–E. Aalders, "Die Meropes des Theopomp," 317–27.

16 Rohde, "Zum griechischen Roman," 14–19.

17 Murray, "Theopompus," 168.

18 Socrates or Plato, see, for example, *Republic* 3.408D–9D. Of course, Socrates pressed this observation to yield a definition of justice (4.433). It is by no means clear how far Theopompus would have followed this line of argument.

19 When a person is good or bad, he is generally described as living (ζῶν, F213) or passing time (διατελῶν, FF62, 75; διατρίβων, F49; δίαιταν διάγων, FF187, 188) doing this or that. Occasionally, the besotted just exist as such (ὄντες ἀκόλαστοι, etc. FF162, 75, 114); they may be disposed (διάκεινται, F40) toward excess or be born (φύσει ὄντες, FF114, 162; γεγονώς, F121; γίγνονται, F75) or become (γίγνονται, FF62, 90, 99, 100) that way. People can happen to be (τυγχάνειν, FF114, 139; συμβαίνειν, F99) indolent and they can be accustomed to the state (εἰθισμένοι, F62). That the sense meant is a state of being is suggested by such expressions as ἐν βίῳ βελτίονι διετέλουν ὄντες (F62); and twice incontinence is characterized as something (a state) into which a person goes (εἰς τοῦτο . . . προέβησαν ἀσελγείας, ὥστε, F121; εἰς τοσοῦτον προῆλθεν ἀκρασίας, ὥστε, F143). In this state, people may scorn the best pursuits (τῶν βελτίστων ἐπιτηδευμάτων ὑπερορῶντες, F139) and indulge in pleasures (ταῖς ἡδοναῖς χρώμενοι, FF20, 22, 135, 192). Most of the fragments exhibit these rather stereotyped constructions, somewhat hackneyed nouns and adjectives, and passive or colourless verbs.

20 The English sounds awkward because the text is difficult. Perhaps something has fallen out, but emendation is not easy. If, as seems likely, Plutarch was thinking of this passage when he wrote *Mor.* 856B, then he read it approximately as I have translated it.

21 *IG* II^2 141 = Ditt. *Syll.* 263; see also Isoc. *Letter to Timotheus* 8–9. See also Stähelin, "Die Griechische Historiker-fragmente bei Didymus," 149.

22 The Byzantians gave heavy support to the besieged Perinthus before coming under attack themselves (D.S. 16.75–7). To be sure, Olynthus

was betrayed from within, but only after a stubborn fight (D.S. 16.53). But it is not known what Theopompus made of any of this (Flower, "Theopompus of Chios," 108–11).

CHAPTER FIVE

1 Important works in English that discuss this period and give references to the ancient sources include: Pickard-Cambridge, *Demosthenes and the Last Days of Greek Freedom*; Jaeger, *Demosthenes*; Ellis, *Philip II and Macedonian Imperialism*; Cawkwell, *Philip of Macedon*; Hammond and Griffith, *History of Macedonia*, 2. For an excellent critical review of the last three volumes (plus one other), see Errington, "Review Discussion," 69–88. There is a very useful collection of reprinted articles, S. Perlman, ed., *Philip and Athens*. For a recent attempt to establish the precise dates of Philip's reign, see Hatzopoulos, "The Oleveni Inscription and the Dates of Philip's Reign," 21–42.

2 On Bardylis, see Hammond, "Kingdoms in Illyria," 248–53; on Cotys, see Hammond and Griffith, *History of Macedonia*, 2: 195–6: on Jason, see Westlake, *Thessaly*, 67–125.

3 The sensitivity of the age to this issue is well brought out by Perlman in his discussion of Isocrates' "Philippus"; see Perlman, ed., *Philip and Athens*, 114n64. Isocrates avoids referring to the Macedonian contribution to the proposed invasion of Persia as an act of revenge. That was for the Greeks themselves. It follows, in Perlman's view, that the invasion would be a redirection of Macedonian expansionism away from Greece.

4 Ehrenberg, *Greek State*, 110, and, generally, 108–12; see also Hammond and Griffith, *History of Macedonia*, 2: 450–6; and Aeschines "On the Embassy" 113–16.

5 Westlake, *Thessaly*, 116–17.

6 On the settlement see Hammond and Griffith, *History of Macedonia*, 2: 451, 453–6; Westlake, *Thessaly*, 189. Does the remark in F225, "they readily assumed the odium of perjury and cheating in the most august sanctuary," refer to this settlement?

7 Hammond and Griffith, *History of Macedonia*, 2: 220–5.

8 Demosthenes *On the Embassy* 128. They apparently passed a decree denying Philip a share in Amphictionic business (*On the Embassy* 181).

9 On the date of the *Philippus*, see Blass, *Attische Beredsamkeit*[2], 2: 314. The references to the *Philippus* are on ethnicity, 108; on Heracles, 32–4, 105–2.

10 Hdt. 5.22, 8.137; Th. 2.99–100, 5.80. On Philip's Olympic victory, Plut. *Alex.* 3.8.

11 Demosthenes *Third Philippic* 31. On the barbarian is a natural slave: Aristotle *Politics* 1252b; he quotes Euripides Iphigenia in Aulis 1400.

12 Demosthenes *On the Embassy* 302–8.
13 Athenian juries varied in size with the nature of the trial. However, in this case the correct number is not known. Mathieu, *Démosthène*, 14n3 argues for 501 rather than the 1501 usually given. Cases were pleaded in the open and usually drew an audience.
14 Hammond and Griffith, *History of Macedonia*, 2: 9–13.
15 Justin 8. This is a long, highly rhetorical, and somewhat contradictory comparison of Philip and Alexander as historical figures. Theopompus is not known to have treated Alexander in any historical passage. Anaximenes of Lampsacus, on the other hand, wrote on both Philip and Alexander (see note 16, below).
16 Anaximenes of Lampsacus is Jacoby no. 72. Jacoby gives one doubtful fragment from his *Hellenica* and ten from his *Philippica*. He also wrote on Alexander (two fragments survive).
17 Shrimpton, "Theopompus' Treatment of Philip," 124–7.
18 Hammond, "Sources of Diodorus Siculus XVI," 79–91. Further to the subject of "friendship" with Macedonian rulers, Philip and Alexander, the notion (in Greek φιλία and ξενία) had acquired ugly political semantics by 330, when Demosthenes delivered *On the Crown* (51–2).
19 The unfulfilled relationship between Socrates and Alcibiades, if correctly described by Plato, was not typical, however (Dover, *Greek Homosexuality*).
20 Westlake, *Thessaly*, 160–216; Hammond and Griffith, *History of Macedonia*, 2: 285–95, 523–44; see also Demosthenes *Second Olynthiac* 7–8.
21 D.S. 16.14.1–2; Justin 7.6.8–9; Polyaen. 4.2.19 (Griffith's translation); Hammond and Griffith, *History of Macedonia*, 2: 286, 288.
22 Westlake, *Thessaly*, 186–92; Hammond and Griffith, *History of Macedonia*, 2: 292–3.
23 Paus. 1.6.8; 3.7.11; 4.28.4; 7.7.5; 8.7.4–8.
24 *First Olynthiac* 10.15; *Second Olynthiac* 4; *First Philippic* 34–5, 37.
25 Demosthenes *First Philippic* 46, is usually taken as a reference to Chares: Sandys, ed., *First Philippic*, 119–20; Ellis and Milns, eds., *The Spectre of Philip*, 31n75; Theopompus F213 = Athen. 12.532B–D.
26 On the Theoric Fund and its creation or modification under Eubulus: Cawkwell, "Eubulus," 47–67. For Theopompus on the Theoric Fund: Wade-Gery, "Two Notes on Theopompus," 233–8; Connor, "History without Heroes," 68–9; Demosthenes attacks the Theoric Fund sometimes without naming it explicitly, *First Olynthiac* 19–20; *Second Olynthiac* 12–13; *Third Olynthiac* 11–13, 34; *First Philippic* 35. He takes a very different line in the *Fourth Phillipic* 35–42 (if that speech is genuine). There is a good discussion of the whole subject in Flower, "Theopompus of Chios," 114–25.

27 The chronology for the events of the 350s is vexed. See, for example, Martin, "Diodorus," 188–201. Equally, the precise date of Demosthenes' entry into politics is uncertain. This question is complicated by the difficulty of positively identifying some of his early presentations as politically motivated. Despite the date of *On the Symmories* (354), Keydell (*Kleine Pauly*, see Demosthenes 2, col. 1484) sees Demosthenes as "vor allem bis 352 – als vielseitiger Logograph tätig." Cawkwell, "Eubulus," 48, accepts the genuineness of *On the Syntaxis* and dates it to 353/2, but doubts remain. Jaeger, *Demosthenes*, 241–2, outlines the problem and gives a bibliography. Arguably, for Theopompus the critical date was the delivery of the *First Phillipic*. Dionysius' date for this speech (*Epist. ad Amm.*) is 352/1. This has seemed early to some. Keydell puts it in 349; Martin defends 352/1.

28 Connor, "History without Heroes," 67, see also 68.

29 See the references to Demosthenes in note 26, above.

30 There has been some doubt expressed over the genuineness of the fragment. For evidence and discussion, see Flower, "Theopompus of Chios," 128n32. Flower concludes that the fragment is genuine "beyond reasonable doubt."

31 Shrimpton, "Theopompus' Treatment of Philip," 130n15; Connor, "History without Heroes," 38–41, 59.

32 Demosthenes *On the Crown* 258–62; Aeschin. *On the Embassy* 93; *Against Ctesiphon* 171–3.

33 I made this point some time ago (Shrimpton, "Theopompus' Treatment of Philip," 131n19. It has not won universal acceptance (Flower, "Theopompus of Chios," 131), but I see no need to revise it.

34 On Plutarch's tendency to compress his narrative sources, see Pelling, "Plutarch's Adaptation of His Source Material," 127–31, "Plutarch and Roman Politics," 169–75.

35 Lane Fox, "Theopompus of Chios," 116.

36 The opposite view is argued by Flower, "Theopompus of Chios," 132–4. If Plutarch has indeed quoted a denigration and, by adding a few words of this own, turned it into praise, he has done some violence to his source as Flower admits (134). No parallel for this alleged violent misuse of a source by Plutarch is given, and I doubt that one could be found.

37 Demosthenes *On the Crown* 300, 145.

EPILOGUE

1 Lentz, *Orality and Literacy in Hellenic Greece*, 122–44.
2 Gray, "Diodorus Siculus," 72–89.
3 Shrimpton, "Death of Evagoras," 105–11.

APPENDIX A

1 The following is a select bibliography: Underhill, "Theopompus (or Cratippus)," 277–90; Walker, "Cratippus or Theopompus," 356–71; Meyer, *Theopomps*, 120–39; Maas, "Stilistisches zu dem Historiker Theopomp," 1845–6; Wilamowitz-Moellendorff, *Reden und Vorträge* 4: 224; Barber, *Ephorus*, 123–5; Bloch, "Studies in Historical Literature," 303–55, in which a great deal more bibliography can be found; Jacoby, "The *Hellenica* of Oxyrhynchus," 1–8; Gomme, "Who was Kratippos?" 53–5; a good bibliography and discussion can be found in Bartoletti, ed., *Hellenica Oxyrhynchia*, xvii-xxv; Bruce, *Historical Commentary*, 3–27; Pédech, "Un historien nommé Cratippe," 31–45; Lehmann, 'Ein Historiker namens Kratippos,' 265–88; Ruschenbusch, "Theopompea; ἀντιπολιτεύεσθαι," 81–90; Harding, "Authorship of the *Hellenika Oxyrhynchia*," 101–4; McKechnie and Kern, *Hellenica Oxyrhynchia*, 3–24 and 25 for a list of editions.
2 Walker, "Cratippus or Theopompus," 369, a suggestion that has not been challenged as far as I am aware. Nonetheless, it is an astonishing idea. Cnidus is not a natural stopping place, in the middle of the Corinthian War as it is. That both Theopomus and Cratippus ended with it independently is a lot to believe.
3 Gray, *Xenophon's Hellenica*, 56
4 These alleged coincidences do not overwhelm. The form κατᾶραι with long α after τ looks Dorian, and P always uses the pure Attic η (8.2, 21.2). One would have to argue that the ancient lexicographers have cited the form incorrectly, odd since their main concern is with orthography. Again, in F19 Stephanus cites the plural (Carpaseis) from "Theopompus 10" (which usually means *Philippica*), but P's subject is a single Carpasean who led a revolt of Cypriot mercenaries. Another "verbal parallel," κατασκευασμένον καλῶς (21.6, cf. 22–3; Theop. F31), is between P and the *Philippica*. If it means anything, Theopompus picked up a phrase (or perhaps a few of them) from P.
5 As one would suppose, Ionic had not been completely replaced by the Attic *koinē* in Theopompus' boyhood (see Buck, *Greek Dialects*, 187–9, 174–8). I have not been able to find traces of an East Ionic dialect in Theopompus. A couple of apparent Dorian forms are noted in the text, however. Did the Chian upper classes adopt a Dorian posture during and after the Spartan occupation? What does the tradition that Theopompus' father was a Laconizer mean?
6 In general, see chapter 1. For a detailed description of P's style, see McKechnie and Kern, *Hellenica Oxyrhynchia*, 21–4.
7 Two missed opportunities include the bald mention of Aesimus (6.2), who was ambassador to Chios in 384, the time of the negotiation of the

alliance between Athens and Chios celebrated in F104 (Bruce, *Historical Commentary*, 52, and Chapter 2, above), and a similar mention of Cephalus (7.2), who was involved in the same embassy (Bruce, *Historical Commentary*, 56–7); Laqueur, *RE*, "Theopompos," 2190–8.

8 Meyer, "Theopompus," 123, Underhill, "Theopompus (or Cratippus)," 289n1.

9 Bloch, "Studies in Historical Literature," 310–14n1.

10 Ibid., 315.

11 The important ones were Cli(to)demus, Androtion (both c. mid-fourth century), and Philochorus (third century). In general, see Jacoby, *Atthis*, 1–7, and, especially, 71–9, where the political nature of the Atthis is shown. I should have thought that the Atthidographers would have leapt at the chance to speak not just of politicking but antipoliticking as well.

12 See also Harding, "Theramenes Myth," 101–11; and Pesely, "Theramenes and Athenian Politics."

APPENDIX B

1 Pédech, *Trois historiens méconnus*, was unavailable to me.

2 Milns and Ellis, "Theopompus, Fragment 103 Jacoby," 56–60, argue that the text of this fragment is corrupt and should be rearranged to bring together the two references to the establishment of the peace and postpone the reference to the sea fight off Cyprus. Their argument is based primarily on disputable historical considerations, however, and I am not convinced that there is any good philological reason for doubting the order. I intend to deal with the history in a forthcoming article in *Phoenix*.

3 Bosworth, "Early Relations," 169–72.

Bibliography

Aalders, G.J.D. "Die Meropes des Theopomp." *Historia* 27 (1978): 317–27.

Accame, S. *Richerche intorno alla guerra corinzia*. Naples, 1951.

Adler, A., ed. *Suidae Lexikon*. 1886. Reprint. Stuttgart, 1967.

Andrewes, A. "Two Notes on Lysander." *Phoenix* 25 (1971): 206–26.

Badian, E. "Greeks and Macedonians." In *Studies in the History of Art* 10, edited by B. Barr-Sharrar and E.N. Borza 33–5. Symposium Series 1, Macedonia and Greece in Later Classical and Hellenistic Times. Washington, 1982.

– "The Peace of Callias." *JHS* 107 (1987): 1–39.

Barber, G.L. *The Historian Ephorus*. Oxford, 1935.

Bartoletti, V., ed. *Hellenica Oxyrhynchia*. Leipzig, 1959.

Beloch, K.J. *Griechische Geschichte*² 3. Parts 1 and 2. Berlin and Leipzig, 1922, 1923.

Bengston, H. *History of Greece*. Translated by E.F. Bloedow with added bibliography. Ottawa, 1988.

Bickermann, E.J., and Sykutris, J. "Speusipps Brief an König Philip." *Berichte über die Verhandlungen der Sächsischen Akademie der Wissenschaft* (phil.hist.) 80.3. Leipzig, 1928: 1–86.

Blass, F. *Die Attische Beredsamkeit*² 2. Leipzig, 1892.

Bloch, H. "Studies in Historical Literature of the Fourth Century B.C." In *Athenian Studies Presented to William Scott Ferguson*, 303–55. Cambridge, Mass., 1940. Reprint. New York, 1969.

Bosworth, A.B. "Early Relations between Aetolia and Macedon." *AJAH* 1 (1976): 164–81.

Boyce, Mary, *Zoroastrians, Their Religious Beliefs and Practices*. London, Boston, Henley, 1979.

– ed. *Textual Sources for the Study of Zoroastrianism*. Manchester 1984.

Brown, T.S. *The Greek Historians*. Lexington, Mass., Toronto, London, 1972.

Brown, W.E. "Some Hellenistic Utopias." *CW* (1955): 57–62.

Bruce, I.A.F. *An Historical Commentary on the "Hellenica Oxyrhynchia."* Cambridge, 1967.

– "Theopompus, Lysander and the Spartan Empire." *AHB* 1 (1987): 1–4.

Buck, R.J. *The Greek Dialects*. Chicago and London, 1955.

Buckler, J. *Philip II and the Sacred War*, Leiden, New York, Cobenhavn, Köln, 1989.

– *The Theban Hegemony, 371–362 B.C.* Cambridge, Mass., and London, 1980.

Bunbury, E.H. *A History of Ancient Geography*. Vol. 1. 1883. Reprint. New York, 1959.

Burn, A.R. "A Biographical Source on Phaiax and Alcibiades?" *CQ* 48 (1954): 138–42.

Busolt, G. *Griechische Geschichte bis zur Schlacht bei Chaeroneia*. Vol. 3. 1904. Reprint. Hildesheim, 1967.

Campbell, J. *Grammatical Man: Information, Entropy, Language and Life*. New York, 1982.

Cartledge, Paul. *Agesilaos and the Crisis of Sparta*. London, 1987.

Cawkwell, G.L. "Eubulus." *JHS* 83 (1963): 47–67.

– *Philip of Macedon*. London and Boston, 1978.

– "The Foundation of the Second Athenian Confederacy." *CQ* 23 (1973): 47–60.

Connor, W.R. "History without Heroes: Theopompus' Treatment of Philip of Macedon." *GRBS* 8 (1967): 133–54.

Connor, W.R. *Theopompus and Fifth-Century Athens*. Cambridge, Mass., 1968.

Crawley, R., tr. *Thucydides. The Peloponnesian War*. London and New York, 1910.

Cristofani, M. *Saggi d'istoria etrusca arcaica*. Archaeologica Series no. 70. Rome, 1987.

Davis, J.K. *Athenian Propertied Families, 600–300 B.C.* Oxford, 1971.

Dell, H.J. "The Origin and Nature of Illyrian Piracy." *Historia* 16 (1967): 344–58.

Dittenberger, W. *Sylloge Inscriptionum Graecarum*[3]. Vol. 1. Leipzig, 1915.

Dover, K.J. *Greek Homosexuality*. London, 1979.

Edmonds, J.M. *The Fragments of Attic Comedy*. Vol. 1. Leiden, 1957.

Ehrenberg, V. *The Greek State*. Oxford, 1960.

Ellis, J.R. *Philip II and Macedonian Imperialism*. London, 1976.

– and R.D. Milns, eds. *The Spectre of Philip. Demosthenes' First Philippic, Olynthiacs, and On the Peace*. Sydney, 1970.

Errington, R.M. "Review Discussion: Four Interpretations of Philip II." *AJAH* (1981): 69–88.

Ferretto, Carla. *La citta dissipatrice: Studi sull'* excursus *del libro decimo dei* Philippika *di Teopompo*. Genova, 1984.

Flower, M.A. "Theopompus of Chios." Ph.D. diss. Brown University, 1986.

Fornara, C.W. *The Nature of History in Ancient Greece and Rome*. Berkeley, Los Angeles, London, 1983.

Fritz, Kurt von. "The Historian Theopompus. His Political Convictions and His Concept of Historiography." *AHR* 46 (1941): 765–87.

Gardiner-Garden, J. "Ateas and Theopompus." *JHS* 109 (1989): 29–40.

Garnsey, P.D.A., and C.R. Whittaker. *Imperialism in the Ancient World.* Cambridge, 1978.

Gomme, A.W. "Who Was Kratippos?" *CQ* 48 (1954): 53–5.

Gould, S.J. *The Panda's Thumb.* New York and London, 1982.

Gray, Vivienne. *The Character of Xenophon's Hellenica.* London, 1989.

– "The Value of Diodorus Siculus for the Years 411–386 B.C." *Hermes* 115 (1987): 72–89.

Griffith, G.T., see Hammond, N.G.L.

Griffith, G.T. "Athens in the Fourth Century." In *Imperialism in the Ancient World,* edited by P.D.A. Garnsey and C.R. Whittaker, 127–44. Cambridge, 1978.

Guthrie, W.K.C. *The Sophists.* Cambridge, 1971.

Hall, F.W. *A Companion to Classical Texts.* Oxford, 1913.

Hammond, N.G.L., and G.T. Griffith. *A History of Macedonia.* 2 vols. Oxford, 1972, 1979.

Hammond, N.G.L. "The Kingdoms in Illyria circa 400–167 B.C." *BSA* 61 (1966): 248–53.

– "The Sources of Diodorus Siculus XVI." *CQ* 31 (1937): 79–91.

Harding, P. "The Thermamenes Myth." *Phoenix* 28 (1974): 101–11.

– "The Authorship of the *Hellenika Oxyrhynchia.*" *AHB* (1987): 101–4.

Hartog, F. *The Mirror of Herodotus.* Translated by Janet Lloyd. 1980. Reprint. Berkeley, Los Angeles, London 1988.

Hatzopoulos, M.B. "The Oleveni Inscription and the Dates of Philip's Reign." In *Philip II, Alexander the Great and the Macedonian Heritage,* edited by W. Lindsay Adams and Eugene N. Borza, 21–42. Lanham, New York, London 1982.

Heckel, W. "Philip and Olympias 337/6 B.C." In *Classical Contributions*: *Studies in Honour of Malcolm Francis McGregor,* edited by Gordon Shrimpton and D.J. McCargar, 51–7. New York, 1981.

Heisserer, A.J. "Alexander's Letter to the Chians: A Redating of *SIG*³ 283." *Historia* 22 (1973): 191–204.

– *Alexander the Great and the Greeks: The Epigraphic Evidence.* Norman, 1980.

Henry, R., tr. *Photius, Bibliothèque.* Vol. 2. Paris, 1960.

Herbert, K.B.J. "Ephorus in Plutarch's Lives." Ph.D. diss., Harvard University, 1954.

Hercher, R. *Epistolographi Graeci.* Paris, 1873.

Hirzel, R. "Zur Characteristik Theopomps" *Rh.Mus.* N.F. 47 (1892): 359–89.

Hornblower, Jane. *Hieronymus of Cardia.* Oxford, 1981.

Hornblower, Simon. *Mausolus.* Oxford, 1982.

Jacoby, F. *Atthis: The Local Chronicles of Ancient Athens.* Oxford, 1949.

– *Die Fragmente der Griechischen Historiker.* Vol. 2. 1929. Reprint. Leiden, 1962.

– "The Authorship of the Hellenica of Oxyrhynchus." *CQ* 44 (1950): 1–8.

Jaeger, W. *Demosthenes: The Origin and Growth of His Policy.* 1938. Reprint. New York, 1963.

Joinville, Jean de. *Joinville and Villehardouin: Chronicles of the Crusades.* Translated by M.R.B. Shaw. Harmondsworth, 1963.

Jung, C.G. *Answer to Job.* Bollingen Series, no. 20. London, 1954.

Kalischek, E. "De Ephoro et Theopompo Isocratis Discipulis." Ph.D. diss., Münster, 1913.

Kennedy, George. *The Art of Persuasion in Greece.* Princeton, 1963.

– *The Art of Rhetoric in the Roman World.* Princeton, 1972.

Kenyon, F.G. *Books and Readers in Ancient Greece and Rome*[2]. Oxford, 1951.

Keydell, R. "Demosthenes." no. 2. *Kleine Pauly* 1 (1964): cols. 1484–7.

Kirk, G.S., J.E. Raven, and M. Schofield. *The Presocratic Philosophers.*[2] Cambridge, 1983.

Lacey, W.K. *The Family in Classical Greece.* Ithaca, N.Y., 1968.

Lana, Italo. "L'utopia di Teopompo." *Paideia* 6 (1951): 3–22.

Lane Fox, R. "Theopompus of Chios and the Greek World, 411–322 B.C." In *Chios: A Conference at the Homereion in Chios 1984*, edited by J. Boardman and C.E. Vaphopoulou-Richardson, 105–20. Oxford, 1986.

Laqueur, R. "Theopompos." no. 9. *RE* (1934): cols. 2176–2223.

Lehmann, G.A. 'Ein Historiker namens Kratippos.' *ZPE* 23 (1976): 265–88.

Lentz, T.M. *Orality and Literacy in Hellenic Greece.* Carbondale and Edwardsville, 1989.

Loraux, N. *The Invention of Athens: The Funeral Oration in the Classical City.* Translated by A. Sheridan. Cambridge, Mass., 1986.

Luzzatto, M.J., and A. La Penna, eds., *Babrius Mythiambi Aesopei.* Leipzig, 1986.

Maas, P. "Stilistisches zu dem Historiker Theopomp." *Phil. Woch.* (1912): 1845–6.

Markle, Minor, M., III. "The Peace of Philocrates." Ph.D. diss., Princeton University, 1967.

– "Support of Athenian Intellectuals for Philip: A Study of Isocrates' *Philippus* and Speusippus' Letter to Philip." *JHS* 96 (1976): 80–99.

Martin, R. "Diodorus on Philip II and Thessaly." *CP* 76 (1981): 188–201.

– *Tacitus.* London, 1981.

Massa Pairault, F.H. *Recherches sur l'art et l'artisanat étrusco-italiques à l'époque hellénistique.* Paris, 1985.

Mathieu, G. *Démosthène: Plaidoyers Politiques.* Vol. 3. Paris, 1972.

McKechnie, P.R., and S.J. Kern. *Hellenica Oxyrhynchia.* Warminster, 1988.

Merlan, P. "Zur Biographie des Speusippus." *Philologus* 103 (1959): 194–214.

Meyer, E. *Theopomps Hellenika: Mit einer Beilage über die Rede an die Lariaeer und die Verfassung Thessaliens.* 1909. Reprint. Hildesheim, 1966.

Milns, R.D., and J.R. Ellis. "Theopompus, Fragment 103 Jacoby." *Parola del Passato* 21 (1966): 56–60.

Mócsy, A. "Zu Theopompos 39–40." *Revista storica dell'antichita* 2 (1972): 13–14.

Momigiliano, A. "Studi sulla storiografica greca del IV Secolo a.c.l: Teopompo." *RivFC* n.s. 9 (1931): 230–42, 335–53 = *Terzo contributo alla storia degli studi classici e del mondo antico* 1 (Rome 1966): 367–92.

Montgomery, Hugo. *The Way to Chaeronea: Foreign Policy, Decision-Making and Political Influence in Demosthenes' Speeches.* Oslo, 1983.

Moxon, I.S., J.D. Smart, and A.J. Woodman, eds. *Past Perspectives: Studies in Greek and Roman Historical Writing.* Cambridge, 1986.

Müller, F. *Fragmenta Historicorum Graecorum.* Paris, 1883.

Murray, Gilbert. "Theopompus or the Cynic as Historian." In *Greek Studies.* Oxford, 1946.

Nauck, A. *Tragicorum Graecorum Fragmenta.* Supplemented by Bruno Snell. 1888. Reprint. Hildesheim, 1964.

Pearson, L.I.C., and S. Stephens, eds., *Didymi in Demosthenem Commenta.* Stuttgart, 1983.

Pearson, L.I.C. *The Greek Historians of the West: Timaeus and His Predecessors.* APA Monographs 35. Atlanta, 1987.

– *The Lost Histories of Alexander the Great.* APA Monographs 20. New York, 1960.

Pédech, P. *Trois historiens méconnus: Theopompe, Duris, Phylarque.* Paris, n.d.

Pelling, C.B.R. "Plutarch's Method of Work in the Roman Lives." *JHS* 99 (1979): 74–96.

– "Plutarch's Adaptation of His Source Material." *JHS* 100 (1980): 127–40.

– "Plutarch and Roman Politics." In *Past Perspectives*, edited by I.S. Moxon, J.D. Smart, and A.J.Woodman, 159–87. Cambridge, 1986.

Perlman, S. "Isocrates' 'Philippus' – A Reinterpretation." *Historia* 6 (1957): 306–17 (Also in his *Philip and Athens*, 103–6.)

– ed. *Philip and Athens.* Cambridge, 1973.

Pesely, G.C. "Theramenes and Athenian Politics: A Study in the Manipulation of History." Ph.D. diss. University of California, Berkeley, 1983.

Pickard-Cambridge, A.W. *Demosthenes and the Last Days of Greek Freedom 384–322 B.C.* New York, 1914.

Powell, J.E. "Puns in Herodotus." *CR* 51 (1957): 103–5.

Rahn, Peter J. "The Date of Xenophon's Exile." In *Classical Contributions: Studies in Honour of Malcolm Francis McGregor*, edited by Gordon Shrimpton and D.J McCargar, 105–19. New York, 1981.

Raubitschek, A.E. "Andocides and Thucydides." In *Classical Contributions: Studies in Honour of Malcolm Francis McGregor*, edited by Gordon Shrimpton and D.J. McCargar, 121–3. New York, 1981.

Raven, J.E., see Kirk, G.S.

Reed, K. "Theopompus of Chios: History and Oratory in the Fourth Century." Ph.D. diss., University of California, Berkeley, 1976.

Roberts, W. Rhys. "Theopompus in the Greek Literary Critics." *CR* (1908): 118–22.

Rohde, E. "Theopomp." *Rh.Mus.* n.f. 44 (1894): 623–4.

– "Zum Griechischen Roman." *Rh.Mus.* n.f. 48 (1894): 110ff. = *Kleine*

Schriften, Vol. 2. 9–25. Tübingen and Leipzig, 1901.

Rorty, A.O. "Akrasia and Pleasure: Nichomachean Ethics Book 7." In *Essays on Aristotle's Ethics*, edited by A.O. Rorty. Berkeley and Los Angeles, 1980.

Rose, V., ed. *Aristotelis Fragmenta*. Leipzig, 1886.

Ruschenbusch, E. "Theopompea ἀντιπολιτεύεσθαι." *ZPE* 39 (1980): 81–90.

Russell, D.A. *Plutarch*. London, 1972.

– and M. Winterbottom, eds. *Ancient Literary Criticism. The Principal Texts in New Translations*. Oxford, 1972.

Sandys, J.E., ed. *The First Philippic and the Olynthiacs of Demosthenes*. Cambridge, 1897. Reprint. London, 1955.

Sasone, D. "Lysander and Dionysius (Plut. *Lys.* 2)." *CP* 76 (1981): 202–6.

Schmelling, G., tr. *Cornelius Nepos "Lives of Famous Men."* Lawrence, Kansas 1971.

Schofield, M., see Kirk, G.S.

Schranz, W. "Theopomps Philippica." Ph.D. diss., Freiburg, Marburg, 1912.

Schwartz, Ed., "Kallisthenes Hellenika." *Hermes* 35 (1900): 106–30.

– "Daimachos." *RE* 8 (1901): cols. 2008–9 = *GG* 3–26.

– "Ephoros." *RE* 11 (1907): cols. 1–16 = *GG* 3–26.

– *Griechische Geschichtschreiber*. Leipzig, 1959.

Schultze, Clemence. "Dionysius of Halicarnassus and His Audience." In *Past Perspectives*, edited by I.S. Moxon, J.D. Smart, and A.J. Woodman, 121–41. Cambridge, 1986.

Shrimpton, Gordon. "The Theban Supremacy in Fourth-Century Literature." *Phoenix* 25 (1971): 310–18.

– "Theopompus' Treatment of Philip in the *Philippica*." *Phoenix* 31 (1977): 123–44.

– "Theopompus on the Death of Evagoras I." *AHB* (1987): 105–11.

– "Greek Views of Reality and the Development of Rhetorical History." In *Classical Contributions: Studies in Honour of Malcolm Francis McGregor*, 135–43. New York, 1981.

– and D.J. McCargar, eds. *Classical Contributions Studies in Honour of Malcolm Francis McGregor*. New York, 1981.

Smart, J.D., see Moxon, I.S.

Smets, G. "A propos du chapitre XVII de la 'Vie de Lysandre' de Plutarque." *Revue Belge de philologie et d'histoire* (1929): 168ff.

Smith, N.D. "Aristotle's Theory of Natural Slavery." *Phoenix* 37 (1983): 109–22.

Snell, Bruno, see Nauck, A.

Stähelin, F. "Die Griechischen Historiker-Fragmente bei Didymos 55–71." *Klio* 5 (1905): 141–54.

Stiewe, Klaus. "Anaximenes." no. 2, *Kleine Pauly* (1964): col. 340.

Stylianou, P.J. "How Many Naval Squadrons Did Athens Send to Evagoras?" *Historia* 37 (1988): 463–71.

Talbert, R.J.A. *Timoleon and the Revival of Greek Sicily*. Cambridge, 1974.

Thompson, Wesley, E. "Fragments of the Preserved Historians. –Especially Polybius." In *The Greek Historians, Literature and History Papers Presented to A.E. Raubitschek*, 119–39. Saratoga, Calif., 1985.

Tod, M.N. *A Selection of Greek Historical Inscriptions*. Vol. 2. Oxford, 1948.

Turner, E.G. *Greek Papyri: An Introduction*. Oxford, 1968.

Underhill, G.E. "Theopompus (or Cratippus), Hellenica." *JHS* 28 (1908): 277–90.

Uxkull-Gyllenband, U. *Plutarch und die Griechische Biographie*. Stuttgart, 1927.

Van der Meuhl, P. "Direkte Benützung des Ephoros und des Theopomp bei Plutarch." *MH* 11 (1954): 243–4.

Vlastos, G., ed. *The Philosophy of Socrates: A Collection of Critical Essays*. New York, 1971.

Wachsmuth, C. "Pentadenbände der Klassischer Schriftseller." *Rh.Mus.* n.f. 46 (1891): 329–31.

Wade-Gery, H.T. "Two Notes on Theopompus, *Philippika*, X." *AJP* 59 (1938): 129–34 = *Essays in Greek History*, 233–8. Oxford, 1958.

Walbank, F.W. *A Commentary on Polybius*. Vol. 2. Oxford, 1967.

– *Polybius*. 1972. Reprint. Berkeley, Los Angeles, London, 1990.

Walker, E.M. "Cratippus or Theopompus." *Klio* 8 (1908): 356–71.

Wallace, Robert W. "The Date of Isocrates' *Areopagitikos*." *HSCP* 90 (1986): 77–84.

Walsh, James J. *Aristotle's Concept of Moral Weakness*. New York, 1964.

Wardman, A. *Plutarch's Lives*. London, 1974.

Watson, J.S., tr. *Justin, Cornelius Nepos, and Eutropius*. London, 1980.

Weidemann, T.E.J. "Between Men and Beasts: Barbarians in Ammianus Marcellinus." In *Past Perspectives: Studies in Greek and Roman Historical Writing*, edited by I.S. Moxon, J.D. Smart, and A.J. Woodman, 189–201. Cambridge, 1986.

Westermann, A. *Vitarum Scriptores Graeci Minores*. 1845. Reprint. Amsterdam, 1964.

Westlake, H.D. *Thessaly in the Fourth Century B.C.* London, 1935.

Whittaker, C.R., see Garnsey, P.D.A.

Wichers, R.H.E. *Theopompi Chii Fragmenta*. Leiden, 1829.

Wilamowitz-Moellendorff, U. von. *Reden und Vorträge*. Vol. 4. 1926. Reprint. Dublin and Zurich, 1967.

Winterbottom, M., see Russell, D.A.

Woodman, A.J., see Moxon, I.S.

Woodman, A.J. *Rhetoric in Classical Historiography*. London, Sydney, Portland, 1988.

Wormell, D.E.W. "The Literary Tradition Concerning Hermias of Atarneus." *YCS* 5 (1935): 57–92.

Ziegler, K. *Plutarchos von Chaironeia*. Stuttgart, 1964.

Index of Proper Names in the Historical Fragments of Theopompus

This index is intended to be used in conjunction with the fragments themselves. It makes available in a convenient form nearly all the information contained in the historical fragments. Only a handful of aphorisms include no proper names and are, therefore, not represented. They are discussed in a special section of chapter 3 (pp. 112–15). A few Greek expressions are also included.

In many of the fragments there is a serious problem in determining precisely what comes from Theopompus. Most are paraphrases, sometimes demonstrably crude, and some ancient and Byzantine scholars cite more than one source for their information. Therefore, while it is certain that Theopompus treated the subject, precisely what he said is not clear. To offer a little guidance, I have tried to represent the uncertainties by the use of brackets and question marks as explained below, but the scholar is urged to consult the fragments themselves and make a personal judgment in each case.

NOTE ON THE ENTRIES

The purpose of this index is to make available in a brief note what information there is on the subject each time it occurs in the fragments.

1 A simple entry:
   Indara, city of the Sicanians, F371.
2 Explanatory information about the entry is placed in round brackets before the comma:
   Antalcidas (Peace of), its establishment, F103.
3 Sometimes the entry is translated:
   Helius (Sun).
4 An entry in square brackets is a restored reading. Sometimes an alternative reading is shown in round brackets immediately after:
   [Acontius] (or Hyphantius?).
5 Often there was disagreement about a name or its spelling. Where Theopompus is cited as being in disagreement with an author or tradition, it is indicated:
   Achilles (not Aeacus).
6 I have inserted alternative readings and explanations into the entries in a way that should be self-explanatory.
7 All references are to the *Philippica* (= P, definite or probable) except where other-

wise noted, e.g., F5H (H = Hellenica), F248 TPD (TPD = Treasure Plundered from Delphi).

8 Where the fragment number is in square brackets [F28], there seems sufficient reason for an entry, but the attestation is not considered definite. For a Greek index to the fragments see Connor, *Theopompus*, 185–306. This too should be used only with careful consultation of the fragments cited.

Abdymon, of Citium, king of Cyprus dethroned by Evagoras, F103

Achaea, Dyme a city of, F194; Hyperasians (residents of Hyperasia, a city of), [F379]

Achaean(s), founding member tribe (one of twelve) of the Central Greek Amphictiony, F63; turned into Helots by the Spartans, F122; guards of city of Naupactus killed by Philip with A.'s approval, F235a, or killers of guards at Naupactus, F235b; Arcadion, a hater of Philip, F280

Acharni (not Achani), people who live near Scythia, F367

Achilles (not Aeacus), father of Pyrrhus through whom Olympias, Alexander the Great's mother, traced her lineage back to A., F355

Aconae, place near Pontic Heraclea where the poisonous plant aconite grows, F181

[Acontius] (or Hyphantius?), mountain near (Boeotian) Orchomenus at the eastern end of the Hedylium massif, F385

Acoris, king of Egypt, revolted from Persia in support of Evagoras, F103

Acraephnia, (not Acraephia etc.), city (of Boeotia), F362

Acraephnieus, citizen of Acraephnia, F362

Acylina, city in Illyria, F363

Acyphas, city of the Dorian tetrapolis (union of four cities), F364

Adaeus, the Alectryon (Rooster), commander of Philip's mercenaries defeated by Chares during Sacred War, F249TPD

Adrane, city of Thrace situated "a little above Berenice," F360

Adria, city founded by Adrius, F128c

Adrias, river, from which Adriatic Gulf was allegedly named, F129; name of gulf at northwestern tip of Ionian Sea, FF128c, 129, or Adrian, F130

Adriatic (Gulf), northwestern tip of Ionian Sea, shores densely inhabited by barbarian peoples, FF128, 129, 130; Baretium a region of, F234; Eneti (Venetians) live on, make treaties with birds not to destroy their crops, F274

Adrius, king in region of northwestern tip of Ionian Sea, son of Ionius, gave his name to Adriatic Gulf (and a

river?), FF128c, 129

Aeacides (descendants of the hero, Aeacus), Molossians(?), an Epirot tribe (but *see* F355), [F382]

Aeëtes, with Aloeus son of Helius and Antiope, receives half of Helius' kingdom but gives it to Bunus and goes to the land of Colchis, F356b, quoting Eumelus, Corinthian poet

Aegirus (not Aegirussa), Megarian city, F241

Aegospotami, Athenians defeated at Battle of, F5H

Aegyeans (not Aegytae), citizens of Aegys, a city of Laconia, F361

Aenianes, founding member tribe (one of twelve) of Delphic Amphictiony, FF63, 80(?)

Aeoleum (city of the Thracian Chersonnese), possession of Bottica, it shared citizenship with the Chalcidians, F144

Aeolians, part of alliance of mainlanders; with Chalians, Boeotians, Orchomenians, and Thebans, attacked by Chalcidians, F212

Aeschylus, brother of Timophanes' wife and relative of Timoleon, [F334]

Aethicia, F183

Agamemnon, leaves men behind at Pygela, F59; captures Cyprus and drives out partisans of Cinyras, F103; occupants of Methone in Macedonia (not Troezen) refuse to participate in his expedition, F384

Agathocles, former Penestes (kind of serf, *see* F122) of Thessaly, destroys Perrhaebians for Philip, F81

Agesilaus, meets with Pharnabazus but accomplishes nothing, F21H; rejects sumptuous gifts from Thasians, gives them to Helots who are present, F22H; receives and spurns lavish gifts from Egyptians, FF106–7; ridiculed by Tachos, Egyptian king, F108; drives his opponent Lysandridas into exile, and Spartans kill Lysandridas' mother Xenopithea, the most beautiful of all Spartan women, and her sister, Chryse, F240; greatest and most illustrious man of his time, receives high command of both Spartan army and navy, which is without precedent, F321; restrains Spartans from facing "a billowing flood of war" (i.e., the Theban invasion of Sparta), F322; bribes Theban army with ten talents to leave after they had already decided to depart, F323

Agessus, city of Thrace, F218

Agriae (*see* Agrieis), Paeonian race located between Haemus and Rhodope, [F268b]

Agrieis, Thracian people through whose land a river, Pontus, runs carrying a coal-like stone that does not burn when subjected to air from a bellows, flares up when sprinkled with water, and gives off an offensive smell, F268a

Ahriman. *See* Arimanius

Ahura Mazda. *See* Oromasdes

Aïclus (Attic hero), co-[founder] of Eleutheris, F195

Alcibiades, praised, F288(H?); extravagant return to Athens as described by Duris not found in T., F324(H?); with Thrasybulus and Theramenes wins Battle of Cyzicus, F5H

Alea, city of Arcadia, F242

Alectryon (Rooster), nickname for Adaeus, F249TPD

Alexander (of Epirus), dies in Mandonia, F318

Alexander (of Pherae), F28(?); drowned (?) and has his bones returned to his relatives through the agency of Dionysus Pelagios of Pagasae, F352

Alexander (the Great), [F163]; bought a dog, Peritas, (from India) for one hundred minas, and when it died, founded a city in its

honour, F340(P?); mother Olympias traces her descent to Achilles through Pyrrhus and to Priam through Helenus, F355

Allantium (not Allante), city in Macedonia (and Arcadia? but this is probably a gloss), F33

Aloeus, with Aeëtes son of Helius and Antiope, receives half of Helius' kingdom but gives it to Bunus and goes to the land of Colchis, F356b, quoting Eumelus, Corinthian poet

Alphëus (river), grapevine first discovered in Olympia by its banks, F277

Amadocus (father of Amadocus), F101

Amadocus (son of Amadocus), allied himself with Philip against Cersobleptes, F101

Amathusians, name for surviving partisans of Cinyras, F103

Ambracians, Cranea a region of, F229

Ambryseans, Parapotamii a settlement marking the boundary between As and Panopeans and Daulians, F385

Amisus (Cappadocian city), first founded by Milesians, then by a leader of the Cappadocians, thirdly by Athenocles and Athenians, who changed its name to Piraeus, F389

Amphanaea (not Amphanae), Dorian city (also a region of Thessaly), F54

of, F149; old Histiaeans driven from by Pericles, go to Macedonia, new Histiaeans colonize the place from the Histiaean deme in Athens, F387

Eubulus, diligent at collecting money but squanders it on Athenians, F99; aids the Athenian people on the road to greed and corruption, F100; aids Hermeas in capture of Atarneus(?), [F291]

Euclides, Athenian archon for 403/2 when Ionian letters were adopted for public inscriptions, F155

Eugea, region of Arcadia, F243

Euphrates, Thapsacus a city on, F47

Europe, never born such a man as Philip, F27; [F46]; an island in Ocean according to Silenus, F75c; Philip's friends own part of but lust for more, F225

Eurydice, mother of Perdiccas and Philip, wife of Amyntas, entrusts herself and two sons to Iphicrates on Amyntas' death, F289

Eurylochus(?), ambassador to Athens re Peace of Philocrates, [F165]

Eusebe (Saintsbury), fictional beatific place described by Silenus, F75c

Eusebeis (Saintsburgers), carefree inhabitants of Eusebe, F75c

Evagoras (king of Salamis on Cyprus), rebels

against Persia and forms alliance with Acoris of Egypt, surrenders and is later murdered by Thrasydaeus of Elis, F103

Flattery. See Colacea

Ge (Earth), goddess of Delphi before Apollo, F80?

Gela (Chuckle, name of city in Sicily), Antiphemus is told by an oracle that he will found a city, thinking it improbable he laughs, F358; he does, however, and calls it G. (i.e., it is linked etymologically with Gr. γελάω = I laugh), F358

Gelon, Sicilian ruler who helped adorn Delphi, F193

Getae, conduct international negotiations while playing the *kithara* (lyre), F216

Gibraltar. See Pillars of Heracles

Gorgias (of Leontini), [F24]

Gortynia, city founded by Odysseus in Tyrrhenia where he dies, F354

Graestonia (Gastronia?) (= Crestonia), with Amphipolis and Bisaltia exceptionally fertile region of Philip's empire, F237a (Gastronia, F237b)

Gyges, king of Lydia who helped adorn Delphi with treasures, F193

Gylippus, embezzles money, F332

Hades, equated by some Greeks with Ahriman, FF[64], [68]

Haemus, [Agriae] live near, F268b

Halicyae, city of Sicily, F365

Halisarna, city of the Troad, F366

Halisarnaean, citizen of Halisarna, F366

Halonnesus, disputed island, F50

Harpalus, expelled by Athenians, F330

Hecate, her statue carefully tended by Clearchus of Methydrium in Arcadia, F344

Hecatomnos, admiral of Persian fleet in war against Evagoras, F103; father of Artemisia, Mausolus' sister and wife, F297

Hedone (Pleasure), name of a river that flows through Anostus (No Return), a region of Meropis as described by Silenus, F75c

Hedyleum, mountain in Boeotia, F157

Hedylium (mountain), massif extending sixty stades (seven and a half miles) from Parapotamii and the Cephissus to Mt. Acontius near (Boeotian) Orchomenus, F385

Hegesilochus of Rhodes, corrupt leader of an oligarchy on the island, F121

Hegetor (Leader), name the Argives give to Apollo Carnëus because he is the leader of their army, F357

Helenus, son of Priam (not

Dardanus) through whom Olympias, Alexander the Great's mother, traced her descent from Priam, F355

Helius (Sun), husband of Antiope and father of Aloeus and Aeëtes, divides kingdom between his two sons, F356b, quoting Eumelus, Corinthian poet

Hellanicus, [F25]

Hellas, Lysander rules over all of, but still showed great self-control, F20H; Straton of Sidon collects gifts from all parts of, F114; Gelon's gifts to Delphi given at same time as Xerxes' invasion of, F193; no gold in, F193; scum of, flocks to Macedonian court, F224; Athens described as the "town hall" of, F281; invaded by Persia, F285

Hellenes, resent word "tribute," F98; with Agamemnon take Cyprus and drive out partisans of Cinyras, colonize southern Asia Minor, F103; made into slaves by Spartans and Thessalians, F122; Chians first of, to enslave barbarians, F122; duped by Athenian claims to greatness, F153; worst of, attracted to Macedonia, F224; Philip's friends have more than the richest, F225; armaments of, join barbarians in support-

ing Persian king's invasion of Egypt, F263; prayed for by Corinthian prostitutes in war against Persia, F285

Hellenic (city), of the first rank, Cardia, on the Chersonnese, F6H: (race), the assembly of the Central Greek Amphictiony, F63; affairs ignored by King, F87; (oath), allegedly sworn at Plataea, a fabrication, F153; (cities), Athens greatest of, according to Aristophon, F166

Hellespont, Neandreon (not Neandrea) a city on, in the Troad, [F374]

Helos (Marsh), a place in Laconia whence came some of the Helots, F13H

Helots, oppressed slave population subjugated by Spartans, some came from Messenia, some from Helos (Marsh), in Laconia, are called "heleats" (marsh dwellers?), FF13H, 22H, 40, 122, 171

Hera, tells Medea to build temple of Aphrodite in Corinth, F285b

Heraclea, on Pontic (or Euxine) Sea, home of Clearchus, the tyrant, F181

Heracleots, people of Heraclea Pontica, F181b

Heracles, instructs Pherecydes to tell Spartans to avoid money, F71; from whom Philip traced his heroic, Greek descent, F393

Heraclides, with Athenis,

commander of Syracusan forces, F194

Heraclides, son of Archelaus, F307; with brother Python helps Miltocythes raise mercenaries, F307

Heraclids (i.e., sons or descendants of Heracles, often identified with the Dorians), kill Carnus the seer, taking him for a spy when they entered the Peloponnese, F357; afflicted by a plague, they establish the festival of the Carnea to Apollo in response to an oracle, F357

Hermeas (of Atarneus), attacked by T., takes Assos and Atarneus, murders people, gets into a dispute(?) with Chians and Mityleneans, insults Ionians, a moneygrubber, dies violently, F291

Hermes, statue of, carefully tended by Clearchus of Methydrium in Arcadia, F344; Chthonius, to whom the Athenians dedicate the festival called Chytri, F347; they propitiate him on behalf of their citizens who died in the flood, F347

Hermonassa, city (on an island?) in the Cimmerian Bosporus, F370

Herodotus, [F25]

Hierax, ambassador from Amphipolis sent to offer the city to Athens, F42

Hieron, Sicilian monarch sent a tripod and

Paeonia, Agriae a nation of, F268b

Paeonians, their kings make drinking cups of three or four *choes* (more than two imperial gallons) from the enormous horns of their cattle and trim the rims with gold or silver, F38

Pagasae, harbour of Pherae, F53; Dionysus Pelagius of, honours the drowned (?) Alexander of Pherae by instructing a fisherman to return his bones to his family, F352

Pamphylia, Aspendus (or Aspendia) a city of, F9H

Pamphylia, daughter of Mopsus, after whom a region of Anatolia was called, F103

Pandosia, one of four (not three) cities of the Cassopaeans, FF206, 207

Panopeans, Parapotamii marks boundary of Ps with Ambryseans and Daulians, F385

Pantaen(et)us (not Melesias), alleged father of Thucydides, the Athenian politician, F91

Paphlagonia, Thys king of, captured by Artaxerxes, F179; part of, ruled by Mariandynus for a time, F388

Paphlagonians (people on Euxine coast of northern Asia Minor), colonists from whom, on northern most gulf of Adriatic, called Eneti, F130

Parapotamii, a settlement on the Cephissus river, forms the boundary between Ambryseans, Panopeans, and Daulians, F385

Parmenio, ambassador to Athens re Peace of Philocrates, F165; with Antipater among Tetrachorites, F217; receives letter from Philip, F217

Parnassus (mountain in Boeotia), river Cephissus flows between, and Mt. Hedylium, F385

Paseas, of Argos, Macedonian agent, F231

Pausanias, alias Argaeus, alias Archelaus (of Macedon), F29 (or son of Archelaus, q.v.)

Pausanias (of Naupactus), captain of the guard slain either by Philip or by the Achaeans when Philip took the city, F235b

Pedaritus, a Lacedaemonian of the better class, F8H

Pelagius (i.e., Pelasgius?), epithet of Dionysus of Pagasae, F352

Pelasgia, place through which the Pythian Way passes from Delphi to Tempe, F80(?)

Pelasgus, father of Crannon, F267b

Pelium (Mount), home of Centaurs, compared to advantage to Philip's friends, F225

Peloponnese, [F28]; source of courtesans for Straton's court, F114; Pisa a place in, where Oenomaus, father of Hippodamea, holds competitions for his daughter's hand, F350; Heraclids invade, kill Carnus the seer, F357; afflicted by a plague, they establish the festival Carnea to Apollo, F357

Peloponnesian(s), divided in loyalty, some to Thebes, some to Spartans c. 347/6, F164; Xenopithea, most beautiful of all P. women, mother of Lysandridas, killed by Spartans when Agesilaus expels L., F240

Pelops, goes to Pisa to compete for Hippodamea's hand, on way his charioteer Cillus dies, and P. founds Cilla and establishes a shrine to Apollo in C.'s honour, F350

Penelope (Odysseus' wife), after reunion, Odysseus leaves for Tyrrhenia (Tyrsenia), founds Gortynaia, and dies with honour there, F354

Penestae, Thessalian serfs, FF81, 122

Peneus, river in Thessaly flowing between Mts. Ossa and Olympia, FF78, 80(?)

Peparethians, their offering to Apollo of a golden ivy-wreath given to Bromias, Phaÿllus' sexual favourite, F248TPD

Perdiccas, reigned before Archelaus for thirty-five years (others give different numbers), F279; brother of Philip, taken by Eurydice to find refuge with Iphicrates when Amyntas dies, F289

orated with gold and precious gifts by Gyges and Croesus, F193

Pythian Games (celebrated quadrennially to Apollo at Delphi), nearly profaned by Bromias the flute-girl, FF80(?), 248TPD

Pythian Way, sacred route from Delphi to Tempe, F80(?)

Pythodorus, of Sicyon, his son (name is lost) goes to Delphi to dedicate his shorn locks, is prostituted to Onomarchus, F248TPD

Python, son of Archelaus, with brother, Heraclides, helps Miltocythes raise mercenaries, F307

Python, The, creature slain by Apollo when he first went to Delphi, F80(?)

Rhetra, given to Lycurgus, [F336]

Rhode, daughter of Mopsus, after whom Rhodia, territory in Lycia, was named, F103

Rhodians, had no respect for Hegesilochus, but some played his debauched games, F121; part of an alliance with Chians, hostile to Athens and treating with Philip c. 347/6, F164

Rhodope, Agriae live near, F268b

Rome, captured by Celts (Galls), F317

Sacred War, FF156, 312, 247–9TPD

Sagra, at Battle of, Phor-

mio wounded, F392; at prompting of an oracle he goes to Sparta, is cured, and miraculously returns home, F392

Saintsbury, a place in Meropis, F75c

Samian(s), Thebes, a Milesian city near Mycale, ceded to, F23H; have Syros betrayed to them by Cillicon, F111; Archinus of, persuades Athenians to use Ionian letters in inscriptions, F155; Phygela not allotted to, F305

Samos, where Pherecycles predicted the sinking of the ship, FF70, 71; Hyperbolus goes to, while ostracized, F96a–b; Cillicon lives there after betraying his native Syros, F111

Satyrus (not Orthagoras), seer and friend of Timoleon, F334a; (but Orthagoras in 334b)

Scabala, region of Eretria, F151

Sciraphidas, Spartan lawgiver who prohibited the use of money, F332(H?)

Scirus (Aegean island), gives its name to gambling halls (Sciraphia), F228

Sciathian, citizen of Scithae, F375

Scithae, city of Thrace, near Potidaea, F375

Scotusaei, people who live at Scotussa, F271b

Scotussa, place where there is a miraculously healing spring, F271a

Scybrus, region of Macedonia, F376

Scythia, Acharni a people who live near to, F367

Scythians, make a whey from horse's milk, F45

Sellasia, city of Laconia, F11H

Sesostris (not Sesonchosis), king of Egypt, F46

Sestos, small, well-fortified city controlling the sea-lanes (of the Hellespont), F390

Sicania, Miscera a city of, F198

Sicanians, Indara a city of, F371

Sicilian(s) (history), digression on, F184; in general, FF184–207 (with digressions); Pharax, the Spartan, known more as one than as a Spartan because of his promiscuous lifestyle, F192; Gelon and Hieron, F193

Sicily, [F70]; Dionysius corrupt tyrant of, encourages profligate friends, F134; Merusium a region of, F189; Xiphonia a city of, F190; Hieron sends gifts to Architeles of Corinth from, F193; Dionysius flees from, to Corinth in a merchant ship (not a warship), F341; Halicyae a city of, F365

Sicyon, Melandia a region of, [F177]; Pythodorus of, son goes to Delphi to dedicate his shorn locks and is prostituted to Onomar-

Umbrians. *See* Ombrici

Venetians. *See* Eneti
Victory (Nike), statue at
  Delphi, F193

War, myth of, told by
  Philip, F127
Wartown, place in
  Meropis, F75c
West, F335

Xenopithea, mother of
  Lysandridas, most beau-
  tiful of Peloponnesian
  women, murdered by
  Spartans, F240
Xera, city near Pillars of
  Heracles, F199
Xerxes, invasion of

Greece coincides with
  adornment of Delphi by
  Sicilian rulers, F193
Xiphonia, city of Sicily,
  F190

Zeranians, people of
  Thrace, F214
Zirenia, city of Thrace,
  F44
Zeus, equated by some
  with Ahura Mazda,
  [F64]; claims a
  shrine instead of
  nymphs, F69; father
  of Apollo, F80(?);
  frightened when the
  mountain groaned (but
  brought forth a

mouse), F108; with
  Athena worshipped at
  Omarium in Thessaly,
  F137; worshipped at
  Messapeae in Laconia,
  F245; (Jupiter) —
  (oracle to at Dodona),
  F319; the eagle his
  servant, F331; has a
  forbidden shrine in
  Arcadia, and people
  who enter lose their
  shadows, F343; Apollo
  Carnëus called Z. by
  Argives, F357
Zopyrus, helps Persian
  king capture Babylon,
  F66
Zoroaster, [F64b]

Index of Citations of Testimonia *and Fragments* of Theopompus

General Index

Artemis, 138
Asclepius, 66
Asia, 13, 134; abandoned
  by Agesilaus, 39–40;
  Minor, 73, 76, 86, 91,
  99, 108
Aspendus, 20, 73
Assessus, 75
Atarneus, 108
Athena, 107, 135
Athenaeus, 28, 30, 34, 45,
  47, 50, 52–3, 64, 88, 99,
  106, 120, 131–2, 137,
  146, 165
Athenis, 89
Athens (Athenian[s]), xvi,
  9, 11–12, 15, 29, 31–2,
  35–8, 42, 44, 46–7, 52–
  7, 69–71, 74–9, 83–4,
  88, 108–9, 119–21,
  128–30, 132–3, 149–55,
  157–8, 160, 162, 170–5,
  178, 180, 193–4; for-
  eign policy, 84–6; lies,
  79, 82, 100, 286–7n18;
  point of view of P's (or
  Cratippus') *Hellenica*,
  14, 184–5, 189–90;
  probably visited by
  Theopompus, 9
Atthidographers, 193
Attic dialect, 189–90
Atticus, 192
Autariatae, 109, 156;
  probably to be read for
  Ardiaeans, 289–
  90nn11–12

Babrius, 78
Babylon (Babylonians), 17,
  19
Badian, E., 81
Bakis, 19
Balkan peninsula, 92
Barbarian[s], 27, 35, 93–4,
  101–9, 113, 167
Bardylis, 157
Bisaltia, 128
Bithynia(n[s]), 87, 108, 109
Black Sea (Euxine, or Pon-
  tic Sea), 42, 53, 71, 86–7,
  94–101, 109, 193

Bloch, H., 183, 190, 194
Boeotia(n[s]), 39, 83, 88,
  160, 174–5, 186;
  League, 13, 49
Bosporus, 38
Bromias, 133
Brown, T., 7; argues for
  special letter reinstating
  Theopompus, 277n1
Bruce, I.A.F., 41
Bunbury, E.H., 96
Buttocks (disease of), 68,
  120
"By subject" historiog-
  raphy, 38, 40
"By year" historiography,
  38, 40, 45
Byzantium (Byzantian[s]),
  31, 56, 68–9, 93, 153,
  155–6

Cairo fragments (of P),
  183–4, 189
Calchedon(ian[s]), 31, 68,
  153
Callias (or Epilycus) Peace
  of, 35, 79, 81–2
Callisthenes, 12–13, 43,
  69, 184, 187
Callistratus, 56, 71, 141,
  143, 150–1
Caria(n), 76–7
Carpaseans (Carpaseots),
  188
Carthage (Carthaginians),
  73, 92, 122
Cawkwell, G.: on Athenian
  disregard of King's
  Peace, 284n14
Celts (Gauls), 99, 119, 137,
  156
Centaurs, 149, 150
Ceraunian mountains, 98
Cersobleptes, 93, 106
Chabrias, 77
Chaeronea (battle of), 4, 6,
  85, 89, 128–9, 155, 157,
  167, 170, 174, 178–9
Chalcidice (Chalcidian[s]),
  69, 78, 95–6, 157
Chares, 119, 129, 132, 155,
  170

Charidemus, 139–40, 150
"Chian Letters" (by
  Theopompus), 7, 21, 23
Chios (Chian), 3–4, 13–14,
  35–9, 44, 50, 54–6, 69,
  75, 80, 108–9, 152, 188–
  9, 192; Isocrates' school
  at, 9; pottery, 95
Cicero, 20, 22, 131, 192
Cillicon, 118
Cimon, 70
Cinadon, 48
Citium, 73
Clearchus of Methyd-
  ryium, 83, 134–5, 143,
  151
Cleisthenes, 192–3
Clement of Alexandria, 89
Cleommis (Cleomenes),
  151, 154–5, 179
Cleon, 35, 70
Cleopatra, 89
Cleophon, 71
Cnidus, 8, 20, 29, 36–42,
  53, 93, 186, 194
Codex: replaces the scroll,
  xiv, 59
Colchis (Colchians), 97
Colophon (Colophonians),
  74, 153
Connor, W.R., 70, 82, 130,
  152, 171–2
Conon, 8, 13, 29, 39, 186,
  188–91, 194
Corcyra, 95
Corinth Corinth(ian[s]),
  20, 39, 79, 92, 94–5, 98,
  124; War, 186, 189–90
Coronea, 40
Cos, 20, 69
Cothus, 88
Cotys, 109–10, 135, 157;
  "marries" Athena, 106–7
Cratippus, xviii, 14, 184–6,
  188; avoided speeches,
  189–90, 194; could be P,
  194–5; possible source
  for Ephorus, 190–1;
  used by Plutarch, 190
Ctesiphon, 174
Cyme, 36
Cynic School, 144–5

49, 53–4, 64–5, 68–9,
72–4, 76–7, 82–3, 85,
89, 91–2, 94, 98, 101–9,
113, 130, 133, 135, 138,
142, 145, 148, 157–62,
164, 167, 170, 192; Asi-
atic Greeks, 36; focus of
Ephorus' *History*, 12. *See
also* Hellas (Hellenes)
Griffith, G.T., 56, 119
Guthrie, W.K.C., 26
Gylippus, 44

Haemus, 95–101
Hall, F.W., xiv
Halus, 83
Hammond, N.G.L., 163
Hanno, 122
Harding, P., 125, 194
Harmosts, 8
Harpocration, xvi, 68, 89,
107, 135
Hartog, F. 101, 105
Hearth of Hellas, 52
Hecate, 134
Hecatomnos, 77
Hedyleum, 82
Hegesilochus, 74, 118,
123, 148, 150, 154
Helen (by Gorgias), 26
Hellas (Hellenes, Hellenic)
35, 52, 54, 80–2, 91,
101–9, 157, 161, 163–4,
167. *See also* Greece,
Greeks
Hellenica (by Anaximenes),
12
Hellenica (by Callisthenes),
13–4, 43
Hellenica (by Daemachus),
12
Hellenica (by P) = *Hellenica
Oxyrhynchia*, 13, 183–95
Hellenica (by Theopom-
pus), xvii–xviii, 5, 7, 9,
14, 21, 29–57, 92–3,
112–13, 142–3, 179,
184, 192, 194; Aegean
perspective, 43–4; Ath-
ens in, 52–7; location of
major narratives un-

known, 284n10; not a
source for Ephorus,
186–7; plagiarized from
Xenophon, 187; proba-
bly published before
Theopompus' visit to
Macedon, (344/3),
278n7; Sicilian thread,
42; Spartan empire in,
45–51; termination,
40–4
Hellenica (by Xenophon),
5, 12, 37, 43, 92, 189;
plagiarized by Theo-
pompus, 187
Hellenistic, 184
Hellespont, 38, 53–4, 75,
93
Helos, 50
Helots, 48–50, 119–20
Heraclea Pontica, 87
Heracles, 65, 109, 161–2,
164
Heraclides, 89, 106
Herculaneum, xviii
Hermeas of Atarneus, 5,
10, 35, 66, *108–9*
Hermeas of Methymna, 14
Hermes, 134
Herodotus, xv, 17, 19–20,
27, 36, 64, 70, 79, 96,
101–2, 115, 144, 161,
179
Hieromnemones, 85
Hieron, 89
Hippodamea, 150
Hippolytus, 138, 146
Hippolytus (by Euripides),
138
Histories (or *Hellenica*, by
Ephorus), 30, 36, 165
Homer, 89
Homosexuality (of Philip's
court), 166
How to Write History (by
Lucian), 23
Hyperbolus, 54

Illyria(n[s]), 15, 79, 86–7,
92, 99, 107–9, 120, 151,
155

Information theory,
130–1
Ionia(n[s]), 35–6, 45, 53,
57, 68–71, 74, 76, 79,
80–1, 108–9, 158; Sea,
20, *94–101*
Ionius, 100
Iphicrates, 70, 77
Isagoras, 192–3
Isocrates (of Apollonia), 9;
not the competitor at
Mausolus' games,
279n18
Isocrates (of Athens) xvii,
4–5, 7–12, 21, 26–7, 39,
63–4, 71, 76–7, 115,
130, 144, 161, 163–4,
171, 186–7, 189
Issa, 100, 182
Istria, 96, 98
Italy (Italian[s]), 87–9,
93–4, 98–9

Jacoby, F., 41, 45, 66, 75,
83, 88–9, 96, 99, 108,
110, 121, 125, 184
Jason: legendary hero, 97–
8, 99, 182; of Pherae,
76–7, 157–9, 161
Jung, C.: on authorial ambivalence, 289–90n1
Justin, 121–5, 129

Kern, S.J., 191
King (of Persia), 41, 76–7,
79–80, 86, 102–3, 108–
9, 116–17, 125, 189, 194
King's Peace (or Peace of
Antalcidas), 13–14, 41–
2, 49, 53–6, 73, 77–8,
102, 184, 186, 194

Lacedaemonians, 12
Laconia, 38
Laestrygonians, 149–50
Lampsacenes, 133
Lana, I., 143
Lane Fox, R., 41; on
Theopompus' adapta-
tion of speeches from
Xenophon, 283–4n9